The Book of St Day

'The Towne of Trynyte'

Joseph Mills & Paul Annear

HALSGROVE

First published in Great Britain in 2003

British Library Cataloguing-in-Publication Data
A CIP record for this title is available from the British Library

ISBN 1 84114 251 4

HALSGROVE

Halsgrove House
Lower Moor Way
Tiverton, Devon EX16 6SS
Tel: 01884 243242
Fax: 01884 243325
email: sales@halsgrove.com
website: http://www.halsgrove.com

Frontispiece photograph: *'Blind David' Annear delivers water to Mrs Mary Hensley, in Church Street, St Day, 14 January 1928.*

Printed and bound in Great Britain by CPI Bath

Acknowledgements

The authors owe a debt of gratitude to the several institutions whose staff have so generously given time and encouragement during the research: Cornwall Centre, Redruth, Terry Knight and staff; Courtney Library, Royal Institution of Cornwall, Truro, Angela Broome and staff; County Record Office, Truro, County Archivist, Philip Brough and staff. Our thanks are due also to Paddy Bradley, Redruth, for the freedom to choose from his extensive collection of local photographs; to John Probert for his invaluable help in providing a long list of newspaper references for our use; and to Mr and Mrs Richard Williams for permission to photograph and publish the Manor Stocks.

We acknowledge with pleasure the unstinting help we received from the following individuals who each contributed by consenting to be interviewed and with the loan of family photographs and other material: Roy Annear senr, Roy Annear junr, Karl Bray, Roger Bray, Richard Clymo, Valerie Chown, Stephen Edwards, Sue Edwards, Bernadette Fallon, Hayden George, Mona George, Mrs Albert Harris, Malcolm Hume, Mark Johnson, Betty Jones, Arana Jefferies, Alan Kent, the late Ivy Kent, Richard and Marge Latham, Francis Matthews, Keith and Sue Manley, Reagan Matthews, Tony Mitchell, Bernice Williams, Billy Williams, Dennis Williams, Barrie May, Eric Rabjohn, Beryl Stockwell, Moira Tangye, Michael Tangye, Pauline Temple, John Tonkin, Charles Thurlow, Revd Thomas Shaw and Geoffrey Nankivell.

Our thanks go to Halsgrove, especially to Simon Butler and Naomi Cudmore for their special help; and to our wives, June Mills and Michelle Annear, for their great support, encouragement and forbearance throughout the time when we were immersed in the gestation of this book. If we have inadvertently omitted anyone from this list we apologise.

We acknowledge the work of the three earlier local writers, Annie Trevithick, William Francis and Peter Jennings; and D.B. Barton, R.R. Blewett, A. Buckley, N. Chadwick, H.L. Douch, H.G. Dynes, F.E. Halliday, C.C. James, A.G. Langford, Andrew Langford, A.L. Rowse, Hill & MacAlister and Kathleen Piper which we have used freely.

Lizzie Sherdy, 1902. She was born and raised at Creegbraws, St Day. (See also The Book of Stithians.*)*

A two-horse brake in Church Street outside Kinsman's shop with shuttered window. The vehicle, which is not a Jersey car, has an unusual seating arrangement.

A gathering at the Crofthandy Wesleyan Church Sunday-School tea treat, 1915. The tall man in the centre at the back wearing a cap is Sam Jeffery and further to the right the little man in the bowler hat is 'Jampot' Moyle.

Contents

Part One

by Joseph Mills

Acknowledgements 3
Chapter One: 'The Towne of Seynte Trynyte' 7
Chapter Two: St Day Cross 13
Chapter Three: Fairs & Markets 15
Chapter Four: Mining 19
Chapter Five: The Watercourse Mapp, c.1720 27
Chapter Six: Tin & Copper Dues 31
Chapter Seven: Education 33
Chapter Eight: Transport 39
Chapter Nine: Law & Order 45
Chapter Ten: A Digest of Councils & Committees 51
Chapter Eleven: Two Nineteenth-Century Directories 59
Chapter Twelve: Leases & Surveys 71
Chapter Thirteen: Nostalgia: A Miscellany 85

Part Two

by Paul Annear

Chapter Fourteen: St Day Holy Trinity Church 89
Chapter Fifteen: The Challenge of Chapels 99
Chapter Sixteen: A Town of Many Industries 111
Chapter Seventeen: St Day & The Emigration Experience 125
Chapter Eighteen: The Depressed Years of Mining, 1870–1940 133
Chapter Nineteen: Leisure, Entertainment & Self-Improvement 137
Chapter Twenty: Inns & Public Houses 147
Chapter Twenty-One: Prominent Personalities 151
Chapter Twenty-Two: St Day Town Clock 157
Chapter Twenty-Three: The 1881 Census 161
Chapter Twenty-Four: Making a Fortune, or Making Ends Meet 165
Chapter Twenty-Five: Civic Amenities 169
Chapter Twenty-Six: St Day During Wartime 175
Chapter Twenty-Seven: Sporting Traditions 179

Subscribers *190*

Rock House by the church gates in Church Street.

On the right of this Fore Street view is the shop of John Travis Leverton, painter and glazier.

Part 1: by Joseph Mills

One

'The Towne of Seynte Trynyte'

Writing in 1584, Norden described St Day as a 'hamlet'. Henderson (*Ecclesiastical History*) tells us that in 1540 St Day was called 'the Towne of Seynte Trynyte'. In 1750 Hals referred to 'the Town of St Day' and the seventeenth- and eighteenth-century Manor Rent Rolls and Surveys contain frequent references also to 'the Town of St Day'. Later still, in 1910, *Kelly's Directory* tells us that 'St Day or St Dye is a town and ecclesiastical Parish.' Now, 415 years after Norden, St Day has become a civil parish with a duly elected Parish Council, having passed through periods of both prosperity and depression, arriving at the second millennium halfway through a programme of regeneration.

Situated as it was on the medieval pilgrims' road to St Michael's Mount, it became a stopping place for those making the pilgrimage to that important shrine 'Where troops of pilgrims, whilom, enter'd in/To pray St Michael to remove their sin.' ('St Michael's Mount', Wm Hogg, 1811.) The popularity of the shrine at St Day was probably increased by the following instrument issued by Pope Gregory in AD1070 (which, in his *History of Cornwall,* Polwhele noted was the principle cause of the great influx of votaries to the shrine at St Michael's Mount):

> *To all Members of Holy Mother Church, who shall read or hear these Letters, Peace and Salvation. Be it known unto you all that our most Holy Pope Gregory, in the year of Christ's Incarnation 1070 out of his great zeal and devotion to the Church of St Michael in Tumba in the County of Cornwall, hath piously granted unto the aforesaid Church to remit to all the faithful, who shall enrich, endow, or visit, the said Church, a third part of their penance.*

This proclamation was affixed to the doors of the church and in others it was read before the people. We note the phrase 'who shall enrich, endow...'. His Holiness was not lacking in entrepreneurial skills it seems. In his *Parochial History of Cornwall* (*Vol. IV,* pp206 and 312), Lake makes mention of the fact that St Keyne visited St Michael's Mount in the year AD490 and that it was already a place of some importance. If the shrine on the Mount was already founded in the fifth century and St Keyne was on a pilgrimage to that shrine, it is not inconceivable that other pilgrims too would have passed through what was to become the manor of Tolgullow. Eventually (and we do not know when), a shrine was established at Tolgullow, possibly to mark some miraculous event. Such an event may have occurred as early as the sixth century, when the Breton saint They was alive or still remembered, or at any time thereafter, but there is no record known to us of St They having any direct association with the shrine, or the chapel, both of which are mentioned frequently in later records. There is no record of a dedication to Saint They or Saint Day. At that time, and for some time to come, the place name St Day does not appear – such settlement as existed took the name of the manor, namely Tolgulla, which has survived to this day as a farm name, Tolgullow Vean (Tolgulla Byghan).

C.C. James, in his *History of Gwennap,* gives Talgollo as dating from 1005 (the time of Ethelred the Unready), Talgollou Byghan 1256, and Tallgollo Mur 1293. Talgollou Byghan in English becomes Little Tolgulla (ow), which distinguishes it from Tallgollo Mur, that is 'Great Tolgullou', which surely was the settlement around the shrine, observing that the generally accepted translation of 'Tolgulla' is 'brow of light', or in other words 'a beacon on the hill'. St Day, at its highest point, 417 feet above mean sea level, is overlooked on the north, west and south by much higher ground, limiting its usefulness as a site for a beacon. Carn Brea, Carn Marth and St Agnes Beacon are the obvious choices to cover a wider area. However, a beacon on the hill of St Day would be visible from the east, whence came pilgrims on their way to St Michael's Mount intending to stop at the shrine at St Day. Might not the Tolgullow beacon have been a signpost to give the exact location of the shrine (and hospitality) to the approaching faithful? If so, when was it lit? Every day throughout the year, or only at certain significant times when an increased influx of pilgrims might be expected?

There is perhaps another possibility, which many will consider altogether too far-fetched to be admitted. The generally accepted interpretation of Tolgulla, 'beacon on the hill', suggests at once a flame, a bonfire to guide travellers or a warning signal, the customary practice of such beacons, but could the name Tolgulla have a spiritual connotation? Is it a reference to the shrine itself – a spiritual light?

The manor of Talgollo already existed as an Anglo-Saxon manor before the Conquest. During the reign of Edward the Confessor it was held by Alnod, who continued to hold it during the reign of William the Conqueror. At the time of the Domesday Survey (1086), there was land for three ploughs, there were 3 slaves, 4 smallholders, 2 cows and 15 sheep, as well as 2 acres of wood and 60 of pasture. Formerly it was worth 20 shillings but later was reduced to 4 shillings.

Compare this with the neighbouring manor of Tehidy with land for 50 ploughs, 15 slaves, 25 villagers and 30 smallholders, 5 unbroken mares, 10 cattle and 140 sheep. Formerly £8, its value was by this time (1086) £20. Alnod held a number of other manors in Cornwall, mostly in the east and north of the county, but it is unlikely that he resided on any one of them.

No record of a 'manor house' *per se* has come to light, nor is there any indication of former lords of the manor having residence at Tolgullow, although their steward would certainly have had a base where he kept his records, probably in the modest cottage in which he lived. Some time in the mid-nineteenth century a manor office was established in Market Street (present-day Fore Street) on the north side, east of the town clock where the manor books, maps and papers were then housed and remained until the office was closed. The archives eventually reached the Royal Institution of Cornwall where they are available to those wishing to carry out research.

Records survive of hearings in feet of fines, assizes, etc. during the Middle Ages. In 1244, for example, John de Talgollow and Alfreda his wife were named in a suit, and in 1256 Alan Basset and Reginald de Botemer became involved in a dispute over Talgollen Bydghan (Tolgullow Vean), proof of the continued activity around Tolgulla, the area of the shrine, which was always referred to as 'the Chapelle of the Holy Trinity', as it is in Walter Bronescombe's (Bishop of Exeter) Register of August 1269 and again in a survey of the manor made by Order of the Chapter in 1281. It is not until the mid-fourteenth century that the place name 'St Day' appears, as discussed below.

Henderson lists a number of legacies to the Chapel of the Holy Trinity covering a period of 115 years:

1410	*William Bachyler*	*To the Chapel of the Holy Trinity 2d.*
1419	*John Meger*	*lego eglesie Sancti Dye in com't Cornub 12d.*
1420	*John Bakere*	*12d to the Holy Trinity of Seyndey 12d.*
1435	*William Velour*	*item lego Sancte Trinitate 12d.*
1445	*John Carnell Rector of Hacombe*	*Lego instauro Sancte Trinitatis de Synday 6d.*
1447	*John Trevelan Vicar of Perran* [zabulo]	*item lego ad honorem Sancte Trinitatis in capells eiusdem iuxta Redruth 3d.*
1458	*Thomas Catour of Breage*	*item to the Trinity 12d.*
1476	*Thomas Envs*	*lego Sancte Trinitatis 4d.*
1500	*Thomas Killigrew*	*intem stauro Sancte Trinitatis 12d.*
1503	*John Mowla*	*left 8d to the Store of Holy Trinity at Seynt Day and 4d as an offering to the same Holy Trinity.*
1507	*John Nans LLD*	*lego Sancte Trinitatisin Cornubia 12d.*
1508	*John Bevil*	*lego Sancte Trinitatis 40d.*
1510	*John Envs*	*lego Imagini Sancte Trinitatis de Sent Deve 6d et instauro eiusdem ibidem 6d.*
1511	*Peter Bevill*	*item instauro Beate Trinitatis apud Seynt Dey 12d.*
1517	*Thomasvn Bevyll*	*to the Trinitie of Saint Day 12d.*
1517	*Thomas Tregian*	*to the store of the Trinite 12d.*
1525	*Marion Lelley*	*to Holy Trinity 2d.*

Henderson also lists some 18 legacies to the Church of St Piran, including that of Thomas Killigrew of Penryn in 1500, who left 6s.8d. In his will Thomas Killigrew also left the sum of 12d. to the Store of the Holy Trinity.

Henderson observes that with the exception of Thomas Killigrew the legacies to the Church of St Piran were all from that area: 'These bequests show that the popularity of that shrine was confined to that part of Cornwall and was not so general as the shrine at St Day and the Mount.' There were other legacies to the Holy Trinity and St Day throughout the fifteenth and sixteenth centuries. Henderson also tells us that 'Wayside chapels, as at St Day, were used by bishops for Ordination Services on their journeys.' In 1427 Bishop Lacy ordained the following 12 men to the First

Tonsure 'at the Chapel of the Holy Trinity in Wenappa': Richard Gwavys, John Leyte, John Nicoll, Henry Gille, Ralph Nicoll, Thomas Harry, John Spicer (illegitimate), John Vyntow (illegitimate), David Rawlin, Stephen Crane, Robert Crane and John Hunter. These men were not likely to have been natives of St Day but would have come from a wide area, probably the western half of Cornwall, Penwith, Kerrier and Carrick, and were gathered at an important and convenient location, arranged by the Church authorities over a period of time.

C.S. Gilbert, writing in 1820, notes:

Tradition reports that St Daye was formerly a parish of itself and that when its church or chapel became ruinous, the inhabitants added the South aisle to Gwennap Church, at their own expense, and it is observable at this time, that the South aisle is more modern than any other part of the building; but whether this was done through the acquisition of St Daye to the parish or from the increase of population in Gwennap is a matter of uncertainty.

Saint Day, our presumed patronal saint, is usually identified with the Breton saint They, who is said to have died on 19 June 680. There is then a gap of 670 years between his death and the earliest record of the name that we are aware of, i.e. 1350, which is found in the Assize (Plea) Rolls in the Public Record Office in London where it is written 'Seyntdeye'. From the earliest records there are many references to the 'Chapel of the Holy Trinity', a dedication that has persisted to the present day, but we know of no references to 'St Day' until 1350. The 'Tenth Century List of Cornish Parochial Saints', comprising 48 Brittonic names discussed by B. Lynette Olsen and O.J. Padel, makes no mention of St They or St Day (Offprint of *Cambridge Mediaeval Celtic Studies, No.12*, 1986).

We turn now to the will of Tristram Colan, 1517, in which he left three shillings to 'SANCTI Trinitati DEI'. Does this not suggest a contraction to SANCTI DEI as an explanation of the earlier change from 'Holy Trinity'? The Latin 'Dei' is a two-syllable word; observe now the early spellings in medieval sources as well as the first four cartographers quoted below, where we find the spelling 'Daye', indicating a two-syllable word. Does the place name 'St Day' in fact derive from the Latin Sancti Dei, rather than from the Breton saint, They? Such a suggestion will not be received happily by many for whom St Day, the man, is held in great affection – 'St Day, who showed particular love and tenderness to children' (Baring-Gould, *Cornish Dedications*). In 1750 Hals wrote: 'St Dye of Gaul, very famous in that country for his piety and holy Christian living about the fifth century.'

The enigma remains unsolved, and perhaps it will never be satisfactorily explained. Those who want to believe in St Day of Gaul will remain faithful to the man described by W.S. Lach-Szyrma as 'a cheerful Saint, who always took the bright side of religion, which perhaps accounts for his great success as a missionary under trying circumstances.' St Day is our

The Changing Place Name

Date	Spelling	Source
1350	SEYNTEDEYE	Assize (Plea)
1379	St DEYE	Bassett Papers, St Michael's Mount
1380	SEYNT DEYE	Court Rolls
1389	SENDEY	Catalogue of Ancient Deeds
1435	SEINT DEI	Ibid.
1510	SENT DEY	Early Chancery Roll Proceedings
1584	St DAYE	Norden
1646	St DYE	Will of Richard Harris
1651	St DAYE	Court of Action
1750	St DYE	Hals
1820	St DAYE	C.S. Gilbert
1838	St DYE	C.D. Gilbert

NB: *The earliest spellings of the place name always begins with 'SE' and 'DE'. Not until late in the sixteenth century does the 'a' appear, on Norden's map, drawn in 1584 but published later.*

Cartographers Showing St Day

Date	Spelling	Cartographer
1584	S. DAYE	Norden
1607	S. DAYE	William Kip
1611	Sct. DAYE	John Speed
1645	Sct. DAYE	Jan Blaeu
1689	S. DAY	Philip Lea
1695	S. DAYE	Robert Morden
1700	St DYE	Joel Gascoyne, first appearance of this form.
1724	St DYE	Herman Moll
1748	St DAY/St DYE	Thomas Martyn
1755	St DYE	Thomas Kitchen
1810	St DAY	John Wilkes
1831	St DAY	James Pigot & Co.
1836	St DAY	Thomas Moule

NB: *Kip's map of 1607 appears to be based on Norden, whose own map derived from Saxton (AD1579). Nearly a century later, in 1700, Joel Gascoyne s map gives 'St DYE', which appeared previously on a will of 1646, and was used by later cartographers from time to time up to 1755; thereafter it is occasionally met with in the mid-nineteenth century and can be found on several headstones in the old churchyard.*

adopted patronal saint, that cannot be denied. So be it.

Dr Jon Mills, Research Fellow at the Department of Linguistics at the University of Birmingham, is of the belief that:

The reason for the variations in spelling probably lies in the choice of spelling conventions used in the early forms. Any attempt to propose a given pronunciation of a place name is bound to be controversial. A number of linguistic factors are likely to cloud the matter. The spelling conventions of the early forms can be those of either Latin, Cornish, Norman French, or English. It is perhaps significant that the vowel favoured from 1350 to circa 1600 is 'e', but from this time onward 'a' becomes the accepted vowel. This coincides with a change in the spelling used in the Cornish Miracle plays. Compare the spelling of the Ordinalia, *14th century, with that of* Gwreans an Bys, *dated 1611. The apparent change in spelling may be due to the* Ordinalia *using the Latin convention, while* Gwreans an Bys *is written in the spelling conventions of English of that period. The shift in spelling seems to coincide with the activities of English cartographers who presumably used English spelling conventions.*

Norden (1584) dismissed both 'Camburn' and 'Redruth' each with a few words but had more to say concerning St Day:

St Daye. A hamlet. There was sometime a Chappel, now destroyde, called Trinitye, to which men and women came in times paste from far in pilgrimage. The resorte was so greate, as it made the people of the Countrye to bring all kinde of provision to that place: and so long it contynued with increase that it grew into a kinde of market: and by that means it grew and continueth a kinde of market to this daye, without further charter.

Henderson notes:

In the seventeenth and eighteenth centuries the mines developed so rapidly that St Day soon became the capital of a thickly populated area and its former wayside character was eclipsed by the construction of a new line of road through Scorrier and Mount Ambrose.

A stopping place for pilgrims it may well have been in the Dark Ages and into the medieval period, indeed it was so, but what sort of place was it? Were there many houses? Were there streets? Far from it; as late as the sixteenth century Norden had described it as a hamlet – a few scattered hovels around and outside the church enclosure, the lan, is the most likely scenario. The present slate-clad houses at the western end of Telegraph Street may well mark the former boundary of the medieval church precinct. Continue the line of that curve to complete a circle and the site of the old church, as shown on Thomas Martyn's map of 1748, is central to the area described.

Let us go now even further back in history and ask ourselves whether there had been an Iron-Age hill-fort on this site. There are no visible physical remains to give support to such a premise, no hint of a ditch or rampart, and the whole area of the hilltop has been built over and covered with dwellings for hundreds of years, so the likelihood of an exploratory archaeological dig on the site is slim, to say the least. The wider district was certainly inhabited at an early time, a fact to which the Threemilestone Round and the Trebowland Round testify, the latter, like the St Day site, being under the eminence of Carn Marth and at a similar height above sea level. Ian Soulsby (*A History of Cornwall*) tells us that over 600 Iron-Age sites have been identified in Cornwall.

A one-time Roman presence in West Cornwall is borne out by the Roman Villa at Magor, near Camborne, and the Roman inscribed stone, men scryfa, found at Menhir between St Day and Busveal. The latter suggests that they passed along the ancient trackway which later accommodated those making the pilgrimage from Canterbury to St Michael's Mount.

A search of seventeenth- and eighteenth-century field names has yielded nothing to support the suggestion of the previous existence of a fortification on the hill of St Day itself – no 'caer', 'ker' (or 'ger', meaning a fortified place) or 'din' has appeared in that area. However, it is interesting to note that within the present Scorrier estate and shown on the Ordnance Survey at grid reference OS. SW. 7243 is a rectangular dotted outline of an ancient archaeological site. The small fields in the area are named on the 1772 Survey as Little Gear, Round Gear, Wester Gear Croft and Norther Gear Croft (map 4, p.83).

To the north of St Day also, on the 'Watercourse Mapp', we find Wheal Dungey. 'Dungey' may be broken down to two Cornish words, dun and jy (chy) – a fortified house, strongly suggesting an association with the nearby ancient site. We have not been able to find any other reference to a Wheal Dungey Mine in our searches and assume that it was one of those very many small workings of which there were probably never any records. A further possible explanation is that Dungey was the surname of someone connected with the mine working.

The position of the medieval church is shown on Thomas Martyn's map of Cornwall of 1748. It is well within the 400-feet contour, and on the highest part of the hill at 417 feet above mean sea level. Nora Chadwick (*The Celts*, 1970, p.213) has this to say:

The typical monastery appears to have been enclosed within a bank of earth or stone, and so to have resembled a secular ring-fort. Indeed, there is evidence to suggest that existing ring-forts were sometimes converted to religious use.

Whilst there is no suggestion that a monastery existed at Tolgulla at any time, there may well have been a hill-fort providing security for the inhabitants of the site, and later containing the shrine or chapel established at Tolgulla. The internal wooden structures would have been simple. Chadwick goes on to mention the buildings which one would have found there:

> *The principal building... a rectangular wooden church or oratory with a thatched roof: other buildings included guest-house, emphasising the traditional Celtic obligation of hospitality.*

This is compatible with what Norden wrote concerning the growth of 'the resorte' into 'a kinde of market'.

The later, fourteenth-century church replacing the wooden structure would have been built on what was already hallowed ground, that is, the site of the earlier chapel. Martyn's map of 1748 clearly shows us that site, as does the 1770 Survey Map. There are a few carved stones from that building extant, including, in the old stable yard at Scorrier House, what appears to be a section of fourteenth- or fifteenth-century window tracery.

The place name 'Gorland' pertained to a wider area than the present-day bungalow estate and may indicate either a 'sheep-fold' (C.C. James) or 'a church yard', not a 'burial ground – enclathva' (Nance). If we were able to go back in time to visit the residents, we would certainly not understand a word they said. They spoke and understood only Cornish, and Celtic Cornish at that, as evidenced by an account of an action in the Consistory Court of the Diocese on 28 September 1512, when Michael Franke (a Breton?) accused Nicholas Thomas William, described as being of 'the Parish of Wennap', of stealing his 'tynne'. One John Busveal of Wennap stated that he heard the two men quarrelling at a place near Poldyth in Wennap, and that Michael said to William 'Thou art a theff and you stolys mv tynne.' A footnote in Latin reads *'Scilicit in lingua materna hoc est in Cornysh'* which translates into a request to be heard in their mother tongue, Cornish. Again Norden tells us that:

> *In the Weste parte of the Countrye* [Cornwall] *as in the Hundreds of Penwith and Kirrier the Cornish tongue is moste in use amongst the inhabitants, and yet (which is to be marvele) though the husband and wife, parents and children, Master and Servantes do mutually communude in their native language, yet ther is none of them in manner but is able to converse with a Straunger in the English tounge... But it seemeth that in few yeares the Cornish Language will be litle and litle abandoned.*

And so it came to pass.

Let us return now to the place name St Day. There is another, quite separate factor to consider – the fact of the existence at one time of a family bearing the patronym St Dei. The evidence for this is to be found in two separate documents, first, Harleian Ms. 891, at the British Museum, listing 'Certayne Cornish Armes. An Alphabet of Arms of Cornysh Families', in the handwriting of Ralph Brook Pursuivant, who in 1580 was appointed Rouge Croix. The document possibly predates his promotion. The entry reads 'St Dei. Blue. on a fece argent three keyes gules.' The second, at the Cornwall Record Office, amongst the Gregor Collection, is a collection of Coats of Arms, both Cornish and others. There is no title to the MS but it bears the signature and date 'John Moore 10 Nov. 1684.' It reads 'St Dei. Blue on a fess argent 3 keys gules.' Nothing has come to light to inform us as to the origins of this family; it does not appear in any of the nineteenth-century county histories, and it seems unlikely that the family was Cornish.

It is possible that they were refugees, political or religious. With no land of their own their name would seldom, if ever, appear in taxation rolls or any of the medieval records. We note the early form of spelling using the vowel 'e', which was the practice up until the late-sixteenth century and which lends credence to the theory that the Grant of Arms was obtained at an early date, but in what country, by what authority and at what time was the Grant awarded? We must accept from those two manuscripts that there was, assuredly, a 'Cornvsshe Family' bearing those Arms and we must be left to wonder where they lived. Is there a connection between the family St Dei and the community of St Day, or is this a confusing coincidence?

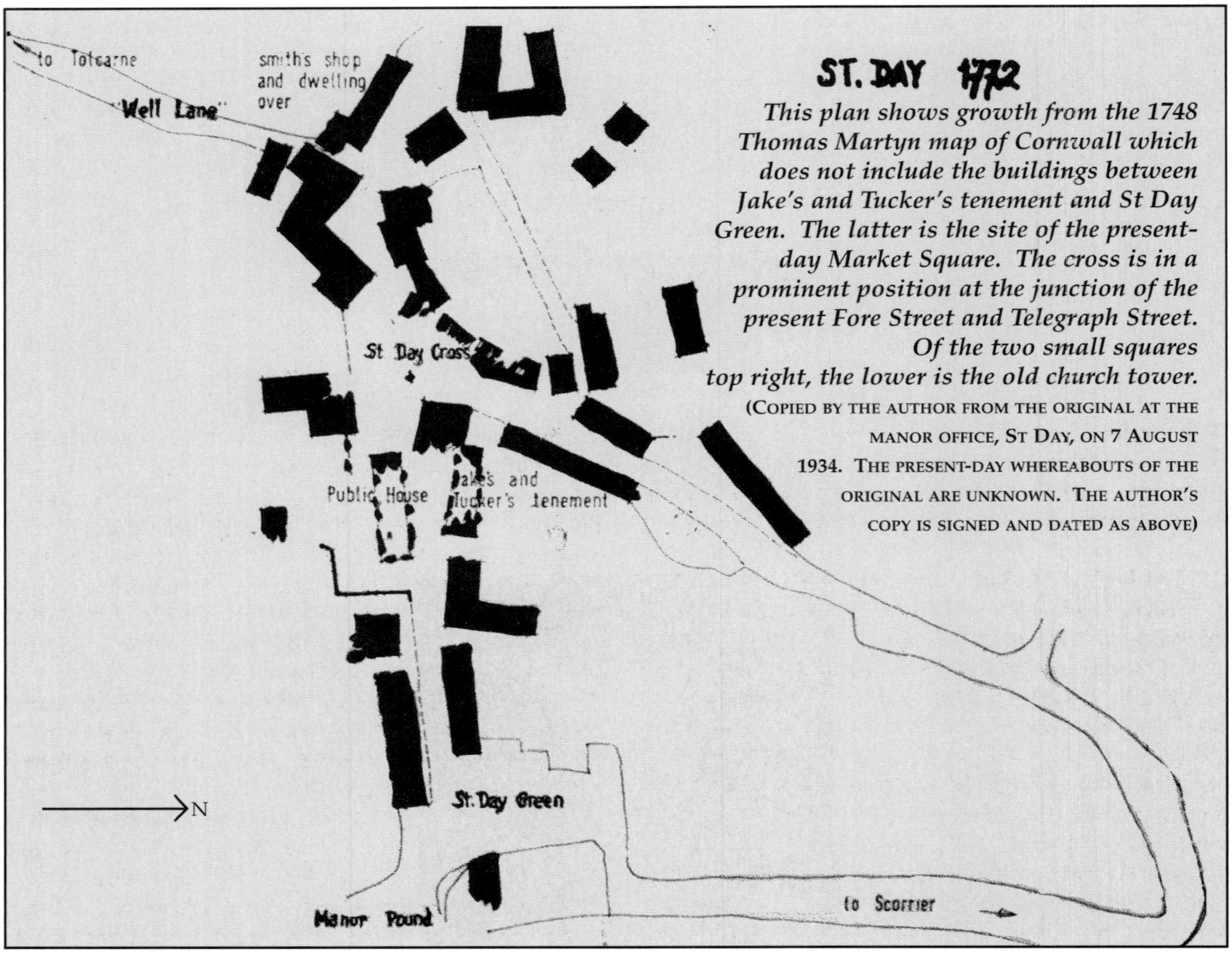

ST. DAY 1772

This plan shows growth from the 1748 Thomas Martyn map of Cornwall which does not include the buildings between Jake's and Tucker's tenement and St Day Green. The latter is the site of the present-day Market Square. The cross is in a prominent position at the junction of the present Fore Street and Telegraph Street. Of the two small squares top right, the lower is the old church tower.

(COPIED BY THE AUTHOR FROM THE ORIGINAL AT THE MANOR OFFICE, ST DAY, ON 7 AUGUST 1934. THE PRESENT-DAY WHEREABOUTS OF THE ORIGINAL ARE UNKNOWN. THE AUTHOR'S COPY IS SIGNED AND DATED AS ABOVE)

to Totcarne
smith's shop and dwelling over
Well Lane
St Day Cross
Public House
Jake's and Tucker's tenement
St. Day Green
Manor Pound
to Scorrier
N

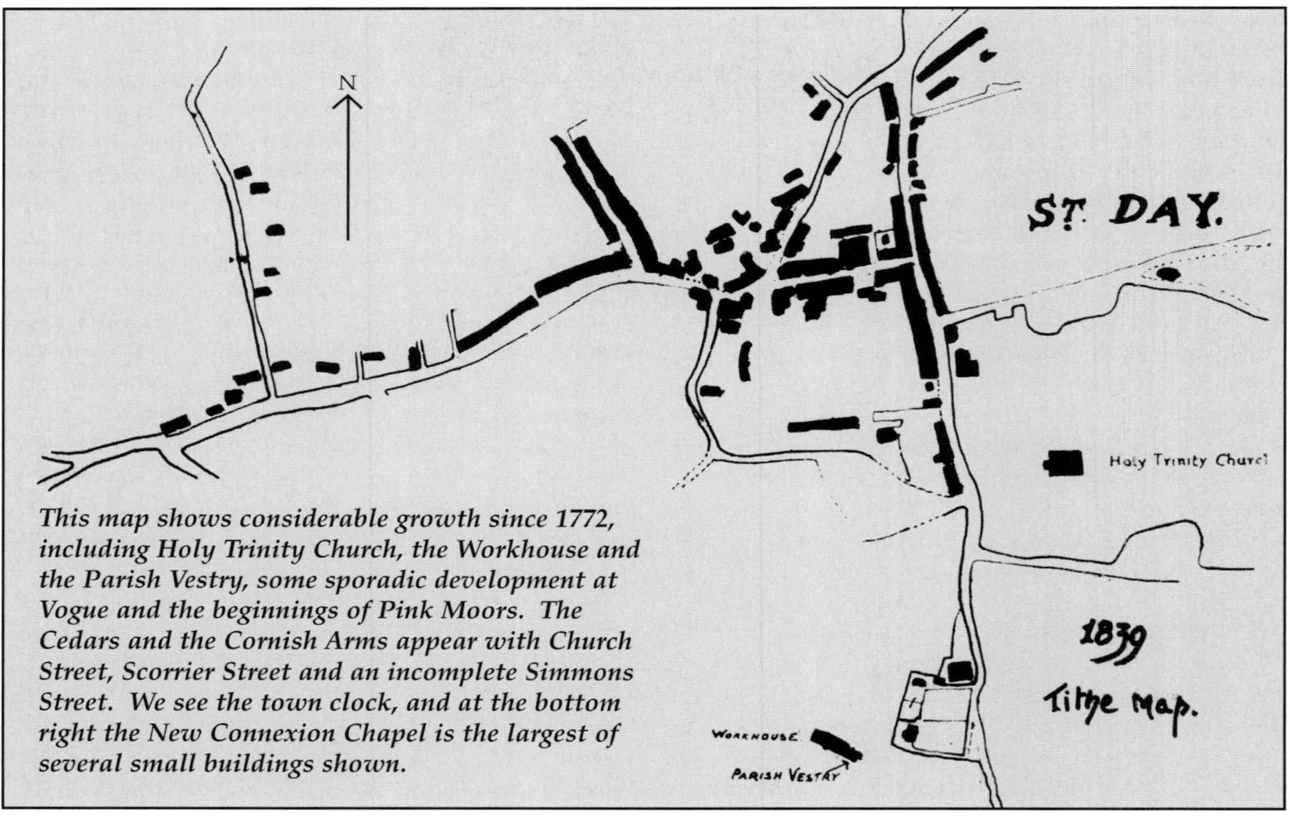

This map shows considerable growth since 1772, including Holy Trinity Church, the Workhouse and the Parish Vestry, some sporadic development at Vogue and the beginnings of Pink Moors. The Cedars and the Cornish Arms appear with Church Street, Scorrier Street and an incomplete Simmons Street. We see the town clock, and at the bottom right the New Connexion Chapel is the largest of several small buildings shown.

Two

St Day Cross

The references below to St Day's cross caught the attention of the author, provoking closer examination of the related map and the plan of St Day with the following title:

> *1772 A Book of the Particulars with references to the Map of the Manor of St Day, in the Parish of Gwennap and County of Cornwall Surveyd in 1772 by F. Welch and mapp'd in 1777 by Wm. Hole.*

On that document is written 'No.16. q. Newton's Tenement by Saint Day Cross. In Lease to Stephen Newton.' This included 'Two Dwellings and Smith's Shop. Garden to the South of and near to the Cross.' On the map a small square with a dot in the centre, at the junction of what is now Fore Street and Telegraph Street, was evidence of the site of 'the Cross', standing well out from the corner. That square, although quite small, appears to be orientated facing north, east, south and west, as does the small square representing the site of 'the Old Tower', both clearly shown on the 1772 Manor Map.

Old Cross Head, now in the church pathway, on an unassociated granite shaft. It was found between St Day and Carharrack in a farm hedge at Chellean Farm during the 1940s.

The orientation of the square plinth is in agreement with, according to A.G. Langdon (quoting Revd W. Haslam, 1847, in *Old Cornish Crosses*), the usual alignment of 'churchyard crosses facing... west according to the invariable rule regarding church crosses.' The same authority informs us that 'wayside Crosses' were erected to 'guard and guide the way to the church' and so were not necessarily orientated east and west but pointed in the direction of the church.

The entry above is the only reference to the cross in the manorial records known to the author, and had those documents not survived it is unlikely that we would have known about its exact site, or even its existence. There is, however, a brief mention of the cross in a little book, *A Londoner's Walk to the Land's End* by Walter White, published 1855, in which the author tells of a visit to Gwennap Pit, thence to St Day, where an old man pointed out a spot where 'a grand old cross stood once, but why it was removed, or whither, he could not tell.' This suggests that the cross was quite substantial. White describes his guide and informant as 'an old man', which surely means he would have been well able, in 1850, to remember the turn of the century and the existence of a 'grand old cross' and where exactly it stood.

We have no indication of the height or form of the cross; the small square does suggest the one-time existence of a square plinth, but again we have no clue as to the type of cross, its size or height.

When was the cross removed from its ancient site, and why was it moved? It is clearly marked on the 1772 map, but does not appear on any nineteenth-century map. It was possibly removed some time before or early in the nineteenth century, probably to clear the way for increased traffic of wagons and carts concomitant with the development of the mining industry. Its removal was likely to have been initiated by the mine owners and authorised by the agent of the lords of the manor (all of the latter were absentee landlords) to speed up communications on the roads, observing that this was a period when Wheal Quick, Wheal Gorland, Wheal Muttrell and others in or close to St Day were at the peak of operations.

When was it erected? A.L. Rowse (*Tudor Cornwall*) suggests that for the most part these characteristic Cornish monuments date from the eighth to the twelfth centuries. It is rarely possible to date them from architectural evidence based on ornament or form. We know that a shrine of some importance was already established here before

AD1269 and its site would surely have been marked with a cross of some distinction, deserving a plinth. Andrew Langdon in *Stone Crosses of West Cornwall* (1999) gives, among other reasons for erecting these crosses, the purpose of marking church sanctuaries.

There are four ancient Cornish crosses in the grounds of Scorrier and Tregullow Houses adjoining St Day. Of the two in Scorrier House grounds one is known to have come from Wendron parish. Of the other, Arthur G. Langdon (*Old Cornish Crosses*, 1896) writes:

> *It is supposed that this cross was removed to these grounds for preservation many years ago, but all enquiries have failed to elicit any particulars regarding its previous site or history.*

The existence of a hole in the front of the head suggests that it was at some time used as a gatepost, a fate not uncommon for crosses, but which precludes any likelihood of this cross having been rescued from St Day. Tregullow possesses two crosses, one of which is said to have come from the crossroads between Ponsanooth and Pengreep. The original site of the other is apparently unknown. Tregullow House was built in 1805 and enclosed in 1826 – around the period when St Day Cross was removed from the town. It is just possible that this Tregullow cross is the cross which originally stood in medieval St Day. There is no evidence whatsoever to support such a premise, but it is certainly a plausible argument that the distance was not great and it is very likely that the Williams hierarchy would have been well aware of the intention to remove the cross, indeed they may well have instigated the movement and arranged for its preservation. Standing almost six feet high, it is certainly 'a grand old cross.'

Neither J.T. Blight's *Ancient Crosses and Antiquities of Cornwall* nor A.G. Langdon's *Old Cornish Crosses* mentions the previous existence of a church cross in St Day. The nineteenth-century authors of Cornish histories, Lysons (1814), C.S. Gilbert (1820), Hitchins and Drew (1824), Lewis (1833) and C.D. Gilbert (1838), all omit any allusion to the ancient cross and in the 1920s Charles Henderson appears not to have seen any reference to such a structure. Was it already gone before the earliest of these writers? It seems likely.

A cross which at present stands on the approach to the old church was discovered some time in the 1930s in a field hedge at Chellean Farm. It was rescued by the then occupier, Tom Peters, and eventually brought to St Day when he moved there. Only the cross head is ancient, the shaft having been provided when it was finally given by Mr and Mrs Swindell to be placed in the precinct of the church.

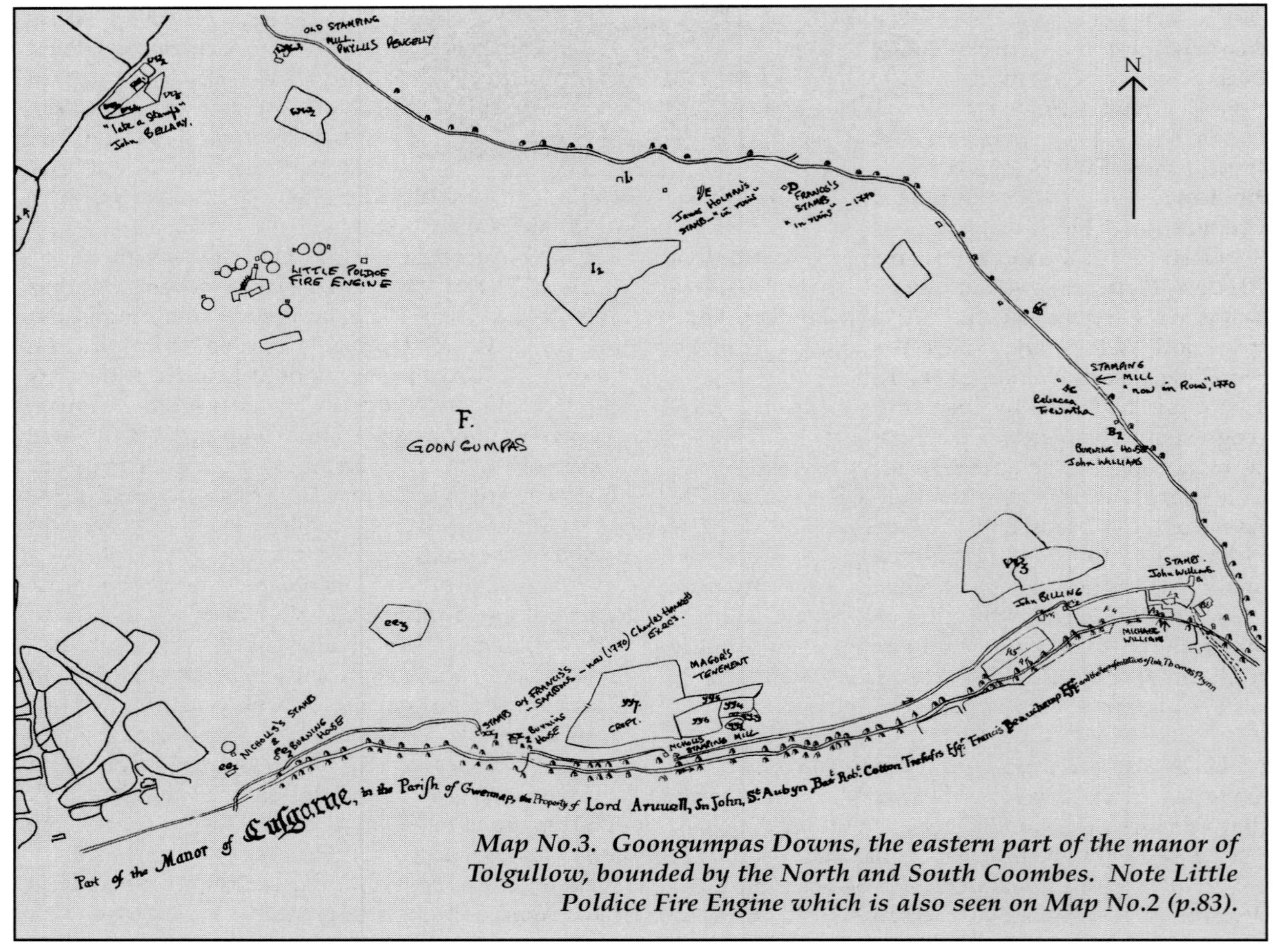

Map No.3. Goongumpas Downs, the eastern part of the manor of Tolgullow, bounded by the North and South Coombes. Note Little Poldice Fire Engine which is also seen on Map No.2 (p.83).

Three

Fairs & Markets

We have seen in a late-sixteenth-century reference (Norden, 1584) that 'a kinde of market' grew alongside the pilgrims' way, an organic growth increasing with passing years, and whilst we see no mention of either market or fair in the seventeenth-century surveys, it may be presumed that the wayside market continued uninterrupted throughout the Middle Ages. Charles Henderson writes:

... as for the growth of a market and then a village around the chapel [at St Day] *we find an exactly similar development at Goldsithney further along the road, near Marazion, where the celebrated Fair grew up by the wayside Chapel of St James.*

Children outside the market building.

He adds: 'St Day is called 'the towne of Seynte Trynyte in the parish of Gwenape' in 1540.'

In a survey of the manor taken in June and July of 1704 by William Longford Esq. and Henry Hill, we find the following entry of a lease: '1704. St Day Fair. Peter Oppy, now Wm. Oppy. Lives: Wm. Oppy. Anthony Tremelling. Yearly Value £2.10.0. Rent 3s.0d.'

The fair had by now become an annual event, recognised and organised by authority, the lords of the manor, who exacted rental for a lease allowing the holder to benefit from the fair. Clearly this 1704 lease was not the first; it transfers an earlier lease held by Peter Oppy to William Oppy, probably the son of the former lessee. Some 25 years later, in 1729/30, William Oppy surrendered his lease or possibly both the 'lives' had died, in which case the lease would have expired with them. The new lease sets out the full terms of the agreement as follows:

St DAY FAIR. Charles Mitchell and John Jeffery of Gwennap, Tinners, hold by Indenture of Lease dated 2nd February 1729/30 Granted by Wyndham Napier Esq. three eighths Parts of and in All the Benefit and Profit of the Fair or Market, alias Saint Dye [sic] *Market belonging to the Manor of Tolgullow alias St Dye usually holden and kept there yearly on the Friday before Easter commonly called Good Friday, together with the Tollage etc. To hold the same unto the said Charles Mitchell and John Jeffery for 99 years determinable on the deaths of Margaret Jeffery [daughter of the said John Jeffery], Charles Mitchell [son of the said Charles Mitchell] and Charles Mitchell [another son of the said Charles Mitchell], Consideration £21.0.0. Rent 1s.1d.*

LIVES: Margaret Jeffery at 19 years. Charles Mitchell at 5 years. Charles Mitchell at 1 year.

The lessees' return on their investment and their work in connection with it appears to have been less than half the benefit and profit of the fair. The greater portion of any profits presumably remained with the grantor, Wyndham Napier Esq.

A further reference to St Day's fair is to be found in the 1772 Survey of the Manor where we find tenement (No.12m) described as: 'A small House on the North side of St Day [sic] Chapple for keeping the Standings in and the Profits of St Day Fair, which is held annually on Good Friday.' This 'small house' is shown clearly on the Manor Map of 1772 *(see page 82)*, the lower-case 'm' beside it confirming it as the store for the standings, etc. The reference to its position in relation to the 'Chapple' helps also to confirm the site of the medieval church.

On Good Friday in medieval times the great Easter influx of pilgrims to the Mount would have been arriving at the Chapel of the Holy Trinity, Tolgulla, a day's march from the Mount. At this time of year those living in the area of the shrine experienced a notable increase in the number of traders from a wider area. In short, it was the ideal occasion for the lord of the manor to establish a fair which would bring increase to his revenues by leasing the benefit and profit of the fair.

The reference above to the 'standings' being kept in that small house suggests that they were owned by the lords of the manor and rented out to traders for displaying their wares. They were the forerunners of the stalls seen in our own times at tea treats and other outdoor events, assembled when and where required then packed away until the next season of events. Did those traders decorate their stalls in some way, perhaps with coloured ribbons and flags to attract attention and to promote a sense of occasion?

St Day Fair was a secular event, initiated for commercial reasons, and not to be confused with 'St Day Feast', the patronal feast which was possibly established to celebrate the dedication to the Holy Trinity of the fourteenth-century church and which is observed on the third Sunday after Whitsuntide.

By the beginning of the nineteenth century local agricultural shows were being held in many localities. An advertisement in the *Royal Cornwall Gazette* of 8 July 1823 gave advance notice of the forthcoming St Day Show which was to be held on 29 July following. The fuller notice, published two weeks later, and shown below, listed the livestock classes with the prizes to be awarded 'by just umpires'.

It is also interesting to note that no inhabitant of St Day, or indeed of the parish of Gwennap, would be allowed to compete:

ST DAY SHOW FAIR. 1823
St Day Show Fair will be held on Tuesday the 29th of July instant, when free ground and every other accommodation will be given to those who may bring cattle; and the following prizes, awarded by just umpires:

For the two best fed oxen, £2.2.0; for the two best working oxen, £1.1.0; for the best bull, £1.1.0; for the best cow £1.1.0; for the best cow and calf £1.1.0; for the best five-years-old saddle-horse £1.1.0; for the best three-years-old colt £1.1.0; for the best half-score sheep £1.1.0; for the best ram, 10s.6d.

The above must have been in the possession of the owners, for the space of two months. No inhabitant of St Day or Gwennap will be allowed any prize, which is done solely to encourage strangers, and it is sincerely hoped that no inhabitant will feel offended, the intention being pure, 25th July 1823.

The fair was an annual event, and meanwhile the daily/weekly 'wayside market' continued to function in the open air until the late-eighteenth century when steps were taken to provide facilities in the centre of St Day in the form of a covered market building. The site was owned by the Chichester family of North Devon, who made the ground available for the new buildings.

The cost of building was met from the tin and copper dues exacted from the mining adventurers as shown in extracts from the 1795 'Account of the Tin and Copper Dues of the Manor of Tolgullow.'

In 1814 Lysons tells us that 'a market on Saturdays, for butcher's meat and other provisions, was established a few years ago by Mr Williams for the accommodation of the miners.' He goes on to say that 'at this place [St Day] a fair was held on Good Friday: It is now a mere holiday fair, and kept on Easter Monday.' Writing in 1820 C.S. Gilbert endorsed this:

... the houses and population having amazingly increased within the last 30 years, the market which had been long discontinued, has again revived and is held weekly on Saturdays... There was formerly a fair held at St Daye on Good Friday, it has been held of later years on Easter Monday and is held for the purpose of amusement only.

Of the market William Lake wrote in 1865 in his *History of Cornwall*:

A market for provisions and articles in general use, is held on Saturdays in the Market Place, which is protected by iron railings. In the centre of the Market Place is a substantial tower containing a clock, it was erected in 1831 at an expense of £400.

In July 1844 the constables applied to the magistrates to close St Day Market at 10p.m. from Ladyday to Michaelmas and 9p.m. from Michaelmas to Lady Day.

It would appear that over the course of time market traders ignored the ruling, failing to cease trading promptly, staying later and later for as long as they had meat still unsold. Eventually, in 1877 on 20 April, the following letter appeared in the *Royal Cornwall Gazette*, its author complaining that the market was left unswept on Saturday nights because the butchers were still trading up until midnight.

Market Cleaning
I find our scavenger refuses to work on Sunday mornings (quite right too!). On Saturday evening the Potato Court and Fore Street, used to be swept after the vendors of cabbages, turnips, etc, had left the market, but now he has not the chance to commence until the Town Clock has struck the last hour for the week. I might mention last Saturday night in particular, when the

St Day Show in 1911 in a field at Vicarage Hill.

clock was striking twelve, seven butchers had not made a beginning to pack their half-bullock heads, hocks of beef etc. In fact the market house gates were not closed until 12:30. Surely the market ought to be closed at 10 o'clock.

Annie Trevithick, in her *Brief History of St Day* (c.1888) writes:

The market of St Day about 40–50 years ago was a big affair; every stall in both market houses was then occupied, the fish market was held in the open space on the north side of the clock, and both potato courts were covered with stalls laden with all kinds of things. Before the West Cornwall Railway was built, a great number of people came from Scorrier and Wheal Rose to St Day Market: and enormous quantities of beefsteak and onions were consumed by the miners on pay night (which fell on a Saturday) at various public houses; the "fry" being well washed down with beer. The mine girls also enjoyed themselves in the same way. On 'Maaze' Monday, ie, the following Monday the miners completed their enjoyment.

The following appeared in the *Royal Cornwall Gazette* on 17 June 1909:

Gwennap Parish Council met on Thursday, Mr George Bray in the chair. It was stated that in the centre of St Day there is an enclosed yard 10 yards square. In olden days this ground was given by the landowners to the inhabitants of St. Day, free of any rent or payment, for a market, and for many years butchers had stalls there. When the mines closed, and Saturday's Market became a thing of the past, no business was carried on in it, and for many years it had been unused. Four or five persons residing near it had keys to the gates, which were old and in a state. The question arose as to the advisability of the Parish Council taking the yard over for the benefit of the inhabitants of St Day. The Committee for Open Spaces were requested to visit it.

In the event the Parish Council decided against taking over the yard and, there being no prospective user coming forward, it was demolished by order of the owners, the lords of the manor.

On 30 March 1911 the *Royal Cornwall Gazette* carried this piece about the Old Market House: 'The Old Market House which has stood for so many years, has been removed. The town clock which stands in the centre of the market, looks very forlorn.'

The following year the paper reported:

The old Market House was the centre of the town's business when the various mines in the surrounding district were in full swing. Holders have gradually fallen away, until only one butcher [Mr Penrose, of Trevarth] has a stall in the Market. The lords consequently determined to pull it down, leaving the Town Clock standing in the centre of the ground. The buildings have been purchased by Mr Joseph Teague Letcher, agent for the Lords. The site which is in Fore Street is one of the best in the town.

The author remembers Mr Penrose of Trevarth still selling meat from his stall in Fore Street in the 1920s, familiarly known as 'Charlie Penrose'. At best, his wares were not exactly top quality and the then accepted practice of selling butchers' meat in the open, in the street, unprotected from dust, flies, etc. would hardly meet with approval from the Public Health Department today.

The market square is referred to as Harvey's Court in the 'Survey of the Division of the Manor', 1826–28, by Richard Thomas, surveyor of Falmouth.

In 1921 a memorial to those men of St Day who lost their lives in the First World War was built on the south side of the town clock in the form of a seated shelter and included a granite tablet recording their names and regiments. At the end of the Second World War a matching tablet was added carrying the names of the fallen 1929–45.

In 1931 the clock movement had been put in good order, and a garden, enclosed by a low wall, was provided through the generosity of W.J. Mills.

The memorial shelter had two seats and was occasionally used by some of the elderly as a meeting-place for a smoke and a chat, and was treated with respect. Regrettably, in the post-Second World War years, vandalism, endemic throughout the country, now showed itself in St Day and the War Memorial was shamefully desecrated. In 1986 the newly formed St Day Parish Council commissioned an imposing pair of wrought-iron gates to protect the memorial tablets within the War Memorial shelter. Every year since the memorial was built a service has been held there in November on Remembrance Sunday. Here at St Day the names of the fallen, of both major wars, are read to the assembled congregation.

St Day Show, 1911.

Above: *Wheal Jewell Row and the nineteenth-century cottages.*

Left: *Group of miners at Wheal Gorland Mine, c.1906.*

Below: *Workings at Bissa Pool, early 1920s.*

Four

Mining

Cornish mining has been well researched and written about by competent authorities over the years; this book therefore only touches on those mines which had a close association with St Day. The present author has relied upon the published works of H.G. Dynes, Hill and MacAlister, A.K. Hamilton Jenkin and others for dates of mine workings, tonnages and varieties of ores raised.

It has been stated by many writers that Gwennap was the greatest copper-producing area in the world during the eighteenth and nineteenth centuries and just as the growth of the industry was rapid so too was the decline from about 1860. The growth and the subsequent decline each had a marked socio-economic effect on the area.

By the end of the 1700s St Day was beginning to expand, an expansion which continued in company with the rapid increase in its associated mining activities, situated as it was in the centre of the world's greatest copper-mining industry, viz the Gwennap mines. This expansion shows up clearly on the succession of maps of the locality from 1772 to the end of the 1800s.

The major surveys of 1682 and 1772 show the increasing population of the manor of St Day. Fresh blood moved into the area from near and far as the news of rapidly increasing activity reached out and St Day found itself at the centre of an area of significant economic growth. Neighbouring villages too enjoyed the growing prosperity. *Williams' Commercial Directory of Cornwall* of 1847 gives an impressive account of businesses in St Day and of the professional men established there

By 1860 the Gwennap copper mines were all but finished and the great exodus began, to the Americas, the Antipodes, South and West Africa, anywhere in the world where there was metal to be mined; Cornish miners, the 'Hard Rock Men', left in droves. The discovery of huge deposits of copper ores in far-flung countries brought the price of copper down to levels which meant that it was no longer a viable proposition to continue mining that metal in Cornwall.

The following extracts from letters addressed to Simon Whitburn, Mining Engineer and Assayer of St Day, from one J. Buchanan Cree, whose offices were at Leadenhall Street in the City of London, throw up one or two matters of interest:

18th April 1879

128 Leadenhall Street, LONDON.
To Simon Whitburn, Esq.,
St DAY

Dear Sir,
I received the enclosed letter from Senor Naldal [from Chile] *with samples of 2 ores, the one is Black Jack and the other I suppose is zinc. I send them also to you & request you to write him in reply as I cannot read or write Spanish. You can inform me if there is anything important in it – zinc, as you know, is a monopoly here* [Chile] *and outsiders can do nothing in it.*

If Chili goes to war in earnest the price of copper may shortly go up again as the overmake of copper by Chili is the chief reason of the low prices.

Yours very truly, J. Buchanan Cree.

The last sentence reveals the reason for the collapse of Cornish copper mining, namely overproduction in Chile. In another letter the same gentleman asks Simon Whitburn to compose a standard formal reply so that he might send it with remittances to his agent in Chile. Cree ends with a postscript: 'I do not think there is any use to look for money at present to carry on. When the market for copper takes a start I shall see what I can do.' (Originals are in the possession of the author, S. Whitburn's great-grandson.)

The writer of those letters confesses to being unable to correspond in Spanish on what must have been commercially sensitive information, and in requiring an assay report he was obliged to turn to a remote little town in Cornwall for Spanish scholarship. Simon is being asked to discuss and advise on technical mining terms in the Spanish tongue – a reminder of the important role played by Cornishmen in the world copper industry.

The popular perception of Cornish mining is concerned with tin, but although this was certainly found and recovered in most of the Gwennap mines, Gwennap was primarily concerned with copper, as emphasised by H.G. Dynes in *The Metalliferous Mining Region of South West England* (1956):

GWENNAP. The area is essentially a copper producer having raised a recorded tonnage of over one and a quarter million tons of copper concentrates as against only 19,000 tons of black tin. Although the overall tin production from the area was small, something like 60% of the mines have raised tin ore, generally in small or insignificant amounts.

Those mines which are closely associated with St Day itself accord with the general pattern of the Gwennap mines in that they produced mainly copper, with tin coming second. Tin mining is, however, of far greater antiquity than copper mining in Cornwall; systematic mining of the latter did not begin before the sixteenth century, continuing in a small way, until the advent of deep mining in the eighteenth century, when with rapid expansion copper overtook the production of tin.

The mining of tin remained the principal industrial activity in the late-seventeenth century, copper not as yet appearing in great quantity in any of the records (although its dominance in the Cornish mining world was not far ahead). Meanwhile, the pattern of industry was of a number of small undertakings – as shown in a survey of 1687 (which can be found in the Courtenay Library at the Royal Institution of Cornwall). This lists the tin stamps in each of the two valleys (the North and South Coombes meeting at Trewinnard Mills), giving ample evidence that mining was already extensively spread over the district. This document makes mention of about a dozen:

Tinn workes that have been wrought within three yeares last past great Quantities of tinngossan.
Little poldice great quantities.
Killicor, great quantities.
The Bissaworke great quantities.
Nanse Gollan great quantities.
Croft Handy great quantities.
Pitts and Parsons.
In the meadows, in several.

Tinn workes now in working on poldiste als noongumpus downs:

Great poldiste.
Little poldiste.
Killavoce.

The Dudman workes, great quantities in the Several
In Tresaddern in the Several.
Besides Severall other Small works.

Of the above, five were located in or bordering the North Coombe. Tresaddern probably refers to Tresaddern Hendy, a tenement north of St Day, where stamps were certainly worked in the mid-eighteenth century, including Tolgullow Higher Stamps. Pitts and Parsons and the Dudman works have not been identified.

Also listed were the following:

Tinn workes now in working on poldiste als noongumpus downs:
Great poldiste.
Little poldiste.
Killavoce.
And Francis's Stamps called Holder's Worke.

Francis' Stamps is seen on the 'Watercourse Mapp', sited in the North Coombe. The foregoing workings were, of course, all within the manor of Tolgullow. Similar activity would undoubtedly have been found throughout the whole of the parish of Gwennap and beyond, to the edges of this great mineral-rich area.

Henderson provides us with evidence of smelting at St Day in 1651 (Henderson Collection, 232.150.RIC, Truro): 'Tinn bought att Gwennap Blowinge House on 12th December 1651. John Gabriell was the Blower. Sited at Tolcarne above St Day.' Again in 1670: '... the watercourse ran first to the blowing-house in Tolcarn.'

That blowing-house was supervised by Francis Paynter, whose family originated at Penryn and was associated with Poldice, their name surviving into the twentieth century at Paynter's Pool at Crofthandy on the Poldice sett. The blowing-house situated at Tolcarne has left us the place name Vogue, in earlier times spelt foge or voge, the Celtic Cornish word for a blowing or smelting work. The blowing-house is not shown on the 'Watercourse Mapp'.

The Mines Around St Day

In St Day itself Wheal Gorland, Wheal Quick and Wheal Jewell were to be found and in its immediate environs were Poldice, Roslabby, Wheal Pink, Wheal Clinton, Wheal Unity and Wheal Unity Wood, St Aubyn United, Cathedral, Trefula, Wheal Cupid, Parc an Chy and others, all a part of the Greater Gwennap Mining Area which itself included the great copper mines – the Consolidated Mines, the United Mines and the extensive Tresavean sett.

In most cases the mine records are only available from the early-nineteenth century to give us positive information regarding the exact tonnages raised and dates of working, as given below for the individual mines named (all of which are taken from *The Metalliferous Mining Region of South West England*).

Wheal Gorland:

Of the mines in the immediate vicinity of St Day which have either declined in their produce of ores or have ceased to be worked, we may notice Wheal Gorland, an ancient mine, which has been subject to great fluctuations, the lode having been so rich at times that the miners have been placed under a strict surveillance lest the Adventurers should be defrauded of the valuable minerals and ores.

With those words William Francis, in a footnote to his poem 'Gwennap', described Wheal Gorland in 1845. It is certainly true that mineral collectors from far afield have long searched the surface wastes of this 'ancient mine' for examples of its rare and beautiful minerals. A few years ago when on a visit to Norway, a lady born in St Day noticed in a museum in Oslo some particularly spectacular specimens labelled 'From Wheal Gorland Mine. St Day. Cornwall.'

C.C. James in his *History of the Parish of Gwennap* mentions some 21 different minerals found in small quantities in Wheal Gorland. In addition to his list may be added gold, silver and uranium, again in small quantities, although the mine was worked principally for copper of which 40,750 tons of ore were extracted between 1815 and 1851, which yielded 3,234 tons of copper. H.G. Dynes records production of 15 tons of black tin and 18 tons of arsenic during the same period. He goes on to give us report of the 1906–09 period when 164 tons of wolfram (tungsten ore) and 18 tons of black tin were recovered from the mine and dumps, in addition to a considerable production of fluorspar. Muttrel lode in this mine was a tin lode and lies under the town of St Day.

Wheal Jewell & Wheal Quick: Dynes tells us that Wheal Jewell sett lies south and south-east of St Day and includes Wheal Quick, a small section lying under the southern parts of St Day town, the northern boundary of the mine lying along Fore Street and Vogue Hill as far as the Star Inn at Vogue.

In a lease dated 1 July 1797 there is a reference to 'the Accounting House belonging to Wheal Jewell Mine' and Wheal Quick is twice mentioned in connection with Francis Quick in the 1772 Survey of the Manor.

During the period 1815–53 the mine produced 58,160 tons of 9 per cent copper ore, 9 tons of black tin and 20 tons of 70 per cent lead ore, the last from a cross-course.

West Jewell: Dynes tells us that West Jewell lies south-west of St Day and includes West Wheal Gorland which was also known as Roslabby and Tolcarne. It produced 12,580 tons of 7 per cent copper ore and 8 tons of black tin between 1831 and 1852 and under the name North Wheal Damsel 580 tons of 8 per cent copper ore and 3 tons of black tin between 1852 and 1854.

Hill and MacAlister tell us that pitchblende and uranite are said to occur at 30 fathoms from surface. A deposit of decomposed granite on this sett was quarried for china clay in the mid-nineteenth century but, lacking the quality of the St Austell deposits, it was used for manufacturing bricks, with over a million bricks being turned out annually. The china-clay deposit was about 50 feet deep and was not distributed over a wide area (see Chapter 16).

Wheal Pink: This mine was worked for a time as Clinton and Pink United and eventually became part of Wheal Gorland with which it shared a common border. From 1815 to 1833 and from 1845 to 1855 Wheal Pink produced 1,830 tons of 7 per cent copper ore. The mine is thought not to have been worked below the 'deep adit level', here 36 fathoms from surface. Wheal Pink is remembered in the place name Pink Moors which borders the sett.

Parc an Chy: This mine adjoins Wheal Pink and Clinton and was first worked in the mid-nineteenth century for copper ore. Production was low, only 36 tons of 8 per cent copper ore being raised between 1863 and 1865. In 1910 it was reopened for wolfram, that ore having been found in the dumps which were worked over but with little success. During the First World War it was again opened for wolfram but closed at the end of the war in 1918. In that year 3,217 tons of ore were crushed yielding wolfram, tin and arsenic. The mine was restarted in 1926 and worked until 1929 as a tin mine, but although some rich values of ore were found these were insufficient to meet the cost of production and milling.

During that final period of working, there being no water at Parc an Chy to service the dressing floors, the ore was transported to a mill built at Poldice Mine for that purpose. Transportation of the ore was by overhead cable.

Wheal Unity: Situated about half a mile north-east of St Day, this mine is believed to have started about 1790 and in 1864 became a part of St Day United, a group of mines formed c.1852. Its western boundary separates it from Wheal Gorland sett. Dynes gives, from 1852 to 1856, 40 tons of black tin, 243 tons of arsenic and a small quantity of lead, but fails to record the amount of copper raised. MacAlister records 108,698 tons of copper ore, yielding 8,836 tons of copper for the period 1815–49.

Unity Wood or West Poldice: Lying three-quarters of a mile north-west of St Day, this mine raised (between 1815 and 1838 and from 1852) some 21,632 tons of 6 per cent copper ore, 570 tons of black tin, 129 tons of arsenic, 21 tons of pyrite and 1.5 tons of lead ore. Later, as Tolgullow United from 1882 to

1903, it recovered 570 tons of black tin, 20 tons of 15 per cent copper ore, 220 tons of arsenic, 152 tons of mispickel (zinc ore) and 185 tons of ochre.

St Aubyn United (including Grambler): One mile west of St Day the engine-house and stack of Wheal St Aubyn stand out in silhouette when viewed from Vogue Hill; this is the only remaining engine-house in the parish of St Day. Between 1843 and 1893 this group of mines raised 12,510 tons of copper ore, 97 tons of black tin and about 300 tons of fluorspar.

New Cathedral: One mile south-west of St Day and adjacent to Gwennap Pit this mine was worked between 1827 and 1842. It was again active from 1874 to 1885 during which period some reclamation was made from the dumps. Between 1874 and 1881 the mine raised 585 tons of 8 per cent copper ore and 1.75 tons of black tin. The deepest level was 84 fathoms below adit, which here was 18 fathoms below the surface, a total depth of 612 feet.

In January 1881 old workings were holed resulting in serious flooding and the loss of eight lives, the bodies not being recovered until the following July, from the 50-fathom level. The names of these men were: Joseph May, Richard Oates, George Richards, John Blackler, William Blackler, William Northey, R. Bennetts and J.H. Farrell. The two last named were boys.

The water from Cathedral Mine was later used to supply the town of Redruth from a reservoir constructed at Sandy Lane.

Wheal Cupid: Situated one mile west of St Day adjoining the St Day/Redruth road, this small mine was worked from two shafts, Engine Shaft and an unnamed shaft. It reached a depth of 65 fathoms below adit which here is 14 fathoms below the surface. Between 1855 and 1862 the mine raised 44 tons of 4.5 per cent copper ore, 6 tons of black tin and 22 tons of fluorspar. The 30″ engine was built in 1851 by the Perran Wharf Foundry for the Great Exhibition in London and afterwards worked at Wheal Cupid.

Trefula: Situated three-quarters of a mile north-west by west of St Day and bordering Wheal Cupid, this mine is thought to have been worked for copper ore and to a depth of 100 fathoms at each of two shafts. There are no records of output.

Poldice Mine & Valley: John Ogilby's Road Map of 1675 shows at the crossroads at Comford *'The Road to Pole Dys'* but does not show St Day. Writing in 1685 Hals noted:

Not far from St Day is that unparallelled and inexhaustible tin work called Poldys which for about forty years space hath employed yearly from eight hundred to a thousand men and boys labouring for and searching after tin in that place, where they have produced and raised yearly at least £20,000 worth of that commodity, to the great enrichment of adventurers in these lands.

Poldice worked from an even earlier age, but while no records exist to show the extent of early mining, there is an account from the mid-1500s of one man accusing another of 'stealing his tynne, at a place called Poldys, in Gwennap'. Later records do exist which tell us that from 1815 to 1849 Poldice produced 108,698 tons of copper ore, and, in addition, from 1837 to 1852 it produced some 1,525 tons of tin ore. It also yielded zinc, wolfram and arsenic (the remains of the 1924 arsenic flue, or 'lambreth', are still there). It was finally worked from 1924–29.

In a 'cost book' of Poldice Mine for June 1798 (in the author's collection) there is an intriguing entry: 'To Messrs. Boulton & Watt for 17 months premium of Oppy's Engine from the 1st January 1797 to the end of June 1798. £1056.11s.' This requires an explanation; it seems to have arisen from a lawsuit successfully brought by Messrs Boulton & Watt against a number of Cornish mines using their pumping engines. The engines were installed in Cornish mines with an agreement that the payment for an engine would include, in addition to actual initial cost, the mine adventurers paying to Boulton & Watt one-third of the savings made between the cost of using their engine and the previous cost of pumping. After some years of honouring that

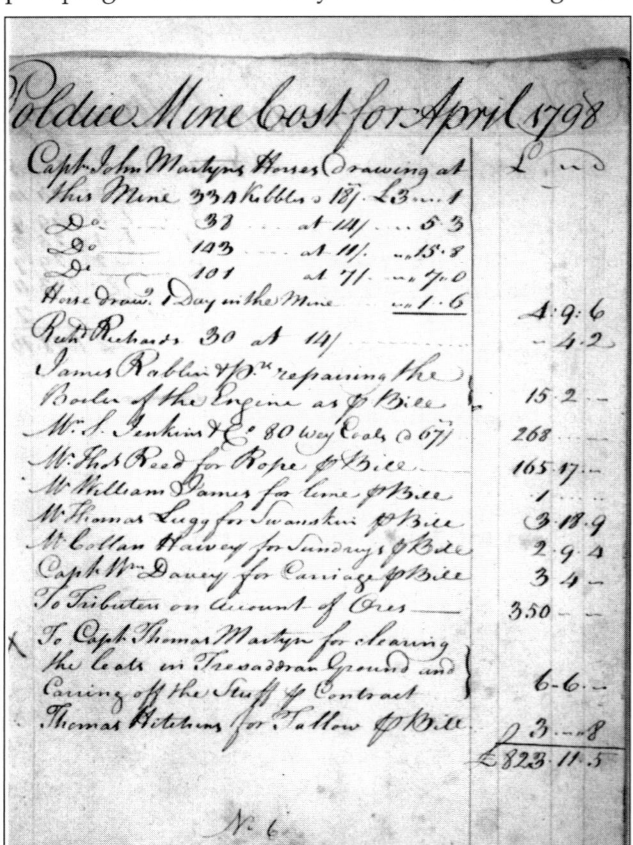

Poldice Mine Cost for April 1798 £ . .
Capt. John Martyns Horses (drawing at this Mine 33 A Kibbles @ 18/. £3....1
Do. 33 at 14/ ... 5.3
Do. 143 at 11/ ..15.8
Do. 101 at 7/ ...7.0
Horse draw. Day in the Mine ...1.6 — 4.9.6
Richd. Richards 30 at 14/ — 4.2
James Rablin & Pr. repairing the Boiler of the Engine as p Bill — 15.2.-
Mr. J. Jenkins & Co. 80 Wey Coals @ 67/ — 268 ..
Mr. Thos. Reed for Rope p Bill — 165.17.-
Mr. William James for lime p Bill — 1...
Mr. Thomas Lugg for Swanskin p Bill — 3.18.9
Mr. Collan Harvey for Sundrys p Bill — 2.9.4
Capt. Wm. Davey for Carriage p Bill — 3.4.-
To Tributers on Account of Ores — 350 ..
To Capt. Thomas Martyn for clearing the Leats in Tresaddran Ground and Carrying off the Stuff p Contract — 6.6.-
Thomas Hitchins for Tallow p Bill — 3..8
£823.11.5
No. 6

Poldice Mine cost book, February 1789.

agreement Cornish mine adventurers together decided to withhold further payment, perhaps being of the opinion that they had paid many times the actual cost of their engine and, driven by the increasing unprofitability of the Cornish mines, that it was time to take drastic action. Boulton & Watt sued and won the day and the mine owners were obliged to settle the outstanding debts. The monthly payment of dues on Oppy's engine amounted to £63.3s.0d. and the cost book shows that amount being paid regularly every month thereafter.

Oppy's shaft was more than 1,200 feet deep. The height of St Day's old church tower to the top of the pinnacle was 85 feet 4 inches above ground level, which means that the church tower would fit into the shaft 14 times!

Amongst other interesting entries in the 1789 cost book we find the following for February: 'Paid Mr. William Murdoch for his invention for boreing pumps. £10.10s.0d.' William Murdoch is better remembered for the discovery of coal gas in 1797 and his harnessing of the same to provide domestic and street lighting. His home in Cross Street, Redruth, was the very first house in the world to be so illuminated, and is now known as 'Murdoch House', the centre for the Cornish Migration Project. Murdoch was resident agent for Boulton & Watt and as such was responsible for collecting the dues from the mines. It will be remembered too, that he successfully built a model steam locomotive. We have no further information regarding the invention for boring pumps.

The 'Tributers Acct of Poldice Ores – sold 26th April 1798' lists the names of 25 individual 'Takers', with the details of the amounts in tons of ore raised, along with entries for the taker's price, taker's amount, subsist, materials, drawings, doctor and balance. The record shows a total of 125 tons, 3 cwts raised. The price averaged at £5.18s.6d. per ton, ranging from £12.6s. down to £2.10s. a ton. The total value was £741.9s.5d. In all 11 of the 25 takers had a varying number of partners. A 'doctor' subscription of 2d. per man per month was deducted from the taker's balance and is shown on the book; thus we are able to arrive at the number of partners working with and sharing with each taker.

The highest nett payment for April 1798 was £62.15s.2d. to be shared between the taker, Sampson Jeffery, and his seven partners. The share per man was worth £7.17s.0d. The lowest payment for that month amounted to £0.9s.2d., paid to Joseph Francis.

In 1798 a record was made of the following:

Richard Ham & 3 partners, firemen at Oppy's Engine
@ 50/per month each. *£10.0s.0d.*
Cleaning the Engine. *6s.6d.*
do flues. *4s.6d.*
Attending Saturdays. *15s.0d.*

Jos.Bray & 7 partners Attending on the Pitwork & Engine @ 42s pr.mth. each
£16.16s.
Attending 4 Sundays. *£1.4s.0d.*

A working month was calculated as 28 days; payments for working Saturdays and four Sundays brought the total of days worked to a calendar month. Firemen would be required every day to keep the pumping engine working and the mine free of water.

These payments are recorded for every month throughout the book, indicating that working Saturdays for firemen and Sundays for the pitmen were outside the customary contract. A regular payment was made to William Kinsman for 'Building the Engine fire place. 10s.0d.' The photograph (*see page 18*) is of workings at Bissa Pool, further down the Poldice Valley, and dates from the early 1920s. Beyond Bissa Pool on the northern hillside stand the remains of Wheal Henry engine-house, which possibly housed one of the earliest steam pumping engines.

Today, Poldice Mine waste, now overgrown, is the home of rare plants, butterflies and dragonflies. Skylarks nested there for many years, but sadly they have apparently disappeared from the area, although they still inhabit the nearby United Mines wasteland. By the beginning of the nineteenth century the feverish searching for mineral wealth underground inevitably had an impact on the surface, with engine-houses and other mine buildings springing up everywhere and the insidious spread of the waste dumps, the mine burrows, covering acres of land, some of it agricultural. It would appear that concern regarding this waste spread had already been voiced in some quarters – thus leading the surveyor, Richard Thomas, to defend the mining interests in his 'Survey of the Mining District' in 1819, a relevant extract from which follows below:

1819 EFFECT OF MINING ON LANDSCAPE.
Richard Thomas. Surveyor and Civil Engineer.
Report on a Survey of the Mining District of Cornwall from Chasewater to Camborne.
John Cary, 181, The Strand, 1819. London.

(p.14) It has been said that the mining operations in Cornwall, destroying the surface and diverting the attention of and the capitals of the inhabitants, have been prejudicial to agricultural pursuits: but this opinion, if any such be now entertained, is erroneous.

The quantity of inclosed ground that has been destroyed in the whole of this district (Chasewater–Camborne) does not appear to be more than 150 acres, part of which was very coarse. But (to say nothing of the encouragement necessarily given to agriculture in general by the demand for the produce of the soil, to supply the great population) thousands of

Mining in St Day

St Aubyn engine-house, abandoned, 1893, the only remaining engine-house in the parish.

Clock tower at Consols Mine with Taylor's Shaft stack in the background, 1985.

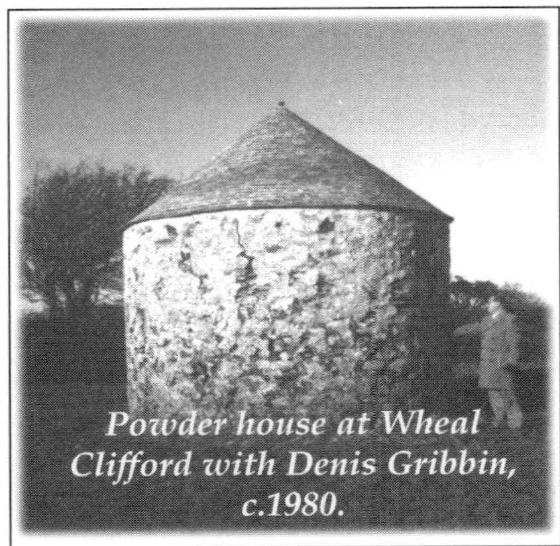

Powder house at Wheal Clifford with Denis Gribbin, c.1980.

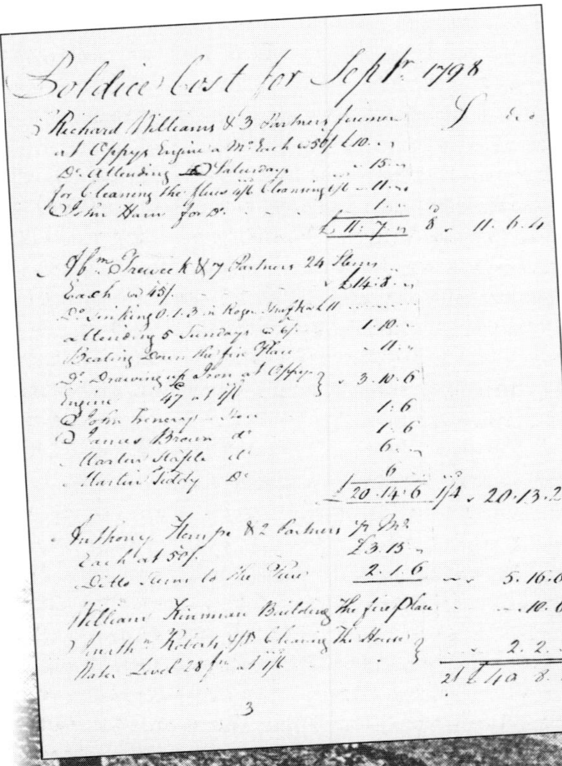

Poldice Cost for Septr 1798

Richard Williams & 3 Partners Enginemen at [illegible] Engine a M^o Each @ 50/ £10. .
D^o Attending [illegible] Saturdays . 15 .
for Cleaning the flues [illegible] Cleaning [illegible] . 11 .
John Harn for D^o 1 .
£11 : 7 . 8 . 11 . 6 . 4

Wm Treweek & 7 Partners 24 [illegible] Each @ 45/ £14 . 8 .
D^o Sinking 0 . 1 . 3 in Roger [illegible] [illegible]
Attending 5 Sundays @ 6/ 1 . 10 .
Beating Down the fire Place . 11 .
D^o Drawing up Iron at [illegible] Engine 47 at [illegible] 3 . 10 . 6
John Henery D^o 1 : 6
James Brown D^o 1 . 6
Martin Staple D^o 6 .
Martin Tiddy D^o 6
20 . 14 . 6 1/4 . 20 . 13 . 2

Anthony Hempe & 2 Partners [illegible] Each at 50/ £3 . 15 .
Ditto [illegible] to the [illegible] 2 . 1 . 6 5 . 16 . 6

William Kinman Building the fire Place . . 10 . 6

[illegible] Roberts [illegible] Cleaning the House Water Level 28 f^m at [illegible] 2 . 2 .
21 £40 8 . 6

3

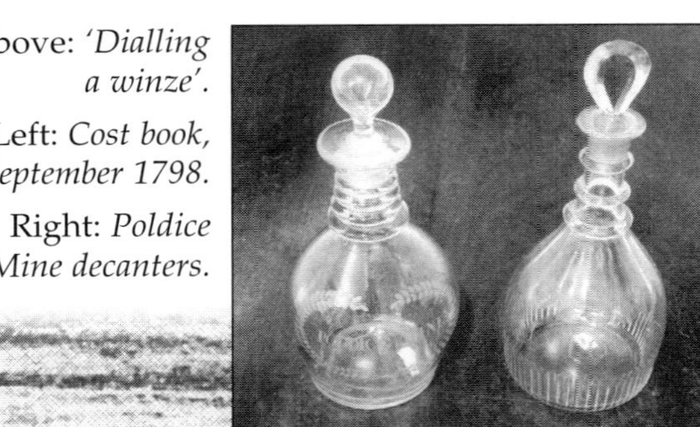

Above: *'Dialling a winze'.*

Left: *Cost book, September 1798.*

Right: *Poldice Mine decanters.*

A mid-nineteenth-century artist's impression of St Day with the town clock on the left, Holy Trinity Church centre and the Consolidated Mines in the background on the right.

acres of downs, commons and wastes, have been inclosed and improved, and are continually inclosing by the miners and others on a small scale generally from three to six acres to a tenement, on each of which, one or two cottages have been erected, which accounts for the great number of detached houses seen in some parts of the Map.

These waste lands, had there not been such a numerous population supported by the miners, would probably have remained in their original state, the soil being too poor a quality (resulting from heathy turf having been cut for fuel), to repay the farmer his expenses for its improvement.

Today's protesters deplore the spread of concrete for new roads and building sites.

The Consolidated Mines & The United Mines (Later to Become Clifford Amalgamated Mines)

A mile east of St Day lie the extensive setts of the above mines, today presenting a scene of desolation, but which in its great period was a hive of activity with the greatest concentration of engine-houses anywhere in the world in such a small area; for many decades this was the centre of the world's copper industry.

Although this great mining area falls outside the manor of St Day proper, its proximity to the town inevitably had a profound influence on changing socio-economic conditions, heralding a growth of population which included not only skilled tradesmen but also the professional men – doctors, engineers and assayers, accountants, chemists and surveyors – concomitant with a growing and busy mining society.

Today that whole mining area is familiarly known as 'United' or 'United Downs', accommodating industrial estates and a County Council Waste Disposal Unit.

The mining history of United Downs is beyond the scope of this volume and we can only attempt to convey some idea of its one-time importance over something like a century, important not only to the immediate community but also in a world context. The following passage taken from Hill & MacAlister, *Geology of the Mining District of Camborne & Redruth*, was written in 1906 and describes United as it was at the beginning of the twentieth century:

... the mineral belt extending from Baldhu to St Day. Although mining operations in the district have ceased, a considerable part of the ground is out of cultivation, and large tracts mark the site of the old spoil heaps which in the district east of St Day cover a considerable area. This wide expanse, that may be described as a vast wreckage, is dotted by engine houses and mine stacks in various stages of decay that still further add to the unsightliness of the landscape. The borders of this tract have in some cases been reclaimed from the dreary features of an abandoned mining district by the planting of timber, as at Gwennap and Scorrier. The extensive nature of the subterranean excavations is vividly brought home in this district by the steam which issues from some of the shafts that reach the heated waters below.

Beneath its surface area of approximately 800–1,000 acres lie abandoned underground workings, shafts, winzes, adits and levels said to total some 63 miles.

A mining plan of the whole area, in the author's possession, shows a total of 165 shafts, most of them named; of these 83 are in the United Mines sett and 82 in the Consolidated Mines sett. The plan also shows and names some 30 lodes worked from those shafts from which an astonishing variety of minerals from so small an area have been extracted.

At the Consolidated Mines the records for 1815–57 show, amongst the viable extractions, copper heading the list with a recorded 750,000 tons of concentrates (the entire Gwennap mining area produced a recorded 1,250,000 tons of copper concentrates). This is followed by 1,050 tons of pyrite, 60 tons of zinc ore, 32 tons of black tin and 7½ tons of arsenic.

The Great Consolidated Mines included, from east to west, Wheal Fortune, Wheal Girl, Wheal East Virgin, Wheal Virgin, Wheal West Virgin. Wheal Virgin is known to have been active in 1757. At Wheal Fortune Davey's Shaft reached a depth of 287 fathoms below adit (the depth of which is not known). (See Buckley, *The Great Adit.*) The United Mines records show similar variations of tonnages recovered as follows: 1815–61, 347,500 tons of copper ore, 1,290 tons of pyrite, 271 tons of zinc, 250 tons of black tin and 158 tons of arsenic.

Copper mining started on the United Mines sett in the mid-eighteenth century as 'The Metal Works'. At Ale & Cakes the lowest level is 250 fathoms below adit, the adit here being 96 feet from the surface. Francis's Engine Shaft, Taylor's Shaft and Garlands Shaft each have levels at 230 fathoms below adit. (The County Adit here is about 30 fathoms below surface.)

Hot Lode is well named, the water temperature here being 96° to 120° fahrenheit and the air temperature even higher at 102° to 124° fahrenheit. At the bottom levels of Davey's Shaft miners' boots are said to have rotted very quickly, this being the result of soaking in the hot water which was acidic (due, in all likelihood, to the presence of pyrite).

To provide steam to drive the pumping engine, water from Hockin's Shaft was used. The acidity of this water was so great that its steam damaged the cylinder of the engine, which proved sufficiently serious to cause the adventurers to seek a source of clean water in adequate quantity. Eldon's Engine-House, situated beside the entrance of the present-day County Council waste tip, contained a 30" pumping engine which raised water from the acid-free higher levels. It was pumped to surface and contained in a rectangular reservoir nearby, the outline of which is clearly visible on the left of the road leading to Bissoe.

The United Mines included, from west to east, Cupboard, Poldory, Ale & Cakes, Wheal Clifford, Wheal Andrew and Wheal Friendship. From time to time we come across the expression 'x fathoms below adit' – this refers to the Great Adit which drains all the mines in the district. Construction began in the mid-eighteenth century, the aim being to reduce the cost of draining the increasingly deep mines. Started in 1748, it was the brainchild of John Williams of Burncoose who managed the affairs of the Hearle family, lords of the manor. Spur adits were driven by mine owners to connect to the Great Adit to take away the water from a depth some distance below the surface, thus saving on pumping costs.

The adit mouth is a little way below Twelveheads and can easily be found and identified by the constant torrent of water issuing from the portal. Starting from this point excavation drove towards the Poldice sett to drain that mine, which it entered at a depth of more than 40 fathoms below surface. Adit level at Jeffrey's Shaft, Poldice, was 48 fathoms from the surface.

Having reached the eastern boundary of Poldice, work continued on the adit, reaching out to include more than 50 mines between Bissoe and Redruth. For a full history and achievement of the Great or County Adit, the reader's attention is directed to A.J. Buckley's comprehensive publication *The Great County Adit*, published by Penhellick Publications, Pool, Camborne (2000).

The following appeared in the *Royal Cornwall Gazette* on 17 July 1818:

> *By immemorial custom, an account day (on a mine) is a species of feast. Such of the adventurers as choose to attend, of whom the merchants and their friends form a decided majority, sit down to an excellent dinner, in which the good old English cheer, of roast beef and plum-pudding makes a conspicuous part. This is followed by flowing bowls of excellent punch, for the manufacture of which mine captains are celebrated. After a full and substantial meal has been properly diluted, by drinking the usual sentiments in this exhilarating beverage, the Manager, who is usually in the chair, produces the Cost Book.*

Certain entries in the Tin and Copper Dues Accounts provide further evidence of account day jollification, with the lords exhibiting unexpected generosity, as on 8 April 1792: 'Paid for a pipe of port for Wheal Unity as a present from the Lords. £85.0s.0d.' (A 'pipe' is a large cask, equivalent to four barrels or 105 gallons.) Again, on 13 July 1805: 'Paid for pipe of Wine for Whele [sic] Jewell £105.0s.0d.' Somewhat less generous was the present recorded in an entry on 17 August 1810: 'Gave Widow Curtis her husband being killed in the Manor £7.0s.0d.' Fatalities in the mines were not uncommon and newspaper reports of inquests show not only deaths of men but also, not infrequently, boys aged 12 or 13 or so being killed 'accidentally'.

Major disaster sometimes struck, with many lives being lost. The *West Briton* of 15 April 1836 made the following report:

> *On the 12th inst. An inquest was held before Mr. Hosken James, coroner, at Chacewater, on the body of James Oates 13 years of age, who worked as a barrow-boy in the Consolidated Mines, Gwennap. Deceased was unloading stuff on a sollar at the bottom of the 188 fathom level, when the timber work which had been erected about three months, gave way and he was precipitated, with his barrow, ten fathoms and killed on the spot. Verdict: Accidental death.*

Again, the *West Briton* carried a similar report on 2 September 1836:

> *An inquest was held on Tuesday before Hosken James, Esq., at Chacewater, on view of the body of Martin Northey, a boy of about 12 years of age, who attended a pair of workmen in the mine. It appeared from the evidence, that on Monday, the deceased was going below at the engine shaft to work, and that on arriving about 12 fathoms from grass he slipped his hold, and falling out of the ladder was precipitated to the depth of 12 fathoms, upon a ladder sollar below and was so much injured by the fall, that he died in about a quarter of an hour. Verdict: Accidental Death.*

On 18 November 1836 the same newspaper made this report:

> *An inquest was held on Wednesday, at the United Mines, Gwennap, on the body of a miner, named Joseph Francis 23 years of age. He was a tutwork-man engaged with others in driving the 140 fathom level west of Hocking's Engine Shaft, where 16 years before other adventurers had driven the 130 fathom level above and taken ore from the bottom of it. Miners were instructed to be cautious lest they cut into water, which might be accumulated in the level above them... When about 45 fathoms from Hockings shaft water was found oozing from the ceiling of the level... And all hastened to the surface. After half an hour, finding no water... they again went below and bored a hole in the ceiling which unexpectedly gave way. All the miners save deceased made a hasty retreat; he endeavoured to escape through a safety door but was caught between the edge of the door and the post, where on the water subsiding his body was found in an upright position. It is supposed the rush of water was too great, and that deceased had not sufficient strength to keep the door open long enough to get safely through. Accidental death.*

Five

The Watercourse Mapp, c.1720

The so-called Watercourse Mapp is neither drawn to scale nor is it properly orientated; it is a rough diagram, reliable only in determining the order in which the numerous stamps and other industrial features occur. It is, in effect, a rough guide for anyone seeking to identify a particular holding, for example, an agent of the lords of the manor needing to weigh or measure the quantity of 'tinn-stuff upon grass' in order to assess and collect the dues from a particular occupier.

The town of St Day is shown as a cluster of dwellings around the church tower, which by this time was all that remained of the original church. Certain identifiable key points are named, for instance, 'the Road from St Day to Redruth', which leads us to the prime source of the streams at what is now called Vogue Shute. Tod Pool, too, is a reliable checkpoint, as is 'The Grist Mill belonging to the Mannor of Tolgullo als St Day' at the junction of the North and South Coombes at Hale Mills near Twelveheads. Grist mills ground corn as opposed to stamping mills which ground ores.

Taking an overall look at the map we see that the South Coombe is the valley stretching from the Pound Crossroads (of today) via Wheal Maid/Consols Hill to Hale Mills where it is joined by the stream from the North Coombe. (Note: Consols is pronounced with the accent on the second syllable.) The North Coombe proper leads from Zimapan via Todpool and Bissa to join up with the South Coombe at Hale Mills. The map also shows an apparent third stream running from Vogue through Poldice to Todpool, and thence to Hale Mills. This is the watercourse to which the title of the map refers, described on the map itself as 'The Watercourse from the Headware to Poldice Engine and Stamping Mills and then to the Greist Mill belonging to the Mannor of Tolgulla als St Day.' Referred to as 'Tresaddern Leats' from time to time, it is mentioned in a seventeenth-century lease and again in a dispute over a watercourse in the 1670s, 'to work an engine on Poldice tinwork or adventure' which states that 'The Watercourse ran first to the blowing-house in Tolcarne, then to the mill, then on to the Plaintiff's mill in Poldice.'

It was a man-made stream, which ran from Vogue to the present-day Crofthandy Chapel area, feeding a number of stamps and 'engines' en route. These engines are distinguished by a simple diagram, a cross within a circle (the term 'engine' being used to denote any mechanical contrivance, whether powered by water-wheel, or horse).

The blowing-house is not shown on the Watercourse Mapp, but the place name Vogue, from the Cornish foge or its mutation voge, 'a blowing-house', suggests the probable site as being near the present Star Inn. The fact that the leat is named 'Tresaddern Leats' several times in leases, etc. suggests at first that it passed through Tresaddern Farm fields, a supposition which is strengthened by the fact that a leat emanating from Vogue Shute passed through those fields until the mid-1950s and is well remembered by the present writer who lived there throughout the 1920s. The Watercourse Mapp, however, puts the leat north of the town of St Day, and further research revealed a tenement listed in the 1682 Manor Rent Rolls Survey as No.2 Tresaddern Hendy als Clibma, which appeared again in the 1772 Manor Rent Rolls as No.6 Tresodren Hendy Debma als Clibma and is shown on the accompanying map sited north of St Day *(see page 82)*.

In 1704 the Manor Rent Rolls record Tresadron East, and in 1742 Tresadron Hendy reappears. In a Poldice Mine cost book for April 1789 (author's collection) there is an entry which reads: 'To Capt. Thomas Martyn for clearing the leats in Tresaddran [sic] Ground and carring [sic] off the Stuff p Contract £6.6s.' The contours for that area show a sufficient fleet to maintain a flow of water from Vogue Shute to the Engine Pool seen near the whipping post.

The name Tresaddern Hendy fell into disuse long ago but with its rediscovery the positioning given of St Day Town makes sense. 'Tresaddern Hendy' translates into English as 'Tresaddern Old Farm/homestead'. Neither the Tresodren Leat nor the later Tresaddern Farm Leat is shown on the Manor Maps but the Watercourse Mapp puts the leat north of St Day Town. That earlier leat ran from Vogue via Tresaddern Hendy to Poldice Engine Pool, thence to the Manor Grist Mill at Hale Mills through

Todpool and to Bissa, feeding a number of Stamps and engines en route.

The later leat ran from Tolcarne along the hillside through Tresaddern Farm and thence to Poldice. In 1860, when St Day Brickworks began production, this leat was probably diverted to allow for the deep clay-pit expansion. It was then carried over the steep ravine next to the road at Tolcarne, by a wooden aquaduct, and through an iron drainpipe under the road at School Hill and on to Tresaddern Farm land. The aquaduct was deliberately destroyed some time in the 1950s. During the 1920s when the author was living at Tresaddern Farm, the leat ran through a number of the farm fields leading towards Crofthandy, and was accessible from most of the other fields, which was certainly an asset to the farm.

The map marks a succession of stamps with their owners' names, starting with 'The Pool belonging to the Engine & Stamping Mills in Poldice.' Reference to the 1772 map suggests that this pool was situated below the present crossroads between St Day and Crofthandy. Close following that is 'Peter Oppy's Stamps', accompanied by the circle and cross motif. The leat is then shown taking some abrupt turns at this part and a succession of stamps sites with their owners' names follow, viz. 'Allen's Stamps', 'Mr Henry Harris of St Day his Stamps', 'John Rabies Stamps' and 'Mr Henry Harris of Cosgarne his Stamps'.

There follows a rectangle drawn with the caption 'The Engine Great Pool here'. In this same area we find 'Mr Coster's Two Stamps here'. The Leat continues to 'Tod Pool' with 'Mr Philip Tom's Stamps', 'Mr Henry Harris of St Day his Stamps', 'Mr Coster's Stamps called Heartsease', 'Capt. Tyack's Stamps call'd Heartsease' and 'Capt. Tyack's Stamps'. Then follow five more stamps ending with Killicor Engine which, like Tod Pool Stamps, is depicted with two of the arms extended indicating a horse-driven whim. Among the names of stamps owners of particular note is Mr Coster with two stamps and further along the leat 'Mr Coster's Stamps call'd Heart's Ease'. The location of Heart's Ease has not been positively identified but possibly lies between Todpool and Crofthandy Chapel.

John Coster set up a copper-smelting furnace on the bank of the River Wye near Monmouth, around 1680, and obtained a lease of the Chacewater mine from Lord Falmouth. As noted by D.B. Barton (*Copper Mining in Cornwall*), he is credited with introducing a number of improvements in the copper mines including the horse-drawn whim.

In all, the Watercourse Mapp names 28 sets of stamps with owners' names; how many were employed in total is not known. The same area recorded in the 1772 Survey gives a total of eight stamps and three burning houses. Deep mining had by that time come into its own and adits driven within the ever deepening mines to connect with the Great Adit cut off the supply of water which had driven the water-wheels, powering the many stamps in the two coombes.

Many names of stamps holders found on the Watercourse Mapp are to be seen later in the manor surveys. The map records a sequence of stamps alongside the stream called the 'South Watercourse', which divides 'St Day Mannor' from the 'Mannor of Tolcarne', running down the valley to the beginnings of the South Coombe. Close to the source of the water at Vogue Shute the map records 'Mr Anthony Cock's Stamps', the first of that sequence.

Among the leases discussed in Chapter Twelve are three sets of stamps called respectively Anthony Cock's lease, 'the Lower Stamps in Voage' (1701), Anthony Cock's lease, 'the Second Stamps in Voage' (1704) and James Harris' lease, 'the Third Stamps in Voage' (1704). All of them are sited 'joining' or 'near the highway leading from St Day to Redruth.'

Further along the map records 'A Greist Mill formerly here in the sd. Mannor [Tolcarne]. The Mill Tenement ends here.' The end of the Mill Tenement is shown near the present crossroads, which is also 'The End of Tolcarne Mannor'.

The North Coombe stream appears to rise in the area presently called Springfield, its course running to Tollgullow where it provided the power to drive Tollgullow Higher Stamps, which was the subject of a lease granted to John Mills and his wife Mary in 1742. Those stamps are not shown on the Watercourse Mapp but are shown on the 1772 Survey Map of the Manor. The lease refers to that Stamping Mill called the 'Tollgullow Higher Stamps', which suggests that it already existed before the date of the lease, 1742.

There are no works of any kind recorded on the Watercourse Mapp in the North Coombe until it reaches Tod Pool where a diagram depicting a horse-whim is shown. Then follow five more stamps ending with Killicor Engine which, like Tod Pool Stamps, is shown with two of the arms extended, indicating a horse-drawn whim, and finally the watercourse feeds the 'Greist Mill belonging to ye Mannor of Talgolla als St Day.' The map clearly shows that the mill was also supplied by the South Coombe stream so that the grist mill was unlikely to have been much affected by the later failure of the North Coombe stream.

Some time after the map was drawn, and before the 1772 Survey, an adit had been constructed from Wheal Unity (c.1770) which took the water away from the North Coombe stream and, by so doing, rendered the stamps of the North Coombe powerless. The following extracts from the 1772 Survey illustrate the effect of the Wheal Unity Adit on the stamps holders in the North Coombe:

No.58.C. A Stamping Mill in North Combe. In Lease to Rebecca Trewartha. Widow. In ruins and as the water is certainly cut off by Wheal Unity Addit never more can be of any value (nor will any of the Stamps in North Combe).

No.59.D. Francis's Stamps in North Combe in Hand and in Ruins.

No.60.E. James Holman's Stamps of little or no value for the reason above given against Mrs Trewartha's No.58.

We are bound to wonder whether the Wheal Unity Adit would have been constructed if the manor grist mill had no alternative source of water power. There is no mention of compensation for Rebecca Trewartha.

The map shows 28 stamps, three engines (Poldice, Tod Pool and Killicor) and two grist mills. The only evidence of deep mining are the three engines named above, which suggest the use of horse-drawn whims for raising ore from shafts. It will be remembered that this device, already in use in Germany for some 200 years, had only been introduced into Cornwall in the very early eighteenth century, probably not many years before the map was drawn up.

The map is principally a record of the stream-works within the manor. In a position opposite 'Mr Coster's Two Stamps' there is a dotted outline with the description 'The Engine Great Pool here'. It is tempting to suppose that the pool was intended to provide water for a steam engine but it was at least 30 or more years too early. Later, on the map of the 1772 Survey, we come across the term 'Fire Engine', which indicated a steam engine, winding or pumping.

Near the source of the leat the map has an intriguing entry which reads 'The Land Mark or The Rock here.' Clearly this was of some importance to warrant inclusion on the map and a special mention. The exact spot is marked with a large, distinct dot. Search for 'The Rock' was made in the area for some time but without success, until a builder doing some work near the Star Inn drew attention to a 'rock', not a stone post, but what appeared to be a small outcrop near the pub. On the rock the letters ST were cut. They resemble the initials cut into the many boundary stones found in the district, particularly on Carn Marth.

The stone is situated at a spot where three manors meet, St Day, Trefula and Tolcarne, and must surely be 'The Land Mark' so carefully recorded on the map. Within living memory there was an iron bar secured to the rock, and the shallow hole which held the bar is clearly visible.

C.C. James draws our attention to the 'Blew Stone' sited where the four parishes of Stithians, Gwennap, Wendron and Redruth all meet. It is shown on Ogilby's Road Map of 1675 which also shows 'Pole Dys' (Poldice) and 'Blow ye Cold Wind' (Coldwind Cross).

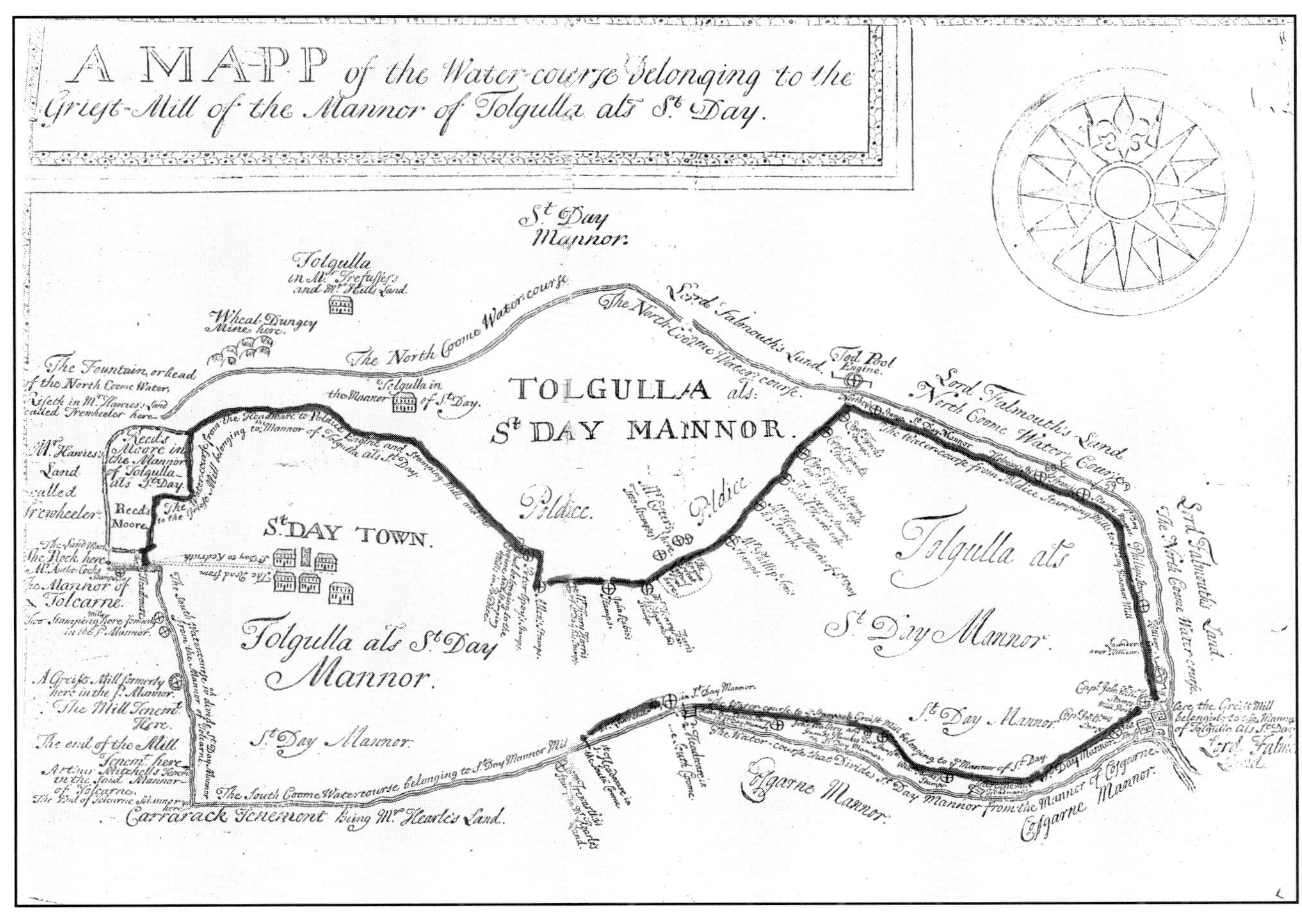

Church Street, St Day, c.1920, with the postman E.J.Pengelly who had one arm, the result of a wartime injury. He delivered post over a wide area outside town. Miss Hooper is to be seen in her shop doorway.

North Street, St Day, now Telegraph Street, showing two shops in the now listed terrace on the right. The shop windows with their multiplicity of panes emphasise the period, c.1910.

Six

Tin & Copper Dues

From very early times mineral rights were owned by the lords of the manor who exacted 'dues' from the tinners who worked the mines. Dues amounted to one-tenth of the recovered mineral and were collected by the agents of the lords of the manor. Accounts of the transactions were meticulously kept. In later years successful entrepreneurial families bought land and sometimes acquired the mineral rights with their acres, but they usually retained the mineral rights under any land which they subsequently sold.

The account of the tin and copper dues of the Manor of Tollgullow, alias 'St Dye', shown overleaf, shows clearly that the dues received by the manor were sometimes used to finance projects for the benefit of the public. Those accounts make several references to the new Market House under construction, the cost of which was borne by the lords of the manor, who presumably had initiated the enterprise.

Granite railroad setts of the Portreath–Poldice Railway of 1819 seen at Little Beside.

The first allusion is dated 23 December 1795, being a payment 'on account' of £52.10s.0d.; this presumably was when the actual work began, providing funds to pay for labour and materials for the start. Three months later, on 5 April 1796, a payment was made of £75.0s.0d. 'paid further on Account of building the Market House,' and finally, on 11 November 1797, two years after the start, we find the balance of £60.0s.9d. being paid, marking completion of the building of 'Saint Dye Market Place', at a total cost of £187.10s.9d.

The town clock tower was not yet built and the new Market House had been built on what was still an open space, 'St Day Green.' The present-day Fore Street was at that time Market Street, and the Potato Market was opposite the covered market with its butchers' stalls, dairy produce, vegetables, etc. The fish market adjoined the covered market on the east side in what is now a private yard which gives rear access to houses in Scorrier Street and Lower Fore Street. It was apparently partly covered, and some of the upright granite roof supports are still to be seen.

From April 1799 and up to 23 October 1800 there were a number of mentions of payments for 'work about the New Market House', the first being 'Paid for Labour & Slate for Repairs of St Dye Market House. £3.17s.2d.' The Market House had been completed only two years earlier, the six payments made in 1800 totalling £18.0s.11 1/2d., suggesting further new building, or an extension of the roofing. The largest payment, £16.14s.3d., was for helliers. Helliers were tilers, engaged possibly to extend the original roof to cover the entire market area, or perhaps the fish market was roofed at this later date? That might account for the plasterers' work being included.

In 1768 a substantial copper deposit was found on the Parys Mountain in Anglesey, a deposit so near the surface and so rich that the cost of recovery was considerably less than that in the Cornish mines. As a result the centre of the copper industry moved from Cornwall to the island of Anglesey. This state of affairs persisted for the next 20 or so years. By the end of the eighteenth century, however, the Anglesey copper deposits had been exhausted, leading to a revival of the Gwennap copper mines, the ores from which had been transported by sea to the smelters in South Wales from the port of Portreath which had been opened earlier by Lord de Dunstanville. Transport from the mines to the port was slow and laborious, the use of pack mules and horses proving totally inadequate to cope with the rapidly increasing production of copper ore from the Gwennap mines following the exhaustion of the Anglesey copper deposits.

That increase in traffic from the mines, coupled with a corresponding increase in the volume of coals from the port to the mines, demanded some improvement in haulage. The ever-enterprising adventurers wasted no time in tackling the problem. An interesting payment from this account in 1796 throws light on a proposal to build a canal connecting the Gwennap mines to the port of Portreath: 'Paid Subscription towards Planning the Proposed Canal from Portreath to the Mines £50.0.0.' However, the terrain posed problems which led to the abandonment of the canal project and in 1819 a tramway using horse-drawn wagons was constructed from the Poldice mine to the port. The line terminated at Crofthandy where the coal yard can still be seen showing that two spurs ran into the yard for unloading direct onto the floor of the yard some ten feet below the level of the railroad allowing the wagons to empty rapidly. The return load of copper ore would presumably have been waiting alongside the line adjacent to the yard. There are no entries in the Tin and Copper Dues Account relating to the new tramway which was financed jointly by the Williamses of Scorrier and the Foxes of Falmouth.

The Tin and Copper Dues Account also records receipts for the lord's dues on tin stuffs, etc. brought to grass by individual tinners, naming among others Henry Kellow, William Kellow, George Richards and John Messer, the latter making considerably greater payments than the other three.

In 1792 John Messer, in company with Captain Davey, paid a substantial sum for 'A bargain of Tinn-Stuff sold them the 3rd January' and 'Capt. John Williams paid for a Bargain sold him the same time.' Clearly Mr John Messer was a man of some standing and substance, being both a tinner and merchant, buying quantities of Tinn-stuff from the Manor. He held on leases 'Tallgullow Higher Stamps, Cottage and Acre formerly John and Mary Mills', and also a 'Tenement in St Day Town. In Lease to John Messer. Including Two Dwellings and Stable. Mowhay. Garden. A Good Dwelling House and five Meadows' (which are tenements nos 3.c. and 20.t. respectively).

Captain John Williams is named as holding the 'Mill Stamps' and 'Burning House' at Hale Mills (tenement No. 57.B1. in the 1772 Survey, see Chapter Twelve).

Extracts from the Account of Tin & Copper Dues of the Manor of Tollgullow (St Dye) (Drawn from the Poldice Mine Cost Book)

1792. July 3rd. Received of John Messer	£210.15s.0d.
Paid Jno. Whitburn Turning & Dressing Tin-Stuff at Wheal Jewell	£ 1. 13s. 4d.
Rec'd of Mr John Messer and Capt. Davey for a Bargain of Tin-Stuff sold them the 3rd January	£ 68. 0s.0d.
1793. Rec'd of Capt. John Williams for a Bargain sold him	£ 95. 5s.0d.
1794. August 12th Received of John Messer	£ 50. 10s.0d.
Received of John Messer	£ 48. 0s.0d.
1795. Dec. 23rd. Pd on Acct of the New Market House now Building	£ 52. 10s.0d.
1796. Received of Henry Kellow	£ 8. 13s.0d.
1796. Paid Subscription towards Planning Canal	£ 50. 0s.0d.
1796. April 5th Paid further on ac't of building the Market House	£ 75. 0s.0d.
1797. Nov. 10th Paid for repairing Saint Dye Old Tower	£ 7. 11s.0d.
1797. Nov. 11th Paid for repairing George Richards's House, damaged, by the falling of the Old Tower	£ 13. 9s.0d.
1797. Nov. 11th Pd William Kinsman for taking down the Old Tower	£ 0. 7s.6d.
1797. Nov. 11th Pd the Balance of building Saint Dye Market Place	£ 60. 0s.9d.
Feb.1s. Paid Capt Jno. Dennis for labourers taking down the Old Tower at Saint Dye	9s.6d.
1798. May 5th. Received Dues of Wm. Kellow	£ 2. 4s.8d.
July 20th.	12s.6d.
1798. August 18th Paid Carriage of Posts for St Dye Pound	16s.0d.
Paid for building the walls etc.	£ 3. 13s.6d.
Paid for a Gate, Ironwork &c for do	19s.9d.
1799. April 24th Pd for labour & Slate Repairs St Dye Market House	£ 3. 17s.2d.
1799. October. Pd Geo. Richards Damages to his Ground by Mining	£ 2. 2s.0d.
1800. Feb. 25th By Paid Jno. Lidgey for Crease and Hair for Market House	
1800. Apr. 19th Paid Wm. Harvey for Work about the Market House	4s.0d.
1800. Oct. 23rd pd. J. Lanksbury for Helliers & Plasterers	£ 16. 14s.3d.
Pd Wheal Jewell Adv'r's for 8 Bushels of Lime for do	12s.0d.
Paid Collan Harvey for 2 Bushells of lime	3s.0d.
1802. Dec. 10th Received of Henry Kellow	£ 38. 3s.9d.
1802. May 22nd Paid for Carpenter's work about the Market House	7s.0d.
1802. October " " " " " " " "	6s.6d.
1803. Feb. 11th Received of George Richards	£ 9. 18s.2d.

Seven

Education

There is no mention of any school in either the 1682 or the 1770 Survey of the Manor. The earliest reference to education for children in the ecclesiastical parish of Gwennap is to be found in a questionnaire sent to the vicar of Gwennap by the Bishop of Exeter in 1745, in which he asks, 'Is there a school of any kind?', to which the vicar replied, 'No, only several small schools where children are taught to read.' (C.C. James, *History of Gwennap.)* We may assume that the 'several small schools' referred to were what would in time become known as dame schools. Dame school classes were held in one room of the dame's home.

Common day schools also existed in the early-nineteenth century and were attended by the children of tradespeople – shopkeepers, mechanics, farmers and the like. Four pence (old pence) a week was charged for the scantiest of education. (Kathleen Piper, *History of St Day School,* 1979.)

The quality of education provided in all schools was universally poor and the teachers were unqualified and, at best, provided only the very basic rudiments of learning – an introduction to the three Rs and, for girls, some sewing lessons.

In the late-eighteenth century a number of societies had already attempted to make education available to a wider catchment, including the Society for Promoting Christian Knowledge, the British and Foreign Schools Society, and the National Society for Promoting the Education of the Poor in the Principles of the Established Church.

The Anglican and Methodist churches each set up Sunday schools to encourage the 'working class' children. Opposition from some politicians was raised, arguing that to educate the labouring class would be dangerous. Despite this argument, Sunday schools thrived and increased in number, accelerated by competition between the Anglicans and the Methodists for members.

Opposition to education for the masses was still very much in evidence 100 years later, however, as the following letter, published in 1881 in the *Royal Cornwall Gazette,* demonstrates:

Why has the Wesleyan Improvement class, which was started last winter, become defunct? Last year it proved highly successful, and was a means of conferring a great boon to the Working-Classes. It is characteristic that any thing devised for the intellectual improvement or recreation of the young only survives a short time owing to lack of support of some 'well-to-do' people.

In 1802 the introduction of the Factories Act further advanced education for the masses by the inclusion of the provision that 'apprentices were to be instructed in some part of every day in reading, writing, and arithmetic.' The employer was to bear the cost.

The National Society aimed to establish day schools in every parish in the kingdom, and in 1814 set up a national school at Gwennap Churchtown. This was followed by another at St Day, sited behind the present Parish Church, and is identified in St Day Town Trail (No.14). It was on two floors and is said to have accommodated 200 pupils, a figure in excess of the total number of boys (58) and girls and infants (91) reported by Peter Jennings, the first headmaster of St Day Board Schools, shortly after the Board School opened on 13 May 1878:

A National School [in St Day] *is supported by subscription, for the instruction of 120 girls; and 20 boys are gratuitously instructed by subscription, in a School in which the other scholars pay for their education.*

Lewis, 1833.

In his *Notes on St Day* Jennings tells us that William Rickard, the first headmaster of the national school in St Day, had a wooden leg and was very strict. Apparently he 'did not spare the rod'.

Historically, women had been deprived of education, but already by the early-nineteenth century there were more forward-looking individuals who saw the need for change.

The Gwennap Parish Vestry Minutes for 14 February 1837 record the sponsorship of a school 'for girls of poor families' at Gwennap Churchtown as follows:

It is proposed and unanimously agreed to vote the sum of Twenty Five Pounds towards the erection of a Girls'

Schooling in St Day

Left: *St Day School girls, 1910/11.*

Lesson 10.—Adjectives.

An adjective is a word that qualifies a noun. In some cases an adjective may qualify a pronoun.

Adjectives qualify nouns in three ways.

First way.—When the adjective stands before a noun, as—
A good boy.
In this way the adjective is said to qualify the noun attributively.

Second way.—When the adjective enters into the statement or predicate, as—The boy is good.
Here the adjective qualifies the noun, boy, predicatively.

Third way.—When the adjective stands after the noun and expresses an effect, as—
The good things made the boy happy.

Below left: *St Day School class, 1908.*

Below right: *A St Day School class of 1898.*

Bottom: *St Day School class with Miss Hetty Hensley the teacher, March 1908.*

School at the Churchtown to be paid out of the Parish funds, on condition that ten poor girls be received gratuitously into the same for education.

A lady present remarked, 'It is important that the future mothers be educated how else will they see that their sons are educated?'

The standards of education accepted at that time were considerably lower than are required today. The only known evidence of work done at Rickard's school is a sampler, worked in very fine, small stitches by 'Susan Richards. Finished 19th December 1832 aged 13 years.' The sampler *(see page 38)* is an interesting item. It is the earliest illustration known of the then almost new church, which is the central motif. It was drawn by someone having some skill in draughtsmanship, perspective and proportion, with the possible exception of the top spire which is a little too large.

Susan Richards, orphaned granddaughter of George Richards, yeoman, had an allowance from her grandfather's will upon his death in 1832 'to continue her education and accustomed comfort until she attains the age of nineteen', at which age Susan married William Mills. She was the great-grandmother of the author.

In the Tithe Apportionment of 1838 for Gwennap parish we find two schools listed in St Day:

The National School. William Rickard, Master. Assisted by Mary Dingle.
William Downing's School for Boys, Chapel Street, occupying the last two houses on the left at the North end of Chapel Street.

A third school, situated on Carn Marth, west of Gwennap Pit and kept by Joseph Morcom, is listed in the Apportionment Book as 'School Room and waste, an area of 17 perches.'

Kathleen Piper in her *History of St Day School* refers to that school thus: 'In connection with the Church at St Day there was a Free School at Carn Marth, patronised by Miss Williams of Scorrier House.'

On 6 January 1834 a boarding and day school for Young Ladies was opened at Scorrier by Miss Elizabeth Dennis, a native of Devon. The school bore the name the 'Scorrier Seminary' and was under the patronage of Miss Williams of Scorrier House.

Peter Jennings, in his annotation of the 1866 *Directory*, draws our attention to a school in Church Street, St Day, on the west side, 'Miss Williams's free school for girls.' It would appear that Miss Williams took a keen and active interest in the education of girls. It is possible that she was the lady present at the Gwennap Parish Vestry Meeting on 14 February 1837 who remarked, 'It is important that the future mothers be educated, how else will they see that their sons are educated?'

In the *Royal Cornwall Gazette* of Saturday 24 December 1835 we find the following report:

***Gwy yn Erbyn y Tyd* [sic].**
Truth against All the World.

We learn that the Seminary for young ladies lately established at Scorrier, closed on Wednesday for the Christmas holidays, previous to which, Miss Williams of Scorrier House, gave prizes to such as made the greatest progress in the different branches of their education, the rapid improvement made by the young ladies fully demonstrates that the school is conducted with much ability.

The census return for 1851 lists nine boarding scholars, the head and one assistant teacher, as follows:

Elizabeth Dennis. Head, unmarried, age 53, Schoolmistress and Teacher, born Devon.
Maria Burnley. Assistant, unmarried, age 21, Asst. Teacher, born Yorks.
Maria L. Jenkins. Scholar, unmarried, age 13, born Truro.
Mary I. Harris. Scholar, unmarried, age 15, born Hayle.
Celia Waters. Scholar, unmarried, age 13, born Angarrack.
Eliz. A. Youlton. Scholar, unmarried, age 14, born Wh. Rose.
Caroline H.B. Myle. Scholar, unmarried, age 12, born Chacewater.
Mary A. Henwood. Scholar, unmarried, age 12, born Perran Wharf.
Emily A. Nancarrow. Scholar, unmarried, age 13, born Pool.
Emily Waters. Scholar, unmarried, age 11, born Wh. Rose.
Phillippa Roberts. Scholar, unmarried, age 9, born Brazil. British Subject.
Grace Gidley. Servant, unmarried, age 28, House Servant, born Scorrier.
Mary A. Jenkins. Servant, unmarried, age 28, House Servant, born Stithians.

Serving the area at this period there were two other boarding and day schools for boys within reach, and offering a much wider range of subjects, including several foreign languages.

First, Redruth Grammar School, situated at the west end of the town, was founded in 1801. It had 60 scholars each paying £2 a quarter, to include stationery and 'coles'. The curriculum included Greek, Latin, French, drawing, mathematics and geography. In 1805 lessons in Hebrew, Chaldee and German were offered 'if required'.

The second, Trevarth House Grammar School, between Carharrack and Lanner, was founded c.1821. For further information about this school the reader should refer to *Lanner* by S. Schwartz and R. Parker, published in 1998.

Williams' 1847 *Commercial Directory of Cornwall* records William Rickard's school and we find it again in *Kelly's Directory* of 1852/3. (See Chapter Eleven: Two Nineteenth-Century Directories.) Rickard was eventually succeeded by John Bawden, as shown in Richard Symons' *Directory* of 1866, and he was later listed as 'Schoolmaster and Auctioneer.' According to the Census of Eduction, by 1851 most children nationally were receiving some day school education at Church of England schools. An Education Report of 1840 (the Tremenheere Report on Education) makes comparisons of the percentages of the total child population attending school in a number of districts. The figures given for St Day are:

Percentage (of total child population) attending school	*15.1%*
Redruth	*5.5%*
St Agnes	*13.4%*
Percentage of girls to all children attending:	
St Day	*47.2%*
Redruth	*8.3%*
St Agnes	*28.0%*

The extent to which the very high percentage of girls attending schools in St Day was due to the exertions of Miss Ann Williams is not known.

Kelly's Directory of 1853/3 lists the following schools in St Day:

Miss Dennis. Boarding. Scorrier.
Wm. Downing. St Day.
FREE SCHOOL St Day. Sophia Guy. Mistress. Near the Church.
John Hawken. Boarding. Trevarth.

In the 5 August 1864 edition of the *West Briton* it was reported that:

St DAY. On Wednesday last, the children belonging to the girls' free school of St Day, numbering 160, were, with the teachers, treated to their annual tea by Mrs and Miss Williams in [sic] *the lawn at Tregullow, where swings were erected and other amusements provided for them.*

Just before leaving they assembled in front of the terrace and sang several little pieces, after which Miss Williams distributed several books as prizes to those most deserving, and regular in their attendance.

The 1866 *Directory* records Mrs Cara as the schoolmistress. Peter Jennings notes that the 'Schoolroom where [the] present billiard room is (1910) [was] Miss Williams's free school for girls.'

The *Directory* also records Thomas Cara in Church Street, west side, as goldsmith and church organist. He was a native of Crowan. P. Jennings' *Notes* tell us that he was 'conductor of brass band, and taught Music.'

The Education Act of 1870 introduced compulsory education for all children, thus opening the door of opportunity, if only a chink, to the children of so-called 'working-classes'. Following the passing of that Act, parish vestries (there were no parish councils yet) were required to set up school boards and Gwennap School Board was formed and held its first meeting in April 1874, in the Vestry Room at St Day (that being the end house of Burnwithian Terrace, the old workhouse) to consider the provision of suitable schools at St Day, Lanner and Cusgarne.

In a period of already declining population through the collapse of the copper-mining industry, with mass emigration following, this proved to be a perplexing problem. After consultation with a Government Inspector of Schools it was resolved to build a school for 400 children at St Day, a second at Lanner for 300 and a third school at Cusgarne.

In an 1878 edition of the *West Briton* it is reported that:

The Architect says; These schools are to be erected near St Day for the Gwennap School Board. The site is about one and a half acres in extent, on high ground and in close proximity to the public road leading to Carharrack. Situated in the centre of an important mining district, engine houses, tall chimneys and debris arrest the eye in every direction. The staple commodity here – tin – being low in price unhappily so that many mines are not in active operation as could be desired; but with a rise in the standards increased activity would be certain to follow, as the district still abounds in vast quantities of mineral wealth.

The buildings will provide accommodation for 400 children in separate schools for boys, girls and infants, with the requisite playgrounds and lavatory space and appliances.

The masonry will be in local stone, with granite dressing, roofing of Delabole slate, and the woodwork internally wrought and varnished. A dado boarding is carried around the building internally to the level of the window sills and the necessary provision for heating and ventilating.

Above the original entrance to the school building on the south wall is a circular granite stone with the inscription: 'Gwennap School Board. St Day & Carharrack School, 1877.' The Board School opened on 13 May 1878. The Board charged parents 1d. per week for children under 6, 2d. per week for children under 9, and 3d. per week for children over 9. The school-leaving age was 13. These school fees were finally abolished in 1891.

The 14 June 1895 edition of *The Cornubian* records the following summary of an Inspector's Report of achievement at St Day Board School:

The boys had passed a praiseworthy examination, but

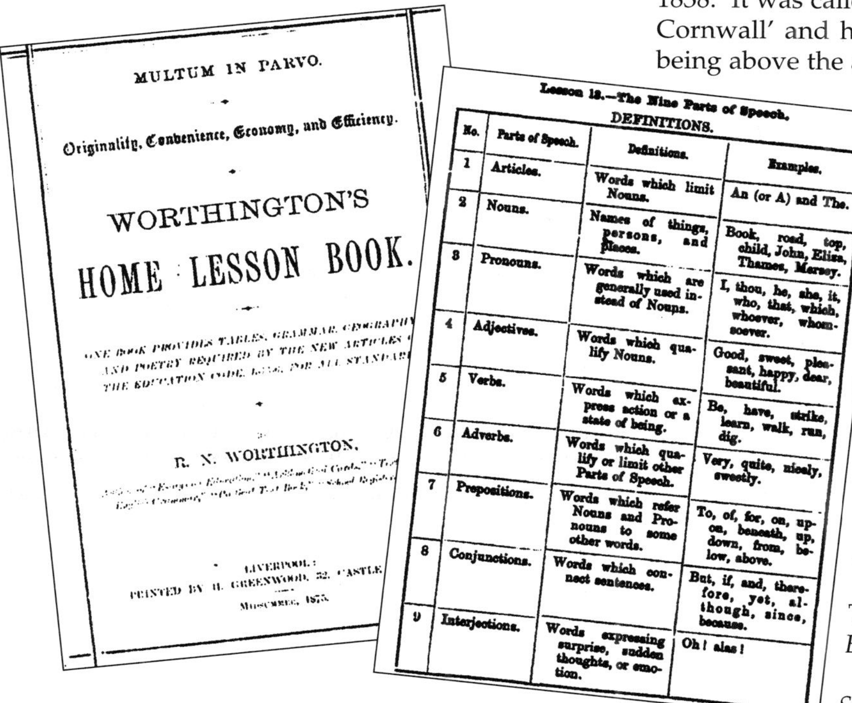

MULTUM IN PARVO.

Originality, Convenience, Economy, and Efficiency.

WORTHINGTON'S
HOME LESSON BOOK.

R. N. WORTHINGTON.

LIVERPOOL:
PRINTED BY H. GREENWOOD, 32, CASTLE

Lesson 12.—The Nine Parts of Speech.

DEFINITIONS.

No.	Parts of Speech.	Definitions.	Examples.
1	Articles.	Words which limit Nouns.	An (or A) and The.
2	Nouns.	Names of things, persons, and places.	Book, road, top, child, John, Eliza, Thames, Mersey.
3	Pronouns.	Words which are generally used instead of Nouns.	I, thou, he, she, it, who, that, which, whoever, whomsoever.
4	Adjectives.	Words which qualify Nouns.	Good, sweet, pleasant, happy, dear, beautiful.
5	Verbs.	Words which express action or a state of being.	Be, have, strike, learn, walk, run, dig.
6	Adverbs.	Words which qualify or limit other Parts of Speech.	Very, quite, nicely, sweetly.
7	Prepositions.	Words which refer Nouns and Pronouns to some other words.	To, of, for, on, upon, beneath, up, down, from, below, above.
8	Conjunctions.	Words which connect sentences.	But, if, and, therefore, yet, although, since, because.
9	Interjections.	Words expressing surprise, sudden thoughts, or emotion.	Oh! alas!

reading and arithmetic were the weak subjects. The Girls had passed a remarkably good examination, and the Infants were also very good.

The Inspector thought it was a pity that a musical instrument was not provided for the St Day infants' school.

The Gwennap School Board continued to administer the school until 1903, following the passing of the Education Act in 1902 which abolished board schools in the county. From that time Cornwall County Council has been responsible for all the old board schools.

There follow extracts from the school log-book:

Book 1. p.189. 18 October 1901.
Admitted four children this week. There has been a very good attendance all week. Messrs Mills and Chipman visited the school on Tuesday afternoon. Work as usual.

Book 2. Infants' School. p.276. 8 October 1908.
Owing to the closure of a small private school in St Day seven new scholars were admitted on Monday morning.

'Further Education', as it is known today, was already available in the nineteenth century. Officially called 'Adult School', and popularly 'Night School', it provided opportunities to learn something of the sciences pertaining to the world of mining. Several writers have commented on the fact that Cornish miners were superior to workers in other industries, especially those in other counties.

The *Journal of the Statistical Society of London* published a paper, which was read by Sir Charles Lemon, Bart. M.P., F.R.S., to the society on 19 March 1838. It was called 'Statistics of the Copper Mines of Cornwall' and he referred to the miners' education being above the average:

With respect to education, I will only observe that the miners are fond of instruction, and are educated in their different grades far beyond the average of most counties, but they possess no especial opportunities. I know of only one school on a mine particularly for the benefit of those there employed; it was established by the late Mr Borlase, who was a member of this Society. About 100 scholars attend it, and the advantage to the mine and neighbourhood is said to be immense. It is at Wheal Vor, near Helston.

The following appeared in the *West Briton* in September 1897:

St Day, Gwennap & District.
Technical Instruction.
The Committee have arranged the following Classes:
Monday Evenings: Blowpipe Analysis.
Wednesday: Human Physiology, Advanced & Elementary, Freehand & Model Drawing
Saturday Evenings: Inorganic Chemistry and Mineralogy.
The whole to be held in the Board School, St Day.
Friday Evenings: Shorthand & Mensuration & Geometry.
Saturday Evenings: Machine Construction.
Church Schoolroom, Carharrack.

During the second half of the nineteenth century two private schools were opened at Carharrack, each drawing pupils from a wider area, including St Day.

In 1870, W.E. Edwards, a native of Crowan parish, opened a school for boys offering a wider range of subjects than the national schools provided. An advertisement in the press offered as an extra option, the services of 'Mr Crosby, Music Master'. The school closed in around 1904.

In a surviving Euclid textbook from the school, Tommy Mills, uncle of the author, wrote in the bottom margin of one page, 'I don't like Euclid' and at the bottom of another page 'Euclid is a Turk to learn.'

Miss Helen Johns' school, situated in the Anglican Church Meeting Room between 1893 and 1925, drew pupils from the district including St Day. The school took girls from five to 14 years old, and boys from five to eight years old. Familiarly known as 'Nellie Johns' she retired in the mid-1920s and the school was taken over by Miss Goldsworthy, in whose hands it continued until it finally closed in the mid-1940s.

In her *History of St Day School* Kathleen Piper lists the names of the masters and mistresses of the Board School from its start in 1878 to 1978, its first 100 years. From that list we particularly notice Peter Jennings, the first headmaster, who held office for 39 years, from May 1878 until his death in March 1917. For the next three years the post was held by three different teachers until May 1921, when Richard Rodda Blewett was appointed headmaster, a position which he held until September 1943 when he retired after 22 years as the head of St Day School. We are indebted to both these distinguished teachers, firstly for the records kept by Peter Jennings, which tell us much about the St Day of his time, and secondly to Richard Blewett for the many entertaining talks he gave, at the Church Hall and the Women's Institute, on St Day's past and his observations of life in the district which were published in the monthly church magazine under the title 'These Things Have Been'. Equally worthy of notice is Kathleen Piper's informative *History of St Day School* which also, with her permission, has been freely used in this volume.

Above: *Sampler made by Susan Richards.*

Left: *The Board School. Note the chimneys and belfry which have since been removed.*

Below: *St Day girls' school – all in clean white aprons, 1908.*

Eight

Transport

By the seventeenth century some of the wealthiest families possessed a private coach but they were rare indeed. The Trewinnard coach seen in the Royal Cornwall Museum in Truro is an example of the earliest of these, dating from c.1700. By the end of the seventeenth century stagecoaches had come into being and towards the end of the eighteenth century the first mail coach appeared, carrying His Majesty's mail from London to the busy port of Bristol. By the mid-seventeenth century the growing mining activity in the manor of St Day inevitably brought greatly increased road traffic, pack-horses at first, conveying ores from the mines to the smelter at Tolcarne. When the traffic reached tonnage proportions carts began to be seen on the roads, and, very soon after that, bigger four-wheeled wagons came into use demanding further improvements in road building and surfacing.

Four-wheeled wagonette with family party, c.1910.

As has been mentioned, the cross was removed from its site in about 1800, no doubt to make it easier for the ore-carrying wagons to negotiate the street. It was already becoming abundantly clear that the rapidly increasing output from the mines called for drastic improvement in haulage facilities to the ports of Portreath and Devoran. Pack-horses and wagons found it increasingly difficult to keep up with mine output, and as a result a backlog of ore heaps built up.

At first a canal from Poldice to Portreath was proposed, and when that was shown not to be feasible a horse-drawn tramroad was constructed. That was followed by the Devoran to Redruth railway which was built in 1832.[1]

By the middle of the nineteenth century a wide choice of private carriages for the wealthy and the well-off new middle class had arrived, the broughams and landaus, the phaetons, dog-carts and ralli traps – designed and built by the newly emerged coach-builders who specialised in elegant carriages. As always, fashions were set in London, but provincial coach-building was not long to follow, and every town had its own wheelwrights and coach-builders. In West Cornwall, Truro and Penzance were home to the leaders in the changing styles. Here at St Day a coach-building enterprise *(see p.41)* was established in the late-nineteenth century and grew into a sizeable concern employing wheelwrights, blacksmiths, carpenters, painters and trimmers for the upholstery. Inevitably coach-building at St Day mainly consisted of the building of commercial vehicles rather than 'carriages', with the businesses turning out light-sprung and heavy unsprung farm carts and wagons while carts designed for heavier loads of coal and building stone from the quarries were the main output. However, some carriages – mainly light traps and jingles – were produced for family use, but it is unlikely that any of the elegant carriages such as phaetons, landaus or broughams were actually made at St Day.

Associated with this enterprise was a considerable haulage business carrying coals from the railhead at Scorrier to the mines and coalyards and dealing with general haulage throughout the district, as well as providing a variety of carriages for hire, cabs for weddings and funerals, and wagonettes, brakes and Jersey cars for organised parties. The wagonette was a small, single-horse-drawn version of the brake; in each of those vehicles the driver sat on a high seat, which gave him a good view of the road ahead, whilst his passengers sat on two long seats facing each other. Entry was by mounting two steps at the rear and through a small door kept closed during journeys. The brake, a larger vehicle, was often drawn by two horses. The Jersey car was unusual in having the transverse seating mounted very high, giving an uninterrupted view of the countryside for its passengers. Access to the seating was by a short ladder, or steps put into position by the

Horse Power

Jersey car and four-in-hand; Simon Mills with 'the ribbons' – off to the seaside.

Miniature hansom cab and Shetland pony with Hugh Mills outside and Susan Temple inside, 1950s.

Above: *A covered trap, a commonly used tradesman's vehicle.*

Left: *Granite milestone, c.1860–70.*

Far left: *A Cornish jingle, the rear door of which gave ladies and children easy access via a single step. This was known as a governess car throughout the rest of England.*

'steps boy' who occupied a seat at the back of the vehicle throughout the journey.

Jersey cars were usually four-in-hand, i.e. drawn by four horses, especially if the journey included long or steep hills. Handling a four-in-hand in narrow streets and roads called for great skill and the drivers employed would have had considerable experience before being entrusted with passenger carrying. If the route was not too arduous then three horses, a 'unicorn', would be hitched up to the car. In its heyday 60 horses were kept by the St Day enterprise, stabling was to be found in various parts of the town and Tresaddern Farm provided much of the grazing.

Regular public transport services were provided by 'carriers' like Walter Penna whose horse bus left St Day for Falmouth every morning except Sunday. Richard Penna's bus took people from St Day to Truro every Monday, Wednesday and Saturday. Times of departure and return are not listed in *Pigot's Directory* of 1844.

Successful tradespeople kept a horse and trap for everyday family conveyance, while farm carts, market traps, bakers' vans, light-sprung wagons, milk floats, etc. served the transport needs of commerce and industry. Slightly up-market were such light vehicles as ralli traps, and a variety of gigs for the smart and the sporty, as well, of course, as the Cornish jingle (or 'governess car'), which was low slung on springs and with a low step to the rear door to assist children and the elderly getting into the vehicle.

The writer seems to remember that two or three bells hung from the collar of the pony pulling his grandfather's jingle (hence the name?). Church and chapel annual Sunday-school outings to the seaside were made by brake or Jersey car, with the hymn-singing passengers being carried to Porthtowan, the most popular beach within easy reach, or further afield to Falmouth, Newquay or St Ives.

By today's standards travel was painfully slow; for instance, in 1915 Carharrack Band entered a contest at St Newlyn East, to which they travelled in a Jersey car drawn by three horses (with Jimmy Chynoweth driving). On the way one of the traces broke and a stop was made at Zelah for repair, refreshment and practice! Newlyn East was reached by midday, six hours after leaving home. It may be of interest to the reader to know that the band took first prize on the march playing 'Follow Me' which perhaps made the tedium of the journey worthwhile. On August Bank Holiday that year, the same band entered a contest at Newquay and this time they travelled the 15 or so miles in one of the newly acquired GWR motor charabancs. This time the journey was completed in one hour.

The Great Western Railway completed its line through to Penzance in about 1852 which provided access to the main railway line at the little station at Scorrier for the convenience of passengers and the despatch and collection of goods. This signalled the end of the stagecoaches which were unable to match the speed and lower fares offered by the railways. Coaches were reduced to providing links to the main-line stations from remote towns and villages.

By this time steam road locomotives, traction engines, had made their appearance on the roads in Britain following the introduction of the first heavy-duty steam road locomotive by Charles Burrell of Thetford, Norfolk, in 1856. By the 1870s traction engines were becoming widely used, not only for haulage of heavy loads (being capable of pulling a number of heavily laden wagons), but they were also now beginning to be used in agriculture for ploughing and hauling threshing machinery from farm to farm. The author remembers clearly when, as a boy in the 1920s, every autumn Sid Carlyon's (of Little Beside) threshing set drawn by a steam traction engine pulled into the farmyard at Tresaddern and negotiated the sharp corners leading to the mowhay.

Later in the nineteenth century steam road-rollers were introduced to flatten the stone road surfaces and, up until the late 1920s, piles of road stone could still be seen deposited at strategic sites by the roadside, waiting to be broken down into suitable size by the 'stone-cracker' wielding long-handled hammers, ready to be rolled flat by the 12-ton steamrollers.

Travelling showmen were changing over from horse-drawn vehicles to the powerful steam traction engines, which, in time, they decorated with brass fittings and a full-length canopy overhead, also equipping their vehicles with a powerful dynamo to generate electricity for lighting and power. Many of these splendid road locomotives have been restored and preserved and are to be seen at rallies throughout the country. Meanwhile, waiting in the wings, not quite ready to appear, was the greatest revolution in world transport and men whose names were yet to become known worldwide – Daimler, Benz, Morris, Austin, Ford – future designers and leaders in the forthcoming motor-car industry which would have the greatest impact ever on world commerce by exploiting the capabilities of the internal combustion engine.

From St Day horse-drawn buses still ran to Redruth daily until the mid-1920s and the writer remembers clearly going from St Day to Redruth in the horse bus run by 'Jimmy' Chynoweth. The entrance door was one step up at the back, the two seats facing each other, carrying about five passengers each.

The GWR ran a motor-bus service from Redruth to Carharrack via St Day, with one trip in the morning, leaving Redruth about 10.00a.m., and one in the afternoon, leaving Redruth about 4.00p.m. The service was introduced by the GWR some time before the First World War and withdrawn in 1929 when the newly formed Western National

Jersey cars with all male passengers set to go on an outing to the seaside, mid-1920s.

The charabanc of Mr Dunstan of Troon with the Crofthandy Chapel members on their annual outing to the seaside, mid-1920s.

Omnibus Company took over the principal operators throughout the South West.

In the mid-1920s Cornwall Motor Transport ('CMT') provided bus services starting at Truro via Chacewater, through St Day, Carharrack and Lanner to Redruth every hour. Between the towns and villages buses would stop to pick up or drop passengers when asked, anywhere on the route, and it was not unusual for a driver to stop and wait for a minute or so if some regular user was not already waiting at the end of their lane! Summer excursions to the seaside and popular events brought out the charabanc, an open-top motor vehicle with transverse seating right across the body looking forward, entered from one end of each row. In inclement weather the folded hood would be brought forward and secured to the windscreen framing. Sidescreens were also an option.

A few independent operators ran small buses, 12–15 seaters, on short very local routes in the area. One such, Mr Goldsworthy based at Carharrack, next to what is now the Mills' Hall, ran a regular service to Redruth in the late 1920s and in the summer ran to Porthtowan on Saturdays. It was not unusual for these one-bus concerns to name their vehicle, Mr Goldsworthy's little 15-seater bus was called 'The Royal' and was painted livery green, passengers sitting on two seats running the length of the vehicle, one each side facing inward.

Nationally, public transport by bus expanded rapidly, opening up wider horizons for the country dweller, and bringing towns and villages closer together socially. Double-decker buses, previously a feature of the bigger towns, now began to appear on rural routes.

Right up to the outbreak of the Second World War people walked; they walked to Redruth from its surrounding district to shop, then walked home again, from St Day they walked to Carharrack or Chacewater perhaps, to visit friends, to Gwennap Church, indeed to anywhere within a few miles or so. Even up until the late 1930s time was not so pressing as it has since become and 'Shanks' pony' was much more exercised.

For those who owned or had access to a horse, or a donkey, riding was an option, although the latter animal was more amenable to being driven in a shay. Miners were to be seen driving to work or returning home with their little donkey and shay, a simple vehicle consisting of a board mounted on two light wheels, more often than not a pair of bicycle wheels, and often another miner would be given a lift to and from work, both men sitting on the one board, the passenger facing backwards.

The ubiquitous bicycle served a wide section of the public and could be obtained in a variety of forms, for instance, the lady's bicycle which had no crossbar and was fitted with a chain-guard as a precaution against grease from the chain. The very real danger of a lady's long skirt getting caught in the rear wheel was prevented by a screen of cords, each side, stretching from rear mudguard to hub in the shape of a fan. Then there was the tradesman's bicycle with a capacious basket in front of the handlebars and sometimes another behind the rider. Various handlebar shapes were offered, from the upright to the extreme downswept 'racing handlebars', appealing to those who thirsted after speed.

In the minutes of the Gwennap Parish Vestry of March 1898 it was decreed that any constable who owned a bicycle was permitted to use it in an emergency, where speed was of the essence! By the second quarter of the twentieth century private cars were seen more and more on the roads and motoring for pleasure increased, allowing, and indeed encouraging, family outings to seaside resorts and social events previously out of reach. At the same time smaller lightweight commercial motor vehicles were being introduced in the form of tradesmen's delivery vans and 'pick-ups', bringing town and country ever closer.

NOTES:

1. Barton, D.B., *The Redruth and Chacewater Railway*, 1624–1915.

Market Square railings with a donkey cart on a cobbled surface. The corner shop was, from the 1840s, a 'druggist's' and later, in the 1880s, a doctor's surgery.

Market Street, St Day, at the junction of Church Street. Note the young lady proudly showing her (new?) bicycle with its chain guard.

Policeman smart in uniform with button-up jacket and belt in Chapel Street before the First World War. Above him, between the bedroom windows, can be seen the small plaque denoting CORNWALL COUNTY POLICE.

Nine

Law & Order

Until well into the nineteenth century those unfortunates who were found guilty of any one of a wide catalogue of offences were sentenced to punishment, oftimes of outrageous severity. It will no doubt surprise many to learn that in England burning at the stake continued up until 1789 and that branding was still carried out until 1834. The pillory was commonly used until 1837, and for another 30 or so years offenders could still be sentenced to being confined to the stocks. Deportation for comparatively trivial offences was by no means uncommon. The quality of justice was questionable, to say the least.

At a meeting of the Gwennap Parish Vestry on 22 March 1836 13 parish constables were appointed, of whom one, Charles Hawke, was 'especially confined to the service of the assistant overseer'. It was further proposed to give the constables a gratuity of £20 for the previous year for visiting the beer shops and the public houses, according to the directions of the Vestry, on Saturday nights and Sundays.

At the May meeting of the Vestry it was resolved to start legal proceedings against Elizabeth Bray, Elizabeth Selkirk and James Knight 'for violent proceedings and assault in the workhouse on Friday night and Saturday last.' Conditions in the workhouse at that time would have provided little comfort, either physical or mental, to those unfortunate inmates, and it is not surprising that some were finally driven to violence and assault.

At the Vestry meeting in June 1836 the overseers were 'desired to enquire if any of the young women who occasionally infest the workhouse will volunteer to go to Australia.' The minutes of that meeting fail to record under what conditions they would go, and what awaited them on landing. The following month Tristram Powning, one of the constables, was requested to call James Oppy, John Blamey, Walter Roberts, John Grigor, John Davey, William Allen and William Waters before the magistrates for breaking the Sabbath. We are not told in what manner they did this. At the December 1842 meeting the names of the parish constables responsible for each of the four 'districts' of St Day, Carharrack, Lanner and Cusgarne are recorded. For St Day four constables were appointed, namely, Jonathan Bawden, Davis Trebilcock, John Hawke and Charles Hawke. John Hawke's baton is dated 1834 and is, at the time of writing, in the possession of the author. Lanner had six constables, Carharrack three, and Cusgarne four. Presumably the Lanner district, being more widespread, required more constables. It surely was not more lawless!

Mr Thomas Martyn was appointed superintendent of the constables and was to be paid £5 per annum. Each constable's book was to be produced to the superintendent every Monday morning or the week's pay would be forfeited, and if it was not produced for four weeks he would be disqualified.

In March 1844 the Vestry set aside £30 for one year for the payment of two efficient constables whose duties would be to enforce general order and make frequent visits to all beer and spirit houses and prevent persons from assembling in the different villages and public highways. Thomas Martyn was to become constable to receive reports. Jonathan Bawden and Benjamin Bargwanna were to be officiating constables at 20 shillings per month each. Fines were to be paid to Thomas Martyn and appropriated as decided by the parishioners assembled in Vestry.

In July 1844 the constables applied to the magistrates to close St Day Market at 10p.m. from Lady Day to Michaelmas and from 9p.m. from Michaelmas to Lady Day. In 1846 28 constables were appointed along with five officiating constables, the latter five to receive £7 each per annum. In 1839 the County Police Act authorised magistrates at Quarter Sessions to appoint paid police forces, if it was thought desirable. On 5 January 1858 in Cornwall it was reported that the force was nearly complete.

Detected crime was largely of the petty type and the majority of those arrested were illiterate. Small larcenies such as stealing a watch, or poultry, clothing and small sums of money were dealt with at Assizes or Quarter Sessions. Sentences varied considerably from three months to a year in prison. For stealing a sheep, which only a few years before carried the death penalty, a man could be transported for 20 years. Arson was punishable by death until 1838 when the penalty was reduced to transportation for life. At the Cornwall Lent Assizes in March 1837

George Wallis, aged 22, was indicted 'for having... unlawfully and maliciously set fire to a certain stack of hay, the property of Hugh Barratt.' The following was recorded in the *West Briton*:

> *Hugh Barratt kept a beer shop at Gwennap.* [He] *Had a stack of hay 72 yards from his house. On the 18th November last, he was alarmed by a person coming at night, knocking at the door, and calling fire:* [he] *came down and saw the prisoner and William Slanter. Went to the rick, and saw it so enveloped in flames that it could not be approached. Stephen Mitchell works in Poldice Mine. On the 18th November prisoner came to the Blacksmith's shop, about seven o'clock at night. He lighted the fire with a rope, as is usually done in mines. John Penrose came with the prisoner, and they had a feat of strength with the anvil. Prisoner took up a piece of rope and lighted it. Witness took it away and threw it back. Prisoner lighted it again. Penrose asked what he was going to do with it? He said he only wanted it a few minutes, and went away. Witness looked after him until he got 264 yards off (measured the distance next day) saw him 120 yards beyond the engine-pool. The rope was alight then; the wind caused it to blaze. A little after he saw the rick on fire... Death was recorded against Wallis.*

In this case the judge was able to recommend mercy but only because the rick did not adjoin a dwelling-house.

Magistrates showed no mercy when dealing with child offenders. In 1857 two boys aged 13 and 15 were sent to prison for 14 days for hawking without a licence. For stealing a half-pound of horse-hair, three boys aged 12, 15 and 15 years were committed to prison for one month, two months and two months respectively. On 7 April 1865 at West Powder Petty Sessions Richard Burrows, of Creegbrawse, was summoned by Elizabeth Evans, of Bissoe Pool, for assaulting her on 11 March. The complainant's statement was:

> *... that defendant entered her house, caught her by the throat, and brandished a stick over her head, saying, "I'll take your life." Burrows, when asked what he had to say, replied "I thought the woman was a witch. I think she ill-wished me, and I pretended to give her a scratch. I have heard that if you go and bring blood they can never hurt you any more. I was not well in body and mind: and she pretends to do witchcraft, and takes money.*

The bench remarked on the ignorance of the defendant, and fined him 1 shilling and costs.

In 1857, when the creation of a National Police Force was anticipated, 13 parish constables for St Day and Lanner were appointed to receive 'a salary as for last year, for four months or until the Police take office, if such salary be legally chargeable.'

Parish constables were still being appointed in 1865, in which year 21 constables were nominated. On 24 March 1870 parish constables were appointed for the last time. In 1873 the salary of a constable of the National Police Force 1st Class was £1.3s.4d. per week and a 3rd Class constable was paid £1.0s.5d. a week.

The following nineteenth-century extracts from, among other newspapers, the *Royal Cornwall Gazette* provide an insight into transgressions of those times, some of them amusing, others less so:

> *DISTURBANCE. 14th July 1832. Cornwall Quarter Sessions. 16th October 1832.*
>
> *John Morcomb, Thomas Gribble, John Rogers and Joseph Whitford were charged with having riotously assembled at St Day on Saturday 14th July last, for the purpose of lowering the price of potatoes and other vegetables, and also assaulting the constables in the execution of their duty. A great body of people assembled at St Day, they came into the place shouting and swearing that they would have the potatoes at 6d a gallon.*
>
> *In the beginning of the Market they were 8d a gallon, then the price was reduced to 7d, but the mob insisted on having them at 6d.*
>
> *Morcombe was the ringleader and said he would upset the carts if potatoes were not sold at that price; the mob cheered and urged him on; on attempting to upset a cart he was taken into custody. But immediately rescued from the constables, who were assaulted by Thomas Gribble and Joseph Whitford, they were knocked down two or three times.*
>
> *The constables showed their maces to the mob who tried to take their maces from them. Rogers was called on by a constable to assist him, but he took part with the mob. Morcombe was sentenced to 12 months, the others to 6 months imprisonment, at hard labour.*

NB: In Cornwall potatoes were sold by the 'gallon' (of 10lbs weight) up to well into the second half of the twentieth century.

In a case heard at the Truro Petty Sessions reported in November 1836 a miner successfully sued his employer for failing to pay the wages due direct to him. The full newspaper report, published on 4 November in the *West Briton* read:

> *At Truro Petty Sessions, before Edmund Turner and H.P. Andrew, esquires, Justices of the Peace for the County, a complaint was made by William Thomas against Mr Henry Francis, the Agent for Wheal Prosper Mine, for non-payment of wages.*

It appears in evidence that Thomas took a bargain (worked for a percentage of the value of ore raised) in the mine, and there was due to him and his partners about £4. On his applying at the counting-house for his wages he was told that one of his partners had authorised an innkeeper of the neighbourhood to take up the money, which was paid to him. The account continues:

Thomas applied to the innkeeper for his part, and was offered the balance, after deducting the amount of the public house bill incurred by him and his partner, which he refused to take. The magistrates highly disapproved of payment of poor men's wages to innkeepers, and ordered the manager of the mine to pay Thomas, as the Taker of the bargain, the whole of the wages.

The following report, from the *West Briton* dated 1 October 1845, with its mention of the Stannary Court, is a reminder that this ancient tradition, dating from the twelfth century, was peculiar to Cornwall and Devon tin miners. Presumably Stephen Blamey was in dispute with mine owners in the locality and the Stannary Court had awarded against him. We have no record of the original hearing nor of the outcome of the mêlée. The report reads:

Thomas Terrell, 53, Middleton Kitto, 25, Thomas Jacka, 44, and Richard Bawden, 36, were indicted for obstructing Thomas Eyre, a bailiff of the Stannary Court, in the execution of his duty (to seize goods of Stephen Blamey, at St Day Market)... Eyre had asked Terrell if the stall at which he was standing was Stephen Blamey's. Terrell replied that the Stall was Blamey's, but most of the hats on it were his. Eyre then told Terrell he was about to seize the whole of the property as Blamey's... Kitto, who was standing by the stall, said to Terrell: "You are not such a d – d fool as to let the hats go"; and also told the people who were standing by to "push on, push on"... The prisoner Bawden, who was standing behind Eyre, called out, "d – n the bailiff, let us kill him. Knock down the bailiff and kill the constable." Bawden also held up his fist to Eyre, and said he would peel the skin off his body if he could get at him... By this time there was a mob of 500 people, who kept hallooing "knock down the constable; kill the bailiff and trample him underfoot." It was pay day at Consols.

This report appeared in the *West Briton* on 23 June 1865:

On Tuesday last, before Mr William Williams of Tregullow, William Cookman, apprentice of Mr John Thomas, boot and shoe maker of St Day, was brought up in custody of PC Timmins, charged with absconding from his master. It appeared that Cookman had left his master for some time; there was a warrant issued for his apprehension, and on Monday last he was apprehended by PC Timmins at Truro. On his promising to return to his master, and not abscond again, he was discharged.

The *Royal Cornwall Gazette* reported on an incident of 'Stealing at St Day' in February 1881:

At the County Petty Sessions at Penryn on Wednesday, before Mr M.H. Williams and a full Bench, Catherine Smith, the wife of a shoemaker residing at Gwennap, answered to her bail, and was charged with stealing on the 18th Instant a £5 Bank of England note, the property of the Rev. Wm. Radnor, Primitive Methodist minister of St Day. It appears that the Minister and his wife left the house in charge of the servant girl [who for some time went out] *and returned late in the evening. On entering his study he found his papers disarranged, and also missed the note. Information was also given to the police. The prisoner afterwards sent for the prosecutor, admitted her guilt, which she confirmed in court, and pleaded for mercy. The Bench sentenced her to six weeks imprisonment. 'Forgive us our trespasses?'*

In 1889, on 7 November, the same paper reported on a St Day policeman:

After about six years good service, Mr. Tonkin the St Day policeman, has been removed from us. He is gone to Mawgan. His successor is Mr. Hooper of Camborne. Let us hope that now the long winter evenings are about to settle in, when the "larkins" are up to a little mischief, they will stand in fear of our new policeman. It has been often the case that whenever there was a row in the previous policeman's time, that 'Mr Bobby' could not be found; but perhaps now one public house is closed there will be less need for a policeman. The one I refer to is the Market Inn, lately owned by Mr. B.M. Moyle. I would suggest that it be turned into an Institute and Public Library, as there is no such thing in the place. Perhaps our worthy and esteemed friend, Mr. Conybeare, will take the matter up, as he has a large share of voters in this place.

Mr Conybeare was the MP for the constituency and lived at Tregullow House. In the Chief Constable's General Orders for 11 July 1888 a PC Samuel Tonkin was promoted to PC 2nd Class, but we are not told where he was stationed.

Following the establishment of the National Police Force (County Police Act 1839) by Sir Robert Peel, the new police constables were familiarly known as 'peelers' in the London area at first, then more widely they became 'bobbies'. And well within the author's memory the honorific 'mister' was rarely used; it would be 'Bobby Ough' (during the 1920s) and his successor 'Bobby Babbage'. One 1859 newspaper report about the police read as follows:

On Saturday last, John Cundy of St Day, and lately of St. Austell, was apprehended by Inspector H. Coombe, charged with being drunk and creating a Disturbance in the streets of St Day; also with resisting and assaulting Inspector Coombe in the execution of his duty. He was taken to Tregullow on Monday 15th instant before Mr W. Williams and Mr F.M. Williams and fined 30/ including costs.

St Day stocks, last used in the 1850s.

In 1883 'William Trenear of St Day was sentenced to four days Hard Labour for sleeping in the open air.' Ten years later, in 1893, 'Zacharias Mitchell of St Day was arrested in an outhouse at East End (Redruth?) and sentenced to seven days' Hard Labour.' In 1910 the following report was printed in the *Royal Cornwall Gazette* regarding an incident of drunk driving:

William Bailey, Frogpool, was summoned at Penryn on Tuesday for driving without a light at 11.15 pm on July 16th. P.C. Burrell said he stopped the horse and found Bailey, who had evidently been drinking, asleep in the trap. Fined 10s. and 8s.6d. costs.

The Whipping Post

Not far from Great Poldice Fire Engine on the St Day side stood a whipping post. These instruments of punishment were introduced during the reign of Elizabeth I, prior to which vagrants were, under the direction of the Whipping Act of 1530, carried to some market or other public place and tied to the end of a cart, naked, and beaten with whips throughout the town until they bled. Men and women alike were thus treated until the year 1577 when the Act was altered so that offenders were stripped from the waist upwards then whipped until the blood ran. It was at that time that whipping posts were introduced in place of the cart. It was not until 1791 that a statute was introduced forbidding the whipping of female vagrants. It has been stated that the latter change did not lead to an increase of crime amongst women and girls.

Whipping was not confined to vagrants, the punishment being awarded for a variety of offences including drunkenness and theft and was still practised in various parts of the country until well into the nineteenth century.

It has been said that it was the custom in Cornwall in the eighteenth and nineteenth centuries for miners, after serving sentence for theft from the mine, to be publicly whipped on the mines where they formerly worked. This probably accounts for the St Day whipping post being erected on Poldice Mine sett.

The Stocks

Stocks were already in use in the sixteenth and seventeenth centuries and were used as punishment for a variety of offences. They were to be found in every town or village and used as a form of punishment for quite minor offences, including drunkenness. Like their contemporary, the pillory, the principle involved was to expose the culprit to public degradation and humiliation.

The stocks could be used to confine both hands and feet, and although this was not commonly done, when used it could cause extreme pain to the victim. Extreme injuries, too, were often suffered by the victims, who were pelted by potatoes, turnips and stones, etc. Fatal injuries were not unknown and exposure to cold during the period of sentence sometimes led to death after release.

The Gwennap Parish Vestry minutes for 1836 record that a certain Captain Richard Nicholls (a mine captain no doubt) enquired if 'the friends of the boys who were found gambling on Sunday last, will consent to the boys being placed in the Stocks.' The *West Briton* of 27 February 1863 reported that a 'young man named John Williams, was placed in the Stocks in the Market Place, St Day, for six hours, for non-payment of fines and being drunk and disorderly.' Annie Trevithick in her *Short History of St Day* (c.1888) tells us that the St Day stocks were kept near the church gate 'and of course the prisoner was an object of observation to all who attended church.' She noted that many could 'remember seeing [the stocks] in the churchyard within the last quarter century.'

Stocks were still widely used until the 1860s, the last recorded use in Cornwall being at Camborne in 1866.

Clink or Lock-Up

The ground floor room of St Day town clock, built in 1830, was used for the overnight holding of prisoners charged with drunkenness, before they were escorted to Penryn the following morning to appear before the Justices. It was the duty of the parish constables to escort prisoners to Penryn, a distance of eight miles, which meant a 16-mile round trip walk for the duty constable. Doubtless there were occasions, particularly in bad weather, when the prisoner was released unofficially!

Batons

Parish constables were issued with batons of office which for most Cornish parishes were square in section, whereas elsewhere in the United Kingdom they were usually round. These batons, or 'truncheons' as they are often wrongly called, were decorated with the Royal Arms, the name of the parish, the year of issue and the name of the constable. Some of the Gwennap maces can be seen in the Royal Institution of Cornwall at Truro.

Building St Day Pound

1798. August 18th Paid Carriage of Posts for St Dye Pound. *16s.0d.*
Paid for building the walls etc. *£3.13s.6d.*
Paid for a Gate, Ironwork &c for do *9s.9d.*
1799. Sept. 23rd. By Paid Nath. Weeks for work about the Pound. *12s.3d.*

The payments for building St Day's pound were for the manor pound situated below St Day Green, shown on the 1772 Plan of St Day. There are no further references to that structure, either in terms of repairs or animals being impounded there. There is a reference to a 'Pound Meadow' in the 1682 survey in that part of Burnwithian Tenement, which is given as being only one rood in area. The tenement of Burnwithian at that time included the area adjoining St Day Green at the junction of the present-day Fore Street, Scorrier Street and Church Street.

Some 30 years later the overseers of Gwennap caused a parish pound to be built 'in the neighbourhood of St Day and Carharrack', which still exists, and is in need of restoration. Stray animals were impounded and released to the owner on payment of the required fine for 'herbage'. We have no record of the scale of fines exacted or of any incidents of its usage. Fines went to the lords of the manor.

Three entries made in November 1797 record payments concerning the derelict church tower, all that remained of the medieval Holy Trinity Church. Thomas Martyn's map of 1748 gives us a clear plan of St Day and shows the church tower standing alone. Martyn was meticulous when depicting churches, where there was a spire, he drew a spire, where, as at Gwennap, the tower was a separate building, he showed it as such, and in the case of St Day his drawing gives no indication of anything other than the tower remaining in 1748. Was the tower originally separate from the chapel itself or had it been integral with the building? On 10 November 1797 the lords paid £7.11s.0d. for repairs to 'St Dye Old Tower'. On the following day, one George Richards received damages amounting to £13.9s.0d. for repairs to his house caused by 'the falling of the Old Tower'. And on that same day William Kinsman was paid £0.7s.6d. 'for taking down the Old Tower'. The final payment was made on 1 February 1798 to Capt. John Dennis for labourers taking down the 'Old Tower at St Dye'. The family of Kinsman is first recorded in St Day in 1728 and from then on the name occurs not infrequently and usually in connection with building work, for they were a family of builders, known to have built many of the mine engine-houses in the district.

George Richards was the possessor of many leases on land and buildings within the manor. It was he who acquired a lease on Goongumpus Downs (a sizeable area) for the consideration of enclosing the land. In addition to the payments which the manor made to meet the cost of providing public amenities like the pound and the Market House, it also accepted responsibility for damages to George Richards' house by the falling of the old tower, further to which the manor paid the cost of repairing and, finally, taking down the structure.

The parish pound which was built in 1832.

Fore Street, St Day, c.1911. On the left is the rubble from the dismantling of the old 'St Day Market'.

Left: *Vogue Terrace showing the street lamp placed to illuminate both Chapel Street and Vogue Terrace. Note the original glazing in the windows, 1904.*

Church Street with a horse-drawn light four-wheeled wagon.

Ten

A Digest of Councils & Committees

From the early-nineteenth century and throughout the twentieth, the people of St Day were active in sustaining and improving social and civil facilities. From time to time public meetings were arranged to air whatever need had arisen and to form a committee to deal with the matter. The minutes of some of these organisations have survived – providing us with a telling insight into local life in those times.

From Annie Trevithick's *Short History of St Day* (c.1898) we learn that street lamps were provided in the parish in 1887 to mark the Golden Jubilee of Queen Victoria, at a total cost of £30, the money being raised by voluntary subscriptions. The lamps were of copper frames, glazed on all sides and raised on cast-iron standards. Fuelled by paraffin oil and wicks, they were positioned at strategic sites throughout the town.

The first minute-book of the Clock and Lamps Committee has, regrettably, been lost. Fortunately, however, some records have survived, the earliest amongst them being a minute-book dating from October 1907. As its title suggests, the main business of that committee was the condition of the town clock and the ongoing problems of street lighting. The duties of the lamplighter were demanding and the job was poorly paid at 1s.10d. a month per lamp. With about 15 street lamps to attend to, the lamplighter might expect to be paid about £1.7s.6d. a month. To earn this he was expected not only to light every lamp every evening at a stated time, but it was also his duty to 'put them out at 9pm Sundays, 10pm Mondays to Fridays and 10.30pm Saturdays.' In addition he was required to fill them daily with the paraffin oil supplied, trim the wicks and, of course, clean the glass chimneys as well as the glass on the lamp frames.

To make quite sure that these conditions were observed each committee member was responsible for the lamps in his district 'to see that they are kept lighting and properly cleaned and report same to the Secretary if not done.' It is not surprising that there were frequent changes of lamplighter.

The project was financed by residents paying dues collected by committee members, each of whom was responsible for specific streets or areas. At a committee meeting on 10 November 1911 the following collectors were appointed to the respective districts: Messrs Richards and Bickford, Vogue Terrace, Fore Street and Church Street; Messrs Hancock and Marshall, Scorrier Street, etc.; Messrs T.R. Mills, W.J. Mills, Pink Moors, Tolgullow, etc. From time to time we find that lamps were re-sited 'to the opposite side of the road', etc. to see if it would make an improvement. Bunt's Lane and Pink Moors were frequently the subject of complaint. Another, not infrequent entry in the minutes is a plea to the collectors to bring in 'urgently needed' cash. The committee existed and worked under the strain of a hand-to-mouth state of finance and they appeared to have no capital resource whatsoever. They derived no income from taxes, either from the Redruth Rural District Council or the Gwennap Parish Council, so unless the collectors were successful there would be no lights. From time to time we find that the Lamps Committee were in desperate straits, being driven to raising funds through concerts given by local organisations and jumble sales. Instances of this are disclosed in the minute-book. For example, on 14 February 1913 a letter of thanks was to be sent to the St Day Choral Society for its donation of £2.10s.0d. and in the same minutes there was a proposal that 'Redruth Operatic Society be asked to give a pastoral play in the summer months to raise funds.'

Prior to that at a meeting on 9 November 1910 it was proposed 'that Mr Bickford be asked to insert in the papers an appeal to the St Day Boys abroad for help towards the Town Clock and Lamps.' A similar appeal in February 1914 was aimed at the 'St Day Boys in South Africa'. By May 1914 debts amounting to £5 needed to be cleared and a jumble sale was proposed to raise necessary funds 'or any other means of clearing the debt.'

At the annual meeting on 25 August 1914 it was decided to print posters asking the public whether or not 'the clock be kept going and the lamps continue to be lit during the coming year.' The First World War had just started and the coming year was as far ahead as they needed to plan; little did they know what the coming four years held in store for them. In the event the public opted for continuing to light the lamps and keeping the clock going as usual.

Each year the lamps were lit in October and continued to be lit until late March; the supply of paraffin oil for the lamps for the ensuing six months was put out to tender in good time and discussed at the next meeting. The names of those offering to supply and at what price were all faithfully recorded in the minute-book. Several brands of oil were offered, White Rose, Royal Daylight, Royal Standard, Homelight and Crown Diamond. Prices over the years ranged from 6½d. in October 1907 to 8½d. per gallon in 1913 with very little difference between brands.

On 3 October 1913 at a public meeting in the Church Schoolroom it was:

Proposed by Mr T.R. Mills, seconded by Mr A.B. Rowe that the Rev. W.W. Bickford, J.R. Rooke and J.T. Letcher to see the manager of the Electric Supply Co. on conditions &c of bringing it in this town and that their report be given at a Public Meeting.

The representation to higher authority appears to have fallen on stony ground, for we find no further mention of the matter until 1926.

On 25 June 1917 a new committee was elected with a number of new names, not seen previously but destined to be prominent in St Day affairs for the next 20 or more years. Thomas Rogers Tripp, Herbert Barrat Veale and Nicholas William Hensley now appeared and were to remain in the forefront of St Day affairs for many more years to come. The last recorded meeting of the old Clock and Lamps Committee took place in the Literary Institute on 15 January 1920. The last resolution of the Clock and Lamps Committee reads: 'Proposed that Mr Hockey and Mr J. Reed be asked to Collect the Town.' It was winter, oil was needed for the street lamps, and the lamplighter had to be paid.

There is then a gap of six and a half years before the next recorded meeting which was a public meeting held in the Church Hall on Thursday 27 May 1926 'To Consider the question of the Town Clock and any other Public matter that might arise.' About 40 or 50 people were present, Mr T.R. Tripp, JP, CC, was elected chairman and the following committee of ten formed: Mr J. Potter, Mr T.R. Tripp, Revd Evan Thomas, Mr W. Kinsman, Mr Wm. Hensley, Mr H. Teague, Mr Farrer, Mr R.R. Cullen, Mr T. Simmons and Mr R.R. Blewett. Richard Rodda Blewett now appeared on the scene and was appointed honorary secretary of the new committee. Headmaster of the St Day and Carharrack Council School, energetic and enthusiastic, he was to be deeply involved in St Day affairs from this point on.

The committee was to take charge of the clock and tower and the Market Square, in addition to the lampposts and lamps. At its first meeting on Monday 31 May 1926 held in the Church Mission Hall it assumed the name 'St Day General Purposes Committee'. All members were present. Application was made to both the St Day Feast Committee (through H.B. Veale) and the Gwennap Show Committee (Mrs Johns) for funds for the clock repairs. The question of a water supply was discussed and a deputation of three was to meet Major John Williams of Scorrier to enquire under what terms Vogue Shute could be used as a source for water. He agreed to make it available for the sum of £16 a year along with a site for a pumping station at Tolcarne. A public meeting held on Monday 21 June attracted about 100 people and a resolution was made to 'advise the Redruth Rural District Council to arrange with Major Williams for the possession of Vogue Shute water.' The Redruth RDC was further asked:

... to cause Plans and Estimates to be made for a Water Supply for St Day using Vogue Shute as source and that those Plans and Estimates be presented to a Public Meeting of the St Day people for their consideration and approval.

At that same public meeting it was resolved that the General Purposes Committee should henceforth be responsible for the organisation of the Hospital Sunday events.

Several communities in the area had for decades held an annual event to raise funds for the hospitals, usually including the St John Ambulance and the local Nursing Association. On 15 August 1926 St Day Hospital Sunday included an evening open-air concert held on the lawn of The Cedars by permission of Mrs Hannay. The takings that day amounted to £16.12s.7d. which was distributed as follows: Redruth Hospital £6, Truro Infirmary £6 and Redruth Ambulance £3.

On 8 March 1927 at a joint meeting of the GP Committee and the Feast Committee it was agreed to amalgamate. At the meeting of 12 April 1927 R.R. Blewett proposed 'That the provision of a Playing-Field and recreation ground be part of our programme.' The proposal was seconded and carried unanimously. The secretary wrote to J.C. Williams Esq., on 10 July following, to enquire on what terms they might acquire the corner field of Tolgullow Vean Farm at Crossroads. A reply was received by return on 14 July. On Tuesday 16 August 1927 the chairman, T.R. Tripp, and secretary, R.R. Blewett, met Major Godfrey Williams of Perranwell, secretary of the National Playing Fields Association, and Mr W.W. Teague, steward to J.C. Williams Esq. of Caerhays Castle, on the field. A letter was read from Mr Peter Michael Williams (actual owner of the field and son of J.C. Williams) handing over the field to the General Purposes Committee, subject to conditions set out on an attached sheet.

On Sunday 21 August 1927 at the evening concert held in the grounds of Carew House, an

Opening of the playing-field in 1928 by Peter Michael Williams, who is seen here bareheaded in the gateway. On his right is Herbert Veale with a bowler hat and T.R. Tripp wearing a trilby. Next to T.R. Tripp is Harry Teague senr (bowler hat) and the bowler-hatted man on the far left is Joseph Mills, brother of W.J. Mills.

official announcement of the gift was made to an audience of about 500 people. Mr P.M. Williams was thanked for his generous gift and the field was officially accepted.

The last meeting of the General Purposes Committee was held in the Church Mission Hall on Friday 26 August 1927 at which it resolved to take responsibility for the playing-field. Eleven new members including seven ladies were elected (the first time that ladies were elected) and the name of the committee was changed to St Day Community Council.

The new council began at once to formulate plans for laying out the new playing-field and to make arrangements for a formal opening which eventually took place on Feast Monday, 18 June 1928. Mr Peter Michael Williams, the donor, performed the opening ceremony.

The activities at St Day caught the attention of the press, which suggested that many other places in the West might with advantage follow the example 'set by the little Cornwall town of St Day' as published in the *Western Morning News*, 16 September 1927. A week later the *Western Weekly News* had this to say:

> *The little Cornish town of St Day sets an example that Torrington and other places might follow. Instead of having a Ratepayers' Association which spends its energies on criticism, St. Day has a Community Council (ie an improvement committee) that does things and so keeps down the rates in a practical way. The committee was set up a year or so ago to restore the town clock to working order and to find means of improving the local water supply. Having successfully grappled with the first of these tasks and induced the Redruth Rural District Council to put new energy into the study of the second the committee turned its attention to other matters, including the provision of a Playing-Field which was brought to fruition by the gift of four acres of land by Mr P.M. Williams.*

William John Mills, a native of St Day living at Torquay, having already provided a playing-field pavilion for shelter, next offered to provide a free tea for all the old people on Feast Monday, the occasion of the opening of the playing-field, and to present them each with a parcel of provisions. In addition he was to spend about £250 on planting and road-making in the field. These gifts marked the beginning of the modern form of the St Day Feast celebrations. Invitations to tea were sent to about 160 old people and every child of school age was to receive a traditional saffron tea-treat 12oz bun and a new shilling bearing the date of the current year.

In 1930 the W.J. Mills St Day Benevolent Fund was established and thereafter provided endowment for all Feast Monday celebrations. About this time Mrs John Williams of Scorrier House wrote to the Community Council offering the Infant Welfare Building and the caretaker's house as a gift to be used as a community centre. The gift was accepted by the Community Council. During its time, the Community Council provided three sets of trustees: for the playing-field (eventually transferred to the Camborne/Redruth Urban District Council); the W.J.

Left: *Feast, 1945. The under-fives collect buns and shillings.* Left, front: *Reg Barrett;* centre, back: *R.R. Blewett.*

Right: *St Day Feast Committee in Church Street leading the procession to the playing-field on Feast Monday, 1990s.*

Mills Street

The formal opening of Mills Street, 3 July 1933, by John Charles Williams, Esq., the Lord Lieutenant of Cornwall. Holding the ribbon are Misses Marian and Pauline Mills, great-nieces of W.J. Mills.

Right: *Mills Street, formerly Simmons Street, which was acquired by William John Mills and the houses refurbished for the old people of St Day. The plaque records the gift by William John Mills of a street of 28 almshouses: 'This Street is an Endowment made by William John Mills and Dedicated by him to the people of St Day for their Benefit and Comfort in Memory of his Mother and Father William and Susan Mills and his Sisters Elizabeth Ann Petherick and Mary Rule Mills. July 3rd 1933.'*

Clockwise from centre left: *The 50th anniversary of Mills Street with W.J. Mills and Enid Mills, his sister; Mrs June Mills, who made and decorated the anniversary cake shown. Also in the picture is her husband Joe Mills; St Day Majorettes; the anniversary cake and Miss Enid Mills.*

Mills Benevolent Fund; and St Day Community Centre.

In September 1928 a cheque for £145 was received from W.J. Mills for the following purposes: £113 to buy Consols to hand over to the Parish Council as an endowment for the town clock; £25 to put the clock in good order before handing over; and £7 for a memorial stone to the late T.R. Mills to be erected on the clock tower. The trustees of the Benevolent Fund found it impossible to carry out the enormous amount of work demanded by the terms of the deed and were obliged to turn to the Community Council for support which was given freely. The organisation of the Feast celebrations, including keeping a register of old persons up to date as well as general advice, became the province of St Day Community Council from then on.

The most notable gift from W.J. Mills to St Day was a street of 28 well-built houses. He bought them from the lords of the manor, the Chichester and Champernowne families, had them reconditioned, water laid on, the gardens planted out and the pavements re-laid. The houses were formally opened by the Lord Lieutenant of Cornwall, J.C. Williams Esq., on 3 July 1933.

Managed by trustees, 22 houses were for the use of old people of St Day, the remaining six to be let and the rents applied to the upkeep of the street. The street was renamed Mills Street, dedicated to the memory of Mr Mills' parents and two sisters, this being recorded on the bronze tablet seen illustrated on page 54.

In 1983 the 50th anniversary of the gift of Mills Street was celebrated with a splendid street tea party organised by the Feast Committee. The centre of the street for its whole length was occupied by a table covered by white cloths and laden with cakes and other goodies. June Mills made and decorated a birthday cake for the occasion which was cut by William John Mills and his sister Enid Mills and distributed to the residents of Mills Street.

Now, in the new millennium, the term 'Community Council' seems to have died a natural death and the old title 'the Feast Committee' is again in favour verbally.

Silver Jubilee, 1977

A public meeting was held at St Day Community Centre at 7.30p.m. on Thursday 10 February 1977 to discuss the possibility of a public celebration of the Queen's forthcoming Silver Jubilee. Some 50 people attended the meeting. Mr Leslie Smitheram, District Councillor, and Mr Leslie Martin, Feast Committee, addressed those present. After discussion it was unanimously agreed to celebrate the Queen's Silver Jubilee despite the inability of Kerrier District Council to help with funds. Many suggestions were made from the floor, such was the enthusiasm – these included presenting every child under the age of 16 years with a jubilee mug. Fund-raising was the first hurdle and various suitable events were proposed to meet that requirement, such as a band concert, raffles, a 'mile of pennies' and a sponsored walk. Raffle prizes were offered by a number of those present.

It was decided that a committee should be formed at once to organise the events and volunteers were called for. It was left to the committee to elect their own officers. The committee members were Mrs D. Blackmore, Mrs Tremayne, Mrs A. Angove, Mrs M. Richards, Mr T. Richards, Mrs Morrish, Mr and Mrs W. Williams, Mr E. Pettit, Mr V. Vanstone, Mr and Mrs J. Mills, Mr and Mrs K. Temple, Mrs Paget, Mr N. Long, Mrs M.L. Mitchell, and Mr and Mrs D. Williams. The following officers were elected: chairman Joe Mills, vice-chairman Billy Williams, secretary Ed Pettett, treasurer Mrs Marlene Richards and auditor Mr J.G. Gilbert.

A general discussion ensued during which various ideas were put forward and it was agreed to consider these items and produce other ideas at the first formal committee meeting which would be held at the Church Mission Room on Thursday 17 February at 7.30p.m. The meeting then concluded.

They had 18 weeks to plan and organise in detail their intended programme for the day. In that time they met in full committee 18 times, in addition meeting twice after Jubilee day to confirm that all clearing up had been completed satisfactorily and to disperse the remaining funds. There were no 'passengers' on that committee, each member had positive input; in addition to their individual contributions, the ladies' sub-committee took responsibility for catering for an estimated 1,500 people in Fore Street and Market Square. The *West Briton* published a glowing report of the day's happenings:

St DAY PUTS ON A DAY OF SPLENDOUR

Few of Cornwall's smaller towns could have matched St Day. Its narrow streets were a riot of colour, bunting and flags seeming to hang from every house and window. Centre of the celebration was the Market Square, in front of the distinctive Town Clock, a square created by two huge arches of greenery, each spanning the road and some 20 ft. high. Interlaced in the arches were flags, patches of colour against the dark green background, and beyond the flags laced across the wide square. St Day's energetic Silver Jubilee committee had raised nearly £800 [actually £948]. *and no expense was spared. Mr Joe Mills, chairman, sporting grey bowler and red carnation, was delighted with the whole day – even the weather.*

MASSIVE

The street party was a massive affair. Something like 2000 people enjoyed a free tea. True 1500 sandwiches were made by a firm, but everything else was homemade

Left: *Jubilee Day, 1977; the opening event in the morning, with a horse-drawn vehicle led by Joe Mills and his daughter Sally Mills.*

and that included 1200 sausage rolls, dozens of cakes and a wide range of other fare.

"It has been a marvellous day", said Mr Mills, "Everyone has enjoyed themselves and we have had marvellous support."

St Day Action Committee: Telegraph Hill

In 1978 a subsidence at the top of Telegraph Hill, St Day, led to the County Council putting a temporary closing order on the road. There had been subsidence in the area previously, in February 1970 and again in October 1977. In June 1978 they announced their intention to close the road permanently; that news was at first greeted with dismay by the inhabitants of the town, quickly followed by a feeling of outrage and refusal to take the County Council's decision lying down. A public meeting was called for 8 June 1978 at the Community Centre at which it became clear that the inhabitants were prepared to challenge the County Council's decision. That evening saw the birth of a new force, the St Day Action Committee, which was destined to join in battle with the County Council for the ensuing seven years.

The new committee consisting of 11 members met formally for the first time after the Public Meeting that same evening. It appointed its officers, the chairman Joseph Mills, the secretary Richard Angove and elected four members as delegates to meet the county surveyor at the earliest possible date. The meeting closed at 9.55p.m.

That was the first of the several hundred meetings which would be held over the next seven years before victory was achieved. Professional advice was sought, legal, civil engineering and of course mining, all of which had to be paid for.

St Day Ladies' Action Committee undertook to raise the funds and were very successful, the legal fees alone amounting to more than £1,200. Action Committee members met District Councillors and County Councillors face to face from time to time and enlisted support from them as well as from MPs.

In 1982 the Department of Transport appointed Major General J.C. Woolett, CBE, MC, as Inspector to head a public inquiry into the objections to the proposed closure of Telegraph Hill, St Day. The inquiry was held at the Community Centre, St Day, on 18 and 19 May 1982 and an inspection of the site and surroundings took place on 20 May 1982. Kerrier District Council, St Day Action Committee and the Cornish Assembly appeared at the inquiry. The Inspector reported:

> *The main grounds of objection were that there is a statutory duty to repair the highway, that the alternative routes are unsatisfactory, that the causes of the subsidence have not been adequately investigated and that the estimated cost is excessive.*

The County Council accepted that it had a duty under the Highways Act (1980) to repair the road but pleaded that 'no highway authority could be expected to keep a road open regardless of expense.' Referring to the Highways Act, Kerrier District Council pointed out that the statutory duty to repair did not alter with financial restraint: 'There are a number of reasons why a highway may have to be closed but the cost of repairing is not one of them.' The Action Committee did not accept that there was any evidence that the cavities extended to any great depths and noted that four years had elapsed since Telegraph Hill was closed, yet the people had not given up their efforts as shown:

> *... by the way that they have been able to raise a four-figure sum to oppose the closure order, and by the large attendance at the inquiry. St Day is thought of as a town rather than a village.*

The committee had obtained various estimates and reports, not all of which had been produced at the inquiry – 'These estimates of £30,000 to £60,000 are all a fraction of the very expensive Council's estimate at £250,000.' In his summing up the Inspector observed:

> *... the prolonged loss of this old and familiar route has cast a blight on this ancient and proud community, affecting property values and creating a feeling of isolation and this should be taken into account.*

His final recommendation was that the proposed 1982 Order, when made, should be reviewed after a fixed period. A period of two years was at first suggested but was amended to one year.

That, however, was not the end of the story; the Action Committee continued to put pressure on the County Council. Slowly, empathy between St Day Action Committee and many of the Councillors became more and more apparent, culminating in a proposal by the Chairman of the Transportation Committee at a meeting on 12 January 1984 to do a 'proper job'. And so it was, and a 'proper job' was done and Telegraph Hill St Day was repaired and fully reinstated. The formal reopening took place on Saturday 26 October 1989.

On 2 September 1992 the Action Committee met for the last time and decided to disband, the remaining funds to be given to the St Day Community Centre to be used at the discretion of the Management Committee. Meanwhile, the Ladies Action Committee remained and pursued an active policy of fund-raising for the Community Centre and selected charities for a further five years. The *West Briton* of 16 October 1997 reported on the closure:

> *END OF THE ROAD FOR FUNDRAISERS*
>
> *A locally well-supported fundraising committee of ladies has disbanded at St Day as members feel it has achieved much of what it set out to do.*
>
> *The small and hardworking body headed by June Mills, held Easter, summer and Christmas sales, coffee mornings and other events. The Summer Fair in the old vicarage gardens held annually for several years was always a popular occasion. Peggy Singleton, Secretary, said in the last decade that they raised £3,770 for the Centre, spent £1543 on furniture and curtains and had contributed £405 to the Air Ambulance and £440 to St Day Pre-School Playgroup, £400 to Children in Need as well as help to the Band, the St Day Christmas Lights appeal and money to send a local disabled boy to Florida. Their final act was to spend the £260 balance on new chairs for the centre.*

St Day Residents' Committee

This committee came into being following an open meeting in mid-November 1981 sponsored by the Devon and Cornwall Constabulary who wished 'to enter into discussions concerning the future policing of St Day' following complaints of rowdyism received. The meeting was chaired by Chief Inspector Stephens of Camborne Police Station. A list of 16 volunteers to serve on the new organisation was drawn up and a date set for its first formal meeting, 2 December 1981. Chief Inspector Stephens again took the chair to open and the election of officers followed in due course for treasurer, secretary and finally chairman, in that order. Ian Brinkley was elected treasurer, Julia Dagley secretary and Joseph Mills chairman.

It was agreed that a meeting-place for the over-16s was the priority for the committee. There were few suitable sites in St Day and only two possibles, one the vacant area opposite the Primary School (now the school car park), the other a plot on high ground at the Vogue playing-field. Enquiries were made to the Education Committee who held out some hope by not dismissing the request outright but pointing out that it was county policy to sell any surplus land on that area on the open market and, as the site had planning permission for one dwelling, the plot would be expensive.

The District Planning Officer at Kerrier District Council drew attention to the fact that St Day Football Club had already on two occasions been refused planning permission to build changing rooms on the Vogue playing-field site 'in view of the prominent position of the site and local opposition.' At the same time a search was being made to find a suitable prefabricated building to fulfil the need.

A number of organisations, including The Prince's Trust and the Cornwall Rural Community Council, were approached for grant funding 'but unfortunately did not qualify for financial support.' It became clear in time that grant funding was not going to materialise for the Residents' Committee and eventually it was dissolved and its funds were handed over to the Community Council.

European money was to become available 15 years later and the programme for the regeneration of St Day included a successful application for finance for a Youth Club and Sports Centre which was built on the Vogue playing-field site and formally opened on Saturday 4 November 2000.

St Day Parish Council

In 1980 the Boundary Commission considered the then existing parliamentary, county, county borough and parish boundaries. It also looked at the many instances of 'unparished' areas. St Day was one of the latter and a public meeting was called by the present writer 'to discuss the desirability or otherwise of having a Parish Council for St Day.' The Parish Clerk of St Feock explained the duties and responsibilities of a Parish Council and the advantages of such a status.

A vote at the end of the meeting was unanimous in favour of the motion that St Day should apply to be parished; accordingly a letter was sent to Kerrier District Council asking that St Day be recommended and outlined suggested parish boundaries.

About five years later the District Council informed St Day that the application had been approved and an election for seven Parish Councillors was arranged by the District Council to take place on Thursday 28 March 1985. The first annual meeting of the council was held on 23 April 1985 at the Community Centre, St Day, and the newly elected Parish Councillors Mrs A.D.V. Hillman, and Messrs B.C. Braddon, W.E.G. Dymond, J. Mills, K.D. Temple, P.E. Tregoning and V. Vanstone were all present. The meeting was chaired by S.G. Stevens, Chief Executive and Proper Officer of the Kerrier District Council. The assistant secretary of the District Council, J.P. Goldsworthy, was also present. Mr Stevens called for nominations for the election of chairman of the Parish Council.

Councillor J. Mills was elected to be the first chairman and made his declaration of acceptance of office and took the chair which he was to occupy for the next 14 years. Then followed a number of resolutions necessary to the proper running of the Parish Council, including advertising for a Parish Clerk, salary to be agreed by negotiation. The next meeting was to be held on 22 May following. Awaiting the new Parish Council was a letter from the Parochial Church Council with the information that the churchyard was full and could accept no more burials. It placed the responsibility of providing a new burial-ground firmly on the new council. Some burials had taken place using one of the paths, but this practice was not only undesirable, it was a very limited area, capable of accommodating only a small number of graves.

The value of having a Parish Council was clearly demonstrated here, making it possible for St Day to provide a burial-ground for the immediate locality. The choice for the Parish Council was either to do nothing, in which case burials of St Day inhabitants would be at the cemetery at Trewirgie, Redruth (extremely inconvenient and difficult for people wishing to visit family graves), or, alternatively, to acquire suitable land at St Day and get planning permission to create a new burial-ground, which would have to meet regulations governing such sites. (It must not overlook or be overlooked by domestic dwellings, it must not drain into streams and in a much mined area, the ground must not be liable to subsidence.) But before it tackled these details of law, the Parish Council had to find a site, not too far from St Day itself, which the owners thereof would be willing to sell at an acceptable price within the resources of a small Parish Council. Land touching the town would have building-site value if planning permission could be obtained, and this would be prohibitive.

A field to the south of and adjoining the old churchyard was outside the area in which building could be allowed and would not therefore attract building-site values. The owner was approached and agreed to sell, having eventually accepted that building development in that field would not be allowed. The site was bought, and a new boundary wall was built without charge, by the Redruth Methodist Community Project using Cornish stone paid for by the Parish Council. On Friday 3 June 1988 the new burial-ground was consecrated by the Bishop of Truro, the Right Reverend Bishop Peter Mumford, and officially opened for use.

The late Stanley Martin, for many years secretary of the Community Council, drew attention to the growing misuse of the War Memorial shelter and suggested that gates to protect the memorial should be provided. The Parish Council wrote to Kerrier District Council to obtain permission to do this and then placed an advertisement in the papers inviting designs and costings. At the February 1987 meeting they discussed the ten tenders and designs received. One of the two designs submitted by Hamish Miller of Hayle, a wrought-iron artist, was the unanimous choice, and the present splendid and impressive pair of gates was commissioned and was erected some months later in time to be dedicated before the Remembrance Day service

The Parish Council met monthly, continuing to deal with the minutiae of parish affairs, planning applications, attending site meetings, requests for grants received from local and other organisations, faulty pavements, gutters and suchlike.

In the mid-1990s, the term 'regeneration' began to be heard, and a forum, ACCESS TO ACTION; TOMORROW'S HERITAGE, organised by the Civic Trust in conjunction with Redruth 2000, was held at Redruth on Saturday afternoon 18 March 1995. Among the 41 delegates from all parts of the county was the then chairman of the Parish Council. Following that meeting he wrote to Groundwork Kerrier, who had been present at the forum, inviting them to come to St Day and walk the town. This they did on Tuesday 18 July 1995 and as a result a small steering committee, including representatives of the District Council, was formed to put together a regeneration programme for St Day. The Old Church Restoration Project would be included and would attract significant grant aid.

Bids were made for improvements to the Market Square, an important focal point, and for the area fronting Buckingham Terrace. Additional areas in need of improvement were identified and at the final count a sum approaching £1million had been received and put to good use.

Eleven

Two Nineteenth-Century Directories

In 1910 Peter Jennings, headmaster of St Day and Carharrack Board School (1878–1917), recorded notes which throw light onto a number of individuals remembered by him. He used both the *Williams' Commercial Directory* of 1847 and Rd. Symons' *Directory* of 1866 as framework for his commentary, providing convenient lists of active inhabitants of the town. He came to St Day 31 years after the publication of *Williams' Directory* and presumably would have used the memories of some of the older residents of the town to help colour the picture of life in a small mid-nineteenth-century Cornish mining community. Those notes have survived, thanks to one of his successors, Richard R. Blewett, who became the headmaster at St Day in 1921 and, finding the documents among other papers, preserved them, eventually handing them over to the then Secretary of St Day Feast Committee, the late Stanley Martin whose widow was kind enough to allow the author to make copies which are here reproduced.

There follow abstracts from pages 162/3 of *Williams' Commercial Directory of Cornwall*, 1847, as annotated by Peter Jennings, whose comments are underlined:

CLERGY and GENTRY.
Gilvey, Rev. George. Vicar of Gwennap.
Stothard, Rev. William. Curate of Chapel of Ease.

NAME and PROFESSION.
Adams, Henry. Blacksmith. *Familiarly called 'Old Adams'.*
Arthur, Samuel Pellew. General. Pract. MRCSE. 1830. LAC. 1830. *Lived in Mrs Lanning's house in Telegraph St. Mrs Jno. Cooke's house was the Surgery. Dr Pellew later moved to Vogue House.*
Barnett, William. Shopkeeper, Church Street, *two small windows, one each side of the door. Edward Newton lived here later. He eventually moved to Camborne, setting up business there as watchmaker. Mrs Jno. Phillips was the next occupant and finally Miss Murton.*
Blamey, William. Tailor.
Bray, John. Grocer and Tea Dealer.
Chegwidden, Thomas. Beer-retailer *where A.B. Rowe's Drawing-room is. Michael R. Michell bought it and added it to his new house.*
Chynoweth, James. Shopkeeper. *He was Mrs James Hart's father. Where Mrs Fred J. Hart now lives.*
Chynoweth, John. Tailor, *first in Church Street where Jos. Kinsman lives. Mr J.M. Whitford lived there afterwards.*
Cock, Henry. Mercer and Tailor, *where Jn. Leverton lives. John Chynoweth succeeded him.*
Cocking, John. Hatter and Eating-house Keeper. Fore Street, *where Mr Martin, Outfitter lives.*
Corfield, T.J. Chemist and Druggist.
Davis, William. Victualler. 'Lion Inn'.
Downing, John. Cabinet-maker and Upholsterer. *Workshop at Lichfield House.*
Downing, William. Shopkeeper. *Brother to John. Shopkeeper in Scorrier Street. Father of Geo. Downing of Truro.*
Dryden, Joseph. Beer-retailer. *Behind the Town Clock.*
Dunstan, Henry. Grocer, Tea-dealer, Corn and Provision Merchant.
Edwards, John. Grocer and Tea-dealer. *Mr Hensley succeeded him.*
Goldsworth [sic], John. Boot and Shoemaker.
Gray, William. Earthenware dealer.
Grenfell, Joseph. 'Market Inn.' *Between Mrs Hensley's and Mr T.R. Mills's. Is now [1910] two houses. He was Mrs Jno. Edwards's father. Capt. Rd. Magor, who came home from Mexico, then Joanna Thomas, Chenalls afterwards landlord. W. Ninnis in 1857.*
Hamlin, William Jones. Grocer and Tea-dealer. Scorrier St. *Part of Red Lion. Two large Chinese figures in window, would nod heads, attraction to children.*
Harvey, James & Co. Wholesale Drapers, Grocers, Tea-dealers and General Merchants. *Their shop was where Mr Legg lives; their warehouse was on the other side of the street and is now used as the Masonic Lodge. Their stables were in Mr Jos. Mills' yard in Church Street and their dwelling-house was Carew House.*
Hawke, John. Grocer, Tea-dealer and

Ironmonger. *If sold pattens and clogs was 'ironmonger'. Where Mrs Clift Matthews lives. A good painter.*
Hunt, Thomas. Doctor. Gen. Pract. MRCSE. 1839. LAC. 1840.
Jacka, Thomas. Baker. *At Mr Jos. Kinsman's Church St before Jno. Chynoweth. His wife was a gossip. He would say 'Oh! My dear! She's a Jacka! She's a Jacka!'*
Jacka, William. Black and Whitesmith.
Johns, Henry. Mercer and Tailor.
Kendall, John. Fore Street. Chemist. Druggist. Grocer. Tea Dealer. Ironmonger. *Two little windows. Where Mrs Whitford now lives. Three steps up.*
Kinsman, James. Grocer, Tea-dealer and Earthenware dealer.
Kitto, Mary Ann. Earthenware dealer, where Post Office now is.
Kitto, S.K.M. Grocer, Tea-dealer and Earthenware dealer.
Litcher [sic], Mary. Shopkeeper. Fore Street, *where Mrs Hooper's Pork shop now is. Two small windows. Steps to shop door. Aunt to J.H. Letcher.*
Luke, Henry. Victualler, 'Queen's Arms'.
Major, John. Victualler, 'Britannia'. *Afterwards John Bull, he could not read.*
Michell, George. Painter, Glazier, Auctioneer and Appraiser.
Michell, Michael R. Draper. *Pulled down the corner shop and bought Th. Chygwidden's kiddleywink. The present Drawing-Room was Store Room and spaces between pairs of kerbstones are still to be seen. They were so placed to allow wagons to get nearer the window. Mr John Barratt, Mr Simon Whitburn, R.H. Chynoweth and A.B. Rowe, were successors.*
Michell, Nanny. Shopkeeper. *Carried on a good business in thatched house in front of space* [occupied by Trinity House in 2000].
Michell, Thomas. Victualler, 'Commercial Inn'.
Michell, Thomas. Mercer and Tailor.
Mills, William. Currier and Leather-cutter. *Scorrier St, where now Mr Chynoweth lives, was then a small shop entered by descending steps.*
Mitchell, Richard G. Boot and Shoemaker. *(R.G.) Where Mrs Greenwood has just died* [13 Jan. 1910]. *In Scorrier Street.*
Perryman, William. Beer-retailer.
Philp, John. Draper. Church Street. *Where Mr Jane lives. Baptists. Large family. Respectable, but too proud.*
Provis, James. Ironmonger, Fore St. *Succeeded Jno. Kendall. Eccentric.*
Rickard, William. Schoolmaster. *Wooden leg. Did not spare the rod. In Mission Room on site of present* [1910] *Anglican Church Schoolroom. John Bawden, Auctioneer, succeeded him.*
Rooke, John. Draper and Tailor. *Built big shop in Scorrier St.*
Rosewall, John. Draper and Grocer. Scorrier St. *Followed Hamlin (at his death) at part of Red Lion.*
Simmons, Thomas. Draper, Fore St. *Where Mr Arthur Kinsman Jr. lives. Married daughter of William Wilton.*
Stephens, Michael. Shopkeeper. *Thomas Dennis took his business in Church Street when he went to Australia. Where Richford now lives.*
Tabb, John. Victualler, 'Cornish Arms'. *Capt. Simon Toy succeeded John Tabb (father of Mrs Simon Whitburn and Mrs Davey Lanner) James Verran (Vogue) successor to Simon Toy.*
Teague, Harriet. (Honor?) Dressmaker. *Aunt to T.H. Letcher, sister to his mother.*
Tiddy, Joanna. Postmistress. *(Cross Post once a day.) Post Office and Shop where Capt. Annear died. Scorrier St. Had a good business.*
Tiddy, Susan and Joanna. Shopkeepers. *Susan – Mrs Annear. Mary Tiddy kept shop at Lowertown Cusgarne. Made little fortune in shop.*
Tonkin, John. Beer-retailer. Scorrier St. *Lived where William Gilbert lives and then crossed street to where Mrs Nicholls lived.*
Tregaskis, Thomas. Agent to Britannia Insurance Office.
Truscott, William. Saddler and Harness-maker. Church Street. *Where Mrs Spriddell lives.*
Veale, John. Watch and Clockmaker.
Whitburn, Mary. Straw-hat Manufacturer.
Williams, Henry. Shopkeeper.
Wilton, William. Church Street. Mathematical Instrument, Watch and Clock Maker. *Where Mr T.R. Mills lives. Many going men* [still following their trade] *served their time there: Kistler, Tom Carah, the Truscotts, etc.*
Yeoman, John. Boot and Shoemaker. *Where Mr A. Kinsman lives, a very tall man. Mr Trevethick succeeded him.*

POST OFFICE.
Joanna Tiddy. Postmistress.
INSURANCE OFFICES.
'Britannia'. Thomas Tregaskis. Agent.

ANALYSIS.

Shopkeepers.	*7*
Grocer and Tea-dealers.	*9*
Tailors.	*6*
Drapers.	*6 (incl. 1 w'lesaler.)*
Mercers.	*3*
Dressmakers.	*1*
Chemists and Druggists.	*2*
Medical Practitioners.	*2*
Blacksmiths.	*2*
Ironmongers.	*3*
Earthenware Dealers.	*4*
Named Inns.	*6 See below.*

Beer-retailers. See below.	4	*Kiddleywinks.*
Watch and Clock Makers.	2	
Auctioneers.	1	
Boot and Shoe Makers.	3	
Straw-hat Manufacturers.	1	
Saddler and Harness Makers.	1	
Painter and Glaziers.	1	
Cabinet and Upholsterers.	1	
Hatter and Eating-houses.	1	
Corn and Provision Merchants.	1	
Bakers.	1	
Mathematical Instrument Makers.	1	

NAMED INNS: 6

Lion Inn.	*Britannia.*
Commercial Inn.	*Cornish Arms.*
Queen's Arms.	*Market Inn.*

Some of Peter Jennings' comments above are mildly amusing and all are of interest to present-day readers. Such references as 'came home from Mexico' and 'when he went to Australia' serve to remind us that travel to and from the far-away mining camps scattered throughout the world was commonplace.

The notes were written in 1910 and the frequent expression 'now lives' refers to that year. In all, the directory itself names 63 individuals, including two clergymen and two medical practitioners.

There are 24 business categories listed but most individual shopkeepers sold a variety of widely differing merchandise. As an example, John Kendall, chemist and druggist, was also listed as a grocer, tea dealer and ironmonger. Peter Jennings tells us that if a shopkeeper sold pattens and clogs he was an ironmonger, and those grocers who sold tea were 'Tea Dealers', just as those who sold earthenware were 'Earthenware Dealers'. The four 'Beer retailers' kept the Kiddleywinks, licensed premises selling only beer, usually home-made.

There were still self-employed dressmakers plying their skills in the late 1920s, but they were already a dying trade. In St Day, we remember well the Misses Luke of Church Street, still making dresses and doing 'alterations', putting in a 'tuck' here and 'letting-out' there to meet the changes of middle-age spread. The advent and spread of the multiple shops with new fashions and well-cut off-the-peg garments was, however, too strong a competition and dressmakers soon disappeared from every locality.

The coming of the motor car brought a great reduction in the requirement for saddlers and harness makers, as it did for the skill of wheelwrights and coach builders, who, in company with the straw-hat manufacturer, the hatter, the boot and shoe maker, the drapers, tailors and mathematical instrument makers, were all no longer to be found in St Day after the First World War.

Apparently there never were banking facilities in St Day, nor is there an accountant listed in the directory, as it seems that Redruth supplied those wants when needed.

Cross referencing the above directory with the *Book of Reference to the Plan of St Day* produced by R. Symons, Surveyor, Truro, in 1866, shows that of the names listed in *Williams' Directory*, ten were still in business in St Day 13 years later, as follows:

Arthur Samuel Pellew.	*General Practitioner.*
T.J. Corfield.	*Chemist.*
William Jones Hamlin.	*Grocer and Tea-Dealer.*
James Harvey & Co.	*Wholesalers. General Merchants.*
John Hawke.	*Grocer, Tea-Dealer, Ironmonger.*
Mary Litcher.	*Shopkeeper.*
Michael R. Michell.	*Draper.*
James Provis.	*Ironmonger.*
Harriett Teague.	*Dressmaker.*
William Wilton.	*Mathematical Instrument Maker. Etc.*

It has not been possible to identify exactly where in St Day most of these businesses were sited, but we are able, by cross-referencing, to locate the premises of some. For example, Samuel Pellew was a doctor. In 1847 he was located in Telegraph Street, in 1866 he occupied Tresaddern Farm (R. Symons, 1866) and later lived at Vogue House (Peter Jennings).

T.J. Corfield was listed as a chemist and druggist. He worked in Church Street, where the business of 'Chemist' remained in the Corfield family for three generations. On the death of the last Corfield ('Old Charlie Corfield' as he was affectionately known in the mid-1930s), the premises were used as a chemist shop by Alexander McPhee, who lived in the little house attached to and behind Vogue House. He was the last chemist in St Day, remaining until the late 1930s, and was a familiar sight, driving his three-wheeled Morgan.

William Jones Hamlin was a grocer and tea dealer, situated in Scorrier Street. His premises were a part of the Red Lion, formerly a beerhouse (Kiddleywinks) situated on the corner of Barracks Lane and Scorrier Street. It was licensed in 1839. In 1912 it was popularly known as 'Michael Duff's', he being the landlord at the time. In 1948 it was a greengrocer's shop kept by 'Willie' Williams, also known as 'Woodbine Williams'.

Harvey & Co. was located in Fore Street, opposite the present-day Masonic Hall, which was built as their store. Of the others it is known that James Harvey occupied Carew House, Mary Letcher was in Fore Street, Michael R. Michell worked from the corner of Fore Street and Church Street, in the present-day Amber House, and William Wilton was in Church Street. Little is known of Harriet Teague or John Veale and William Wilton was in Church Street.

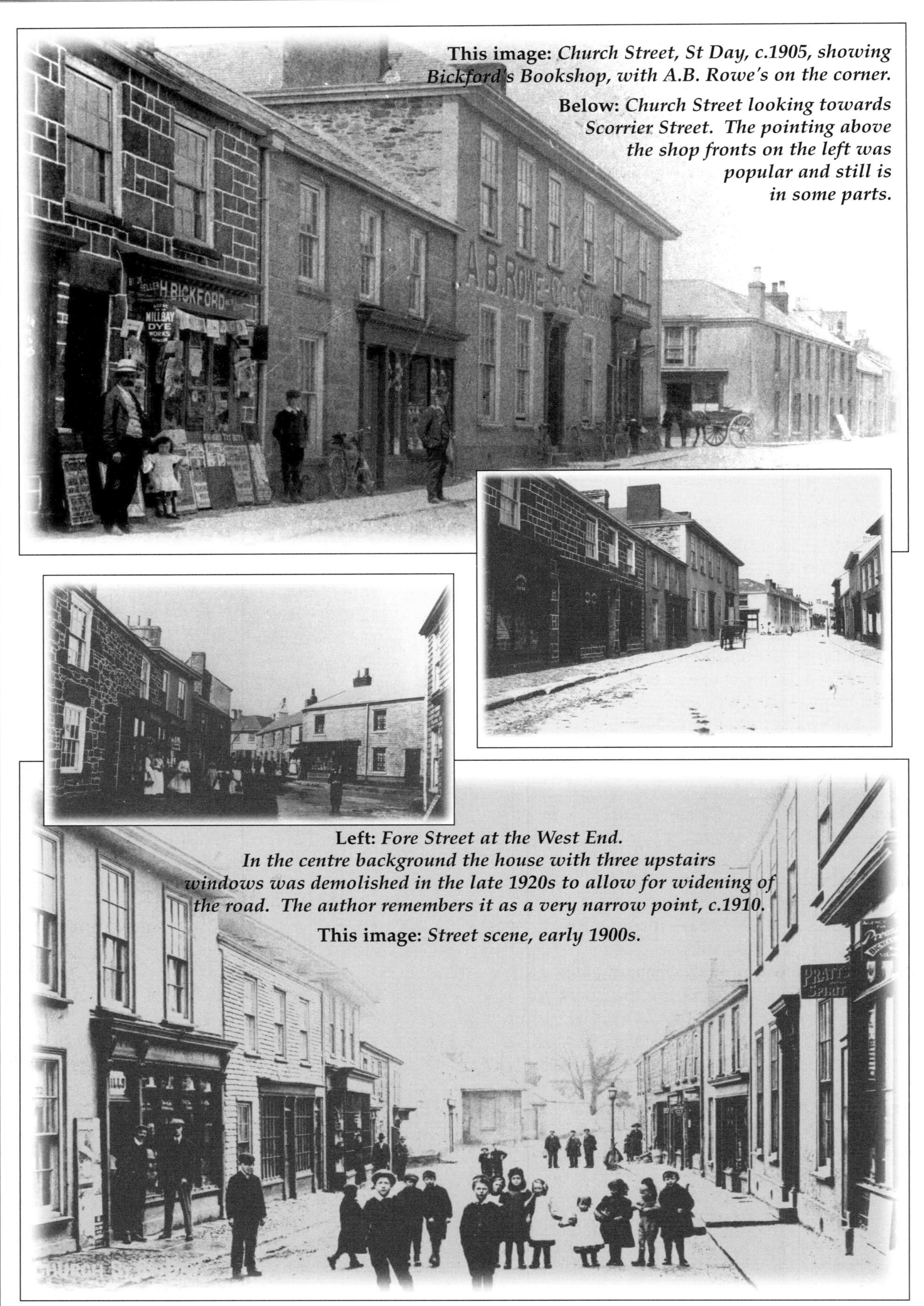

This image: *Church Street, St Day, c.1905, showing Bickford's Bookshop, with A.B. Rowe's on the corner.*

Below: *Church Street looking towards Scorrier Street. The pointing above the shop fronts on the left was popular and still is in some parts.*

Left: *Fore Street at the West End. In the centre background the house with three upstairs windows was demolished in the late 1920s to allow for widening of the road. The author remembers it as a very narrow point, c.1910.*

This image: *Street scene, early 1900s.*

The 1866 Directory

Peter Jennings' annotations of the 1866 directory give information about the wider district, including Busveal, Crofthandy, Little Beside, Ninnis, Tolcarne, Tolgullow, Tregullow and Vogue. Further extracts are taken from this directory, and again his annotations are underlined and italic:

BURNWITHIAN HOUSE

Philip Rogers. Assayer, *afterwards at Trefula.*

CHAPEL STREET [SIC]

Rev. Henry Wheeler. Prim. Meth. Minister.
John Leverton. Gardener
Henry Potter. Shoe maker and engine man, *grandfather to James Hy. Potter, builder.*

CHURCH STREET, EAST SIDE

John Edwards. Grocer *now* [1914] *Hensley.*
John Thomas. Market Inn. *Afterwards Chenhalls. John Thomas uncle to John Thomas, postman.*
Wm. Hy. Wilton. Jeweller. *Now T.R. Mills. Mr Wilton built the house, its predecessor was a small shop with two windows. Mr Wilton died and Mrs Wilton 'broke his Will' to give money to scapegrace son. Quarrel ensued.*
Richard Skinner. Printer and stationer and machine ruler. 'Account books made to order on the premises at the shortest notice. Orders per Post promptly executed, and carriage paid on all orders to the amount of Ten Shillings and above.' *Now Mrs Richards. His printing house was behind in garden. Miss Holman burnt papers there and in the night the house burnt down.*
Thomas J. Corfield. Chemist and Druggist. *Lived where Mr Tom Martin now* [1915] *has outfitter's shop.*
Edward Harris. Grocer. *Now Mrs Hooper, draper.* *(Mrs H. still there c.1930. JM.)*
George Lewis Coachman to Mrs Andrew. The Cedars Lodge.
Mrs Zaccheus Andrew, *daughter of James Harvey She lived at Rock House. James Harvey, her father, died at The Cedars and then Mrs Andrews moved thither. Very stout. Her two daughters had the bulk of Mrs Harvey's fortune, £10,000 per year each. One died and the survivor, Mrs Hewitt has £20,000 a year!*
Benjamin Matthews. Mine Purser. Rock House. *Commander Mann removed there from Vogue Hill where Dr Michell lives. One of head clerks of Messrs. Harvey.*

CHURCH STREET, WEST SIDE

Mary Ann Skewes. Milliner. *Succeeded Philp, draper. A remarkable shop, all along front of house. She removed to Bristol.*
Ann Francis. Grocer. *She was formerly Ann Dennis. Mr Stevens had the grocer's shop before Mrs Dennis and became bankrupt there.*
The Rev. Henry Wheeler's daughter, Mrs John George [brother to Richard George], kept fancy shop in Mrs Collins' house, now [1915] *Miss Whitford's store, then removed to opposite side of street to Mrs Whitford's present shop. Mrs Phillips bought the business and brought it to Church Street. Mrs P. formerly used the shop as store, then took premises previously to 1866 where library now is for store.*
John Veall. Watch and clock maker. *Brother to Herbert Veall's father.*
William Annear. Mine agent. *Post Office was here and shop, hence big window. Misses Tiddy kept it.*
Joseph Jacka. Baker.
John Goldsworthy. Grocer. *His shop is now part of Jos. Kinsman's draper. He was brother of Capn. Dick G. of Trevethan.*
Jane Barnett. Confectioner. *Lived where Mrs Phillips now lives.*
James Gray. Mine agent. *Husband of Mrs Gray almoner of Lady Williams.*
Thomas Cara. Goldsmith and church organist. *Mrs Cara, schoolmistress, schoolroom at present billiard room. Miss Williams' Free School for girls. Lived under same roof where Mr Rd. Morcom now lives, Mr Cara conductor of Brass Band.*

MARKET STREET [FORE STREET], NORTH SIDE

Edward Newton. Jeweller and Mathematical Instrument Maker. *He was apprenticed to Wilton and married his daughter. Newton succeeded Wilton and removed to Wilton's house [now T.R. Mills' premises] then removed across the street to where Miss Murton keeps shop, then to Mrs John Nicholls' shop, Scorrier St., and from there to Camborne.*
Thomas Polkinhorne. Shoemaker.
Rd. Powning. Grocer and draper. *At present Post Office, one storey, with gallery to store room .*
John Chynoweth. Tailor. *Mr and Mrs Hy. Cock before Chynoweth. Pay day drinking. Put into Klink. One Saturday night man 'run in', by Sunday morning he broke one quarter of window, high up, with lead sashes, got out, had rope to lead from window to roof, slid down to market house roof. Never captured. Man would climb to top of tower and play pranks with clock. Mrs Cock would say ' 3 or 4 men were put into Klink last night, they must be hungry, I'll give them something to eat.' It was her hobby. Mystery is how she got it in!* [High steps?]
Joseph Yendell. Grocer and stationer.
Elizabeth Bennett. The 'Hotel'.
Jane Benbow. Greengrocer. *Where Mr Joseph Barnet lived. His aunt?*

Above: *Scorrier Street with two shops and elegantly dressed ladies, c.1912.*

Left: *Slate-hung houses in Telegraph Street with a thatched cottage in the distance. The boys wear caps and knickerbockers and in the foreground the boy with a hoop is carrying an oil can to collect paraffin-oil for the lamps at home, c.1910.*

This image: ***Fore Street, showing the market building which was demolished in 1911 and which is shown in front of the clock tower. The shop front on the right was the manor office.***

Edwin Teague. **Butcher.**
John Hawke. **Painter, glazier and oil-man.**
Charles Trengove. **Gardener.**
Jane Davey. **Grocer.** *Where Mrs Fradd lives.* [Mrs Fradd still there in mid-1930s.]
Henry Carbis. **Carpenter.**
William Jones Hamblyn. *Post master, in house now occupied by Mrs Hockey, before removing to Mr George's [now Mr Martin's, draper]. Window nearest the corner was that of room used as post office.*
Eliza Hamlyn. [sic] **Dressmaker.**

MARKET STREET [FORE STREET], SOUTH SIDE

Michael Michell. **Draper.** [Present-day Amber House]
James Provis. **Ironmonger.**
John Trenerry. **Draper in Arthur Kinsman's shop.** *The Red Lion in Scorrier Street was two shops, Trenerry kept draper's shop in one before removing to Fore Street.*
Elizabeth Mardon. *The 'King's Arms' and her sister, maiden ladies.*
Nanny Whitburn. **Grocer,** *afterwards removed to where Mr Jos. Letcher lives at corner of Fore Street and Scorrier Street.*
William Whitburn. **Mine Agent.**
Caleb George. **Baker and confectioner,** *Mr Corfield had chemist's shop here, after serving for 12 mths. with Dr. Arthur, then Mr T.H. Letcher used it as workshop.*
John Jacka. **Confectioner.**
John Yeoman. **Shoemaker.** *Very tall man. Mr Trevethick worked for him and succeeded him. Mr A. Kinsman Sr. lives there.*
Mark Davey. **Grocer.**

NORTH ROAD [PRESENT-DAY TELEGRAPH STREET]

William [Thomas] Henry Letcher. Builder, *when married lived where Mrs Blewett lives.*
James Letcher. **Glazier.**
James Kinsman. **Mason.**
Jonathan Bawden. **Relieving officer.**
Prudence Penna. **Van proprietor.**
William Bennetts. **Dairyman.**

PARSONAGE HOUSE

Rev. John Bannister. M.A. *His Glossary of Cornish Names was shortly to be published, based mainly on the Rev. Robt. Williams's newly published Lexicon Cornu Britannicum. The Glossary was to have been followed by a larger and more critical work on 'Cornish Nomenclature', in which Mr Bannister was to have been assisted by Mr Williams. The profits were 'to be given towards establishing at St Day a Boys National School.' It was never published.*

POLDICE HOUSE

Charles Bawden. **Mine broker.**

SCORRIER STREET, EAST SIDE

Richard Hewitt Thomas. Jeweller.
Thomas Sims. **Hairdresser.** *Quaint character. A Captain of a mine cheated him, would say 'I'll pay you next time.' At last Tom said 'I'll do for'n.' He shaved one side and lathered the other and said he would shave it when the Cap'n paid. Wore broad brimmed hat. Died where Miss Holman lives.*
William Downing. **Grocer.**
William Mills. **Shoemaker.** *In small house on site of Mr Chynoweth's shop. Steps to go down to it. Came from Falmouth. Had 12 or 14 men working for him. Made a lot of money, but had extravagant wife. Mr John Thomas's father was his foreman.*
Thomas Michell. **Tailor and outfitter,** *shop now converted into 2 dwelling houses. Capt. John Nicholls lives in one.*
Richard Dennis. **Hairdresser.**
John Bawden. **Grocer, auctioneer, schoolmaster.** *Opposite Mrs Nicholls' butcher shop. Mrs Bawden was the grocer, he was the auctioneer and schoolmaster. Succeeded Rickard in Mission Room on site of present* [1915] *parish church Sunday School.*
Elizabeth Ann Petherick. **Milliner,** *sister to Mr T.R. Mills. Very conscientious.* [née Elizabeth Ann Collins Mills] [Unrelated to William Mills, shoemaker.]
James Collett. **Draper and tea-dealer.** *Next door to the Red Lion.*
Thomas Hawke. **Plumber.** *Came from Falmouth, clever tradesman.*
Honor Teague. **Dressmaker.** *Next door to Mrs Gill's shop; aunt to T.H. Letcher.*
Samuel Youlton. **Grocer.**

SCORRIER STREET, WEST SIDE

William Trebilcock. **Photographer,** *from Chacewater, bachelor.*
Peter May. **Shoemaker.**
Richard Apps. **Shoemaker.**
Edward Harvey. **Saddler.**
John Luke. **Grocer.**
Richard G. Michell. **Shoemaker.**
Esther Ann Grey. **Milliner.**
James Kinsman. **Builder.** *Built many houses in St Day; but leasehold and fell away.*
Richard Rooke. **Tailor and draper.** *Many houses in this street were low and thatched. Rooke's was and had little garden patch in front. Old woman kept shop here, green grocery and good sweets. Mrs Hambly, who lived opposite bought all her sweets. Rooke enlarged or re-built it.*
James Thomas. **Beer seller** [Kiddleywinks] *kept last of all by Jeffery, one-legged shoemaker, who worked for Peter Benjamin May.* [The author's father remembered him as 'Old Ben May'.]

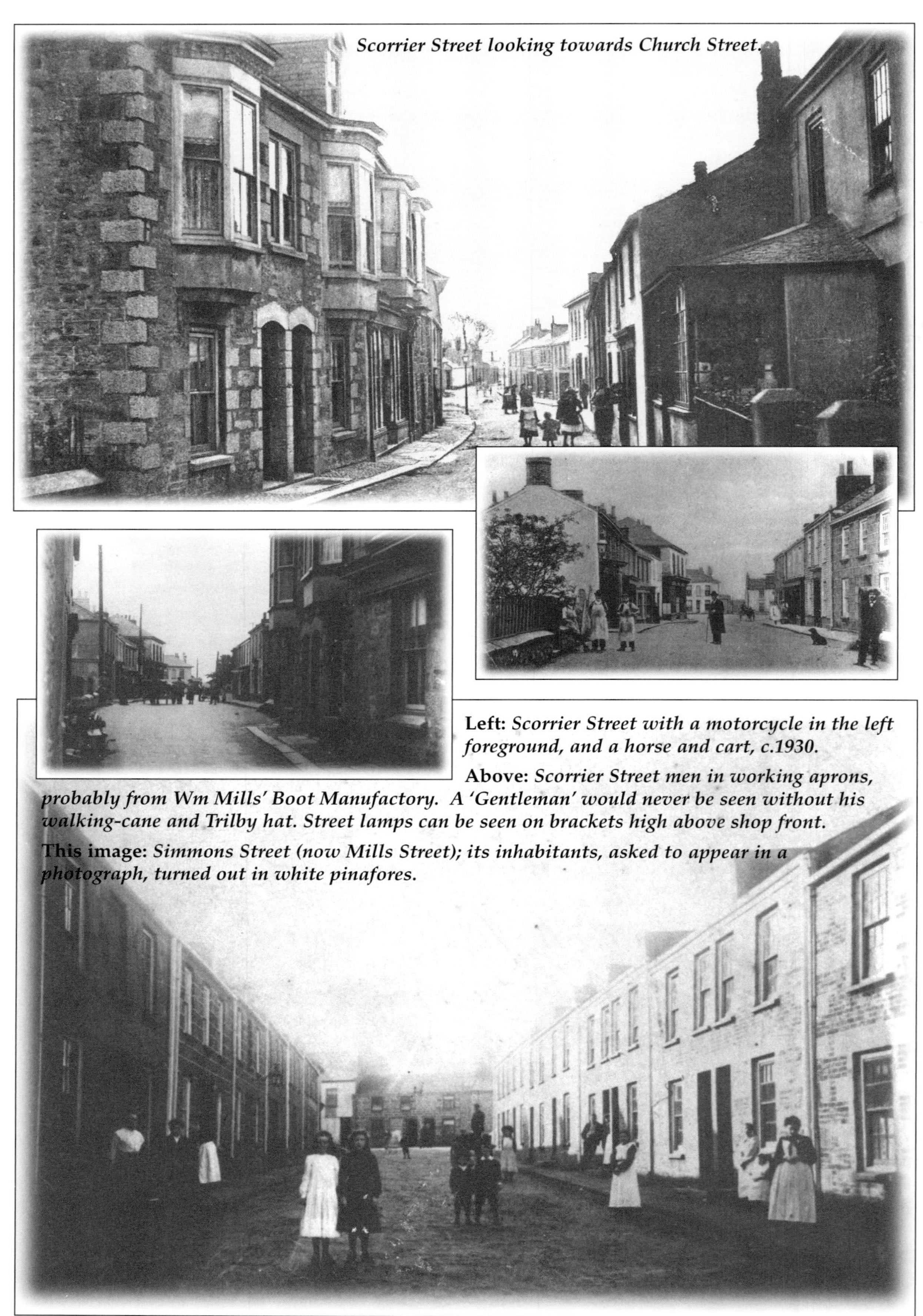

Scorrier Street looking towards Church Street.

Left: *Scorrier Street with a motorcycle in the left foreground, and a horse and cart, c.1930.*

Above: *Scorrier Street men in working aprons, probably from Wm Mills' Boot Manufactory. A 'Gentleman' would never be seen without his walking-cane and Trilby hat. Street lamps can be seen on brackets high above shop front.*

This image: *Simmons Street (now Mills Street); its inhabitants, asked to appear in a photograph, turned out in white pinafores.*

Samuel Trengove. **Smith.** *Dwelling house and blacksmith's shop on site of Mrs Morcom's house – Litchfield House.*
Grace Richards. **Greengrocer.**

SIMMONS STREET

Simon Kinsman. **Mason.**
Philippa Vivian. **Milliner.**
John Downing. **Tea-dealer.**
William Luke. **Carrier.**
John and William Kinsman. **Builders.**
John Kinsman, jr. **Mason.**

VOGUE TERRACE

John Hawke. **Smith.**
Thomas Jones. **Van proprietor.**
George Michell. **Surgeon.**
James Williams. **Grocer.**

WEST END

John Nicholls. **Butcher.**
Joanna Pope. **Green grocer,** *in thatched house on triangular piece before Trinity House. Lived afterwards in Wheal Jewell Row. Fellow classmates. Before Mrs Pope, Granny Michell was greengrocer here.*
James Hodge. **The Britannia Inn.**
Henry Pearce. **Painter.**
William Tregellas. **Retired miner.**
Joanna Chynoweth. **Grocer,** *where Mr Hart lives. Mr John Chynoweth's mother, and therefore grandmother to Richard Hart Chynoweth.*

BUSVEAL

William White. **Farmer,** *near the Pit.*
John Davey Sr. **Mine agent.**
John Davey Jr. **Mine agent.**
William Davey. **Farmer.**
John Notwell [sic]. **Farmer.**
Harriet Christopher. **Grocer.**

CROFTHANDY

John Barnett. **Grocer and draper.**
Joseph Higgins. **Mine agent.**
James Ham. **The Miners' Inn.** *[see p.75]*
John Vine. **Mine broker.**
Edward Murley. **Grocer.**
John Bray. **Smith.**
Joseph Cock. **Mine agent.**
James Verran. **Carrier.** [Later emigrated with his brother-in-law, John Kellow, to New Zealand and founded a haulage business there at Thames, N. Island. The business still survives in the 21st century.] [J.M.]

LITTLE BESIDE

Richard Michell [' Painter Dick']. **Merchant.**
Hugh Barrett. **Beer seller and grocer.**
Edward Hawke & Co. **Safety Fuse Manufacturers.**

NINNIS

James Trembath. **Farmer.**
John Davey. **Butcher.**
Elizabeth Davey. **Housekeeper.**
William Davey. **Clerk.**
Jane Endean. **Housekeeper.**

TOLCARNE

Richard Dryden. **Retired miner.**
John Brown. **Mine agent.**
James Bawden. **Farmer.**
James Martin. **Farmer.**
William Thomas. **Mine agent.**
Mary Michell. **Housekeeper.**

TOLGULLOW

Edward Hawke Sr. and Jr., **Rope manufacturers.**
Edward Williams. **Clerk.**
John Mayne. **Mine agent.** *Lived where Mr Bennett lives at Tolgullow. His son, John Mayne courted Miss Edwards and is reported to have been afraid to go home, down Bunt's Lane, in the dark, and would give any boy 6d. to escort him.*
James Tregoning. **Clerk.**

TREGULLOW

William Williams. **Gentleman.**
Hugh Sims. **Clerk.** *Lived at Fourburrow House, a clerk to Mr* [afterwards Sir] *Wm Williams.*
Elisha Trewartha. **Clerk.** *Head clerk to Edward Hawke.*
John Cornelius. **Gardener.**
William Brown. **Hind.**
Jane Vinnacombe. **Housekeeper.**
Alice Coombe. **Housekeeper.**

VOGUE

Samuel P. Arthur. **Surgeon.**
Henry Bray. **Builder.**
Maria Curtis. **Grocer.**
Josiah Jewell. **Mine agent.**
George Kinsman. **Retired miner.**
Daniel Hodge. **Smith.**
Joseph Stevens. **Farmer.**
John Thomas. **The Star Inn.** *In Redruth Parish.*
Julia Pearce. **Housekeeper.**

ANALYSIS

Assayer.	1
Auctioneer.	1
Bakers.	2
Boot and Shoe makers.	7
Builders and Carpenters.	6
Butchers.	3 [including John Davey, Ninnis]
Carrier.	1
Chemist and Druggist.	1
Confectioners.	3

West End line-up of children, the girls in white pinafores. The lady of fashion on the right proudly shows the high elegant perambulator with the child sitting up to look at the photographer. Who was she?

Dairyman.	*1*
Drapers.	*4*
Dressmakers.	*2 None mentioned as living in other parts of Gwennap.*
Farmers.	*4 all on the outskirts of St Day.*
Gardeners.	*2*
Glaziers and Oilmen.	*2*
Greengrocers.	*3 all women.*
Grocers.	*17*
Hairdressers.	*2*
Inns and Beerhouses.	*8 including Little Beside.*
Ironmonger.	*1*
Jewellers.	*3*
Mathematical Instrument Maker.	*1*
Milliners.	*4 Twice as many as dressmakers, none mentioned in other parts of Gwennap.*
Mine Agents.	*8*
Mine Broker.	*1*
Organist.	*1*
Painters.	*2*
Photographer.	*1*
Plumber.	*1*
Postmaster.	*1*
Postman.	*1*
Printer.	*1*
Stationer.	*2*
Relieving Officer.	*1*
Rope Manufacturers.	*1*
Saddler.	*1*
Safety Fuse Manufacturer.	*1*
Schoolmaster and Mistress.	*1 of each;*
Smiths.	*3*
Surgeons.	*2*
Tailors and Outfitters.	*3*
Tea Dealers.	*2*
Van Proprietors.	*2*
Watch and Clock Maker.	*1*
Inspector of Nuisances for Gwennap.	*1 James Kinsman, St Day.*
Relieving Officer for Gwennap.	*1 Jonathan Bawden, St Day.*

Neither the 1847 or 1866 directory gives any indication of the existence of a manor office, where, presumably, the manor archives would have been kept. In the early-eighteenth century John Williams (the first) settled at Burncoose and was active in mining enterprises, also becoming manager of the Hearle family properties in St Day Manor. Burncoose, therefore, may well have held the Manor Rolls from then on and up to the mid-nineteenth century when Thomas Henry Letcher became Under-Agent to the lords of the manor, the families of Chichester, Hearle and Champernowne. Thomas Henry Letcher is listed in the 1866 directory as a builder in North Street, the present-day Telegraph Street. He was succeeded eventually by Joseph T. Letcher who remained as the agent until his death in the mid-1930s. His office was in Fore Street on the north side and next to the then Post Office, and housed the manor archives including the Rent Rolls from 1682, and the Manor Map of 1772 with its schedule and a number of leases. The author enjoyed the privilege of being allowed access to the manor papers (perhaps because of a family connection

Simmons Street, c.1910, with Mrs Gill's corner shop. Mrs Gill is in the doorway, her son-in-law Fred Williams is wearing the cap and his son George is the smallest child (apparently dressed as a girl as he always was!).

with the agent), which undoubtedly sparked an interest in local history.

Additional information from the 1866 directory provides an insight into some of the social organisations extant in the second half of the nineteenth century, a few details have been paraphrased as follows:

St Day Temperance Society

Meetings were held in the Temperance Hall in Scorrier Street. The Temperance Society took over the original Baptist Chapel, a single-storey thatched building which became the Town Hall when the Temperance Society vacated the building. In 1858 the Primitive Methodists demolished the old building and built a new chapel on the site. That building still stands at the time of writing and is unoccupied.

The secretary was W.H. Richards of St Day and treasurer was Francis Terrill of Vogue. He was an engine man who came from Lincoln and returned there later, and also the superintendent of the Wesleyan Sunday School for many years.

Freemasons' Lodge

'Tregullow Lodge No. 1006' was formed in 1864. Meetings were held in the Masonic Rooms, Fore Street, on the third Tuesday in each month. Members were:

Worshipful Master.	*Bro. Edmund Michell. Jr.*
(Captain at Tresavean Mine, who lived there)	
Past Master.	*E.H. Hawke, Jr.*
(Rope manufacturer)	
Senior Warden.	*Josiah Ralph.*
(Mine agent, from Carn Marth, east side)	
Junior Warden.	*John Michell.*
(Farmer from Treviskey)	
Town Clerk.	*Farmer.*
Chaplain.	*Dr John Bannister. D.D.*
(Vicar)	
Treasurer.	*John Burgess*
Secretary.	*George Michell (Surgeon)*
Senior Deacon.	*Richard Skinner.*
(Printer, Church Street)	
Junior Deacon.	*Thomas Hawke.*
(Plumber, Scorrier Street)	
Organist.	*Thomas Cara.*
Inner Guard.	*Joseph Jewell.*
(Mine agent, Vogue)	
Stewards.	*John Grenfell, Thomas Trewartha. (Hare and Hounds, Scorrier)*
Tyler.	*Stephen R. Trebilcock.*

Gwennap Horticultural Society

The society was established in 1858, the society's show being held annually at Tregullow on the second or third Tuesday in August. Patron was Mr William Williams, of Tregullow, president was Revd Saltren Rogers of Gwennap Vicarage, and secretary was E.T. Newton, from St Day (watchmaker).

St Day Cricket Club

President	Mr Edward Hawke junr, Tolgullow.
Vice-President	Mr E.W. Michell, M.R.C.S.
Captain	Mr T. Michell.
Secretary	Mr J.R. Pearce.
Asst Secretary	Mr S. Michell.
Treasurer	Mr J.H. Mayne.
Committee	Messrs. Cara, Teague, Nicholls, Trenerry and Davey.

Bond of Administration, December 1669

A Bond of Administration of the estate of one John Williams sentr of St Day, Gwennap, dated 1669 is of great interest, being an inventory of his goods and chattels with their estimated values as follows:

An Inventory of all the goods and Chattels of John Williams late of St Day in the p'ish of Gwennap ...de... taken and appraised the 16th day of December Anno Domi. 1669 by Richard Harris als Crowsier and George Wassley as followeth:

Item:	£	s	d.
3 kine, Heifer and a weaning calf at	8	10	0
Sundry goods of Pewter dishes 5 flaggons 2 pints			
4 Candlesticks, 4 cupps, 2 Chambersticks, 6 Porringers			
2 C...s and one Salt.	2	15	6
2 old crock potts. 2 iron potts.	0	12	0
8 Brass Panns 1 Cauldron. 3 Skillets.	5	10	6
3 cuppoards.	1	10	0
1 Feather Bed. 3 Bolsters. 3 Pillows.	4	0	0
4 Coverletts old. 4 old Blanketts.	2	10	0
4 Bedsteads. 3 Table Boards & Frames.	1	10	0
4 Bedsheets old.		10	0
2 old carpets.	0	2	0
2 Chairs.	0	2	0
1 C....l to old d....	0	2	0
6 pewter spoons. 5 wooden dishes.	0	0	11
3 Brandis irons.	0	10	0
2 old horses	1	10	0
3 Piggs.	0	6	0
His wearing apparrell.	1	10	0
Tinn Stuff upon the grass at	9	0	0
For.........................but forgotten..	0	5	0
	£40.15s.11d.		

Richard Croucher. George Wassley.

Debts due att his death which the Accoumptant hath paid and discharged viz:

Item paid:			
Hosken debt upon Bond	£24	0	0
William Oppy for same.	£30	0	0
John Lawer of Passow gent.	£ 7	2	6
Henry Gregor, gent.	£ 9	0	0
Anthony Cock, Merchant.	£ 3	7	0
	£73	9	0

NOTES:

The five debts settled by 'the Accoumptant' include one of £30, a quite considerable sum, which was owing to William Oppy. In 1704 William Oppy was named in a lease which transferred St Day Fair to him from one Peter Oppy, possibly his father.

A table of equivalent values of the pound, which sets out to show changes in the value of money over a period of 700 years, gives the figure £74.73p (as at September 1998) required to buy goods which would have cost £1 in 1670. This gives a present-day total value of John Williams' debts at £5,522, leaving £3,045.25 as the total value of his goods and chattels.

The inventory makes no mention of any freehold property, as only the lords of the manor owned land freehold; all others held property on lease only. Neither are we informed about any money which may have been left, even though the fact that his debts were settled indicates that sufficient funds were available.

Twelve

Leases & Surveys

It was the custom in Cornwall from medieval times until well into the nineteenth century for leases to be drawn up on the basis of 'three lives', the prospective lessee naming three persons, and the lease remaining in force until the expiry of the last to survive. In the event of a premature death of one of the lives, it was sometimes possible to name a substitute on payment of an agreed 'consideration'. Norden comments on this practice of leasing: 'they generally prefer Lives before yeares, presuming upon long life in response to the healthsome ayre wherein they live.'

The following mid-eighteenth century example (RIC. Brookes, 45) demonstrates the practice followed in Cornwall for possibly more than 400 years:

John Mills of Gwennap, Yeoman, holds by Indenture of Lease dated 7 September 1742 granted by Arthur Champernowne Esq., and Francis Champernowne, Clerk, three eighths parts of and in All that Stamping Mill commonly called the Higher Stamps on Tollgullow, with three eighths of the plot of Ground thereunto adjoining as it had been then lately mark'd out and allotted by one John Williams and allow'd by All the Lords of the Said Premises to be a Stamps Plot to and for the Said Stamping Mill. Which Said Premises are part of the Tenement of Tollgullow, belonging to the Manor of Tolgullow als Saint Day together with the liberty of erecting any other Stamping Mill on the Said Premises and the use of the Water and Watercourses belonging to the Said Stamping Mill. Excepting Timber Trees Tin Copper and other Ores &c And also the above Water when wanted, upon paying 22½d per week for the same. To hold the Said Premises unto the Said John Mills for 99 years determinable on the Deaths of The said John Mills Mary his wife and John their son.
Lives: the Sd John Mills at 38 years. Mary Mills at 33 years. John Mills Jnr. 9 years. Consideration: £122.7s.6d. Rent: 7s.6d. Capon. 4½d.

Note: The 1999 equivalent value of £1 in 1742 is £78.29. The consideration sum of £122 equates to £9,551.38 in 1999, this being the cost of the original lease. (Taken from 'A Historical Series 1270 to 1998. Equivalent Contemporary Values of the Pound.')

John and Mary Mills both died in 1764, the lease remaining in force in favour of the remaining life, their son John, by this time 31 years old. Presumably he worked the property for the next six years for we find a reversion of the lease dated 1770 in favour of John Messer as follows:

John Messer of Gwennap, tinner, holds by Indenture etc.... dated the 2nd day of February 1770 Granted by Rawlin Champernowne Esq., the Stamping Mill and Premises above... etc. etc. for 99 years determinable on the Deaths of him the said John Messer and Anne his Wife. In reversion of the above named John Mills Junr. Consideration: £27.0s.0d. No Herriot Due.
Lives: The said John Messer at abt. 31 years. Anne his wife abt. 26 years.

The £27 consideration shows a substantial drop in the value of the property from the time that the initial lease was taken up 28 years earlier, in 1742. Herriot was an obligation sometimes required to be paid to the lord of the manor. In earlier times the herriot was often a service in military terms. By the eighteenth century payment was met by a sum of money agreed when the lease was drawn up, as we see in the leases below, relating to stamps at 'Voage' taken by Anthony Cock of Redruth at the beginning of the eighteenth century.

The following leases (CRO.DDSN.209) show a burst of activity at Vogue c.1700 when Mr Anthony Cock was named as the owner of newly built stamps close to the stream source, today's Vogue Shute, adjoining the road from St Day to Redruth, and which appear later on the Watercourse Mapp of 1720.

Anthony Cock's Lease. Dated 1701. 29th day of September 12th year of William III. Mannor of Tolcarne. Rent 6s.3d. Herriott 6s.3d. on the death of every Life and every surrender.

Between Jonathan Trelawney of Coldrinick in the County of Cornwall and Anthony Cock of the Parish of Redruth in the Said County.
Consideration: £17.3s.9d. for 5/16 parts of and in one Stamping Mill newly built called the Lower Stamps in

Voage joining with the highway road leading from St Day to Redruth, parcell of the Manor of Tollcarne and situated within the Parish of Gwennap and now in the possession of said Anthony Cock.
To have and to hold for ninety nine years and from the date of these presents if the said Anthony Cock Elizabeth and Anthony their Son shall happen to live. Anthony Cock. Seal. 1701

1704. Anthony Cock's Lease for ye second Stamps in Tolcarne. Lives: Elizabeth his Wife. Anthony and Jane their Son and Daughter.
Rent: 6s.4d. Herriott 13s.4d. on the death of every life and every surrender or Assignment.
Made in the 3rd year of the Reign of our Sovereign Lady Ann [sic] *by the Grace of God etc etc.... newly built called the second Stamps in Voage near the highway leading from St Day to Redruth parcell of the Mannor of Tolcarne and situated in the Parish of Gwennap.*

1704 VOGE STAMPS. James Harris in Tolcarne Counterpart for the Third Stamps in Tolcarne.
Lives: James Harris. Francis Harris. And Loah Harris.
5/16 parts of and in one Stamping Mill newly built called the Third Stamps in voage [sic] *not far from the highway leading from St Day to Redruth.*

1730. Lease between Charles Trelawney to John Russell of the Town of Redruth and Samuel May, Taylor of Redruth. All that Stamping Mill commonly called or known by the name of Voage Stamps.

Notes: In 1704 Anthony Cock expanded his interests in St Day with a lease on new stamps called the Second Stamps in Voage near the highway leading from St Day to Redruth.

Anthony Cock was a member of an old Redruth family of standing, already established there during the reign of Henry VIII. In 1666 Anthony Cocke of Redruth issued farthing token coins, specimens of which are be to found in the Royal Institution of Cornwall, Truro. (Taken from Thurstan C. Peters, *Redruth Parish Registers*, 1894, p.109.)

The Hawke lease below distinguishes between St Day Downs and St Day Common:

25th Jan. 1736. James Hawke of the Parish of Gwennap, Tinner... all that Dwelling House and two acres of land situate upon St Dye Downs one acre thereof the said Dwelling House and the other Acre of Ground was to be included from St Dye Commons [by the said James Hawke] Together with the liberty of cutting Furze and Turf, and also a Right of Common upon St Dye Downs aforesaid... which said Premises are situate in the parish of Gwennap and are Parts and Parcels of the Manor of St Dye alias Tolgullow.
Consideration: The Expense of inclosing the Ground.

There is no positive identification of either St Dye Downs or St Dye Commons on the 1772 Map of the Manor; however, the Watercourse Mapp, c.1720/30, gives us Reed's Moor in the area immediately north of Vogue Shute which at first seemed a possible location of one or other of the sites. St Day Green, No.61F in the Apportionment, is too small being only one rood 30 perches in area, but Mungumpus Common (Goongumpus), No.62G, is shown as being 176 acres 3 roods in extent and seems much more likely to be the St Day Common of the 1736 Hawke lease.

Adjoining Goongumpus to the north lie Killicor, Nancegollan and Wheal Gassek, which names appear in a document in the County Record Office (DD EN 1528) concerning a proposal to drive an adit to Killicor from Nansgrows Bottom, etc. The Tin Bounds through which the proposed adit would have proceeded included, among others, 'East Killicor in St Day Downs. Nancegollan in St Day Downs and Wheal Gasseck in St Day Downs.' That document fixes the location of St Day Downs. Assuming that Goongumpus Common and St Day Common are one and the same, the Hawke lease straddles the boundary between Downs and Common, the lessee's two acres comprising one acre in each, making a single tenement.

Triplett

25th Jany. 1749. Anthony Bawden of Gwennap, Yeoman, holds by Indenture of Lease... commonly called Triplett's Tenement, formerly Two Crofts or Closes of land and one Moor under the Same containing in the whole six acres of land or thereabouts [more or less] and whereon were several houses then lately built.
Lives: Richard Bawden 26 yrs. Peter Bussow 16 yrs. Sarah Bussa 14 yrs.

An entry in the Gwennap Marriage Register for the year 1608 records the marriage of Katherine Triplett of Gwennap to John Hocken of St Pinnock. She was probably born about 1585/90, suggesting that the Tripletts were already in Gwennap parish in the sixteenth century. In 1625 another marriage is recorded for this family when Julia Triplett married Henry Gidnal on 17 November 1625. No other entries for Triplett appear in the Gwennap Church Registers but certain leases from the manor show that the Tripletts held land near St Day until about 1640 when their holding or tenement passed to Constance Patherick, after which it was referred to in subsequent leases as 'Patherick's Tenement, formerly Tripletts.' There was a further change about the year 1700 when it passed to a Shelston and the lease identifies the fields as 'Shelston's Tenement, formerley Petherick's, alias Triplett's.'

Reference to the Manor Map of 1772 identifies the land as being near the bottom of what is now Telegraph Hill, adjacent to Todpool and bordering the North Coombe opposite Unity Wood. The road leading from Todpool to Crofthandy has long been known as 'Triplett'.

The Redruth Church Marriage Register contains entries of Triplett marriages throughout the eighteenth century as follows:

4th February 1733. Thos. Lidgey & Margt. Triplett
5 June 1734. George Triplett & Ann Tynner.
3 February 1740. William Vincent & Elizabeth Triplet. [sic]
21 December 1767. Thos. Pollard & Elizabeth Triplett.

Tresaddern Lease, 1749

Jany. 1749. Granted by Arthur Champernowne Esq. and Francis Champernowne, Clerk, three eighths Parts of and in All that Messuage and Tenement commonly called or known by the name of Tresaddern situate in the Parish of Gwennap and Parcel of the Manor of Tolgullow als St Dye Excepting thereout Allen's House Two Meadows and a Garden and also Two other Plots of Ground to the South of Said Meadows and one Croft or Slip of Ground further to the south of the Said last-mentioned Plots usually called the Stream Marks. And adjoining to a Close or Field on the said Tenement called the Farm-Field and the Premises to be bounded and divided by a Gurgery-Hedge between the Said Stream-Marks and the Farm-Field above mentioned. Lives: John Bawden 8 years. Elizabeth Bawden 10 years. Collan Bawden 5 years

Note: The term 'gurgery hedge' has not been met elsewhere in the manor records, it is pronounced with hard gs and defined by Jago as being 'a low hedge or boundary'. M. Courtney's book *Cornish Dialect* defines it as 'A rough fence for wasteland'.

Mitchell's Tenement

1st July 1789 John Williams of Scorrier House, Gent. All that Barn, Stable and Cooper's Shop situate in St Dye Town and Four Garden Plots behind the same – and the Wastrel on the North Side of the said Cooper's Shop and the Backlet and Lane adjoining the said garden. And also all that Plot or parcel of Ground called the Outer Meadow [one acre].
All parts of Mitchell's Tenement.

This tenement was held in 1682 by one John Mitchell, his age given then as 55. A second life given was Honor Mitchell, aged 58, probably his wife (although her status is not revealed). The tenement was again listed in the 1772 Survey when the barn, stable and cooper's shop were shown where the present (2002) Post Office is in Fore Street, opposite St Day Cross. The tenant at that time was Mr Henry Harris, who appears also on the Watercourse Mapp as owner of three sets of stamps. Henry Harris was a member of one of the prominent families in the parish at that time; it is highly unlikely, therefore, that he was the cooper in occupation and nothing has come to light to reveal the identity of that worthy. An entry in the Poldice Mine Cost Book for February 1789 names a cooper, James Rabblin, who was paid for work on behalf of the mine: 'James Rabblin & prs. Making, Binding, repairing Kibals & Barrels.' (The OED defines 'Kibble' as follows: 'Kibble. 1671. Mining. A large wooden or [later] iron bucket, for carrying ore or rubbish to the surface.')

Collan Harvey

The following lease to Collan Harvey (RIC.Brookes.45, p.65) gives the date of Carew House being built:

1 July 1797. Collan Harvey of St Dye in the Parish of Gwennap, Granted by Arthur Champernowne Esq... all that Messuage or Dwelling House and Garden in Saint Dye Town and sundry small fields or parcels of Ground [formerly in One Field] *thereunto belonging Situate nearly adjoining to Poldice Ball and containing about Three Acres and Three Quarters of Ground* [be the same more or less]... *also a plot of Ground containing about or under a Quarter of an Acre* [more or less] *being part of a certain Field called Hallwidden Field belonging to the Tenement of Hallwidden and lying near the Accounting House belonging to Wheal Jewell Mine near the Town of St Dye aforesaid. On part of which said plot of Ground He the Said Collan Harvey hath lately erected and built a House and Warehouse.*

The tenement of halwidden is identified by the letter l on the 1772 Approtionment and is shown on the map sited where Carew House presently stands. The 'house and warehouse' were probably the present-day Masonic Hall and the shop and dwelling opposite, which served as warehouse, offices and retail outlet for the firm of Harvey & Co. On the south side of Church Street the imposing residence, The Cedars, hides itself behind a high wall which also encloses spacious gardens. The date 1809 is cut into one of the roof timbers and may well be the date of the building, observing that the area was open fields on the manor map of 1772. The Cedars was the residence of James Harvey, brother of Collan.

Surveys

Surveys of the manor of Tolgulla were made from time to time, the earliest surviving such document *(see page 76)* known to the present writer dating from 1682. In this nine tenements and their occupants are named, with details of field names, acreages and annual rent values also being listed. The lives named in the leases are given with their ages as well as the tenant's own name and age. At this time the manor was divided among three parties who were the lords of the manor: 'Lady Smith the moiety thereof, one third part to Mr Hunt and one sixth to Mr Chichester.' Lady Smith was the widow of Sir John

Smith, named in the title paragraph of the 1682 Survey. A moiety was a half share, the remaining half being divided between the other two lords having two sixths and one sixth respectively.

The survey of 1697 names 14 tenements including some of those in the former list. In 1772 another full survey of the manor was made which indicates considerable growth of population and enclosure of land, listing some 60 tenements with their details. The growth of both population and the number of tenements applied chiefly to St Day itself. The Book of Apportionment of the 1772 Survey is accompanied by a detailed map which gives the reference number of each feature clearly marked, be it field, garden, croft or cottage. From this we are able to confirm the exact sites of such features as St Day Green, the pound, the cross, the chapel, etc., as well as individual tenements.

The earlier surveys, as far as we are aware, had no relevant maps; thus there was no requirement for such code letters. The major surveys demonstrate clearly the growth of population which took place alongside the expansion of deep-mining activity.

In addition to the principal surveys there are references to minor surveys made in 1687, 1689, 1704 and 1743 recording a number of changes concerning individual tenements occasioned by either change of lessee or of the terms of an expired lease. In addition there is an interesting plan, c.1720, of the watercourses emanating from the present-day Vogue Shute which is discussed elsewhere.

A survey of 1687 lists various stamps in the South Coombe – Burnt Stamps, Ben Stamps, Stribley's Stamps, Pinter's Stamps, Bissa als Francis' Stamps, The Little Stamps, Christopher Nicholas's Stamps and Gabriell's Stamps. Upon lease, each paid a yearly £20 conventionary rent. It would require £78 at the time of writing to equal the purchasing power of £1 in 1690, which means that each of those stamps would pay to the lords of the manor £1,560 per annum rent in today's money, that is £30 a week.

In 1687 Trewinnard Grist Mills (Hale Mills) were leased to Marke Sampson, the then occupier of Tresaddern. Their yearly value was £15 and the lease was for the lives of James Robins (60) and John Harris (44). In 1704 the yearly rental was increased to £16.0s.0d. Trewinnard Mill was the most important grist mill in the manor, described in the title of the Watercourse Mapp as 'the Greist Mill belonging to the Mannor of Tolgulla als St Day.' Traces of the mill house were still to be seen on the site in the 1930s when the present writer made frequent visits to the area. It stood at the confluence of the Watercourse and the South Coombe streams, shown on the map at the mill end. The map reads: 'The Watercourse from Poldice Stamping Mills to St Day Mannor Mill', with a similar inscription alongside the South Coombe approaching the mill: 'The Watercourse belonging to Ye Stamps & Greist Mill belonging to Ye Mannor of St Day.' The South Coombe stream was the boundary between Cusgarne and Tolgullow Manors.

The Sampson family were already settled in Gwennap parish in the late-sixteenth century at Tresodron (Tresaddern), and were in possession of a number of stamping and grist mills. A colourful individual, Mark Sampson was said to have been 'a man of great dealings in Tynworkes and Tyn adventures.' He found himself in trouble with the Church and was fined for brawling in the churchyard at Gwennap. He was several times summoned to pay the cost he had been taxed by the Consistory Court but still failed to pay. He was next ordered to appear at the Court at St Nyott (St Neot), but again failed to appear and was then charged with contumacy (failing to acknowledge authority). The Church then applied its ultimate sanction, Mark was excommunicated, which event was published in Gwennap Church.

Mark Sampson was born in 1638 and died in 1695. Would he have been Royalist or Roundhead? He was certainly rebellious. In a survey taken in 1704 we find 'Tresaddron East' as one of the tenements, with the intriguing description 'heretofore the Overseers of the poor of Gwennap'. This is the only time that the qualification 'East' has been encountered and it is the only reference to the overseers of the poor in any of the surveys.

The earlier surveys of 1682 and 1697 both list

Survey of the Mannor of Tolgullow als St Day as it was taken in June & July 1704 by William Longford Esq. and Henry Hill. Total Acreage 328 acres. Yearly Value £231.9s.4d.

Tresaddron East heretofore the Overseers of the poor of Gwennap.
Francis Winter now Philip Toms.
Lives: Philip Toms 43.
Philip 9 & Wm. his sons 6.

Two houses and Gardens
The Farme Croft
The farme field
Tresadrons meadow
Lower field
Close above the Moor
The Moor
Another meadow
A Close above the Meadow or Middle Field
A Croft
The Higher Field

Totalling 26 acres.
Value £20.13s.2d.

'Tresaddron Hendy als Penross & Clibma' which appears again in the 1772 Survey (No.6.f.) as 'Part of Tresodren Hendy Debma alias Clibma.' Reference to the 1772 map accompanying the apportionment identifies that site positively, north of St Day, but in the absence of any earlier map we are unable to locate reliably Tresaddron East which was the domain of the overseers of the poor in the seventeenth century, but which is not mentioned in the earlier surveys. The present-day Tresaddern Farm is the most likely area, being south-east of St Day and appearing in 1772 as No.13.n., also as No.27.&., the latter having an area of 26 acres corresponding to that given to 'Tresaddern East' as shown below.

In earlier times religious houses provided hospitality to wayfarers and pilgrims and to the aged, infirm and the poor. Most of the monasteries, abbeys and shrines had a hospital attached to provide succour and shelter for the needy, which often included medical care, giving rise to the present-day usage of 'hospital' and 'hospice'. The fall of the monasteries and abbeys following Henry VIII's Reformation left the country without resources for the care of the destitute. Towards the end of the reign of Elizabeth I parishes were required by law to make such provision for their own people, and vagrants could and would be sent back to their native parish to be cared for. The parish priest, the squire and other leading citizens became the governors (or overseers) of the poor and were held responsible for providing shelter, food and sometimes clothing to the destitute. The tenement Tresaddern East covered an area of 26 acres which seems excessive. Was the tenement farmed by the overseers, using 'the poor' as labour and the proceeds of sales to meet the costs? The 1772 map shows five fields reminiscent of the medieval 'strip fields' (i.e. numbers n4, n5, n6, n7 and n8). Were those fields survivors of an earlier area of cultivation?

Seventeenth-Century Surveys

Seventeenth-century surveys were as follows for 1682: 1. Tresoddern Handy, 2. Debmine, 3. Burnwithian, 4. Woolcock's or Dingle's, 5. Triplett's or Patherick's, 6. Leonard Nicholls (sometime Tucker's), 7. Bray's, 8. Wassley's, 9. Smith's Shop. Those for 1697 included: 1. Talgollow Farme, 2. Tresaddern Hendy als Clibma, 3. Groce's Tenement, 4. Mitchell's Tenement, 5. Debmine, 6. Bray's Tenement, 7. Roose's Tenement, 8. Talgollow part to Edmund Bawden, 9. Jake's Tenement, 10. Menargwin, 11. Constance Patherick's, call'd Tripletts, 12. Burnwithian, 13. Smith's Shop, 14. Phillips' Tenement. They are listed on the following pages.

Above: *Tolgullow Vean Farm, Little Beside Farm.*

Below: *Thatched house at Crofthandy, formerly the Miners' Inn. Standing in the doorway is the author's godmother, Agnes Dunstan, c.1900.*

Below: *An eighteenth-century house at the entrance to Forth an Eglos.*

Higher Trevethan, a house with an external round chimney of a style believed to be peculiar to the district within a 10–15-mile radius during the nineteenth century.

1682. Talgullow als St Day. A Survey of the Manor of Talgullow als St Day in the Parish of Gwennap in the County of Cornwall. Taken by Richard Stephens and John Peter, September 1682, the moieties thereof belongeth to my Lady Smith and third part to Mr Hunt and one sixth pt. to Mr Chichester.

1. TRESODDERN HANDY. *als penross & clibma. The* Executors of John Littleton Gent. *Lives: William Oppy 55. Mary Littleton 30.*

2 houses, garden & mowhay.
Park an bannel.
The clibma, The meadow,
Tresaddron fields in Crofthandy
A house & garden & croft.
3 houses & 3 crofts.

2. DEBMINE. *James Phillips (late John Jeffery). Life: Edmond Jeffery. Age 45.*

	No. of acres	*Ann.value*
House, Garden, Mowhay.	*0.1*	*£1.13.4.*
3 Debmins.	*7.0*	*£5.10.0.*
a meadow.	*0.1*	*£0.6.6.*
Turndavor.	*2.2*	*£1.5.0.*
Turndavor Moors.	*1.3*	*£0.8.0.*
TOTAL	*11.3*	

3. BURNWITHIAN. *Richard Harris, a third life on ye moietie granted by Sir J. Smith. Lives: Mary Nicholas 65. Loveday Harris 65. John Harris 35.*

	No. of acres	*Ann.value*
a house a garden		*£1.0.0.*
Park an gorland	*3.2*	*£3.10.0.*
Pound meadow	*0.1*	*£0.6.8*
pk. michell	*2.0*	*£1.6.8.*
pk.golla	*2.0*	*£2.3.0.*
The hill close in 2 parts	*2.0*	*£2.0.0.*
burnwithian meadow	*1.0*	*£1.0.0.*
croft & chare	*0.2*	*£1.0 0.*
2 other crofts & a plot	*3.2*	*£0.13.4.*
the Moors	*2.0*	*£0.13.4.*
TOTALS:	*16.3*	*£13.1.8.*

4. WOOLCOCK'S *or* DINGLE'S *Tenement. John Harris. 2 lives after 1 ye 3d granted by Sir J. Smith to Jo. Dingle for 10th in April 1656. Lives: Joan Dingle 56. Henry Harris 20.*

House and Garden
mowhay
The meadow
Well Lane Close
The long close
The 3 corner close
Stone close
park an fold
The croft
The moore

[In 1704 the tenant was Mr John Harris. Lives: John Harris junr 24. Henry Harris 20]

5. TRIPLETT'S *als* PATHERICK'S *Tenement. Constance Patherick. 2 lives after 1 in the moitie granted by Sir J. Smith for 4th to R. Harris. Lives: Said Constance Patherick 17. Nicholas Patherick 20.*

House, 2 gardens & orchard plot
A little house, 3 gardens & plotts
the meadow
2 crofts & land
the higher croft

[1704 Lives: Constance 40. Nicholas Patherick 44. One life in Reversion.]

6. LEONARD NICHOLLS [sometime TUCKER'S] *Tenement. Will'm Oppy. 'Did not see his Lease.' Lives: Mary Littleton wid. 30. Wm. Oppy Jnr. 17. Anthony Tremellyn 18.*

House & garden
Ye meadow between the lands
Ye meadow next the little land
3 crofts
Miller's house & plot

7. BRAY'S *Tenement. Arthur Spargo. 'Did not see his Lease.' Lives. Arthur Spargo 50. Stephen his son 14. Mary his daughter 18.*

2 houses and a smith's shop
2 meadows

8. WASSLEY'S *Tenement. Geo. Wassley. Lives Said George Wassley 50.*

a house and 2 gardens and back
2 meadows

9. SMITH'S SHOP. *Said George Wassley. 'Did not see his Lease.' Life. Said George Wassley. 50.*

An eighteenth-century house at Tregullow, possibly the farmhouse of Tresadron Hendy als Debma No.6.f. in the 1772 Survey which was leased by Edmund Jeffery with 24 acres in 1772.

The Survey of 1697 Lists Fourteen Tenements which Include Most of those on the Earlier List.

(There are no reference numbers on any of the seventeenth-century records and no maps.)

1. Talgollow Farme. Constance Penrose. Widow, now her son. Lives: Mark Bawden 66 yrs. Edmund Bawden 44 yrs.

House, garden, orchard, and mowhay
Meadow under the House
Park an crock
Quarry Close or Middle Penty karne
Little penty karne
The Little Wood
Park an Crogg
The Little Mead
The Wood and three crofts
Two Higher Moor plotts
A Stamping Mill
A little house, meadow and garden
Two Lower Moor plotts
A Wood
A Stamping Mill
Two other Stamping Mills

46 acres. her part. Yearly value: £28.19s.10d. Including a stamping mill.

Edmond Bawden's part [No. 8] *Granted by Sir John Smith by deed dated 20th February 1654.*

[The above tenement is the farm presently called Tolgullow Vean and appears to have been split, Number 8 below is Edmund Bawden's part of the entire holding. It is noted that Mark and Edmund Bawden are the named lives on both properties.]

2. Tresaddern Hendy als Clibma. The Exectrs. of John Littleton. Gent. Now Mr. John Harris, Tenant. Lives: Mark Jeffery in Reversion of Mary Groby, heretofore Littleton, 45 years and Joan her daughter now Bowden 22.

Two houses, gardens and mowhay
Park an Bannel
One house and garden
The Clibma
The Meadow
Tresadron Fields in Crofthandy, viz A house garden and croft.
Three houses and three crofts
Two houses and gardens

3. Groce's Tenement. The Exectrs. Of John Golsery. Life: Spargo 20 yrs. ['In St. Day Town', 1772]

4. Mitchell's Tenement. John Mitchell. Lives: John Mitchell 55 yrs. Honor Mitchell 58 yrs. 'Did not see his Lease.'

5. Debmine.

6. Bray's Tenement.

7. Roose's Tenement.

8. Tallgullo part to Edmund Bawden. Lives: Marke Bawden 66 yrs. Edmund Bawden 44 yrs.

9. Jake's Tenement. Richard Harris.
Lives: John Harris 40. Hope Harris. 16.
'Now in John Harris.'

10. Menargwin. Mark Sampson. Lives: Mary Trewollow. 40. Mark Sampson. Jnr. 23. Edmd.Sampson 19.

11. Constance Patherick's, call'd Triplets
Lives: Constance Patherick 23 yrs. Nicholas Patherick 27 yrs.

12. Burnwithian.

13. Smith's Shop. A Smith's Shop. George Wassley 50 yrs. 'Did not see his Lease.'

14. Phillips' tenement. Richard Harris. A house, garden, three meadows. Matilda Hank 40 yrs. now Munday.

A Book of the Particulars with References to the Map of the Manor of St Day, in the Parish of Gwennap & County of Cornwall. Surveyd in 1772 by F. Welch & mapp'd in 1777 by Wm. Hole.

No.1.a. Scorria alias Scorrier. In Lease to Benjamin Perriam and John Bowden.

a1. Farm House and Courtlage and four small Dwellings.
a2. Garden at the Back of the House.
a3. Another Garden adjoining the last mentioned.
a4. Another little garden.
a5. Orchard.
a6. Lower Cock's Close.
a7. Higher Cock's Close.
a8. Town Field.
a9. Lower Parkengue.
a10. Higher Parkengue
a11. Grandmother's Field.
a12. Middle Field.
a13. Higher Field.
a14. Lower Dry Field.
a15. Higher Dry Field.
a16. Croft Vean.
a17. Great Teague's Croft.
a18. Teague's Garden.
a19. Little Gear.
a20. Round Gear.
a21. Potatoe Garden.
a22. Wester Gear Croft.
a23. Norther Gear Croft.
a24. Tame's Croft.
a25. Souther Tame's Croft.
a26. Little Tame's Croft.
a27. Great Tame's Croft.
a28. Great Croft.
a29. Junan's Field.
a30. Benjey's Field.
a31. Scorrier Down
a32. Moiety of Scorrier Green with Fra's Beauchamp, Esq.

Total Acres. Crofts: 121a.3r.31p.
Arable & Pasture. 24a.1r.32p.
Total Content. 147a.3r.36p.
[p = perches]

No.2.b. Tallgullow. In Lease to John Bawden.

b1. Dwelling House and Outhouses.
b2. Garden.
b3. Garden.
b4. Mowhay.
b5. Potatoe Garden.
b6. Middle Field.
b7. Coarse Field.
b8. Tallgullow Moor.
b9. Stamps Cottage and Garden.
b10. Meadow.
b11. Plot formerly an orchard.
b12. A meadow.
b13. Lower Moor.
b14. Higher Moor.
b15. The Wood. Bushes and furse.
b16. Hill Meadow.
b17. Wood Field.
b18. Moiety of Pednicarne Moor.

Total Acreage: 12a.3r.39p.

No.3.c. Tallgullow Higher Stamps, Cottage and Acre. In Lease to John Messer [formerly to John/Mary Mills].

No.4.d. Pednicarn. In Lease to John Edwards.

d1. Stamps.
d2. Cottage.
d3. Garden.
d4. Stamps Acre Plot.
d5. A Moiety of Pednicarne Moor.

Total Acreage: 1a.3r.1p.

No.5.e. Part of Tallgullow. In Lease to Elizabeth Bray.

e1. Dwelling House and Outhouses.
e2. Garden.
e3. Garden.
e4. Mowhay.
e5. Town Field.
e6. The Meadow.
e7. Park an Crock.
e8. Quarry Park.
e9. Middle Field.
e10. Calf's Meadow.
e11. Jeffrey's Field.
e12. Pednicarne.
e13. Lamb's Close.
e14. The Wood – Bushment and Furze.

Total Acreage: 33a.3r.13p.

No.6.f. Part of Tresodren Hendy Debma alias Clebma. In Lease to Edmond Jeffery.

f1. Four Dwellings, Stable, Barn and Garden
f2. Two Dwellings and one little Garden.
f3. Another Garden..
f4. Garden or Orchard.
f5. Lower Town Meadow including the Garden
f6. Higher Town Meadow.
f7. Town Field.
f8. Middle Field.
f9. Higher Meadow.
f10. South Parkanbannal including the Garden.
f11. Lower Parkanbannal.
f12. Three cornerd Field.
f13. Long Field.
f14. Moory Meadow.
f15. Garden Adjoining.
f16. Long Garden.
f17. Another Garden Adjoining
f18. Do.
f19. Another Garden Adjacent
f20. Another Garden adjacent Westward.
f21. Dwelling House, two little gardens.
f22. Garden at the North thereof.
f23. Field and Garden.
f24. Tallgullow Moor.
f25. Garden.
f26. Lower Wester Meadowe.
f27. Higher Wester Meadow.

Total Acreage: 24a.2r.13p.

No.7.g. Woolcock's alias Dingle's Tenement. In Lease to Colan Bawden.

g1. Two Small Dwellings at Tallgullow.
g2. Garden.
g3. Another Garden Adjoining.
g4. Meadow.
g5. Easter Parkan bal.
g6. Higher do.
g7. Wester do.
g8. Two Dwellings Two Stables and Shop with a Courtlage and Mowhay in St Day Town.
g9. Another Mowhay or Garden.
g10. Garden.
g11. Little Meadow.
g12. Well Lane Close.
g13. Great Long Close.
g14. Quacker's Field.
g15. Little Long Close.
g16. Stone Close.
g17. Croft.
g18. Norther Moor.
g19. Souther Moor.

Total Acreage: 17a.0r.32p.

No.8.h. Debmine Tenement. In Lease to Charles Hawke & Margaret Knava.

h1. Garden.
h2. Hither Meadow.
h3. Yonder Meadow.
h4. Easter Debmine.
h5. Long Debmine.
h6. Dwelling House and Garden in St Day.
h7. Meadow.
h8. Little Tandava.
h9. Great Tandava.
h10. Meadow.
h11. The Moor. [1a.3r.33p.]

Total Acreage: 14a.3r.21p.

No.9.I. Burnwithian. In Lease to Mark Jeffery's Widow with right of Common.

i1. Great Parkangawland.
i2. Garden.
i3. Little Parkangawland.
i4. Easter do.
i5. Garden.
i6. Ruins by and about St Day Green.
i7. Publick House in St Day Town and Courtlage behind.
i8. A Garden.
i9. Pound Meadow.
i10. Norther Parkan.
i11. Souther Parkan.
i12. Easter do.
i13. Boss Close.
i14. Easter Hilly Field.
i15. Hilly Meadow.
i16. Great Croft.
i17. Moor.
i18. Little Croft.
i19. Garden at the Bottom of the Green. A Note beneath this entry reads: 'This part of the Tenement belongs to Mr. Champernowne and Mr. Hearle...' followed by 'A mistake It Being only a Division between the tenants themselves.'

No.10.k. Groce's Tenement in Saint Day Town. In Lease to Rebecca Trewortha. Total Acreage: 7a.1r.0p.

No.11.l. Helwiden. In Lease to Charles Mitchell Jnr.

l1. Dwelling House in St Day Town.
l2. Garden at the North End of the Chapple Yard.
l3. North Helwiden.
l4. South Helwiden.
l5. New Inclosure.

Total Acreage: 2a.0r.29p.

No.12.m. 'A Small House on the North Side of St Day Chapple for keeping Standings in and the Profits of S. Day Fair, which is held annually on Good Friday.'

No.13.n. Tresadron. In Lease to Henry Williams.

n1. Smith's Shop and Dwelling over.
n2. Garden. n1 & n2 together is a Tenement of itself & lyes in St Day Town.
n3. Little Furses.
n4. Great Furses.
n5. Norther Tresordron.
n6. Norther Middle do.
n7. Souther Middle do.
n8. Souther Tresodron.
n9. Dwelling House and Courtlage.
n10. Garden Adjoining.
n11. Higher Meadow.
n12. Sandy Plot.
n13. Little do
n14. Higher Town Field.
n15. Long Meadow.
n16. Two Gardens.
n17. Dwelling House,
n18. Orchard.
n19. Lower Town Meadow.

Total Acreage: 13a.3r.6p.

[A Farmyard was called a 'Town Place' and fields leading direct from the Town Place were identified by the name 'Town Field', as above.]

No.14.o. House and Garden in Saint Day Town. In Lease to Charles Hawke's Exors.

o1. Two Dwellings and Plot behind them.
o2. Garden.

No.15.p. Venson's House with a Smith's Shop etc. and a small garden in St Day Town. In Lease to Charles Hawke's Exors.

No.16.q. Newton's Tenement by Saint Day Cross. In Lease to Stephen Newton.

No.17.r. Jake's and Tucker's Tenement in St Day Town. In Lease to Henry Harris.

Dwelling House and Stable.
Higher Field.
Garden.
Meadow.
Higher Field.
Lower Field.
Oppie's Croft. Furze and Shafts.

Total. 7a.0r.23p.

No.18. Leonard's Tenement in St Day. In Lease to John Edwards.

No.19.s. 1. House and Garden in St Day Town. In Lease to James Gatty.

s1. Two Dwellings.
s2. Garden.

No.20.t. Tenement in St Day Town. In Lease to John Messer.

t1. Two Dwellings and Stable.
t2. Mowhay.
t3. Garden.
t4. Another Garden Adjoining.
t5. A good Dwelling House.
t6. Meadow behind it.
t7. Higher Meadow.
t8. Little Middle Meadow.
t9. Great Middle Meadow.
t10. Lower Meadow.

Total: 6a.3r.39p.

No.21.u. Hoar's or Rosewarne's Tenement. In Lease to Richard Williams.

u1. Two Dwellings and a Garden in St Day Town.
u2. Poldice Higher field.
u3. Poldice Lower field.
u4. South Meadow near Wheal Quick.

No.22.v. Roose's Tenement in Saint Day Town. In Lease to Francis Quick.

v1. Four dwellings in St Day Town.
v2. Garden.
v3. Quick's Meadow.
v4. Garden.
v5. Another Garden.
v6. Wheal Quick. Rubbish Ground.

Total Acreage: 0a.3r.33p.

No.23.w. Mitchell's Tenement in St Day Town. In Lease to Mr. Henry Harris.

w1. Barn, Stable, and Cooper's Shop.
w2, 3, 4, and 5. Gardens.
w6. Little Meadow.
w7. Outer Meadow.
w8. Well Lane Close.
w9. Garden.
w10. Voge Lane Field.
w11. Little Voge Meadow.

Total Acreage: 7a.2r.3p.

No.24.x. A Tenement. In Lease to Mary Bray.

x1. Dwelling House and small Gardens in St Day Town.
x2. Bray's Field.
x3. Garden.
x4. Another Garden.
x5. Lower Bray's Field.
x6. Bray's Rubbish Plot.
x7. Field adjoinng.
x8. Another Field to the East.
x9. Parkan crock.

No.25.y. Part of Leonard's Tenement. In Lease to Charles Mitchell.

No.26.z.1. A Tenement near Poldice Ball. In Lease to Mark Jeffery.

z1. A Dwelling House.
z2. Garden.
z3. Lower Field.
z4. Higher Field.

No.27.&. A Messuage and Tenement called Tresoddron. In Lease to John Edwards. Farm House, Out Houses, and Courtlage. Dwelling House consisting of two Dwellings.

&1. Garden.
&2. Mowhay.
&3. Garden.
&4. Orchard.
&5. Pump Field.
&6. Little Hilly Piece.
&7. Great Hilly.
&8. Easter Hilly Piece.
&9. Wester Moor Close.
&10. Croft.
&11. Middle Moor.
&12. Orchard.
&13. Skew's Field.
&14. Town Field.
&15. Higher Town Field.
&16. Lower Farm Field.
&17. Whiteford's Field.
&18. Lower Moor.

Total Acreage: 26a.3r.24p.

No.28.aa. Messuage and Tenement. In Lease to James Curtis.

aa1. Dwelling House.
aa2. Garden.
aa3. Orchard.
aa4. Long Meadow.
aa5. Little Plot Adjoining.
aa6. Middle Field.
aa7. Saffron Plot.

aa8. Field.
aa9. Another Field.

Total Acreage: 2a.0r.20p.

No.29. Messuage and Tenement. In Lease to Richard Mannell.

bb1. Two Dwellings.
bb2. Garden.
bb3. Field Adjoining.
bb4. Lower Field.
bb5. Garden.
bb6. Dwelling House, Smith's Shop and Orchard.

Total Acreage: 1a.1r.29p.

No.30.cc. Stamps. In Lease to John Lawrence Esq.

No.31.dd. A Tenement near Wheal Maid. In Lease to George Gregor.

dd1. Two pretty little Dwellings and Courtlage.
dd2. Orchard.
dd3. Little Orchard.
dd4. A Field.
dd5. Another Little Field.
dd6. Easter Field.

Total Acreage: 1a.1r.35p.

No.32.ee. Nichols's Stamps with the Burning House and plot in South Coombe. In Lease to John Bawden.

Total Acreage: 0a.2r.0p.

No.33.ff. A Tenement in South Combe. In Lease to Christopher Kneebone.

1. Dwelling and Plot before it.
2. Orchard.
3. Homer Field.
4. Outer Field.
5. Croft.

Total Acreage: 3a.1r.34p.

No.34.gg. A Tenement in South Combe. In Lease to James Williams.

gg1. Public House and Plot round it.
gg2. Orchard.
gg3. Plot to the Eastward.
gg4. Garden.
gg5. Another Garden.
gg6. Another Garden.
gg7. Norther Field.
gg8. Middle Field.
gg9. Easter Field Field.
gg10. Great Field (0a.2r.38p.)
gg11. Wester Lower Field.
gg12. Easter Lower Field..

Total Acreage: 3a.0r.15p.

No.35.hh. Part of Crofthandy. In Lease to Henry Noel.

hh1. Dwelling House and Plot round it.
hh2. Garden.
hh3. Field under.
hh4. Two Dwellings and Barn.
hh5. Garden.
hh6. Field Adjoining.
hh7. Western Field.
hh8. Higher Field.
hh9. Another Field.
hh10. Another Little Plot Adjoining
hh11. Another do.
hh12. Two Poor Dwellings.
hh13. Garden.
hh14. Town Meadow.
hh15. Wester Field on the other side of the road.
hh16. Another Plot Adjoining.
hh17. do. To the North.
hh18. Easter Plot

Total Acreage: 4a.1r.29p.

No.36.ii. A Tenement in South Combe. In Lease to Richard Williams.

ii1. Two small Dwellings and Courtlage.
ii2. Garden.
ii3. Garden.
ii4. Field Adjoining.
ii5. New Inclosure.
ii6. Field behind the House.
ii7. Wester Field.
ii8. Higher Field.

Total Acreage: 4a.1r.29p.

No.37.jj. A Tenement in South Combe. In Lease to Elizabeth Whiteford.

jj1. Two good Dwellings and Plot round them.
jj2. Field before the Door.
jj3. Little Field.
jj4. Lower Field.

Total Acreage: 1a.1r.1p.

No.38.kk. A Tenement late Francis Richards's. In Lease to Thomas Hitchins.

kk1. Two Dwellings.
kk2. Garden.
kk3. Garden.
kk4. Lower Meadow.
kk5. Middle Meadow.
kk6. Higher Meadow.

Total Acreage: 1a.3r.7p.

No.39.ll. Part of Crofthandy. In Lease to William Real.

ll1. Public House, Outhouses and Courtlage.
ll2. Garden.
ll3. Garden.
ll4. Long Meadow.
ll5. Wester Little Meadow.
ll6. Little Meadow.
ll7. Lower Meadow.
ll8. Black Croft.
ll9. Lower Field.

Total Acreage: 5a.2r.11p.

No.40.mm. Courtis's Tenement near Poldice Ball. In Lease to Christopher Kneebone.

mm1. Dwelling House and Courtlage.
mm2. Garden.
mm3. Field.
mm4. Easter Field.
mm5. Great Field by the South Bound of Poldice Ball.
mm6. Little Field.

Total Acreage: 2a.1r.4p.

No.41.nn. Part of Crofthandy. In Lease to Frances Halse, widow.

nn1. A Poor Dwelling House and Courtlage.
nn2. Garden.
nn3. Field adjoining.
nn4. Three cornerd Field.
nn5. Middle Field.
nn6. Wester Field.

Total Acreage: 0a.3r.35p.

No.42.oo. A Tenement on the South Side of Poldice Ball. In Lease to Stephen Mitchell.

oo1. Two small Dwellings and Little Plot adjoining.
oo2. Easter Plot.
oo3. Another Plot adjoining.
oo4. do.
oo5. Oar Field.

Total Acreage: 1a.0r.34p.

No.43.pp. A Tenement on the North Side of Poldice Ball. In Lease to Thomas Tregurtha.

pp1. Two Dwellings, one of them a Publick House and Courtlage.

pp2. Gardens.
pp3. Orchard.
pp4. Field.
pp5. Fields.
pp6. Another Field.
pp7. Croft.

No.44.qq. A Messuage and Tenement on the North Side of Poldice Ball. In Lease to Martin Skinner.

qq1. Two Dwellings.
qq2. Another Dwelling.
qq3. Garden.
qq4. Another Garden.
qq5. 6, 7, 8, fields.
qq9. Shut Close.

Nos 45 and 46.rr. Two Tenements Part of Shelston's. In Lease to James Williams.

A list of 20 items includes:
rr1. Two Dwellings
rr2, 3 & 4. Gardens.
rr5. Orchard.
rr6. Meadow.
rr7. Town Meadow.
rr8. Four Dwellings, Stable and Courtlage, two Gardens,
rr9. Orchard behind.
rr10. Orchard above.
rr11. Another Orchard.
rr12. Middle Meadow.
rr13. Higher Souther Meadow.
rr14. Souther Part of the Four Acres. (2a.1r.6p.)
rr15. Norther Part do. (2a.2r.15p.)
rr16. Higher Little Beside Croft.
rr17. Lower do.
rr18. Higher Park Tubby.
rr19. Lower Park Tubby.

Total Acreage: 16a.3r.35p.

No.47.ss. Triplett's Tenement. In Lease to Peter Bussoe and Elizabeth Bowden.

Lists:
SS1 Two Dwellings and SS20 Dwelling House. Three Orchards, Three Gardens, Potato Garden one Croft and a total of fourteen fields.
SS 20. Dwelling House.
The whole measuring only 11 Statute acres.

No.48.tt. Part of Shelston's Tenement. In Lease to Gregory Raby.

tt1. Dwelling House. With 2 Orchards, 2 Crofts and 5 fields.

No.49.uu. Part of Shelston's Tenement.

No.50.vv. Tenement late a Stamps in North Coombe. Dwelling house etc.

No.51.ww. Tenement late an old Stamping Mill. A poor dwelling house and garden.

No.52.xx. Stamps & Burning House in South Coombe near Poldice Ball, formerly Francis's & Sampsons.

No.53.yy. Magor's Tenement in South Coombe. Dwelling House etc.

No.54.zz. Nichols's Stamping Mill in South Coombe. In Lease to Mr James Williams.

No.55.&&. Drew May's Stamps in South Combe. In Lease to Mr. Michael Williams.

&&1. Burning House.
&&2. Stamping Mills.
&&3. Burning House Plots.

No.56.A. Trewinnard Mills [Hale Mills] In South Coombe. In Lease to Mr. Michael Williams.

A1. Two Poor Dwellings, Mill House in Ruins.
A2. A Pretty Dwelling and Orchard.
A3. Garden and three meadows.

No.57.B. Mill Stamps. In Lease to John Williams.

B2. Burning House.

No.58.C. A Stamping Mill in North Combe. In Lease to Rebecca Trewartha. Widow. In Ruins and as the water is certainly cut off by Wheal Unity Addit never more can be of any value (nor any Stamps in North Combe).

No.59.D. Francis's Stamps in North Combe in Hand and in Ruins.

No.60.E. James Holman's Stamps of little or no value for the reason above given against Mrs. Trewartha's at No.58.

No.61.F. Mungumpas Common.
Statute Measure: 176a.3r.0p.
Customary Measure: 148a.2r.12p.

No.62. G. Saint Day Green.
Statute Measure: 0a.1r.30p.
Customary Measure: 0a.1r.19p.

No.63.H. Menarguin Tenement. In Lease to William Read. Farm House, Outhouses and Townplace. A List of some 15 items, incl. 'Wester Pease Meadow'.
Total Acre. Statute: 29a.0r.24p.
Customary: 24a.1r.8p.

SUMMARY *of the* 1772 SURVEY

The 14 tenements named in 1682 Survey are all named again in 1772 Survey.

Total Stamps in North Coombe:	*5 including three 'in ruins'*
Total Stamps in South Coombe:	*3*
Burning Houses:	*3 plus one Burning House Plot*
Public Houses:	*3 plus one in St Day Town*
Smiths' shops:	*4*
Coopers' shops:	*1*
Orchards:	*15*
'Houses':	*4*
'Cottages':	*2*
'Dwellings':	*67*
Tenements:	*63*
Gardens:	*93*
Potato Gardens:	*4*
'Tenements' in St Day Town:	*19*
'Dwellings' in St Day Town:	*35*
Saffron plot:	*1, at Crofthandy*

St Day Green, an open space, lay at what is now the bottom of Fore Street, on part of which the Market House was built, followed by the Post Office and adjoining houses and the row of houses and dwellings opposite.

These maps are taken from the Tregullow and St Day 'Map of the Mannor' surveyed by Welch and Hole in 1772. (CRO Ref.No.XI 48/1)

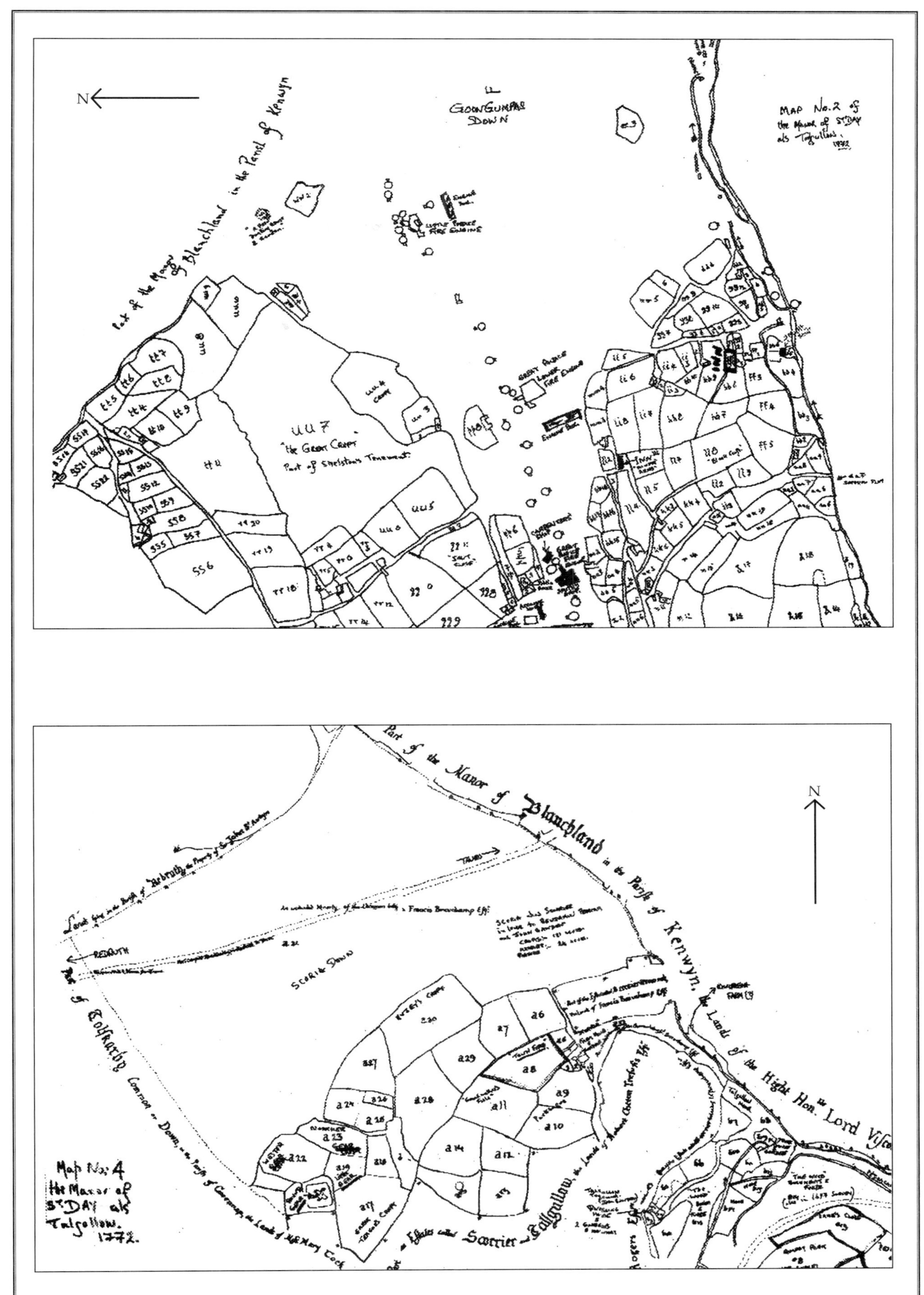
N
Part of the Manor of Blanchland in the Parish of Kenwyn
GoonGumpas Down
Map No. 2 of the Manor of St. Day als Tolgullow. 1772.
UU7
"the Great Croft"
Part of Shelstons Tenement
Little Pearce Fire Engine
Great Pearce Lower Fire Engine
N
Part of the Manor of Blanchland in the Parish of Kenwyn.
Lands of the Right Hon. Lord Visc
Scorier Down
Redruth
Truro
Part of Gwinear Common or Down, in the Parish of Gwennap, the Lands of Mrs Mary Cock
Estates called Scorrier and Tolgullow
Map No. 4 the Manor of St. DAY als Tolgullow. 1772.

A good crowd at Crofthandy Sunday-School tea treat, 1915.

West End, now Forth an Eglos, which was known as Well Lane in the eighteenth century. The blacksmith was John Eustace. A smithy on this site is recorded during the seventeenth and eighteenth centuries. The man on the far left in the foreground is believed to be A.B. Rowe, c.1914.

Thirteen

Nostalgia: A Miscellany

'Fings aint what they used to be' – those words from a one-time popular song carry some truth; 'things' have certainly changed, and mostly for the better it must be said. Who wants to go back to earth closets, and a water supply from an itinerant horse-drawn barrel, times when diphtheria and scarlet fever struck and children had rickets?

My memory goes back to the very early 1920s when nobody in St Day had a wireless set or a motor car. However, most houses had a gramophone, the grand ones of the community would own a floor-standing console, others contenting themselves with a table model or even a portable. On Sundays, in many houses, only 'sacred music' was allowed to be played either by the gramophone or on the ubiquitous harmonium, and the purest of the pure covered all such items with a cloth on Saturday nights before retiring to bed. The cloth remained in place until Monday morning. Hallelujah!

One of the tearooms at Porthtowan, the nearest beach to St Day.

Private telephones were few, so telegrams were sent from and received by the Post Office and delivered by the telegraph boy, who would ask if there was a reply and, if so, wait to receive the message. Rag-and-bone men travelled the country around, calling out in the streets, for 'old rags or bones' and paying a few pence for a sackful; glass jam jars also had their own market and were saved and sold to 'Jampot Moyle.' Conservation and reuse of raw materials is not just a latter-day phenomenon.

During the Second World War 'make do and mend' was practised by economical housewives when clothing, etc. could only be bought new with coupons issued by the Government who published posters with those words on for display in shop windows, etc. Prior to the war the General Election in this constituency was largely two-party and when the count was over we listened, and if the Conservative candidate won, Redruth Brewery 'hooter' was blown, as also was Treseavean Mine hooter. The sound of the Cathedral Boot and Shoe Factory siren signalled a Liberal victory. They could be heard over a wide area and the news spread fast, to the joy of some and dismay of others.

Porthtowan was the nearest beach and was popular, people walking there at weekends for a day at the coast, with pasties. Cold pasty for a picnic, in my experience, was almost always parsley pasty. Tea could be bought from several establishments sited on the edge of the high-tide mark. Sunday-school parties would travel in a brake, the two steep hills of Millpool and Navvy Pit required the men and boys to get off and walk down and shoe-drags were put under the back wheels to hold the vehicle back. On the return journey once again the men and boys got off and walked up the hills to lighten the load for the horses. At Easter girls had new dresses and boys had a new tie and a ball, as well as Easter buns, specially rich, saffron buns: with a cross cut across the top. A few St Day families still observe the tradition.

I had cousins living at Crofthandy and I attended the chapel Sunday school there, although my parents were Anglican. Highlights of the chapel year included the Sunday-school anniversary, for which special services were held, the womenfolk, young and old, dressed out in their finery – for most of them the occasion meant a new dress and hat. Preachers were chosen for their 'drawing power' to fill the chapel.

In the mid-1920s it was customary at Crofthandy to hold the anniversary evening service on St Day Feast Sunday outdoors in a field called 'Buck's Head Field', sited opposite the present Crofthandy Village Hall. The men of the chapel built a platform in the field against the hedge farthest from the road to accommodate the organist and the visiting preacher. The timber for the platform, uprights and flooring was stored throughout the year in a little stone building, 'the weighbridge', on the corner of the road to Tripletts. Special anniversary hymns were sung from words printed on leaflets obtained for the occasion.

Crofthandy Wesleyan Church Tea Treat, 1915

Above: *Tea treat group. The bearded man, William Annear, was born during the reign of William IV and died in the 1920s in his late nineties. He is well remembered by the author who visited him frequently.*

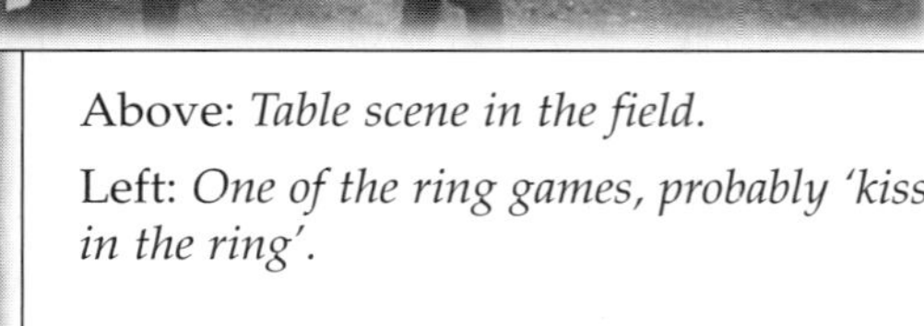

Above: *Table scene in the field.*

Left: *One of the ring games, probably 'kiss in the ring'.*

Right: *The crowds enjoy themselves in Capt. Tamblyn's field.*

The annual Sunday-school tea treat would take place on the following Saturday; this was the event the children really had been looking forward to. Buck's Head Field was still available, and the platform, already built, carried Carharrack Brass Band. The celebrations began after dinner (midday) when the scholars of the Sunday school gathered outside the chapel and formed into a procession headed by the elaborate Sunday-school banner with its long tassels, held high on two poles by two of the young men and steadied with guy ropes held by four more young men. The banner declared 'CROFTHANDY METHODIST SUNDAY SCHOOL' and the procession 'marched' up the hill to St Day with the banner, band, elders of the chapel and the children in that order. At the crossroads people would come out to watch them go by, and assess whether there were more or fewer in the school, reflecting its growing or declining strength and that of the chapel itself.

The procession wound its way through St Day along Scorrier Street, Telegraph Street, Vogue Hill and as far as the Star Inn, thence returning to the field at Crofthandy. Arriving at the field the band took up position on the platform, hampers of tea-treat buns were opened and the saffron buns given out to the children eagerly awaiting. Mugs and cups from home were used for the sugary tea (in itself a special treat, for taking sugar in tea was not usual in Cornwall, a custom dating back to the anti-slavery movement). Music from the band was enjoyed and the traditional games were played in the field (see C.C. James, *History of Gwennap*). The day ended at 9p.m. with 'The Serpentine Walk' headed by the band, everyone falling in behind and all being led in an intricate pattern around the field. Keen eyes noted who had paired with whom – a pointer, perhaps, to a forthcoming romance?

It was the custom during the tea-treat season to visit neighbouring Sunday-school tea treats which meant walking to places like Twelveheads, or Hick's Mill or Carharrack, and for the older and more adventurous as far afield as Redruth or Lanner. A brass band from out of the immediate district would always draw people from neighbouring villages, especially bands from the china-clay district such as those from Stenalees, Foxhole, St Dennis, Indian Queens or perhaps Bugle.

The Sunday-school annual prize-giving was another event to which we looked forward. Attendance at Sunday school was recorded and marks awarded to each scholar which accrued and determined the value of the book prize to be received. I still have one of my prizes, *The Life of David Livingstone*. Those were the days when individuals, adults and children sang solos, gave recitations and performed small sketches at concerts in the chapel. Occasionally these concerts were taken to neighbouring chapels on winter evenings, including Frogpool, Hick's Mill, Wheal Busy and Twelveheads. Meeting at Crofthandy Chapel, the party would then walk to the venue for that evening, and afterwards walk back home, a few miles each way.

There were idiosyncrasies of speech, still in use by many, but worth recording. When referring to other places one of four prepositions would be used, for example you went UP to any place beyond Truro, UP Newquay, Sen Austell, Sen Columb, Probus, Tregony and Bodmin, and if it was beyond the Tamar it was UP COUNTRY. It was IN Truro or Redruth, and 'in Town' was Redruth. You went OUT Illogan, Mount Hawke, Sen Agnes and Camborne and OVER Carharrack, United, Baldhu, Creegbrawse, Scorrier Wheal Rose and so on. The survival and continued usage of the Celtic Cornish Sen, equivalent of the English Saint, was, and is, the norm. Thus we still hear Sen Day, Sen Ives (no T sound), Sen Columb, etc. in everyday speech. Nicknames were commonly used, some being attached to a family; thus every male Knowles was 'Peano Knowles' and 'Swiss Hocken'. There was Roughy Richards (an allusion to his prowess at wrestling and on the rugby field?) and Ratty Hampton, Woodbine Williams and 'O Be Joyful'!

The policeman was 'Bobby'; we remember Bobby Ough in the 1920s – portly, easy-going, affable. He was followed by Bobby Babbage, a more active officer who carried out his duties conscientiously. Then there were the quite inexplicable Wuppy Di Doh and Boojy Bah (the latter from Carharrack) and Coomer Vincent. A story is told of Coomer that he intensely disliked being called by this name and on one occasion was so incensed that he resolved, with a stutter, 'I'm going to tell Bobby Babbage' and went at once to the police house in Scorrier Street, knocked and Bobby opened the door with the greeting 'Hullo Coomer, what can I do for you?', to be answered in fury with 'You're as bloody bad as the rest of them!' Coomer then turned and went. Poor old Coomer! He is well remembered with his beautifully-kept donkey and shay, his great pride and joy.

There was a curious expression 'Cut your 'and boy?' which was directed to anyone seen eating a pasty outdoors. The meaning and origin of this have not been discovered by the author. A dog chasing a cat was 'coosing' the cat and a farm-hand would 'meat the pigs'. Wasps were 'apple bees', woodlice

Procession with the band in Scorrier Street.

were 'grammar sows' and snails 'jan jakes'. Storm water from the roof was collected in 'launders' (not gutters) and where a stream was carried under a path or roadway it went through an iron pipe of suitable diameter called a 'cundard'. The cupboard under a stairs was the 'spence' and the landing at the top of the stairs was the 'planchen'.

The season of good will witnessed some purely Cornish customs, in most homes the Christmas tree was holly, many of the Christmas carols were Cornish ones written by nineteenth-century Cornish composers, among them Merritt, Broad and Nicholls, as well as carols of unknown age or composer like 'Star of Bethlehem', 'Steren Bethlehem Yma'. Throughout the Christmas period these would be heard in the pubs and outside in the streets, always pitched accurately and always in four-part harmony.

From Chapel Street came the Matthews family (about 20 of them) who, every Christmas without fail, came out into the streets of St Day and entertained the populace as a choir. They made a well-balanced choir, with strong basses (a prerequisite for a Cornish Choir), good tenors, altos and sopranos. They visited Carharrack and outlying farms and for many years were undoubtedly an established part of the Christmas scene in the district.

Here ends Part 1 in which I have set out a small selection of personal memories. I end with a line from *Henry IV*: 'There is a history in all men's lives.'

Memories of Four-Legged Friends

Above: *Church or chapel outing to the seaside by Jersey car.*

Above left: *'A-Hunting We Will Go'; Simon Mills and George Hicks, 1950s.*

Above: *The carnival queen's carriage harnessed to six skewbald horses supplied and driven by Simon W. Mills* (seen on the box).

Right: *Group of spotted horses bred at St Day by Simon Mills, with grey Shetland pony Coco and her foal in the foreground.*

Part 2: by Paul Annear

Fourteen

St Day Holy Trinity Church

Origins

By the early-nineteenth century St Day had clearly become established as the new service centre for the Gwennap mines. The population swelled at a staggering rate, shops appeared and trade flourished, forming a new industrial town. Nonconformity had become widespread within Gwennap, particularly at St Day. The Church of England responded to the situation with an impressive campaign of church building. The process was given a boost when a government grant of £1 million for this purpose was made available in 1818 as a 'thanks offering' for victory over the French at the Battle of Waterloo. Often we hear of the 'million fund' or 'Waterloo' churches which relate to these times. Realistically, it was an attempt to assert some influence and perhaps control from the 'established' Church of England over the rapidly growing industrial masses.

In 1826, during the reign of George IV, 'His Majesty's Commissioners for the building of additional churches and chapels' made grants available to the rapidly growing districts of St Day and Chacewater. The formative years of these churches run striking parallels. Both were funded, designed, built and consecrated by the same architect, mason and bishop, at more or less the same times. By April 1826, £6,000 had been raised for the buildings.[1] Charles Hutchins, an architect based at Torpoint, offered tenders for the building of both churches inviting glaziers, carpenters, painters and plumbers to inspect plans and specifications at the relevant parish vicarages before 22 July 1826. Shortly after, the designs were approved. Of the many tenders presented, that of J.L. Rickard of Devonport was chosen as the most suitable, with the exception of the plumber's work being contracted to J. Hearle of Plymouth.[2] The site had already been outlined at the southern end of St Day and progress was not delayed.

The next major event was the laying of the foundation stone, which was a massive, formal affair. Over 8,000 spectators crowded the scene and looked on as Mr F.H. Rodd (a lord of the manor of St Day) laid the foundation stone on Friday 6 October 1826. For a district that had fallen heavily to Methodism, this was a rather remarkable event and the Methodists reacted in a decisive manner. The Primitives took the initiative and set themselves about building their small thatched chapel 'down Backway' in 1827 while the Wesleyans decided to build a chapel, which they completed in 1828, though probably finishing last. Chapel Street and Church Street enter the map of St Day. It must have been an incredible sight as the local community laboured tirelessly. The strain was also felt financially, as during this period the town was taxed to the full. However, the Gwennap mines were in full swing and new migrants appeared at Gwennap and St Day every week. Economic prosperity was enjoyed by many and the 'competition for souls' was fierce.

The consecration of the new church was held on Friday 1 August 1828 by Dr Carey, the Bishop of the Diocese of Exeter. The petition for consecration was presented by the Right Hon. Lord Dunstanville, who in a 'neat and well-delivered' speech thanked those involved in the achievement. The *West Briton* concluded:

> *The church of St Day is a building of great strength, admirably well calculated for the accommodation of a very large congregation, and does great credit to those who have been the means of effecting so praiseworthy an undertaking.*[3]

Charles Hutchins chose a rather unusual 'Gothic' design which impressed the imagination of one of our finest Poet Laureates, Sir John Betjamin, who in the *1965 Shell Guide to Cornwall* commented:

> *The church (Holy Trinity) stands apart from the hilltop Town and its chapels. It is a most fanciful granite square of*

Left: *St Day Church, c.1910.*

Previous page, top: *Print of St Day Church c.1904 with surveyors in the foreground.*

Previous page, bottom: *St Day Church.*

1828, in quite unsophisticated gothic, with two storeys of perpendicular-style windows, a flat triple front with a pinnacled tower and a spirelet and turrets at the corners. It looks like an ecclesiastical toy fort.

The church was undoubtedly stunning and the people of St Day felt proud to boast of one of the most architecturally daring local structures of the period. The total cost of the building was approximately £4,000 and it held a seating capacity for 1,500 people. Initially the church was consecrated a Chapel of Ease to Gwennap before being 'carved' from the same parish, when St Day was granted ecclesiastical independence on 1 April 1835; with the same boundaries more or less surviving today.[4] As important was the provision of a cemetery, as opposed to that used at Gwennap Churchtown, which had probably been the custom since the dissolution of St Day's medieval chapel.

Music, Missions & Challenge of Methodism

The church at St Day has a rather musical past, having produced instrumentalists and choirs of a high calibre. Organs were such a prominent feature of church life and the original church organ was given to Carharrack Mission Church when it opened in 1884. This had already been replaced by another built in 1858 at a cost of £600 which was later enlarged in 1880, only to be in need of restoration by early 1890. The usual concerts and fund-raising continued for ten years before the organ was completely renovated in 1900 by Heard & Sons, organ builders of Truro. However, by this time the organ was sited in the north-east side of the church, instead of in the gallery.

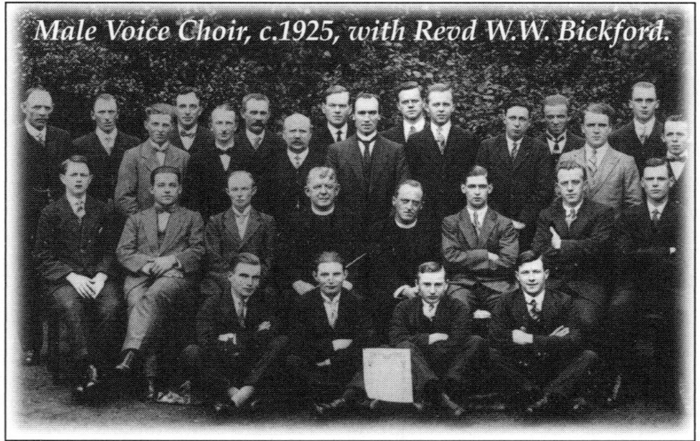
Male Voice Choir, c.1925, with Revd W.W. Bickford.

Musical entertainment for the people of St Day was regularly provided by the church, with instrumentalists and vocalists giving concerts, often at the church Schoolroom. These grew very popular and were usually well attended; there were occasions when the hall was totally full and people were turned away. Miss Williams of Tregullow was a particular patron of the church choir during the 1870s. She took a lively interest by supporting events, concerts, outings, etc., with great generosity.

A 1920s group photograph of St Day's Male Voice Choir can still be found in many homes in the parish. Mr Rutter Stephens reminisced about the early days when the group formed in a small house opposite 'the Crofthandy Shop'. Soon the choir outgrew the premises and the church adopted the group under the musical directorship of St Day's vicar, Revd Walter Bickford. At times up to 60 men strong, the choir would practise twice a week in the church Schoolrooms (the present church building). The programme of concerts was busy and would often list venues at Carharrack, Redruth, Stithians, Camborne and Illogan, amongst others.

The population of St Day peaked around 1851 with 3,907 inhabitants. Population figures would have been calculated when the provision was made for seating 1,500 people in 1826. The new industrial population would mainly have consisted of the mining classes, so it is difficult to speculate on class distinctions within St Day's church. Certainly the town had its share of wealthy patrons, who maintained their seat-rents before they were abolished in 1891. Undoubtedly class distinctions would have been reinforced by the gentlefolk who probably occupied the box-pews in the gallery, casting glances down below to the more humble worshippers segregated by inferior seating. By the 1880s emigration had dwindled the population considerably and perhaps the existence of a predominantly Methodist community concerned the higher clergy of the Anglican Church. Missions therefore continued well up to the 1900s, remaining an important part of church life, and were to some extent supplemented by evangelical groups such as the Low Church Kensit Preachers, who toured annually, visiting St Day on their travels. This Low-Anglican group would appear on a mid-week evening in Market Square, singing and engaging in public debates about theological issues and doctrine. They were, it seems, always well received at St Day.[5]

In 1851, the first and last religious census was conducted across the country. Its aim was to determine two issues: how many people attended a place of worship and which denominations they preferred. The census was held on Sunday 30 March 1851. Returns for St Day can be seen in the table overleaf:

Religious Denomination	Numbers Attending	Percentage of Total
St Day Anglicans	350	21.40
St Day Wesleyan Methodist Assoc.	181	11.07
St Day Wesleyan Methodists	654	40.00
St Day Primitive Methodists	450	27.52

From these figures we can see that a total of 1,635 church and chapel attendances were recorded for that particular Sunday at St Day. When we consider that the population of the town was 3,907 for the same year, we calculate that at most only just under 42 per cent of the people attended that day (and we must bear in mind that some may have attended two or three times).

Of the four denominations at St Day in 1851, the Wesleyan Methodists appear the most popular, attracting an overall 40 per cent of the church-going population. The Wesleyan Methodist Association who had moved into the thatched chapel in Scorrier Street (vacated by the Baptists three months earlier) received the least attendance, a respectable 11 per cent. The Primitives 'down Backway' maintained a steady 27.5 per cent. Collectively the Methodists accounted for 78.5 per cent of all church and chapel-goers and a total 33 per cent of the population of St Day.

The Anglicans, who accounted for 21 per cent of the church and chapel-going community, only attracted 9 per cent of the town's population. Accordingly, St Day was overwhelmingly a Methodist community. In the other industrial areas of Cornwall, the results were more or less the same as at St Day. The census further revealed that Anglicanism was often stronger in rural areas, with Nonconformity more active in urban areas. Methodism showed a particular strength in Cornwall and South Wales. Overall the census illustrated that more people stayed away than attended, and of those who chose to worship the majority were Nonconformist.[6] At the start of the twenty-first century an average Anglican attendance at St Day would probably amount to 35, with the Methodists at 45. In total these amount to around 5 per cent of the total 2002 population. Compared to the 1851 census figures, we could safely say that the Victorians were religious in a way that we are not. For the Anglicans the result was concerning, reducing them nationally to merely 'another' denomination amongst several. The various social authorities and legal privileges they had assumed and enjoyed for so long were now about to be challenged. From this time onwards, the Anglicans could take little for granted and were forced to seek new approaches towards reaching their community.

The new church extension, c.1966.

The Church Interior

Church interior, c.1900.

Internally, the church consisted of chancel, nave, north and south aisles, and south, west and north galleries. The arcades comprised five four-centred arches supported on pillars. The stone font stood on a square-based octagonal shaft. There were three western doors and a 'priest door' at the east end. The tower contained one bell.[7]

At the eastern end the apse accommodated three stained-glass windows forming a triptych, illustrating Christ at the centre of the four evangelists. Below were minor compositions. The centre window (as viewed internally from the west end) was a dedication to Sir William Williams, Bart. and related to the eighth chapter of St Luke's Gospel, in which Christ whilst on his way to a ruler's house passes a women who touches his garment as a cure for her infirmity and then kneels in supplication before him. The window to the left was a dedication to his wife Caroline depicting the raising of the daughter of Jairus from death, from St Matthew 9: 23–25. The tracery at the top was filled with angels. Underneath were the words 'Daughter, be of good comfort: St Luke viii, 48.' At the base was an inscription: 'To the Glory of God, and in dutiful and loving memory of Caroline, Widow of Sir William Williams, Bart. Died at Tregullow, 17th February, 1866; aged 90 years.' The window, unveiled on Christmas Day, 1886, was intended as a companion to the window on the right, dedicated to Mrs Hornby Buller, and was the work of the firm Taylor & Son, late O'Connor and Taylor, 4 Berners Street. Below the windows was a large brass commemorative plate. Around 1970, Richard Blewett got Miss Anne Kinsman as his research assistant to gain permission to enter the disused church and record the inscription. It read:

In memory of Sir William Williams, Bart. of Tregullow who died March 24th 1870 aged 79. These windows are erected by his widow and children who mourn a beloved husband and affectionate father, while the poor and the needy deplore the loss of a kind and benevolent friend. He that hath pity on the poor lendeth unto the Lord.[8]

There were several other monuments listed by William Lake in his *Parochial History of Cornwall*, mostly relating to the Harveys of St Day, most prominantly Collan Harvey.

Church interior, c.1900.

Renovations

Since its construction in 1828, the church has undergone the usual renovations typical of any church, the years 1875, 1890, 1897 and 1901 perhaps being the most active. In January 1874 it was reported that a thorough restoration of church and cemetery was necessary. About 18 months later, in July 1875, E. Halligey and Olver, surveyors of Falmouth, estimated that repairs would cost £400. The *Royal Cornwall Gazette* reported:

The tower is in a wretchedly dilapidated condition, and in a worse state than any other part of the edifice. The woodwork is gradually giving way, and if something is not done, the tower must come down with a crash. New windows will be put in and the church will be thoroughly renovated and painted.[9]

At this time £200 was raised by a bazaar in the grounds of Tolgullow House, which featured a show by the Royal Marine Band. There were special excursion tickets by the West Cornwall Railway Co. to Scorrier Gate Station. Lord Champernowne donated £25. Several concerts to aid the fund were held at the Druids Hall, Redruth, and as far as the Polytechnic Hall in Falmouth, throughout 1877. Only ten years later the church was again in need of repair and new heating. The financial stress placed on the greatly diminished population was badly felt. On this occasion another £200 was necessary. Within 12 months enough money had been raised, work proceeded and the church must have appeared quite different:

The interior of the church is the result of much recent alteration, and presents a much improved appearance. The altar has been enlarged and raised, and is now the most prominent object in the sacred building. Choir stalls have been fitted in the chancel and the nave seats cut down and stained, a convenient choir vestry has been screened off at the west end.[10]

Much of the original church interior was removed at this time. A person signed as 'A Careful Restorer' wrote the following account in *The Cornishman*, after a visit to the church in October 1892.

I have visited the St Day church for the first time since its restoration, and I am heretical enough to say that alteration is not improvement in this particular instance. I recall some 20 years ago when, as a boy, I sat and slumbered in the old high back pews during sermon time, and awoke in time to join noisily in singing the beautiful old hymns. Then there were flaming chandeliers, with their family candles in winter time to lighten the gloom, and there was a solemn dignity about the old, high, carved pulpit and carved reading desk, where the parson read from the top storey and underneath him the clerk droningly uttered the responses. Where are the relics of this old time?

I confess though I am not antiquarian, that I felt saddened on Sunday to see the austere plainness of the church, with its little brass reading-stand, its altar with cross and other paraphernalia, and its paraffin lamps instead of burning wax candles.

Even the Ten Commandments, beneath the beautiful stained-glass memorial windows, have been obliterated: and in huge incongruous letters are the words 'My flesh is meat indeed' and 'My blood is drink indeed'. I imagine the words of the Ten Commandments are of more importance than these metaphorical utterances. But I admit the new seats, set widely apart, are more comfortable than the old ones; the surpliced male choir sang commendably; and Brother Cannon, one of our oratorical Townsmen, read sonorously and impressively, the lessons.

I am told the old pulpit was sold by public auction and so much firewood; and that a small and low pulpit will be used when someone is generous enough to present it; but forgive me if, progressive as I am in many ways, I consider that the spirit of over-restoration has been busily at work in St Day church.[11]

The same year two 'tortoise' stoves were installed to help warm what must have been – in the winter – a very cold church. Perhaps the most ambitious project during this decade was the erection of a new pulpit, dedicated in December 1897. The event was planned to coincide with Queen Victoria's Diamond Jubilee celebrations. Subscriptions towards the fund were invited throughout the year and were well supported by patrons at home and abroad. By November, H. Hems & Sons of Exeter were contracted to build the new pulpit, which was to be installed in the north side of the 'sacred fane'.[12]

When we view original photographs and postcards of the church interior, these final renovations are what we see. The original interior must have been quite different. The addition of stained-glass windows, the raised and enlarged altar, relocated pulpit, the screened choir vestry and new seating, all added splendid colour, function and comfort in contrast to the former whitewash, stone and plain furnishings.

The Sunday Schoolrooms

The Anglicans, like the Methodists, always understood the importance of Sunday schools. The Education Acts of the 1870s made provision for compulsory schooling. Before this time Sunday schools were, for many children, the only form of free education available. For local clergy it was to remain a means by which they could, perhaps, secure young minds that were encouraged to think and grow spiritually in the doctrine of the Church. The importance of Sunday schools in fulfilling a social role within the parish, by promoting secular as well as Christian knowledge must also be recognised.

By the 1890s, it was reported that the Sunday Schoolrooms at St Day were 'very dilapidated' and unfit for use. The Church had its eye on the plot of land opposite Rock House (now the present vicarage) and applied to Mr Mallock, MP, who generously donated the land.[13] It was fortunate for the community that around this time, Passmore Edwards, a successful businessman from Blackwater, was donating large sums of money towards the building of various academic, religious and public buildings around the county. His contribution to the county's amenities was broad enough to encompass St Day, and when the Revd J.J. Murley asked him for help in September 1892, he obliged by agreeing to fund most of the project. His personal motive was that he 'wished [to do] this in memory of his uncle who had lived in St Day and had been connected with various Sunday schools for 50 years.' He agreed to build the Schoolrooms, leaving the parishioners to furnish the interior. The news was received with delight by the people of St Day. John Symons, also of Blackwater, designed the building and built it.

The Clergy

Having touched on some aspects of St Day's church life throughout the nineteenth century, we should observe something of the lives of the clergy at St Day. These men, some of whom worked with deep religious conviction, should be recorded for posterity. The first vicar of the new St Day church was the Revd George Birch Baraston, MA, previously vicar to Wendron. He was succeeded in 1828 by the Revd James George Wulff, BA, who left in 1833 to become vicar of Illogan. The Revd Alexander Allen Vaudrey, MA, continued in 1833 for 13 years until 1846, undertaking the first curacy of St Agnes. From 3 September 1846, the Revd William Stothart, BA, maintained the incumbency for eight years before moving to Thorpe Hesley in Yorkshire. He was followed by the Revd Thomas Henry, who stayed for three years before moving to Kirt-Christ-Lezayne, on the Isle of Man. Little is known about these early clergymen who witnessed the great growth and boom years as St Day prospered as a busy mining town.[14]

St Day then saw the arrival of the Revd John Bannister, perhaps one of the most celebrated clergymen within the community, on account of his major research and contribution towards Cornish history, in the publication of his *Glossary of Cornish Names*. Dr Bannister was a graduate of Dublin University and Cambridge where he had taken honours in Mathematics and Classics, in particular studying Hebrew. It was therefore no surprise that when he arrived in Cornwall in 1857 from Belper in Derbyshire, he immediately became interested in 'old Cornish and the kindred branches of the Celtic language.' Due to lameness, he was unable to travel about the parish, so he threw himself into the labours of collecting and recording Cornish place names. He left a library containing many unusual editions of work relating to theology, early typography, philology (especially Hebrew and Celtic) and antiquities amongst other subjects, together with a considerable collection of minerals and fossils.

However, Dr Bannister's academic achievements must not overshadow his 16-year contribution to the community at St Day as curate. Despite his physical disabilities he fulfilled his duties with enthusiasm. He worked for the poor and needy at St Day, who held him in great affection. Clearly he observed no class distinctions and was concerned for the temporal and spiritual welfare of each and every one of his parishioners. Locally, he became involved with the Freemasons, which interested him immensely. He was always willing to partake in the various ceremonies. His Mother Lodge was the Tregullow, 1006, of which he was a regular attendant. He was taken ill with congestion of the lungs at the early age of 57 and died on Saturday 30 August 1873.[15]

St Day continued to be blessed with enthusiastic clergy, with the appointment of the Revd Edward Olivey, who was well known in the county as an excellent judge of cattle and horses, an authority on agricultural matters and one in constant demand at agricultural meetings. He was a fine athlete, a superb cricketer, and declined participation in football matches only because he felt it 'unseemly for clergy to enter the pulpit with black eyes from such a match.' The Revd Olivey established rugby, football and cricket clubs during his time at St Day as well as a reading room and technical instruction classes for young men. The 1870s must have been difficult years for the people at St Day as almost every mine closed in the vicinity of Gwennap. Undoubtedly the Revd Olivey felt that some technical or educational opportunities might improve prospects for

Vicarage front lawn, c.1900, the scene of events such as fêtes.

men 'of all classes' who began to leave St Day seeking employment elsewhere.

Hard times fell heavy and the Revd Olivey with his wife, fulfilled another important social role; that of providing for the poor and needy. In January 1879 we find:

Our Vicar (Revd Olivey) has been supplying soup to the poor for the last eight weeks and Lady Williams of Tolgullow, Mr Harvey of Torquay, Mrs Andrew of St Day and a few other kind ladies have [given] *over 20 tons of coal to the poor of the neighbourhood.*[16]

In April 1891, after 17 years, the vicar announced that he was leaving St Day. He had decided, with the consent of the Lord Bishop of the Diocese, to exchange livings with the Revd J.J. Murley of St Merryn. By September, the vicar and his wife were ready to depart. A formal presentation in the crowded church Schoolroom with the gift of a clock left the couple to bid farewell to a community whom they helped through mixed fortunes, and a community that would miss them greatly.

The lasting bonds of friendship were, however, to continue. For the next 30 years the Revd Edward Olivey and his wife returned to St Day at Christmas and on Feast Days with seasonal gifts, especially tea and sugar for the elderly people, which were usually distributed by Mr S. Kinsman, draper of St Day. Reminiscences of their kindness were always recalled, especially by the sick whom the Revd Olivey and his wife would take out in their 'wagonette and pair' to provide fresh air to help them recover from their illness. May these extracts record such good deeds, not to be lost in the mists of time.

The community at St Day seemed to look on with great expectations as they received their next incumbent. During his 20 years at St Day the Revd John James Murley's contribution was significant, especially his duties to the poor who undoubtedly benefited from his kindness. His generosity towards so many in the parish can be illustrated in his involvement in the annual 'treat' for the children of Chapel Street, which he usually supervised. Whether the children of each street in the town enjoyed an annual tea party is uncertain, but clearly Chapel Street enjoyed this church-inspired event:

Favoured with fine weather, the West End was on Wednesday the scene of great excitement owing to the annual treat of the Children of Chapel Street, [who] *this year to the surprise of the inhabitants, were treated to a knife and fork tea, with a quantity of fruit. This was mainly due to the noble efforts of J. and H. Mathews and Mesdames Teague, Davey, Trengrove, and friends. The whole proceedings passed off in a most satisfactory manner under the supervision of the worthy Vicar (the Revd J.J. Murley), Capt. Gidley, Mr Theo. Michell, and others.*[17]

The Revd J.J. Murley must always be remembered for his great church-renovating activities, which benefited St Day; in particular the new Sunday Schoolrooms, which have served St Day so importantly since, were largely the results of his negotiations and hard work. During his stay many societies flourished at St Day, among them a Choral Society considered to be one of the finest anywhere. When he was offered the living at his native St Erth, he accepted, as he felt a 'decided call' to the parish. On 2 May 1912, the vicar and his wife enjoyed a celebration of their times and tireless work at St Day.[18]

From this period the Revd W.C. Reeder acted as curate-in-charge, until July 1913, when he became curate-in-charge of St Martin-in-Meneage, and later curate of Crowan. This interim period was concluded by the ordination of Claude B.D. Gale, of Chichester Theological College, who was ordained as deacon and licensed to the curacy of St Day on St Matthew's Day by the Bishop of Truro.[19]

However, each of these clergy was temporary, and a permanent incumbent was needed. The Revd Walter W. Bickford of St Anne's, Gunnislake, was appointed in March 1912. He was considered a 'high Churchman and a successful worker amongst men.'[20] Within a year the Revd Bickford was making efforts to establish the Male Voice Choir, recruiting men from all over the district. Within a short while attendees to his choral class numbered around 50 and the group was of a high competition standard. The vicar had a particular interest in music and choral groups – most notably the Male Voice Choir of 1922, whom he trained in the Schoolrooms.

The Revd Evan Thomas arrived at St Day in 1923 and occupied the curacy for the next 20 years. During his time at St Day, the church was restored, the organ renovated, electric lighting installed and an electric organ blower fitted, all at a cost of £2,000. Wartime found the Revd Thomas as Air Raid Patrol Warden (he began the group at St Day). After his resignation he became vicar of Boconnoc-with-Braddock, near Lostwithiel.[21]

While the Revd Thomas had ministered only two churches in 30 years, his successor, the Revd Leslie Verne Jolly, had, in the space of 20 years, held rather more posts. He was ordained priest in 1923 in Montreal, Canada, was priest-in-charge of St James Old Town, Maine, USA from 1924–25, and was subsequently curate of Padstow, St Austell, Isles of Scilly, St Winnow, Calstock, Towednack and St Eval, before arriving at St Day. The fact that he was also an ex-serviceman makes this exhaustive list even more remarkable! On 16 December 1943, he was instituted by Dr J.W. Hunkin, Bishop of Truro, who quoted:

The Revd Jolly had had considerable experience of life. He had travelled far and wide and had worked under various, sometimes discouraging conditions, but he never lost heart. He kept up his studies in a remarkable way, and was a preacher of unusual ability.[22]

In May 1946, the Revd Frederick Ernest Charman, at the young age of 33, became the new vicar at St Day, and the youngest incumbent in the diocese of Truro. He was an accomplished tenor vocalist, pianist and organist, after graduating from the Royal College of Music. Five years later the Revd Charman departed from St Day, having accepted the living of Woodlands, near Wimborne, Dorset.[23]

As usual, the vacancy was quickly filled; however, this time by a Cornishman all the way from a parish in Wynberg, Cape Town, South Africa. The Revd ? Hancock was installed in front of a large congregation on Saturday 25 August 1951. Mr E.J. Eustice (senior churchwarden) welcomed the vicar and his wife, commenting that St Day had never had a 'Cousin-Jack' as vicar before.[24]

In 1955, Revd Eric Hall arrived to his new St Day ministry. He was to become one of the most controversial figures in the church's history. Within six months of his arrival, the church was condemned, locked, and for over 40 years was to remain unoccupied. It was a difficult time, but this man labelled 'vicar-militant' pushed the parish forward with positive drives of energy, bringing about successive changes which have since become integral to our community.

As a young man the Revd Hall felt he had been destined for the ministry, but gave up his early theological training to become a teacher at the Lawn School, St Austell, for four years. The Second World War saw him serving in the RAF and his administrative abilities led him to promotion as Squadron-Leader. He held a welfare post in India where he was responsible for the building of a 500-seat cinema for the troops in Delhi. Before the project was complete, government expenditure was suspended. The Revd Hall furiously challenged the crackdown – and won – to complete the troops' cinema. These same qualities were to stand by him all his life at St Day, where he consistently challenged and defeated local authorities who denied the people of St Day an adequate water supply in the 1950s and sewerage in the 1960s. He left the Forces at the end of the war and was ordained within the Church by the Bishop of Exeter, before becoming a curate at Okehampton.[25]

More recent clergy have included the Revd Timothy Van Carpiett, Revd Paul Foot and the current Revd Andrew Gogh, all of whom have continued to build strong spiritual and pastoral links at St Day, as well as lead the church within the community.

Church Closure

One of the greatest controversies in the history of St Day was undoubtedly the closure of the church in August 1956. Father Hall maintained that he was told the church was 'in a good state of repair'. Yet when he arrived, 'he found the Church of the Most Holy Trinity and Mission Halls in a sad state of disrepair.' The vicar soon called upon the opinion of 'three of the foremost ecclesiastical building specialists in the West of England' to examine the church to see if the acoustics could be improved. There followed a full-scale survey in which one of the architects, T. Henwood-Hicks, reported:

The spire and pillars have been defying the accepted laws of science for a number of years, during which time the likelihood of structural failure has been worsened. In the unpredictable future there may be a collapse without warning.[26]

He added:

... that the failure, which could bring the 70 tons of masonry down on top of the congregation, would be most likely to occur as the result of frost, or during the vibrations when the organ was played at full volume.

The architect condemned the church as dangerous:

... walls were found to be of 'pot' granite already decomposing, pillars were of disintegrating brick, pillars were bending under the weight of a shifting roof, arches were of an inferior timber plastered over, plaster was dropping, lead guttering had been removed, water poured in over the choir, a rusted hot water system needed a £1,500 replacement.[27]

Although the roof structure seemed to cause most concern, the tower presented a host of problems which appeared only 20 years after construction when it had to be bolstered with two metal pins.[28] Retrospectively, the community of St Day was thrust into turmoil. Several leading community members openly criticised Revd Hall; they felt the church was not constructed of 'pot-granite' and was not beyond repair.

Today, the church tower is still standing. The roof is not intact because of a scare in 1985; dynamite was used to demolish it after it was discovered children were occasionally playing inside the structure. Chris Massie, a consultant civil and structural engineer of the partnership, Massie, Ludnow & Jenkins, conducted a survey on the Holy Trinity Church, St Day, in November 1991, for the St Day Historical and Conservation Society. He considered that with all the correct remedial works and procedures, the church could again be made available to the public:

The church is constructed of thick masonry outer walls formed on the outer surface in dressed square micro-granite. Micro granite is a fine grained rock formed either in veins or on the chilled margins of a larger intrusion. Despite the ravages which the structure has been subjected to, the outer walls are in remarkably good condition generally.[29]

Further complications had arisen when Revd Hall failed to secure the necessary insurance, as he was unable to find a company prepared to insure the building for public use. An estimate of £3,000 for immediate repairs followed by another £7,000 to bring the building up to an acceptable standard, put the issue beyond resolve. The Bishop of Truro, Dr E.R. Morgan, called upon the architect at Exeter Cathedral to give a final opinion. He confirmed what earlier architects had stated, reinforcing the idea of 'pot-granite' as being the 'main trouble'. After several meetings of the Parochial Church Council, the building was condemned as 'unsafe' and closure was enforced. To some extent, the personal views of Revd Hall provoked the closure. He met some challenges from local opinion:

> *Some St Day people tell me they think their church could have been saved. Certainly it could at a £15,000 cost at present-day prices. Could they find the money? And if they could, why perpetuate a building architecturally ugly inside and out?*[30]

On that fateful Wednesday night in August 1956, Revd Hall moved into the Mission Room. Chairs were taken from the church and borrowed from a local St John Ambulance hall. Other furnishings were removed and placed in storage. A makeshift altar was arranged and a few modifications gave the Mission Room the appearance of a place of worship. The move was of course temporary, but soon other problems emerged. The Mission Room was too small and inadequate. Revd Hall discovered:

> *The difficulty now is that we cannot get all the people in the room on a Sunday evening and have to pack the chairs in the aisle. We have had both weddings and funerals there, but practically all the chairs have to be moved out for a funeral, and a wedding becomes a pretty hectic business.*[31]

Towards a New Spiritual Vision

It appears that around this time the population at St Day was beginning to rise slightly. With his determined attitude and by becoming immediately involved in parish politics, Revd Hall began to win a deeper appreciation and respect from the community. He became a 'voice' for St Day, battling hard against local authorities in attempts to improve the water supply and help secure a much needed sewerage scheme. Each was a necessary and important

Above: *Confirmation at Holy Trinity Church in 1973.*

Above right: *Market Square Palm Sunday service, early 1960s.*

Right: *St Day Church Hall, 1958.*

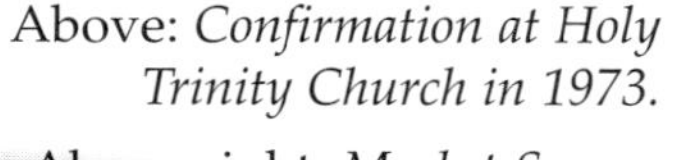

This image: ***Father Hall leads the St Day Feast procession through Church Street, 1968.***

project and Revd Hall combined these with his effort to improve his place of worship. He was a man of ideas. Within two years he acquired an ex-Army hut as a Village Hall. Today, parts of this can still be seen incorporated into the church complex. To some extent this relieved pressure on the temporary church facilities, but it was still inadequate. The vicar opened a world-wide appeal for the cause. The response was a variety of contributions that came from home, abroad and diocesan funds. The costs for a sufficient development amounted to £10,000.

By 1964, around £5,200 was in hand for some of the work to begin. The architect, Mr Giles Bloomfield, an expert in modern church design, of John Crowther Associates, Truro, prepared plans in 1966 and a year later work began.[32] The enlarged church would seat 160 people – almost double the number of before. One of the main features was to be a free-standing altar, removed from the old church, reduced by two-fifths in width and surmounted on three broad granite steps. This was to become the focal point of the new building. The use of light was thoughtfully considered. A hidden window was incorporated into the ceiling space above the altar at each corner, to produce a natural illuminating effect around the western end. Seating was conveniently arranged at the front and around both sides of the altar, allowing the congregation to feel closer to the clergy within the sanctuary. Now communicants could gather around the communion table for the 'Lord's Supper.' The rear gallery remained, even though it was separated from some of the congregation. The overall effect was one of space and freedom combined with modernity.

Relics and items from the old church were installed into the new worship area. Among them, four brass candelabra hung over each corner of the altar. The hymn reader and an ornate brass crucifix inlaid with copper survive to combine the old with the new, which also includes a large wall-mounted carving of Christ crucified, a cast relief of a scene at Calvary and a wooden carving of the Trinity depicted as Christ in his Father's hands with the Holy Spirit above and present. Sadly funds were insufficient to continue the plans for the 'Old Church'. They were, under this scheme, never to materialise.

The Walsingham Pilgrimages

It was during his ministry at St Day that the Revd Hall felt compelled to reintroduce pilgrimages. In the north-west corner provision was made for a shrine for the devotion of Our Lady. A small statue of Our Lady with the Christ Child is mounted upon the wall and maintains a direct spiritual continuity with the former medieval shrine at St Day. The Revd Hall led a group of 38 pilgrims to Walsingham in Norfolk for the first of many visits in May 1962. At St Day the event was to become an annual festival to celebrate the birth of the Virgin Mary, after which the Statue of Our Lady is carried around the 'Old Church' by four attendants, leading a long procession including priests, servers and lay people. There is a sprinkling of water from the Holy Well at Walsingham. This rather recent tradition continues at St Day.

Conserving Old Holy Trinity Church

Throughout the 1980s–'90s, the St Day Old Church Preservation Society worked tirelessly on the future of the ruined church building. By organising ground clearances and fund-raising, as well as various administrative tasks, the group, led by Mark Johnson and Bernadette Fallon, managed to make real headway in securing a future restoration for the site. By obtaining Objective One funding and linking with the Trevithick Trust, the society managed the restoration of much of the existing structure. Guided by the Cornwall Archaeological Unit, the removal of debris and making safe of the site was carefully conducted. The stabilisation of the walls, tower and other key areas followed. The remains of the stained-glass windows were also given a protective covering. Kerrier District Council, through the Mineral Tramways Project, funded interpretation panels, to develop the whole site into an interpretative centre, which today has become an important focus for visitors to the area.

Notes

1 *West Briton*, 7.4.1826.
2 *West Briton*, 1.9.1826.
3 *West Briton*, 2.8.1828.
4 Trevithick, Annie, *A Short History of St Day*, c.1897, p.6.
5 *Royal Cornwall Gazette*, 19.7.1906.
6 Probert, J.C.C., *Sociology of Cornish Methodism*, (n.d.).
7 Lake, William, *Parochial History of Cornwall*, *Vol. 2.*, 1868, p.135.
8 Blewett, R.R., 'These Things Have Been', Inst. 66 (May 1970).
9 *Royal Cornwall Gazette*, 13.11.1890.
10 *Royal Cornwall Gazette*, 29.10.1891.
11 *The Cornishman*, 20.10.1892. (The visitor was almost certainly Herbert Thomas.)
12 *Royal Cornwall Gazette*, 11.11.1897, 9.12.1897 and 14.2.1901.
13 *Royal Cornwall Gazette*, 3.3.1892.
14 Lake, William, *Parochial History of Cornwall*, *Vol. 2.*, 1868, p.135.
15 *Royal Cornwall Gazette*, 6.9.1873.
16 *Royal Cornwall Gazette*, 3.1.1879.
17 *Royal Cornwall Gazette*, 29.8.1895.
18 *Royal Cornwall Gazette*, 1.2.1911.
19 *Royal Cornwall Gazette*, 17.7.1913 and 25.9.1913.
20 *Royal Cornwall Gazette*, 14.3.1912.
21 *Royal Cornwall Gazette*, 23.9.1943.
22 *Royal Cornwall Gazette*, 17.11.1943 and 22.12.1943.
23 *West Briton*, 22.2.1951.
24 *West Briton*, 27.8.1951.
25 Unidentified newspaper extract in author's possession.
26 Unidentified newspaper extract in author's possession.
27 *Western Morning News*, 12.2.1957.
28 Unidentified newspaper extract in author's possession.
29 Massie, Ludlow & Jenkins. Ref: CDM. R1937R1. Nov. 1991.
30 Unidentified newspaper extract in author's possession.
31 *Western Morning News*, 12.2.1957.
32 *Camborne-Redruth Packet*, 3.3.1971.

Above: *Primitive Methodist tea treat, 1910. This is not Carharrack Band.*

Right: *Primitive Methodist tea treat, 1913, with tea-treat buns and mugs in evidence. Were the boaters part of a school uniform?*

Primitive Methodist tea treat, 1912, outside the chapel door.

Fifteen

The Challenge of Chapels

Early Methodism

The exact origins of Methodism in St Day remain vague, although we know that of the 63 Methodist members listed for Gwennap in the 1767 West Cornwall Circuit Membership Book, four came from St Day, Francis Quick (a tinner), Rebecca Trewartha, Ann Simons, A. Taylor, and Ann Simons, (her daughter); two from Vogue, Margaret Jane and her daughter; and two from Tolgullow, Tristam Powning (a carpenter) and his wife Elizabeth (of 'Tolgula').[1]

Primitive Methodist Sunday school tea treat, 1910.

The existence of a Methodist Society Class may be considered in the light of a will dated 12 February 1796, left by Francis Quick, which contained a condition for John Launder, allowing 21s. yearly 'for permitting the Methodist people... to worship God as they now do and did hereto fore.'[2] Such provision was probably for an early meeting-place in St Day as the Launceston Methodist Chapel Stewards Account Book of 1800–57 contains an entry in 1815 for 'Money received on account of the Chapel [Launceston] – [from Methodists at] St Day £3.7s.6d.'

The Bible Christians and the Primitive Methodist movements were both well received in Cornwall, probably because both appealed to the growing labouring classes and both claimed to return to the 'fundamental' concerns, of which Methodism had lost sight. Primitive Methodism soon made headway after William Clowes (a founder of Primitive Methodism and a Staffordshire potter) visited St Day during his first Cornwall tour in 1825. John Probert in his *History of Primitive Methodism in Cornwall* highlights Clowes' early visits to St Day, as recorded in his diary during October 1825:

> *Monday saw his return to the Redruth area. In the evening he stayed with Mr Dennis of St Day. He tells how, when he formerly preached here, he was wet with sweat and very exhausted and had had to return three miles because noone had offered him food, drink or lodging.*[3]

On a further visit to St Day, one man allowed him to share 'half his bed' and with some determination he managed to establish a 'meeting house' where he informs us that one of the first members was Mrs Jane Richards and her husband who had opened their house 'until a more commodious place' was found. Wasting no time Clowes linked Redruth, Illogan and St Day in the West of Cornwall with the Hull Circuit in the North of England. A Circuit Plan for 1827 lists Sunday worship at St Day, Todpool and Carnmarth, all within Gwennap.

Primitive Methodists Down Backway

With the foundation stone of the new church at St Day laid in 1826, the Primitives quickly set themselves the task of building their own chapel 'down Backway', later known as Telegraph Street. A deed, dated 1827, refers to:

> *... a Chapel built on a plot of ground belonging to John Messer. The Revd Richard Abbey engaged to build it and agreed to pay £1.10s.0d. yearly as the ground rent. The deed cost £6.6s.0d. When the foundation stone was laid Abbey abandoned the Chapel and William Driffield, to preserve it for the Methodists had to build it and make it connexional.*[4]

The chapel is said to have been 'square with a thatched roof'[5] and must have made an attractive addition to the other thatched and whitewashed buildings along Telegraph Street. The Primitives probably just beat the Wesleyan Methodists to the opening of their chapel. Later, in 1828, the Wesleyans placed Chapel Street on the town map; the Anglicans did the same with Church Street when they opened the church. The Primitives seem to have settled in well and in 1832, Hugh Bourne, the other founder member, visited St Day. The following year William Clowes returned, but this time to a more enthusiastic congregation almost too large for the humble chapel down Backway. A hint at harmonious relations between the Primitives and the Baptists emerged when Clowes was invited to use their chapel in Scorrier Street.

The Revd William Driffield was left with the early debts of the chapel. At the back of the Redruth Chapel Accounts Book are two pages that refer to St Day Primitive Methodist finances for the years 1834–37. In 1836, we find a 'ballance hawing to W. Driffield... £29.10s.5d.' A note at the bottom says that the 'St Day Chapel is conveyed to Wm Wasley, St Day. He is the trustee and it is conveyed to the connexion.'

The Primitives had dealings with another Methodist group, the Methodist New Connexion Chapel at Burnwithian, in these formative years.[6] In September 1838, when the New Connexion opened their chapel, it was stated to have been 'purchased' lately from the Primitives.[7] Another source states that the Primitives were the last people to use the chapel at Burnwithian before it was 'taken down'. Possibly the Primitives used the chapel at Burnwithian for services whilst their chapel in Telegraph Street was being 'enlarged' in 1843.

Membership Numbers, 1830–58

1830: 16	*1838: 50*
1833: 11	*1844: 103*
1834: 23	*1845: 156*
1835: 32	*1847: 107*
1836: 65	*1850–58: 70–95 average*
1837: 80	*1850–58: 70–95 average*

The membership of the Primitive Methodist Chapel fluctuated considerably from 16 in 1830, to 156 during what may have been a 'revival' year in 1845. Whilst possibly maintaining over 100 members per year during the 1840s, this dropped slightly during the 1850s, averaging between 70 and 95 people. With a growing membership, they certainly felt overcrowded by the mid-1840s and began to extend their chapel. William Francis, writing in 1845, described the 'enlargement' of the chapel:

... the labours and zeal of the Primitive Race,
are crowned with success, so we judge from the case.
Their Chapel enlarged, and three hundred repair,
On Sabbath to breathe the Primitive air.[9]

The Primitives now had the available space to introduce a Sunday school.

In 1858 the Redruth Circuit was divided and St Day was made head of its own new circuit which included Creegbrawse, Threeburrows, Crosscombe, Goonbell and Mount Horam. The St Day Primitives again set about renovating and extending at Telegraph Street, adding 17 feet in length, a lobby and four extra windows. Originally, the chapel must have had a single window on the north and east sides. Internally, a new ceiling centre-piece measuring 6 feet in diameter was fitted and 100 new seats were added, making a total of 340 seats when the chapel was reopened on 8 January 1860.[10]

By the mid-1880s, the Primitives felt that they were outgrowing the chapel in Telegraph Street and built another in Scorrier Street, the old chapel becoming the Primitives' Sunday school. The memoirs of Miss G.M. Stephens describes other features of the inside of this building, which she attended as a Sunday school before its closure in 1913:

The Schoolroom was a plain building outside, but inside there were signs that it had once been a chapel. Just inside the entrance were several rows of fixed seats, some with draught-proof doors. There was a gallery overhead [which] *was not used because there were no seats. The main hall was bare except for the standing stoves which were used in winter.*[11]

The importance of the early Sunday schools in providing secular as well as religious instruction, illustrates the wider social responsibilities that Methodism met. For many children in the early-nineteenth century, this was the only form of education available. The Methodists maintained a strong hold on education well into the late-nineteenth century as a means of transferring their own moral and spiritual values. Miss Stephens' memoirs highlight a typical Sunday for the young St Day Primitive Methodist 'scholars':

The children sat in a circle of movable forms for the School, which was conducted by the Superintendent Mr Barnett. He had some help from a few adults who sat in among the children and kept some order. The School proceeded with a hymn, prayer, hymn, lesson for the day (introduced by a large picture) and then a Bible reading which also related to the picture. Each scholar who was able to read took a turn and then the Superintendent gave a talk about the lesson that had been read. After the School everybody walked from Telegraph Street down to the Chapel in Scorrier Street for the 11a.m. service which usually included a children's address. The School met again at 2:30p.m. consisting of more adults, male and female, and children in classes according to age. The same Bible lesson was used as in the morning and the session lasted an hour. Sometimes it was addressed by the preacher for the day. At the end of each quarter the lessons were reviewed, the pictures being briefly shown again and questions asked about them.[12]

Top: *Primitive Sunday school women's Bible class, 1913.*

Second from top: *The men's Bible class, 1913.*

Third from top: *Primitive Methodist Sunday school treat, 1910.*

Above: *Primitive Methodist Sunday school treat, 1912.*

Many of St Day's Primitive Methodist Chapel and Sunday-school anniversaries were large affairs, with some even being held at the Gwennap Pit. Large groups, a change of venue and traditions in 'camp meetings', summer weather, etc. were all reasons why the Pit was chosen. Again, Miss Stephens reminds us that by the early-twentieth century, customs had not really changed:

> *The Sunday School anniversary required much practicing of special hymns along with the Chapel Choir. On the day, the children sat on a platform which had been set up in the Chapel and took part in the three services of the day. At the afternoon service we were joined by members, teachers, scholars, from the Wesleyans. Once a year a 'Camp Meeting' was held on a Sunday afternoon. There was no afternoon School on that day and everybody, children and older people, walked around the town to one or two places where they sang hymns and listened to short addresses. The first stopping place was usually Tatey's Court* ['tatty' meaning potato, now Williams' Court], *the space opposite the Town Clock. About 5:30p.m. the procession moved on to Gwennap Pit for the last Service of the day.*

Primitive Methodists, Scorrier Street

By the early 1880s the Primitives felt pressed with the need to move. When the lease for the Old Town Hall became available, they competed with the Salvation Army but managed to secure it. As a former Baptist Chapel (and Temperance Hall) built c.1803, the Town Hall was probably similar in design to the Primitives' chapel down Backway; somewhat plain in appearance, thatched and made of cob. For these reasons the Primitives decided to demolish the building and build a new chapel to their own design that matched their needs. James Hicks, the Redruth architect, was asked for a design while J. Williams of Carharrack was contracted to complete the masonry, and W.H. Moyle of Bissoe the carpentry. In May 1885 it was reported that: 'The Temperance Hall at St Day is shortly to be taken down and on its site a commodious and beautiful Chapel is to be erected by the Primitive Methodists.'[13]

Hicks designed a Gothic façade, with a steep roof, pinnacles and pointed windows inset with tinted glass. Around 450 seats were planned, which with a budget cost of £2 per seat, meant the total cost of the building would be around £900. The foundation stones were laid on Thursday 12 June 1885 and the chapel was completed and opened by 13 May 1886. Many St Day inhabitants remember the bronze-coloured cobble entrance, with the date '1886' set in ivory-coloured cobbles at the front of the building. The heavy debt incurred was immediately felt by the Primitives and so fortnightly 'entertainments', usually in some musical form, with choirs, solos, recitals and various violin and instrumental performances were held to raise funds. A heating system added more financial strain in 1889, despite a boiler being given by Mr Moyle of Tolgullow and the work being carried out by Mr Moody of Truro. In the first three years, between 1889 and 1891, the Primitives lost their ministers annually and in 1891 it was reported that, 'We are sorry to find the circuit is in such a sad state financially and what the Ministers will do to get their money is a query!'[14] (The Primitive Methodists at this time worked a system whereby if the circuit was short of money, the ministers' pay was cut.) Although they worked hard at reducing their debt, it still stood at a considerable £530 in 1902.

North Corner Sunday School Rooms

By 1912 the lease on the Telegraph Street premises was due to expire, so the Primitives decided to abandon these and build a new Sunday Schoolroom on land at North Corner. A Mrs Jeffery had made some provision in her will for the land and probably the building. A deed was drawn up on 18 October 1912 between Francis R. Rodd Esq. of Trebartha Hall and the following Primitive Methodist Trustees: John Leverton (painter), Thomas Crocker (of Ninnis, farm labourer), William Richards (painter), Stephen John Hockey (draper), Joseph Barnet (fruiterer), John Littlejohns (miner), John Eva (of Trefula, farmer), William G. Matthews (of Wheal Rose, blacksmith) and the Revd Thomas Lloyd Page the superintendent minister. It is interesting to note the relatively humble occupations of the Primitive Methodist trustees, compared to the wealthier business owners, which can be found among the trustees of the Wesleyan chapel, perhaps highlighting the appeal of each Methodist denomination to different social groups within the community. The Primitive trustees agreed to purchase for £70 'all that stable yard and premises situated and lying in the Town of St Day, which is now and has been for some time in the occupation of the author.'[15]

These same stables would have housed the Jersey cars and various other horse-drawn vehicles used by the author to transport the St Day Methodists on their numerous anniversary outings, tea treats and concerts.

The Redruth architect Sampson Hill designed the new Schoolrooms and the building measured 56 feet long by 24 feet wide. Inside were two classrooms, separated by a wooden partition. Built by William Hensley of St Day, it cost £600, of which £200 had been raised. On Thursday 19 June 1913, the foundation stones were laid.[16] The Schoolrooms were opened in November 1913 and dedicated to the memory of Mrs Jeffery. The old chapel down Backway eventually became disused for worship and was sold, becoming at different times a garage and coal stores until its conversion to a dwelling house in the 1990s. Despite a large debt of £700 in 1920, the Primitive Methodists continued to strive forward and cleared this by 1923, a remarkable feat.

By 1913 Litchfield House became the minister's manse, also at North Corner, and this continued until the Methodist Union became more focused locally in 1934.[17] Around 1930, St Day was still the head of a six-chapel circuit, with Truro, Falmouth and then Flushing joining to form the St Day, Truro and Falmouth Primitive Methodist Circuit. The Primitives were active with their two usual Sunday services, a Wednesday evening service and a 'Women's Own' gathering on Thursday afternoons. With the local merging of the Methodist Union in 1932, the circuit was divided and returned to the Redruth Circuit where it has remained. During the Second World War, services were held at the North Corner Schoolrooms during the winter, because of the blackouts. At the end of the war, membership numbers continued to decline; its average membership was 16. At this time Probert commented:

> *Only a handful are left in both the large Chapels at St Day. St Day has to a large extent been kept together by two men, Mr R.J. Knowles and Mr L. Wills, who died recently. The future of Methodism in St Day is very much in the balance.*[18]

St Day Primitive Methodist Chapel, c.1897.

Primitive Methodist Sunday school foundation-stone laying, 1913.

First Wesleyan Methodist Chapel, Chapel Street, St Day. Built in 1828, it is now two dwellings. Several features remain on the front of the buildings.

Wesleyan Methodists, Chapel Street

The first Wesleyan chapel was built in 1828. By 1840 the Sunday school was thriving and the Wesleyans were looking to expand.[19] More 'revivals' and increasing membership in the early 1840s encouraged the St Day Wesleyans to move. The Revd Richard Moody of Gwennap wrote to a prominent Methodist figure, Dr Jabez Bunting, in 1842, explaining:

> *Our friends at St Day (near Gwennap) having purchased the seceding James Jones Chapel (at Burnwithian) which was built in the above Town, pulled it down and erected an excellent Chapel and Vestry for the use of the Wesleyan Methodists.*[20]

James Jones was a Wesleyan minister who left the denomination and joined the Methodist New Connexion. He was stationed at the Truro and St Day New Connexion Circuit in 1835. The letter confirms that the Wesleyans built their chapel at the West End of St Day with materials from the Burnwithian chapel by the 1840s. The letter continues:

> *The Trustees are desirous to sell the old premises (at Chapel Street) as they are no longer wanted. The Old Chapel is lease-hold property, very small and much dilapidated, worth not more than forty pounds and belongs to the Trustees of Carharrack Chapel, who wish to sell it and to apply the money to pay off some of the debt of Carharrack Chapel.*

An advertisement appearing in the *West Briton* on 4 February 1842 offered the sale of the chapel, which it purported would be suitable for two dwelling houses or a warehouse. The original chapel today stands as two dwellings.

Wesleyan Methodists, West End

In a deed dated 2 March 1844, the trustees of the new Wesleyan chapel at the West End of St Day are mentioned as James Nancarrow (mine agent), Thomas Mitchell (mine agent), Richard Mitchell (merchant), John Nicholls (butcher), John Hawke (painter) and Richard Michell (cordwainer). The deed was made between these trustees and John Ridgway of Couldon Place, Shelton, Stafforshire Potteries, Esq. 'when purchasing the Methodist New Connexion chapel at Burnwithien.'[21] By December 1844, the chapel was complete and opened at a cost said to be £1,200 and with 550 seats. St Day Wesleyans continued in the Gwennap Circuit, but remained a Class Society to Carharrack for another 14 years until 1858.

The building was large and classical, rather typical of Georgian times. Internally, downstairs were three rows of pews facing the pulpit. Later, when the organ was installed, a rostrum replaced the pulpit. Upstairs, a four-sided gallery offered maximum seating for the congregation. An interesting arrangement was made for the building of the chapel in 1844; it was built by a 'double contract', which meant that in order to get the wall up quickly, the work was given to two masons, who worked skilfully and at high speed. The contractors were John Williams of Carharrack and James Kinsman of Scorrier Street. The fact that the building never featured 'settlement' was a testimony to the quality of workmanship, despite working under such conditions.[22]

The Wesleyan Methodists seemed to promote an outward image of self-help, thrift, hard work, deference, and teetotalism. The Wesleyan Methodist Improvement Society was typical of the role Methodists took upon themselves to advocate among their congregation, offering 'intellectual improvement or recreation for the young'. The Wesleyan Temperance Society was also high on the Methodist agenda for social reform. Of course alcohol was considered a 'social ill' by most Methodists, which led to the introduction of Temperance drinks such as the 'New Era Beer'. This seemed to sell well, probably because the agent for the product was the chapel organist. Sermons frequently referred to the evils and misery which alcohol might inflict upon indulgent persons, as a Wesleyan service held in the Temperance Hall in January 1870 reveals:

> *Mr Uren of Plymouth, in his usual eloquent manner, exposed the fearful miseries of strong drink. He spoke for an hour and the salient points in his address called forth repeated applause.*[23]

Former headmaster of St Day's school, R. Blewett, recounts a charming story of a Wesleyan preacher who he witnessed giving a sermon on the evils of drink. The preacher silenced the congregation, when he produced a glass of whisky and a worm. He placed the worm into the glass of whisky and it promptly died. 'Here we witness the evils of drink', he declared from the pulpit. An elderly lady in the crowd replied, 'Could you please tell me that brand of whisky? I could do with some to clear my worms.'

In a mining district which had around 16 public houses and several beerhouses, the Temperance advocates had a difficult task. Mr Uren campaigned tirelessly for another 20 years and managed to secure 85 teetotal pledges at a Temperance meeting in the Wesleyan chapel in 1895.[24] He was supported by the

West End Wesleyans

Top left: *The Wesleyan Methodist Chapel, c.1900. Note the double 'aisle' entrances and the very fine 'classical' façade.*

Top right: *Interior of the Wesleyan chapel Sunday Schoolrooms, c.1900. The text at the rear reads 'They that hear shall live.' The other displays show the Commandments, the Lord's Prayer and the Belief.*

Above: *The reopening of the Wesleyan Methodist Chapel, September 1913.*

Right: *Wesleyan Methodist outing to Porthlowan, c.1897.*

Above: *St Day Wesleyan Band of Hope Temperance pledge certificate, 1897.*

Right: *Band of Hope procession in Church Street by Cedars Lodge, c.1897.*

Wesleyan Band of Hope, started in 1876 for the sole purpose of enforcing teetotal policies. As late as 1906, the British Women's Temperance Association continued themes of teetotalism, as it formed a branch in St Day's Wesleyan Schoolrooms.[25]

Sunday schools were fundamental to church and chapel alike, but by the early 1880s the Wesleyans felt hard pushed to accommodate their young scholars in the chapel. The Wesleyan Trustee Minute-Book (1881–1913) outlines the beginnings and development of the Wesleyan Sunday school building. In July 1882, the committee ventured to Poldice 'to see if some materials consisting of doors, windows, flooring', etc., would be suitable for the new Schoolroom. Shortly afterwards it was decided that 'a building could be erected' presumably from salvage materials available. The same month also mentions a 'meadow adjoining the Chapel now occupied by John Nicholls, for the erection of a school. The cost must not exceed £200.' In September 1882 Messrs Whitford & Sons were thanked for their 'unsolicited generous gifts of old materials from Poldice.' In March 1883 the committee decided to pay 6s. in lieu for 'the potatoes in the meadow from the ground on which the Schoolroom is built.'

The minutes further reflect the regular activities and concerns of the Wesleyans from the same period. Other entries include:

1884: the organ-blower to be stationed in the gallery to communicate with the organist – this would overcome difficulties with speaking tubes.
February 1885: use of Schoolrooms for Mutual Improvement Classes.
1887: School not to be let for political meetings.
1888: Superintendent of St Day Primitives to speak at meeting.
August 1889: 30 vacant sittings.
June 1890: 44 vacant sittings.
May 1893: Captain Stephen Davey of Dolcoath invited to preach.
1894: Jubilee season – a large collection of £25.27s.0d.
1894: Mr John Rooke of Carew House offered the sum of £50 towards 'the purchase of land for a cemetery' on condition that 'the matter be undertaken in the following 12 months'. (Not carried out)
1896: Organist paid £6 per annum.
1897: More alterations.
May 1900: Reference to 'orchestra' which may suggest that the Wesleyans had a group of instrumentalists before the harmonium.
September 1904: William Bennetts, Richard Chapman, John Hall, John Spurrier, John Thomas, Fred Hart, Joseph Teague-Letcher, made Trustees.
1910: Eight different people were asked 'for the price of oil per gallon'.

These seem busy but typical years for the Wesleyans.

The Wesleyan chapel needed continuous maintenance and improvement. By the early 1880s, the Wesleyans had formed a new trust which looked to organise a complete interior renovation, a new organ and a Sunday-school building. The projects were calculated at £580, of which £255 had already been raised by public meetings, bazaars, tea meetings, etc.[26] As was often the case, appeals went out to St Day exiles abroad, who often seemed to send considerable sums of money as individuals, or from group collections. A sub-group known as the Organ Committee took on the role of providing a chapel organ. For many years the Wesleyans seemed to 'make-do' with a harmonium, but in June 1881 they purchased the Hele No.2 Organ from Hele & Co., Plymouth.[27] The organ took central place in the chapel and enhanced hymn singing which was itself at the very core of Methodist worship. From this period, the Wesleyans seemed to have focused much around the organ and music, with various choirs and musical groups forming, often under the direction of Mr Jeffery, the newly appointed organist.

Heating such a large building was eased with the installation of a new system in April 1888. The company of Wright Brothers of Sheffield installed one of their 'eight-tubed patent air warmers', which was apparently capable of heating 'at once' the chapel, schoolrooms and vestries, all at a grand cost of £60!

In 1908 the chapel debt stood at £405, and a consolidated effort was made over the next three years to clear the outstanding balance, with £203 being received by donations, £156 raised through bazaars and £46 from a new Connexional Fund grant; remarkable sums of money for the times. This cleared the way for another large restoration in the last two weeks of December 1911 and into January 1912, when 19 new memorial windows were fitted, those at the front containing 'cathedral-tinted glass', designed and made by Mr W. Hill, an architect from Redruth.[28]

Methodist New Connexion, Burnwithian

The Methodist New Connexion can be followed through a rather complex range of deeds. In the earliest known deed dated 27 January 1830, Mr Nicholas Tresidder assigned to Mr John Nicholls (amongst other things) 'all that Slaughter House with the room formerly used as a Schoolroom over the same.' Both men are recorded as butchers. This deed appears with two other papers dated 1838 and 22 March 1844.[29] The 'Slaughter House' was the building now known as Chapel House at Forth an Eglos. The later deeds refer to a plot of land at Burnwithian; the same spot where in 1835 an 'Associated Body' built a chapel, financed with money sent from Yorkshire. Finding the funds inadequate for the support of the chapel, they turned it over to the Methodist New Connexion.[30] On 24 June 1838, in another deed, Mr Matthew Moyle, who appears as the lessee, assigned to Mr John Ridgway 'a Chapel in St Day,' for £317 to the Methodist Connexion. This deed refers to another deed dated 24 May 1836 which lists a series of people who were trustees to the Methodist New Connexion Chapel. They included Nicholas Bawden, George Michell, William Wilton (the scientific-instrument maker), William Trebilcock, William Downing, William Long, William Painter and John Stephens. The *West Briton* reported that the New Connexion:

... having purchased the Chapel lately occupied by the Primitive Methodists, reopened the Chapel for divine service on Sunday 30 September, when the Revd Mr Heresford of Sheffield preached at the morning service, the Revd J. Chapel of Penzance in the afternoon, and the Revd T. Robinson of Truro at Six in the evening.[31]

Whether the New Connexion maintained another property than this seems uncertain, for the report also states that 'collections will be made at the services for the purpose of defraying the expenses incurred by the transfer of the premises.' Annie Trevithick believes that the Primitives were the last to occupy the building after the New Connexion, probably while their chapel was being enlarged. We know that by 1843–44 the building had been demolished and the materials purchased by the Wesleyans for their chapel at the West End.

Wesleyan Methodist Association at Scorrier Street

By 1850, the Baptists had ceased to use their chapel in Scorrier Street. By 6 January 1850, another Methodist offshoot, the Wesleyan Methodist Association reopened the chapel and their initial reception at St Day was very encouraging. The Wesleyan Methodist Association magazine of that year reported:

Two sermons were preached by Mr Ellery to very crowded audiences. On Sabbath last, the Chapel was well filled and the prospects are truly cheering. Thus far by the hand of God we have extended our borders and set up our banners and our motto is still 'One and All, onward'.[33]

A Wesleyan Methodist preaching plan for 1850 lists Redruth, Camborne, North Country, Calvadnack, Tolskithy, Hayle, Lanner Hill, Union House, Barripper, Helston, Penzance and St Day in all this geographically diverse circuit. An Association plan of 1852 fails to include St Day, suggesting that the group's success in St Day was relatively short-lived.

Revivals & Local Preachers

Revivals often occurred during particular periods and perhaps from the key dates of chapel and Sunday-school building, enlargement, etc. We can identify three prominent 'revival' periods in St Day as the late 1820s, early 1840s and probably the late 1870s and early 1880s. Up to the 1860s, revivals seemed to come of their own accord, but later there were attempts to organise them. Richard Blewett recounted his boyhood experience of a religious revival in the late 1880s when he lived at Leedstown:

My earliest experience of a revival meeting was at the age of six when my mother took me. Close by the pew where we sat was a lamp burning paraffin and standing on a slender brass pillar. The Chapel was full up and down. The air was full of shouting, screaming, crying aloud and groaning and in front of the downstairs audience was a rail lined with penitents 'wrestling with God' as I heard in after years they were doing, or said to be doing. Suddenly a big fellow rushed down the stairs from the gallery, ran up the aisle to the accompaniment of a loud roar, waving his arms in ecstatic gesticulations and smashed the lamp.[34]

Some chapels would be left open all night as souls were pledged by 'penitent sinners' and emotional hymns were sung. At St Day, similar scenes were enjoyed by the Primitive Methodists in Scorrier Street:

In February 1882, a local preacher from Penryn called Dick Richards conducted a mission here. The Chapel was crowded week after week and nearly 100 were converted. The fervent ginger-bearded preacher locally known as 'Hallelujah Dick' worked up young and old to a great pitch of excitement by his exhortations. Whilst the mission was in progress, bands of people sang through the streets.[35]

Herbert Thomas provides us with other accounts of local Methodist preachers at St Day like John Downing, who was blinded in the mines and made his living selling packets of tea or wheeling water from door to door. He describes how in the pulpit, John Downing prayed feverishly, gave out hymns and quoted scriptures from memory and delivered eloquent homilies. Another at St Day was a shoemaker who also 'held forth' to customers for a chat. Thomas comments:

... in the pulpit with eyes mostly closed, he would shake and his body would rise and fall as he balanced himself on his toes. His was a rapid and impassioned delivery.

Richard Hampton (1782–1858) alias 'Foolish Dick' from Porthtowan was another visiting preacher at St Day. By appearance, he was:

... a short, dumpy man with ill-fitting and untidy clothes, 'Foolish Dick' squinted at the world from beneath the rim of his weather-beaten hat, as he shuffled rather than walked along.[36]

Two of St Day's most popular school headmasters were prominent Wesleyan preachers. Peter Jennings, the first headmaster of St Day's Board School, was a preacher and trustee at the West End chapel. Richard Blewett is still within living memory of many people in St Day. Later in his life Blewett described himself as a 'confessed atheist', but John Probert refers to conversations with Blewett, when he simply would not stop talking about religion. Further, he comments on how sorry Blewett was when the West End chapel closed. In countless cases, Blewett often preached a very short sermon on a Biblical text, followed by a lengthy discussion describing the results of his social research on the living conditions of the people at St Day, leaving the audience apparently spellbound.

It would not seem appropriate to record the history of Methodism without particular mention of one of St Day's leading characters during much of the twentieth century. Renfred 'Peano' Knowles typifies the conversion to Methodism, experienced by many of Cornwall's miners. In his later years, he was said to have been enjoying a Sunday lunchtime drink at

A PLAN

OF THE

Primitive Methodist Preachers,

For Redruth Mission.----Hull Circuit.----1827.

PLACES.	DAYS.	TIME.	OCTOBER 7	14	21	28	NOVEMBER 4	11	18	25	DECEMBER 2	9	16	23	30
Redruth	*Sun.*	2	3C	1	4L	3	1C	4	3	1,2	4	3	1	4	3
		6	4C	3	1	4	3C	1	4	3s2	1	4	3	1	4
Ditto	*T*		3	4	4	1		3	3	4	4	1	1	3	3
Copper House	*Sun.*	2	15	4	3TC	5	4	3	12	4C	3	15	4	3	5
Class Chapel	*Sun.*	8½	3	1	1	4	3	1	4	1,2	4	4	3	1	4
Black Rock	*Sun.*	11	4	3TC	7	12	5	15	14	3C	5	7	15	5	13
Garlands	*Sun.*	2	4	3TC	1	12	5	15	14	3C	5	7	15	1	13
Condurrow	*Sun.*	6	13	5	4TC	6	1	4C	7	14	13	6	5	4	14
Mawla	*Sun.*	10	9	15	4TC	3	15	4	3C	11	15	3	9	4	11
North Country	*Sun.*	2	7	15	10	4TC	15	11	4C	11	15	4	9	17	4
Ditto	*W*			1		3		4		1		3		4	
St. Day	*Sun.*	6	3	12	8	3T	7	10	3C	6	9	3	11	15	3
Ditto	*W*		3C		4		3		4		3		4		3
Twelve Hoads	*Sun.*	2	11	17	16	11	3C	12	13	10	11	16	3	8	15
Ditto	*F*			3C		4L		3		4		3		4	
Carnmarth	*Sun*	6	10	17	16	11	10	12	13	10	4	16	17	8	1
Ditto	*T*			1C		3T		4C		1		3		4	
Ale Beagle	*Sun.*	2	1	10	15	1TC	11	9	1	9	17	1C	16	14	12
Todpool	*Sun.*	6	8	10	15	8	11	9	15	3	17	8	16	14	12
Ditto	*F*		4		3TC		4		3C		4		3		4
Copper Hill	*Sun.*	6	14	13	17	16	9	7	17	1	16	13	7	11	9
Ditto	*W*			4TC		1		3C		4		1		3	
Class—Town	*Th.*		3	3	3	3	3	3	3	3	3	3	3	3	3
Illogan Highway	*M*		4	3TC	1	4	3	1	4C	3	1	4	3	1	4
Class—Hill	*Th*		1	1	1	1	1	1	1	1	1	1	1	1	1
Class	*W*		4	3	1	4	1	1	1	3	1	4	3	1	4
North Downs	*F*		1		4TC		3		1C		3		4		1
Illogan Church Town	*F*			3TC		4		3C		4		3		4	
Redruth Prayer Meetings	*Sun.*		18	19	20	21	18	19	20	21	18	19	20	21	18
Ditto	*M*		19	20	21	18	19	20	21	18	19	20	21	18	19
Ditto	*W*		20	21	18	19	20	21	18	19	20	21	18	19	20
Ditto	*Sat.*		18	19	20	21	18	19	20	21	18	19	20	21	18
Illogan Highway	*W*		19	20	21	18	19	20	21	18	19	20	21	18	19
North Country	*W*		21	18	19	20	21	18	19	20	21	18	19	20	21

PREACHERS.

1 Garner
2 Driffield
3 Abbey
4 Strongman
5 Wedlake
6 Juleff
7 Richards
8 Jenkin
9 Thomas
10 Kemp

ON TRIAL.

11 Blamey
12 Benbow
13 Michell
14 Teague
15 Sandoe

EXHORTERS.

16 Hawke
17 Letcher

T Tickets.
L Lovefeast.
C Collection.

Praying Companies.

18 R. P.—J. T.—J. H.—D. A.—S. E. R. H.—
19 J. P.—T. M.—E. P.—M. D.—S. J. T. B.—A. R.
20 R. W.—W. M.—B. P.—W. T.—B. P.—E. W.—W. P.—L. W.—
21 E. C.—T. T.—W. D.—J. D.—J. K.

Brokenshir, Printer, Truro.

Preparatory Quarterly Meeting at Redruth November 6th, to commence at Three o'Clock in the afternoon.

North Corner Primitive Sunday school, now the St Day Methodist Chapel, c.1992.

the St Day Inn, when he heard a hymn being played. He apparently put down his glass and returned to his wife Annie, herself an ardent Primitive Methodist, and 'turned to the Lord'. 'Peano' was a remarkable character, well known throughout the county. He was a successful rugby player, leading St Day to Cornwall Junior Group Cup success in 1921. He also played senior club rugby at Penryn and Redruth, before becoming a county referee. He worked at St Day Brickworks, before his military service following the First World War led him to work for the War Cemeteries Commission. He then returned to work in several Gwennap and Cornish mines. He was a champion Cornish wrestler and taught local boys the skills near Fiveshoots, where he worked. He was a celebrated 'stickler' (wrestling referee) until his late years. He was awarded various medals for bravery, including the White Cross of St Giles, the highest award of the RSPCA for bravery in the duty of protecting animals. This was gained for his particular skills in saving cats and dogs stranded in disused mineshafts. He used a 'two-handed rope' technique to do this alone. What realisation touched this man and caused him to become one of the most God fearing, respected preachers and hard-working chapel workers in the history of Methodism at St Day?[36]

Into the 1960s & '70s

The decades after the Second World War witnessed a steady fall in the congregation at the West End and Scorrier Street chapels. In the 1960s Richard Blewett described the conditions as 'tragic'. He stated:

> *In St Day at the present time the Methodist 'Gulf' has disappeared because one of the Methodist bodies has disappeared and what has come to be an apparently insoluble problem is whether the Primitive Methodists should occupy the West End Methodist premises and sell the Scorrier Street Chapel. It cannot be solved by reason. Emotion from long-standing usage is too strong.*[37]

Several months of continuous negotiations were held towards the end of 1967. A decision was made that the Scorrier Street chapel should be used for future Methodist worship in St Day.[38] A 'Grieved Methodist' corresponding in the *West Briton* in February 1968 felt that his 'shock' was shared by many at the announced closure of the West End chapel. He argued that although Methodist unity was rather overdue, the superior building at the West End should remain open because it represented in its appearance the 'character and that extra finish which most Wesleyan [and not Primitive] Churches are endowed with.' However, other factors considered for the West End chapel were central heating, four vestries and a Sunday school.

It would be some time before the United Methodists in St Day were to fully accept their differences, and for some things would never truly be the same. Despite this, many focused their attentions on the Scorrier Street Chapel and set about modernising and transferring the organ and other items.[39] Central heating was installed at a cost of £1,000 the following year. By 1975 the average attendance was still only 20 members. The problem of 'today's congregation and tomorrow's finance' again became overwhelming. The strain of maintaining such a large chapel with limited resources was too much and the District Replanning Commission suggested closing the Scorrier Street chapel and using the North Corner Sunday Schoolroom as a possible venue for Methodist worship.

For a while some members felt reluctant and considered the idea of adapting the chapel, but with costs amounting to £12,000 this proved too expensive. The late Gwen Wills, the trust secretary, commented that a move to the Sunday school 'would satisfy needs and produce a compact and adaptable modern premises.' New plans and renovations were carried out shortly after. Proceeds from the sale of the chapel, local fund-raising and the Redruth 'Methodist Circuit Advance Fund' helped to meet the expenses of £5,000 for work done by Mr Croydon Nankivell, Bert Higginson, Jimmy Downing and Billy Curnow. The railings and wrought-iron gates were removed and relocated at the new North Corner chapel. A new electric organ was purchased along with seating, and the new and latest Methodist chapel at St Day was opened 24–25 April, 1976.[40]

At the time of writing, the membership of the Methodist chapel at St Day is around 40 adults and children. The Sunday school, renamed the Junior Church in 1991, uses a variety of modern approaches to reach young children such as Bible quizzes (St Day youngsters have won the shield on several occasions). Summer camp is also enjoyed by many and anniversaries are still enjoyed with saffron buns and visits to the seaside. The chapel encourages instrumentalists to support the singing and musical events which are considered significant to Methodist worship.[41]

The Salvation Army

The Salvation Army were working in St Day c.June 1884, when the Redruth contingent were holding 'Services' at the Market Square.[42] They particularly enjoyed open-air preaching and singing; throughout the summer months they could often be found on various street corners, usually at the north end of St Day.[43]

When the lease and freehold expired on the old Town Hall, the Salvationists tried to obtain the site but failed as the Primitive Methodists secured it first.[44] However, by April 1885, they were in occupation of 'Mr Mills' old coach-house', better known as 'Rooke Flat-Tops', which they adapted as a meeting-house, (probably with the support of their Redruth counterparts).[45] Richard and John Rooke kept buildings referred to as 'Flat-Tops' at the bottom of Simmons Street (Mills Street) and behind the King's Arms, (behind the present Post Office). As the lane behind Simmons Street became, and still is known as Barracks Lane (after the Salvation Army barracks), we can assume that they continued at this site until they ceased in December 1900.[46]

The Baptists at St Day

Of all the Nonconformist denominations at St Day, the Baptists were the first to make their presence known at Scorrier Street, in June 1803; initially this group was a joint association of the larger chapel built at Redruth.[47] Some of the earliest Baptist (and indeed Nonconformist) family names recounted to Peter Jennings in the late-nineteenth century are recorded as: Matthews, Jennings, Michells, Johns, Letchers, Bennetts, Nancarrows, Nicholls, Hensleys, Brays, Tiddys, Annears, Sims, Higgins, Bawdens, Phillips, Hawkes, Leggs and Mills.[48]

Little is mentioned from 1803 until December 1828, when 'Brother John Sprague [was] requested to take the management of the financial concerns at St Day.' In 1832 a Baptist minister, the Revd Spashatt, was appointed, and from October 1832 baptisms were recorded, although many would have been baptised by this time and in the following year there were recorded 18 baptised and 32 'resident' members. Remarkably, by early 1833 the Sunday school had 155 children and 20 teachers, revealing a large chapel membership at what was often noted as a rather humble thatched building.

By 1835 Sunday-school figures stood at 44 boys and 45 girls, with six teachers at what is termed the St Day Station. The Baptists took great delight in securing members from the Methodists or Anglicans. Occasional mention is also made to returning 'back-sliders'. Numbers varied and began to dwindle by 1840 when the minister left for an appointment in Devon. In March 1846, the roof was recorded as 'so much out of repair that it demands immediate attention'. By 1850, the Baptists had ceased worship at St Day; their chapel then became occupied for a short time by the Wesleyan Methodist Association.[49] By 1860, the Total Abstinence Society of St Day used the chapel for teetotal meetings and it became known as the Temperance Hall. It later became the St Day Town Hall around 1866, and was used for lectures by the temperance movements. It also became the venue for the St Day Institute until the lease of the site was sold to the Primitives in 1885.

Notes

1 West Cornwall Circuit Membership Book, 1774–96, CRO/AD/350.
2 Launceston Methodist Chapel Stewards Account Book, 1808–1857, CRO/MRL/68.
3 Probert, John C.C., *Primitive Methodism in Cornwall*, (n.d.), pp.21–23, 3 and 5.
4 Ibid.
5 Ibid.
6 Trevithick, Annie, *A Short History of St Day*, c.1897, p.22.
7 Ibid.
8 Ibid.
9 Ibid.
10 William, Francis, *Gwennap*, 1845.
11 Probert, Ibid. p.22.
12 Shaw, Thomas, Collection of Methodist notes, RIC, Truro.
13 Ibid.
14 *Royal Cornwall Gazette*, 1.5.1885.
15 *Royal Cornwall Gazette*, 19.3. 1891.
16 CRO/DD. WH 3307.
17 *Royal Cornwall Gazette*, 26.6.1913.
18 Probert, Ibid, p.23.
19 Ibid.
20 Trevithick, Ibid.
21 Shaw, Thomas, Collection, RIC, Ibid., Truro, Letter Richard Moody, c.1842. Original at the John Rylands Library.
22 CRO/DD/X33/3.
23 *Cornish Post & Mining News*, 11.9.1913.
24 Blewett, R.R. 'These Things Have Been', Inst. 67 (June 1970).
25 *Royal Cornwall Gazette*, 5.12.1895.
26 *Royal Cornwall Gazette*, 27.9.1906.
27 *Royal Cornwall Gazette*, 9.1.1883.
28 *Royal Cornwall Gazette*, 3.6.1881, 29.7.1881 and 9.9.1881.
29 *Royal Cornwall Gazette*, 18.1.1912.
30 CRO/DD/X33/3.
31 Trevithick, Ibid.
32 *West Briton*, 21.9.1838.
33 *WMA Magazine*, 1850, p.100.
34 Blewett, R.R., 'These Things Have Been', Inst. 31 (November 1966).
35 Probert, Ibid, p.22.
36 Herbert, Thomas, 'Local Methodist Preachers at St Day', *Cornish Post*, 6.6.1940.
37 Mr Francis Matthews and Mrs Bernice Williams (daughter of Renfred Knowles) supplied information on Renfred Knowles.
38 Blewett, Ibid.
39 *West Briton*, 22.2.1968.
40 *West Briton*, 29.2.1968.
41 *West Briton*, 24.4.1976, 8.2.1879 and 1.5.1975.
42 Thanks to Arana 'Ray' Jefferys, c.1993.
43 *Cornubian*, 20.6.1884.
44 *Cornubian*, 16.6.1899 and 18.8.1899
45 *Royal Cornwall Gazette*, 23.4.1885.
46 *Cornubian*, 3.4.1885.
47 *Cornubian*, 21.12.1900.
48 *Cornubian*, 26.11.1902.
49 Blewett, R.R., Ibid., Inst. 30 (October, 1966).
50 Ibid., and *Doidge's Directory of Gwennap*, 1866.

Above: *View of stacks at St Day Brickworks. Note the Hoffman kiln* (right) *and the beehive kiln* (left), *c.1900.*

Left: *St Day Brickworks, c.1905, showing the extent of the pit, the processing gear, Hoffman Kiln and the small-gauge railway.*

Below: *St Day Brickworks with Tolcarne Terrace in the foreground and the Wesleyan chapel and town clock on the skyline, c.1900.*

Sixteen

A Town of Many Industries

China Clay & Brick Production

The sale of clay as a commodity at the St Day Brickworks site was advertised when the 'house, outbuildings and 3 acres of land' belonging to a Mrs Hawke were auctioned at Bennetts Hotel, St Day, on 23 February 1864. The advertisement reads: 'There is a claypit opened in one of the plots and being the only one in the neighbourhood, the returns are paying considerable profit.'[1] Mrs Hawke had sold the business to join her husband John, who had emigrated to the Grass Valley, USA. She died in January 1909, but is remembered as the 'first owner of the claypits' at St Day, when 'her husband and a few other men used to go out with pails, dig up the clay and send it away in carts for sale.'[2] The site is further listed in the sales particulars as being situated at St Day, adjoining the road leading to Tolcarne, and also adjoining the property of Messrs Williams.

Tram at St Day Brickworks, c.1897.

Around 1867 mechanised operations first began at the St Day clay-pit.[3] According to the *Mineral Statistics*, 1869 was the first year in which the clayworks at St Day were significant enough to be entered. The mineral lord and freeholder of the land was Sir W. Williams and the tenant was Nettle & Co., managed by Captain Nettle of Truro, who continued to work the site until 1874–75, when the St Day Co. took over.[4] When William Terrill (a mining student) of the Miners' Association visited the site in June 1869, he recorded 'a long embankment of whitish colour' which could be seen on arrival at Vogue. This was 'overburden' or waste clay. For every ton of clay produced, around seven tons of waste was discarded. A Captain Pascoe assisted their descent into the pit, and Terrill explains:

We were informed that the pit had not been worked a very long time for china clay. The material near the surface, being of course nature and very impure, was used for making bricks. The pit is about 200 yards long, and from about 60 feet to 70 feet deep.[5]

He further suggests that the 'famous water of Vogue' percolating through the rock had been responsible for the forming of the clay; a more likely cause was magnate vapours permeating the rocks when the district was mineralised.[6] Contamination from iron-oxide in the soil had rendered most of the soil as unsuitable for china-clay production because it caused some pink staining, which may relate to the name 'Pink Moors' nearby. Despite this, the clay was very suitable for fire-brick production. Terrill significantly records the process by which the clay is refined:

The separation of Kaolin [china clay] *is affected by washing with a stream of water, which after passing along launders or mica pits, in which the mica grit-like pieces of quartz runs into large reservoirs; the lighter matter remaining suspended in the water, will be found in the most distant reservoir. When the reservoirs are nearly full the supply of water is stopped, and what remains is drained off. The clay at the bottom is, when sufficiently dry, cut into blocks, and afterwards exposed to artificial heat for a few days, when it is fit for the market. The price we are told, varies considerably, ranging from 10s to 30s per ton according to quality.*

The process described adds to our understanding of the site as illustrated in the OS map of 1877 (1:2,500) which reveals a detailed complex of workings. The clay once dug would enter into a refining process to extract unwanted minerals. The clay would then be washed with water from a river which ran east from

St Day Brickworks

St Day Brickworks, c.1900.

BUY YOUR
FIRE AND BUILDING BRICKS
OF THE
ST. DAY FIRE BRICK & CHINA CLAY COMPANY,
LIMITED, ST. DAY, GWENNAP,
THE CHEAPEST & BEST IN CORNWALL.

THE ST. DAY FIRE BRICK AND CHINA CLAY
COMPANY
beg to inform the Public that they have on Sale
BEST FIRE BRICKS,
of all sizes and patterns; Plain and Ornamental
BUILDING BRICKS, FLOORING AND FIRE TILES
of all sizes; also BEST FIRE CLAY.

For prices, &c., apply at the Works, or to
MR. JOHN NETTING,
MERCHANT, ST. AUSTELL-STREET, TRURO.

Left: *Advertisement for St Day Fire Brick and China Clay Co. Ltd, 1874.*

1880 F.G. Tamblyn
ST. DAY St Day
FIRE BRICK AND CLAY Co., ~~LIMITED~~,
ST. DAY, SCORRIER, CORNWALL.

MANUFACTURERS OF FIRE BRICKS
In all shapes, suitable for Tin Smelting Furnaces, Cement Kilns, Gas Works, Foundries, &c.
A LARGE AND VARIED STOCK OF
— BUILDING BRICK OF EVERY DESCRIPTION —
CONSTANTLY ON HAND.
Specialitié in White and Yellow Tinted FACING BRICK for Dressings (well burnt).
FIRE, FLOORING, AND GARDEN TILES,
In Stock, and made to order at shortest notice.
ESTIMATES given for Delivery of Goods by Carts or Traction Engine on any building site within ten miles, or free in trucks at all Cornwall and West Cornwall Stations, and by Vessel to any port in the United Kingdom.
L. TAMBLYN, Manager. [P.T.O.]

Above: *St Day Brickworks advertising card.*

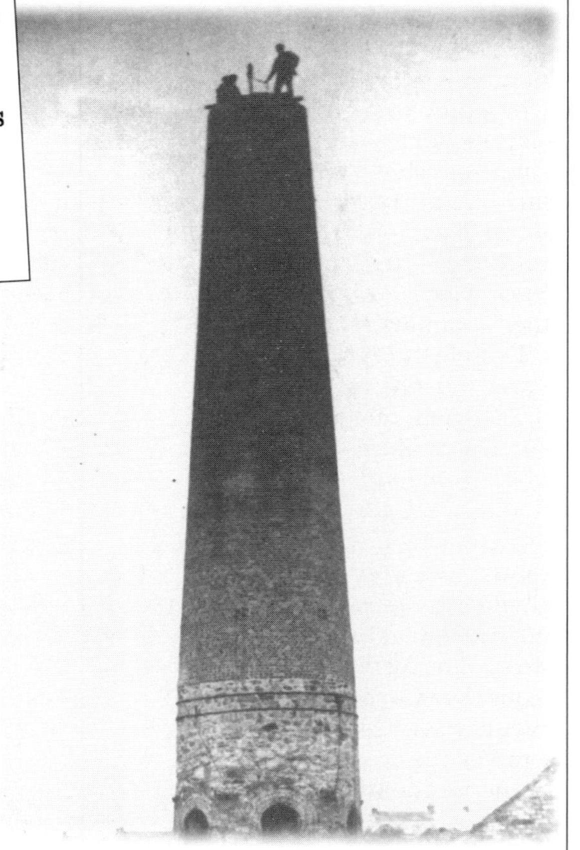

Right: *St Day Brickworks. Two steeplejacks dismantle a stack from Hoffman Kiln, January 1914.*

Vogue Stamps[7] along the 'mica drags' before entering into the mica pits and then kiln tanks. On our 1877 map, the mica drag, three pits and two settling tanks may be seen in the south of the complex behind a long building likely to be the 'dry'.

Some of the clay would then be transported to Devoran and Penryn, where, in the year 1885, the 1,024 tons of clay shipped were believed to have come from St Day.[8] When we inspect the composition of many St Day bricks we often find a heavy quartz content, which suggests that the deposits of the mica drags were used for brick making. Depending on which part of the pit was being dug, bricks could be almost white to dark-red, with many being buff-beige. Dye was sometimes added to produce white or yellow 'facing' or 'dress' bricks used as 'string courses' to complement ornate façades, such as the former Trounson building at Upper Fore Street, Redruth.

Whilst china-clay production may have been the original intent of this industry, the early 1870s witnessed considerable expansion in brick production. The brickworks have at times mainly supplied 'tin smelting and gas companies'.[9] Fireclay products were fired in the kiln to the south behind the 'dry' chimney, but this probably became inadequate to meet growing demands, and in 1874 a hexagonal Hoffman kiln was built to the north-east of the complex.[10]

Tram and incline rail at St Day Brickworks, c.1897.

On the OS map of 1906 (1:2,500), we see clear changes. The title 'china clay & brick works' has now diminished to simply 'brick works', perhaps implying abandonment of the old clay-working section. This seems the case as we notice the disappearance of the mica drag, pits and tanks, as well as the series of reservoirs previously so noticeable within the clay-working section. At the expense of this the brick-working site shows expansion, in particular the appearance of two 'beehive' kilns which have replaced the earlier singular 'pan' kiln. The dry has remained to facilitate rapid brick production, with its chimney more pronounced in this illustration. Another communal chimney services both beehive kilns. Despite the obvious decline in clay production, the works must have still continued to process some clay, for we find in the account book of The Cornwall Arsenic Co. at Bissoe, an entry for December, 1907, recording deliveries of '2 loads [of] brick from St Day' priced at 5 shillings, and '1 load of clay from St Day priced at 2s.6d.' per load.[11]

Almost 30 years of continuous production contributed to the enlargement of the claypit which has nearly doubled, expanding from around one to two acres. The former 'embankment' of waste, probably considered unsightly, had by now been levelled and would have substantially altered the view upon entry to Vogue.

As the works matured, a small-gauge tramway system was used to transport hand-propelled wagons along sections of the claypit. A mechanised winch system hauled full wagons up the steep incline, where the clay was deposited in a 'dry' state. This building probably housed crushing rollers which refined the clay. The mixture was dampened and would then have entered into a pug mill, which forced the clay vertically down into a chamber along an Archimedes' screw and out through an orifice of a predetermined size and shape. A slab of clay in semi-dry state emerged larger than the brick size to allow for shrinkage during firing. A frame containing a series of wires then cut the bricks to a specific size. A press then entered a brick mark, in this case 'ST DAY', upon the face of the brick as a mortar key and also for advertising purposes. The fireclay at St Day was rather coarse and although a brick face was smooth, the edges were usually finished by hand.[12] The bricks would then have been placed on a pallet and entered into a kiln for firing.

The brickworks at St Day manufactured a considerable range of fireclay products, not only the usual range of bricks but also stable paviors (in four or eight panels for stable paving, yards, etc.), garden bordering, flue covers, fire-tiles, brickbacks for household fires, tiles (for flues, ovens and suchlike), as well as special items to customer specifications.

During an average year, output at St Day amounted to one million bricks (20,000 bricks per week), although up to one and a half million bricks may have been produced during good years.[13] As the potential output of the Hoffman kiln was up to five million bricks per year, it can be seen that it never ran at full-steam. With this output, St Day could never have been considered a large brickworks compared to major producers turning out five million bricks per year or more. Despite this, within West Cornwall, St Day was the largest brickworks and the only site to boast a Hoffman kiln. Most of the bricks were disposed of locally, but a significant amount found their way all over England and Wales, with large quantities being exported to France and other foreign countries.[14] When the Truro-based schooner the *Jessie* foundered off Carmarthen Bay, on 17 January 1879, she was carrying a cargo of St Day firebricks. Archaeologist Terry James discovered the *Jessie* when she reappeared briefly in 1993, only to be covered again by the shifting sands. He believes that as ample brick supplies were available in Llanelli, the fire-bricks probably made cheap ballast for ships returning to Wales after delivering coal. Having been used for ballast, they could easily be used in the local metal industries of Wales.[15]

Overall, the business maintained a wide reputation and in 1878 we find the St Day Fire Brick Co. exhibiting at the Paris Exhibition. In 1879 it received First Class medals from the Royal Cornwall Polytechnic Society and (in 1880) the Mining Institution of Cornwall for the quality and diverse range of their bricks.[16]

Most of the advertisements record that deliveries could be made by 'road, rail or water'. Certainly carts and traction engines were used locally within a radius of ten miles, including Scorrier railway station from where the works could link to any other station or port in the country. The brickworks offered some hope to the ailing Redruth and Chacewater Railway in the 1870s, which had become less active since the rapid decline of the copper mines in the district. With the introduction of the Hoffman kiln in 1874, increased production prompted the railway to install a long siding loop, alongside the main line below Carharrack.[17] The average downtrain of the railway in the late 1880s comprised 12 wagons; two or three empties, two or three with ingot tin for Liverpool or with black tin for the Penpol Smelting Co., and the other half-dozen laden with fireclay and bricks from Carharrack. When the brickworks closed in 1912, the lost revenue to the railway was a contributing factor to its own closure.[18]

By the late 1860s, the Cornish copper industry had gone into rapid decline and with it the mainstay employment sector for the Gwennap workforce. The brickworks offered some hope within the parish, employing an average of 20 and up to 50 men during peak years.[19] Unlike their mining counterparts, wages were never exceptional. Around 1877, brick makers would expect to receive 2s.4d. per ten-hour day. This was considered cheap labour even by contemporaries, forcing brick makers into an industry considered to be of low social rank. When Renfred 'Peano' Knowles started work at the brickworks in 1906, aged 14, as a labourer, he worked from 7a.m. to 5p.m., Monday to Saturday (half-day), for 7s.6d. a week.[20] Undoubtedly, 14 years of age seems young, but the 1881 census reveals that John Verran, from Pink Moors, was employed as a 'clay works boy' at the age of 11, along with William James Belman from Gwennap (who may have worked at Pennance Brick Works) who was described as 'brick maker', aged 13. The men of the Browning family residing at Market Street, St Day – father John (from Taunton) and sons George, 19, and John (junr) 13 – found employment as 'brick makers', and Richard Matthews (aged 21) and his brother Thomas were employed as 'clay works labourers'; all perhaps showing the link of family employment. The works for most of the late-nineteenth century were managed by father and son Fred and Llewellyn Tamblyn. The census also lists William Fisher, aged 34, 'brick and clay worker' who may have been the Captain Fisher, manager of the Amelia Clay Works listed in *Harrod's Directory of Cornwall*, published in 1878. The name 'Amelia' is also mentioned in an advertisement (1873–78) by merchant John Netting of St Austell Street, Truro, and by Professor Norman Pounds, c.1940.[21]

January 1912 saw the closure of St Day Brickworks. Changing market forces, in particular competition from the St Austell district, made the works redundant. Despite considerable efforts to establish a new company to rework clay deposits, the venture never materialised and the machinery lay idle until it was scrapped and removed. By January 1913 the site was being demolished and, sadly, no evidence of this once dominant industrial site remains. Occasionally, we find a brick or two which survive to tell of a once thriving industry which served the community at St Day during a fragile period of its past.

PRICE LIST, 188

DESCRIPTION.	On the Co.'s Works.	Delivered at
No. 1 Fire Bricks, 9, 4½, 2½, *per* 1000		
No. 2 do. " "		
Side and End Arch Bricks, No. 1 quality ... ... *per* 1000		
Cylinder Bricks		
Stack Do. "		
Soaps and Splits "		
Fire Tiles ... ... } According to size. "		
Fire Lumps ... ... }		
Flooring Tiles ... }		
Flue Covers ... ... }		
White pressed Facing Bricks—		
Plain ... ... *per* 1,000		
Ornamental ... ... "		
Ordinary Building Bricks "		
Partition do. ... "		
Garden Bordering, any pattern ..		
Gutter Brick (1 ft. lengths)...*per foot*		
Stable Pavors, very hard ..*per* 1,000		
Fire Clay ... ... *per ton.*		

TERMS :—

Safety Fuse Manufacturing

William Francis, writing in 1845, reminds us of the dangers local miners faced as they worked underground at Gwennap:

They used picks and gads, or, by numerous blows,
They bore the hard rocks that their progress oppose,
Then with gunpowder charge as each may require,
And place safety-fuze to convey nitrous fire,
Then with gravel or junk the hole is well fill'd,
Ramm'd close on the charge, as the miner, well skilled,
Will do much with care, lest a spark should be struck,
And ignite the powder confined in the rock,
For then, all expos'd to the terrible blast,
Life's joys and its sorrows for ever are past [22]

Within Gwennap, extensive mining operations prompted a large demand for safety fuse, and in 1846 a group of 'Shareholders and Managers in the Cornish Mines, with mining engineers' co-operated to establish the Unity Safety Fuse Company.[23] With their collective expertise they geared the products to the demands of the markets. The works initially used the original method of spinning by hand using 'primitive appliances' to make 'textile-spun fuse'.[24] Bryan Earl, in his publication *Cornish Mining: The Techniques of Metal Mining in the West of England, Past and Present,* explains methods of production very similar to those used at St Day:

The first safety fuse was made by a man trickling gunpowder from a funnel strapped to his waist into the centre of the fuse rope of jute that he spun walking backwards down a 24 ft 'walk'. This gave fuse in 24ft lengths – and to this day fuse is frequently sold in 24ft units. The fuse burnt regularly at 30 seconds a foot, rather than the unreliable flashing of powder down a straw tube. Later machines were designed to spin the fuse continuously. After spinning, the 'carcass' was treated by running through bitumen and guttapercha [a rubber substance], *and then further counterings put on to give strength. A final dusting of china clay helped show up the fuse where it emerged from the shot-hole.*[25]

The fuse initially manufactured was $^{3}/_{16}$ of an inch in diameter and sold in coils of 24ft, although longer lengths could be supplied by order. Besides the obvious safety factor, the fuse was purported to be far more economical, using only $^{1}/_{5}$ of the gunpowder compared to traditional methods.[26]

By August 1847, the actual manufacturing was managed by Edward Henry Hawke & Co., who by this time advertised the export of safety fuse to 'any part of the world'.[27] Hawke also owned and managed a fuseworks near Lyons in France[28], as well as the Tolgullow Rope Factory (from as early as 1819), with his family. It therefore seems likely that the first Unity Safety Fuse Company may have been associated with the Tolgullow Ropeworks, as rope-making equipment and techniques could be adapted or used for the production of safety fuse.[29] As the site of the first fuseworks post-dates the Gwennap Tithe Map of 1843, it is difficult to say how close the ropeworks and safety fuse factories were. By 1852, Edward Hawke & Co. were listed as the safety fuse manufacturers at the site.

Around 1865 the business was forced to move premises after a serious explosion resulted in the death of the manageress, who was killed after jumping from a window only to be crushed under a falling wall. Several others were seriously injured by the fire.[30] The force of the explosion completely blew out the walls and also blasted a young woman named Ann Davey (who was later to die in the 1875 explosion) into a tree.

The works were then relocated at Wheal Unity Count House which was considered 'old', but had suitably thick walls. This was adapted for the purpose into a two-storey factory measuring 55ft by 25ft, which was the main building along with several others enclosed around a courtyard.[31] The ground floor housed a 'taping' machine which was partitioned from the rest of the room, and at the rear was an escape door which could be opened from the inside. This led into the yard, in case of emergencies, where there were two large doors (for horse-drawn vehicles and which were generally closed) and a small door for pedestrian access. Other buildings around the courtyard were used for 'tarring', and attached to the factory was a building which housed a steam boiler used to generate the machines. On the upper floor of the factory, five or six girls were employed spinning fuse or winding yarn. The room had several windows, each of which could easily be opened to allow workers trapped upstairs an opportunity to escape, but as no outside stairs were provided it seemed escapees were expected to jump. To reduce the risk of grit entering the factory or other units, all the walkways and pathways were laid with bricks.

Nearby was a water reservoir for general use and to draw from in the event of fire. Gunpowder was stored in the fireproof powder-house outside the enclosure, and the magazine was situated half a mile away. The gunpowder was controlled, with only reasonable amounts allocated at regular intervals when needed, to reduce the extent of any accidental explosion.[32]

The main materials used in the manufacture of safety fuse were 'yarns, powder, tar, pitch and gutta-percha'.[33] Undoubtedly the most dangerous part of the manufacturing process (at this time) was the laying of gunpowder on the tapes. This was done by a small wagon filled with gunpowder, which ran along on a small tramway, emitting a regular amount

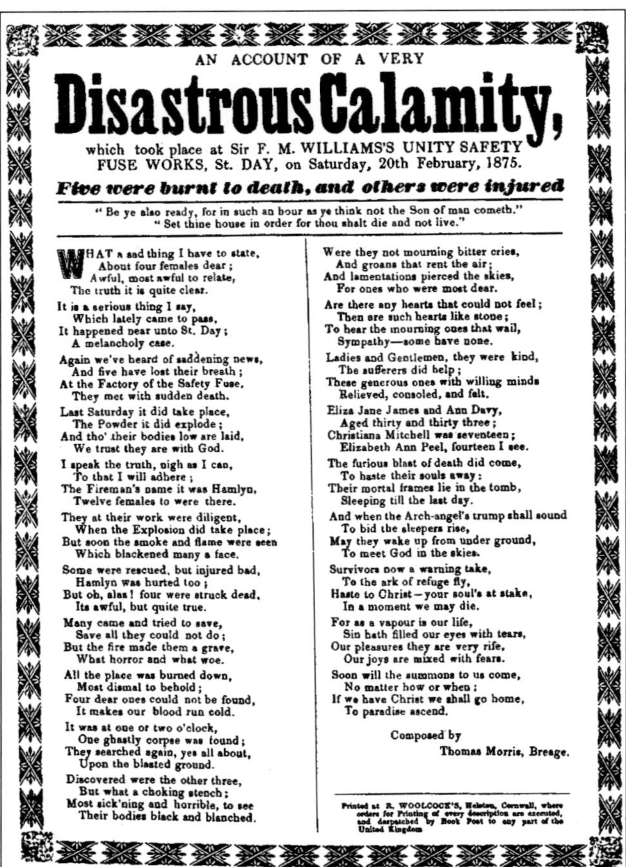

AN ACCOUNT OF A VERY

Disastrous Calamity,

which took place at Sir F. M. WILLIAMS'S UNITY SAFETY FUSE WORKS, St. DAY, on Saturday, 20th February, 1875.

Five were burnt to death, and others were injured

" Be ye also ready, for in such an hour as ye think not the Son of man cometh."
" Set thine house in order for thou shalt die and not live."

WHAT a sad thing I have to state,
About four females dear;
Awful, most awful to relate,
The truth it is quite clear.

It is a serious thing I say,
Which lately came to pass,
It happened near unto St. Day;
A melancholy case.

Again we've heard of saddening news,
And five have lost their breath;
At the Factory of the Safety Fuse,
They met with sudden death.

Last Saturday it did take place,
The Powder it did explode;
And tho' their bodies low are laid,
We trust they are with God.

I speak the truth, nigh as I can,
To that I will adhere;
The Fireman's name it was Hamlyn,
Twelve females to were there.

They at their work were diligent,
When the Explosion did take place;
But soon the smoke and flame were seen
Which blackened many a face.

Some were rescued, but injured bad,
Hamlyn was hurted too;
But oh, alas! four were struck dead,
Its awful, but quite true.

Many came and tried to save,
Save all they could not do;
But the fire made them a grave,
What horror and what woe.

All the place was burned down,
Most dismal to behold;
Four dear ones could not be found,
It makes our blood run cold.

It was at one or two o'clock,
One ghastly corpse was found;
They searched again, yes all about,
Upon the blasted ground.

Discovered were the other three,
But what a choking stench;
Most sick'ning and horrible, to see
Their bodies black and blanched.

Were they not mourning bitter cries,
And groans that rent the air;
And lamentations pierced the skies,
For ones who were most dear.

Are there any hearts that could not feel;
Then are such hearts like stone;
To hear the mourning ones that wail,
Sympathy—some have none.

Ladies and Gentlemen, they were kind,
The sufferers did help;
These generous ones with willing minds
Relieved, consoled, and felt.

Eliza Jane James and Ann Davy,
Aged thirty and thirty three;
Christiana Mitchell was seventeen;
Elizabeth Ann Peel, fourteen I see.

The furious blast of death did come,
To haste their souls away:
Their mortal frames lie in the tomb,
Sleeping till the last day.

And when the Arch-angel's trump shall sound
To bid the sleepers rise,
May they wake up from under ground,
To meet God in the skies.

Survivors now a warning take,
To the ark of refuge fly,
Haste to Christ—your soul's at stake,
In a moment we may die.

For as a vapour is our life,
Sin hath filled our eyes with tears,
Our pleasures they are very rife,
Our joys are mixed with fears.

Soon will the summons to us come,
No matter how or when;
If we have Christ we shall go home,
To paradise ascend.

Composed by
Thomas Morris, Breage.

Printed at R. WOOLCOCK'S, Helston, Cornwall, where orders for Printing of every description are executed, and despatched by Book Post to any part of the United Kingdom

Unity Safety Fuse Works disaster, February 1875 – a poetical tribute to those who died.

of powder. This produced fuse in a semi-manufactured state, which was carried away covered by a piece of hessian. It was removed every other day and kept on the ground floor on the other side of the partition from the tape-machine. About 600 coils, each 24ft in length, were produced each day on six machines.[34]

One of the most important regulations was the wearing of slippers in the buildings, which were specially provided for that purpose, to avoid sparks igniting any loose powder. To walk in the yard, boots were permitted, but upon entry to any building slippers had to be worn. Failure to do this resulted in a fine for the first offence, and dismissal for a second.

After Sir Frederick Williams purchased the works in 1873 (from Henry Backhouse Fox who had purchased most of Hawke's business interests when he died in 1872), he looked to improve conditions and safety for his workers. An inspector of gunpowder works, Major Majendie, recommended a revision in the safety of some areas after a visit in April, 1873, which included:

1. The 'sweepings' in the fuse-room to be placed in a 'closed vessel' instead of an open bucket, and more care to be taken over the spillage of gunpowder (as powder was discovered spilt and lying in crevices of the uncovered part of the floor).
2. That 'made fuse' be removed from the room regularly and not left to accumulate, thus reduce [sic] *the risk of accidents.*
3. In the fuse-making room behind and besides the machines, the walls be wood skirted to a height of four feet and this part of the room be screened off from the remainder, with provision for a clear exit for emergencies.
4. The windows of the 'dry' should be externally protected by wire.
5. That a set of rules and regulations be appropriately displayed and each member of staff be individually issued with a copy to be read and observed.[35]

Operations continued at Wheal Unity Count House until around 1875 when another serious explosion forced the proprietors to consider a more suitable premises. James Tregonning, the agent for the fuse-works on behalf of Sir F. Williams, stated that Major Majendie's recommendations had been adhered to by the time of the accident, except for the printing of the set of rules that were in the process of being printed. The accident in question has been recounted in detail and with five fatalities presented a great shock to communities far and wide.

On Saturday 20 February 1875, one of the female workers was believed to have entered the fuse-making room wearing iron-nailed boots instead of changing into her safety slippers, which may have caused a spark to ignite gunpowder. Flames and flashes from gunpowder combusted into a fire that rapidly spread engulfing the entire building. Thick black smoke made visibility impossible. Those on the ground floor crawled and stumbled to safety into the yard, some with their clothes on fire. Disorientated and fearing for their lives, they tried to scale the large gates, oblivious of the small escape door.

Back inside the building five women and girls were trapped on the upper floor, with the windows their only possible escape, but young Margaretta Long was the only one able to make it. She smashed her hands through the glass and managed to pull up the window. Below her, John Hamlin, the works foreman (himself injured and burnt), beckoned her to jump so he could catch her. She hesitated, so he promptly ran for a ladder. Margaretta looked back, only to see her friends burning alive, their bodies turned black beyond recognition. In desperation, her clothes ablaze, she jumped to her friends who rushed to smother the flames from her body.

The story of the 1875 explosion is confirmed by several witnesses, among them John Pooley, a butcher at St Day (and father of 14-year-old Elizabeth Ann Pooley who died in the explosion). He was in his garden at around 11.30a.m., when he heard a 'slight explosion' and turned in the direction of the factory to see smoke coming out of the roof. He rushed to the scene to find girls scrambling over the large doors and wall. Asking them to jump, he caught each of them. He climbed over the large doors into the yard and found foreman John Hamlin and the girl from the engine-room helping extinguish the flames on Margaretta Long, who then got up and staggered to the road. By this time the alarm had been raised, and a stream of people began to filter from St Day, many anxious relatives of the workers. A large number of miners, headed by Captain Cock, made their way from West Poldice Mine to form a rescue team. Some men repeatedly charged through the flames desperately trying to save the women but were themselves badly burnt. The situation became even more intense when John Hamlin shouted that the boiler might blow. Mr J. Whitford and a Captain Mayne bravely climbed into the engine room and opened the valves to relieve the pressure and then cleared the room of inflammable twine used to make fuse. The inferno continued to rage for an hour before being brought under control.

Then came more difficult moments as every man began to dig and clear the smouldering debris to find the dead bodies. Families looked on and women could only but try to comfort each other. After a while a leg and skull were found. What appeared as corpses came to the surface, black and twisted like 'charred wood'. None could be identified. The remains were placed, respectfully, in an outhouse to await the coroner. Sir Frederick Williams witnessed most of the ordeal and was, like everyone, deeply affected.

Five women died in the fire. They were Ann Davey aged 37; Elizabeth Ann Pooley aged 14; Christiana Mitchell, 17; also Elizabeth Jane James aged 29, and at midnight on the Sunday, Margaretta Long, 18, died from burns and shock. Though the foreman and six other girls were stunned, blinded by smoke or otherwise injured, they all walked home. After the inquest Sir Frederick ordered five oak coffins for the deceased. The following Tuesday, 23 February, the funerals of all but Margaretta Long were held, and St Day fell silent as around 5,000 people formed a procession from the fuseworks to St Day church. The five women were interred in a common grave at St Day churchyard and the following afternoon saw the burial of Margaretta Long in her family grave. A community was left to mourn.[36]

Shortly after this, new premises were acquired at Little Beside (SW 7348 4304). The tragedy at Unity Safety Fuse Company must have preceded the 1875 Explosives Act by mere months, and the proprietor was, by this new Act, required to build the new factory on a single floor only. In 1875, the new works at Little Beside were erected and the business continued successfully, by this time under the management of John Tregonning, the former agent.

The OS map, c.1878 (1:2,500), illustrates the new factory as Unity Safety Fuse Company clearly on the right, travelling down the hill at Little Beside from St Day. The Redruth & Chasewater Railway conveniently sides what appears as a long shed, probably associated with the factory. By around 1888, as a result of increased business, the factory was extended[37] and the OS map, c.1906 (1:2,500), shows considerable detailed expansion. It is difficult to distinguish the function of many of the buildings, other than what appears as a powder-house, detached at the rear to the south of the site. By this time, the works were listed as using 33 buildings, two engines and two boilers among them.[38] Unity Safety Fuse Company had by this time become a major employer in Gwennap, with around 100 workers. When the company was formed in 1846, it boasted the manufacture of 'all kinds of safety fuse of the best quality for use in mining, quarrying, submarine and all other blasting operations.' Success continued and at the turn of the century the works could supply 'a score or more types of fuse' for both home and abroad.

In 1893, William Rich & Son, agents for Nobel's Explosive Dynamite in the West Country, had obtained an interest in the Unity Safety Fuse Company, seeking to extend and expand the works by building an additional factory near the former Unity Count House site.[39] The venture failed to fully materialise, and by 1905, Bickford's Company obtained the largest shareholding. Under their ownership the business was managed and reopened again in 1909 by Captain Bennetts until after the war in 1918.[40]

During the First World War (with a shortage of cordite explosives after foreign imports dried up), the Cornish explosives factories were utilised within the British war-based economy and effort. The factory at Little Beside would probably have been involved in the production of the 'various forms of propellant explosive cordite for big guns'. Bickford's was by this time one of the two factories which kept the Royal Navy supplied with cordite. The factory at Little Beside may also have been involved in such business as the manufacture of 'large compressed guncotton charges for torpedoes' and the 'filling of grenades'. With the end of the war in 1918, demand for such products ceased. Anti-war sentiments set in and, with foreign competition resumed, the works at Little Beside were closed. C.C. James makes reference to the Bickford-Smith dismantling and removal of the machinery[41], probably to his works at Tuckingmill. The loss of a mainstay local industry contributed to the widespread, and already disastrously high levels of unemployment in Gwennap.

The Ropeworks at Tolgullow

Many Cornish parishes, especially those with widespread mining and maritime activity, seem to have maintained a 'ropewalk'. Gwennap, with its ropewalk at Tolgullow, was no exception. The late-eighteenth and early-nineteenth centuries were particularly busy times for the Gwennap mines, so a local demand for the supply of ropes for a variety of mining purposes became essential.

The earliest mention of the ropewalk appears on R. Thomas's map of Gwennap dated 1819, where it is marked between Tolgullow and Scorrier House. A structure like a long, straight building with a continuing 'walk' or path reveals where the site was. The site is better shown on the Gwennap Tithe Map of 1843, where the same long, straight, narrow building, probably a simple roof structure to protect rope workers from the rain and sun, is much more evident. The Tithe Map also shows a small cluster of other buildings probably associated with the site, by this time titled 'ropewalk and yard'. By 1843 the 'walk' extended across three fields in a westerly direction and the site is listed in the *Apportionment Book* (item 968) with six fields detailed as being leased to Edward Henry Hawke by Lord Clinton.

Richard Blewett incorrectly located the ropewalk along the lane leading to Fourburrow, about 75 metres south-west of the actual site. Although none of the former works survive, a site visit showed a remarkably straight wall (approximately 100 metres long) forming part of the garden boundary for the property (presently) called Woodcott.

The business by 1841 was owned by the firm Edward Hawke & Co. Edward himself was the descendant of the 'respectable' Hawke family who had resided around Tolgullow possibly since the mid-eighteenth century. He was born in 1799, so it was likely to have been his father John Hawke who had started the business at some date before mention of it was first made in 1819.[42] Edward, it seems, became extensively involved in the business with a view to succeeding his father. In 1832, his son, also Edward, was born. The family continuity was maintained by Edward junr, who was also groomed to inherit the business. He also became known in the county as a solid and reputable merchant, representing the works all over the country. Both *Kelly's Directory* of 1856 and *Doidge's Directory of Gwennap* of 1866, list Edward Hawke & Son as rope manufacturers at Tolgullow.

The premature death of Edward junr, at the age of 38, after falling from a horse, left his father to form a new partnership with his close friend and business associate Henry Backhouse Fox (of the well-known Falmouth family), who had earlier invested in the Unity Safety Fuse Company (c.1865–73). By the 1870s, most of the major copper mines in Gwennap had ceased working and the local demand for ropes must have fallen dramatically. Despite this, the works were saved from total collapse by the good business relationships Hawke enjoyed in the northern districts of England. The death of Edward Hawke senr in October 1871, at the age of 72, meant the family were unable to continue trading, and around this time Fox completely bought out and then resumed the business.[43]

How the rope was actually made can only be speculated upon, but the process given by R.T. Paige in his publication *The Tamar Valley and its People* (1984), believed to have been typical for many centuries, may not be too unlike the methods used at Tolgullow during the early years:

> *A low, long shed, open to the weather on the south side, was one of the main requirements. To make a 60 yard rope, the shed had to be over 100 yards long, and in order to allow for shortening that resulted from twisting the strands, each strand had to be 80 to 85 yards in length. In addition, allowances had to be made for the twisting machine at the west end of the shed and of the 'jack' at the other end.*

From Thomas's 1819 map and the 1843 Tithe Map we can see that the works at Tolgullow used the customary 'long, low shed', which made up about one-third of the total length of the ropewalk.

The sale of merchandise and plant machinery after the closure in August 1875 lists the works as possessing 'heckles' and a hemp spreader. A rope-tarring machine for tarring single yarns was later used, and about 100 cans, which possibly contained substances such as the oil and grease to make the yarn supple and waterproof, are listed. Copper tar-tanks were also listed at the site. There was a drawing machine, a yarn-winding machine and a large flat hemp rope machine (worked by one man), as well as 'fore-gear with ten crooks' which were all associated with the mechanisation of the later rope-spinning process. Several types of jack are mentioned in the sales list, as well as tram wagons and wheels, which suggest a track for the jack to run as well as transporting heavy items around the site. Other machinery included three spinning machines and 78 iron bobbins, winding drum, warm-water pipes, iron shafting with pulleys, belts etc., turning lathe, vice, ropers' iron tube (tongue and others), sundry tops, dandies, stake heads and posts, improved reels, turntables, several iron equalisers or laying machines and frames, one large for capstan ropes, iron pouch on wood frame, iron winders, welp wheels, large yarn drums, horizontal bobbin frame and a large quantity of bobbins. A 'large iron beam and scales, and several others of various sizes' were for sale as well as a 'large atchet, fitting tools and swivels, etc.' The usual contents of a blacksmith's shop are also listed, along with a cylinder and other parts (including brasses) of a 14½in horizontal iron rack and angle iron, shafting, etc., a long run of iron pipes, iron pumps, grinding stone, tarpaulins, cast steel, lamps, etc.[44]

William Francis, writing in 1845, reinforces the image of the busy scene to which much of the machinery must have contributed:

> *And there, on the left hand, the rope-yard presents*
> *Machinery ample for all its intents,*
> *Where many are made, both large ropes and small,*
> *For the capstan, the whim, the tackle and all.*[45]

Capstan ropes appear to have been a speciality. In 1841, the ropeworks made a capstan 340 fathoms (2,040 feet) long for Tresavean Mine. Weighing almost 7 tons, completely unspliced, and with a 14in diameter, it was at that time reputed to be the largest capstan rope ever manufactured in one length.[46] Francis is again on hand to inform us about materials used:

Thence we receive from the ports of the Czar,
Hides for buckets and clacks, with pitch, oil, and tar,
Grease, tallow for candles, and hemp to make ropes,
These consumed by our mines feed Muscovite hopes.

It seems the industry was, to some extent, dependent on foreign imports of hemp to make rope, in this case Russia, from where such materials were shipped to ports like Devoran, Penryn, Falmouth and Portreath. From the year June 1842 to June 1843 around 1,334 cwt of rope and hemp were consumed by Gwennap's leading mines (not including several smaller ones at a value of £2,668). Such was the value and contribution of this industry during thriving times.

From the 1820s, chains (especially for drawing) were preferred to ropes, and by 1856, we find Edward Henry Hawke & Son described in *Kelly's Directory* as 'improved patent rope and chain manufacturers', also adding wire-rope to their supply items. Hawke's business was clearly innovative and not afraid to change with the times. As Francis mentions, chains were superseding traditional hemp-made ropes and by the mid-1850s wire-rope was considered more reliable for many mining operations. It seems likely that a heavy mechanisation of the works was in place by this time, as the sale list confirms:

... a valuable 15 inch cylinder horizontal rotary engine, 2ft 6in stroke, with governors, fly wheel, shaft, crank, etc, about four tons, also a heavy granite bed etc, and boiler and fittings about nine tons, two wire rope machines (by Bowden Bros, now the Northumberland Engine Company); one wire winding-machine, bobbins for wire ropes, wire ropes reeling machine, etc, stitching machine and frame, and a wire testing machine.[47]

In the yard were housed two horses used for drawing two four-wheeled wagons, and another on springs, all used for transporting merchandise. Nearby was the site office where the business registers, wire gauges, wire pliers, company safe, scales and weights and copying press were kept, amongst other miscellaneous items.

During its time the ropeworks employed 'a large number of hands', although an exact number is impossible to identify. Significantly, the Tolgullow ropewalk was considered 'one of the most successful concerns of its kind in the kingdom', supplying orders not just all over Cornwall, but all over the Lancashire and Yorkshire manufacturing districts.[48] Like so many other Cornish industries at this time, ropemaking, especially if not close to a port or harbour, could become a casualty of the copper-mining depression. This of course highlights the importance of the mining industry, not just for Gwennap but also Cornwall, and the weak postition of industries such as rope making, which depended upon it.

Scientific Instrument Making

Extensive copper-mining activity during the late-eighteenth and early-nineteenth centuries were nowhere more pronounced than at Gwennap. The new 'town' of St Day had rapidly expanded to become a busy service centre for the several mines at work within and around its boundaries and played host to the ever-increasing migrants who had regularly arrived on the streets. One of these migrants was William Wilton. Born in 1801, at Burroppa in the parish of Mevagissey, Wilton became apprenticed to one of the many watch and clock makers who traded in the area. Having acquired the rudiments of mathematical and scientific instrument making, he established a business and workshop in his garden shed at Church Street, St Day, in 1825, setting himself about the task of manufacturing mine-surveying equipment.[49] Wilton particularly sought to adapt existing miners' dials and theodolites (instruments for measuring angles) to the regularities of Cornish mines, which had, on the whole, become deeper and more complex than most other mines of the world by this time. In practice, underground surveying was itself a dangerous occupation as surveyors used foot-boards and were frequently suspended over shafts and inclines to facilitate accurate readings. Tunnels were narrow, space was limited and poor illumination often hampered operations. Thus a demand arose for compactness to ease carriage of heavy and expensive equipment, along with the constant emphasis on, and challenge of, achieving increasing accuracy.

The development and deployment of advanced mine-surveying equipment provided a considerable financial incentive for those capable of exploiting it. In addition, the origins of the Royal Cornwall Polytechnic Society in 1833 were largely based on the principle of improvement within the field of mining-related knowledge and technology, inspiring Wilton and his contemporaries with rewards and recognition for instruments offered to the Polytechnic's annual exhibitions. In 1835 Wilton presented a miners' theodolite which combined 'the properties of the level, with a quadrant to the miners' dial.' Significantly, this latest work was considered a true miners' theodolite on the basis that it realistically

Wilton Workshop remains.

addressed the ever-increasing variety of mine-surveying practice. In short, this instrument adhered to the management of detailed accuracy and stability because it:

> *... was divided into degrees, and the limb to thirds of degrees furnished with large and small sights, and fitted on a tripod stand with adjusting screws and a half-ball joint.*[50]

The exhibit was greatly admired and Wilton received the first award ever given for a surveying instrument by the Polytechnic Society, a bronze medal. The following year saw an exhibit by Mr J. Phillips for 'a dial with a larger compass'. More importantly, Joel Lean looked to seriously address the problem of underground magnetic interference (caused by the presence of iron) and exhibited an instrument capable of 'being used even when the needle was rendered useless by magnetic attraction.' Named the 'circumferentor', this instrument later became known as Lean's Dial and was popularly used until the end of the century. Both Phillips and Lean received bronze medals in 1836 for their contributions. Wilton reacted again the following year by exhibiting a dial which also defied underground magnetism, but further improved accuracy by adding a 'second and supplementary compass plate', but it seems this presented no real challenge to the simplicity of Lean's Dial.

Cornwall could now boast a handful of scientific instrument makers who could between them produce or repair the most advanced equipment available. The acceleration of the collective expertise called for advances in the tools used in manufacturing and, in 1837, an engineer called Jordan designed an 'engine for graduating mathematical instruments'. This further facilitated the accuracy of cutting the measurement impressions made upon instruments. Wilton, too, advanced the graduating engine shortly after. Despite this, instruments were, until c.1850, machined on 'very simple lathes and by hand turning tools.'[51]

Wilton continued to advance variations of his miners' theodolite, seeking perfection and striving for improvement, his success marked by various awards and medals awarded to him almost annually. By the mid-1840s Wilton, by this time advertising as a mathematical and 'philosophical' instrument maker, offered a comprehensive range of mine and land-surveying equipment which included miners' dials, theodolites, quadrants, plain and telescope levels, drawing instruments, pocket dials, circular protractors with or without traversing limb, trigonometers plain and rolling, parallel rulers, plotting scales, measuring chains and tapes, thermometers, barometers, and engine counters 'with the most recent improvements'. His overall service extended to include the 'repair, lacquer, and silver' and total refurbishment of old equipment, as well as the manufacture of sundials 'made to any latitude'. Business expansion included a move to the then mining boom town of Camborne, where Mr Llewellyn Newton, a stationer at Market Place, acted as an agent for the sale of Wilton's merchandise in that area.[52]

Llewellyn Newton himself had a particular interest in engineering and claimed that he 'was to have been' a pupil of Richard Trevithick, and as a boy rode on his engines.[53] In 1824, Newton's son, Edward Tippet, was born, and being of engineering stock he too was encouraged into a career of mine engineering. As a boy he consolidated the Wilton-Newton connection further by becoming apprentice to Wilton at St Day, later marrying his daughter. He learned quickly and at the age of 23 showed considerable initiative by improving the counter attached to pumping engines and used to register the space passed through by the piston. The idea (which Wilton had also achieved notable success with in 1838), was to count and effectively monitor the length of stroke of the piston and thus reduce the 'duty' of the engine. Young Newton's 'improved counter' was deemed more economical during a six-month trial on the 70in engine at North Roskear Mine in 1847.[54] He continued to develop the principle of 'distance-indication' on carriage travel and the speed of machinery, as well as the strokes of steam engines. His pneumatic distance-indicator was recognised by the Polytechnic Society in 1855. Like his mentor, Newton recognised that theodolites always commanded greater accuracy with extra facilities, and sought to improve lathe attachments that would allow finer graduations to be cut, as well as accessories manufactured. His 'compound slide rest', designed for turning lathes and exhibited in 1850, heralded a new era in mathematical and scientific equipment manufacturing.[55] This was only surpassed by his own improved graduating machine, which was a reworking of Wilton's earlier efforts.

By this time, Wilton's own son had served his apprenticeship under the disciplined guidance of his ageing father. Though he was never to display the innovation of his father or Edward Newton, he was still competent enough to be groomed to succeed to his father's business.

In the meantime, the old master still maintained a dedicated enthusiasm and in 1858 Wilton senr exhibited, and received a Royal Cornwall Polytechnic Society Silver Medal for, a theodolite which embodied the 'principle of working with two or three stands' allowing the 'check' technique to be exploited. This technique continued as the most 'approved method' until the 1890s. Sadly, ill-health set in and William Wilton senr died at his home in Church Street on 25 April 1860. As was his wish, his son continued the management of the business with his brother-in-law, Edward Newton.[56] Renamed Wilton & Co., the partners enjoyed relative success exhibiting in 1865 a 'self-levelling dial' which was awarded a Silver Medal.

By 1866 the partnership was dissolved. William Wilton junr was still to be found in his father's home in Church Street, St Day, by now advertising sales and services as a jeweller. His partner Edward Newton moved around the corner to the north side of Market Street (now known as Fore Street), where he too described himself as a jeweller, along with his usual role as mathematical instrument maker.[57]

At this time another creditable young apprentice was to make his appearance. John Teague Letcher, was born at St Day in January 1851. He became an understudy to William Wilton junr in June 1863, at the age of 12. Around four years later, William Wilton junr sold his business to Mr A. Jeffery of Camborne (whom it appears was an assistant to his father), before emigrating to Valparaiso, Chile.[58]

In 1867, young Letcher continued his apprenticeship with Edward Newton for one year, before joining Mr Jeffery at Camborne for the next ten years until 1878. Letcher was also to demonstrate the abilities and talents so praiseworthy of his predecessors. He learned the rudiments of mathematical and scientific instrument making sufficiently to invent his own theodolite and dial in 1876.[59]

At some time along the way, his success attracted the attention of his brother Thomas Henry Letcher. Thomas, born at St Day in June 1836, was the older of the two and started his working life as an apprentice carpenter to John Downing (probably of Litchfield House, St Day) in 1848, going on to become an established builder by 1860. In the true spirit of the Smilesian philosophy, Thomas looked to self-improvement through education by enrolling as a student at the classes of the Miners' Association of Devon and Cornwall. In 1871, he became a teacher at the St Day Classes and re-established classes in mineralogy and inorganic chemistry at Camborne in 1874, reputedly walking from St Day to his lectures. Thomas continued at St Day until 1875, by which time he passed chemistry in the South Kensington Exams, listed fourth out of 60 students. Thomas left his former occupation as builder and carpenter to be an under-agent, overseeing the properties within the St Day manor of the estates of R. Chichester Esq., in 1874. He extended this to include the estates of the Hearle and Champernowne families in 1876.[60]

Shortly after, Thomas joined his brother John who was already working with A. Jeffery at Camborne. The new partnership was called Letcher Bros. & Jeffery[61], but by 1878 Thomas had dissolved the group, having decided to establish a family business at Cathedral Lane in Truro, in company with his brother, making scientific instruments.

Success came immediately to the pair when in 1878 they received a Silver Medal in an open competition presented by the Society of Arts for 'the best set of blowpipe apparatus to sell retail at one guinea.' With an emphasis upon compactness derived from their skills in scientific instruments, the Letcher brothers met the challenge with ease. Further, neither could have failed to recognise the financial potential that such an inexpensive and compact mineral-testing kit could bring. The situation developed into the manufacture of a neat and well-designed blowpipe set, used by mineralogists, chemists, metallurgists, prospectors, mining engineers and surveyors, for the precise identification of minerals. The equipment comprised of a deal-wood box 10½in long by 4¾in wide by 3⅕in deep, containing 'no less than 42 different articles, and all of these packed in a highly ingenious manner.' A 'superior set' in a polished mahogany box, containing additional items of better quality could be purchased at £1.12s.6d. and the 'Best Set' (again in a mahogany box), containing an additional 48 test minerals arranged in a drawer, could be purchased at £2.2s.6d. The equipment proved popular for students and specialists alike throughout the international mining industry, essentially because the set, being so compact, was easily transportable yet with its diverse range of testing kit, enabled practically any mineral to be identified promptly.

Despite their early success, this partnership also dissolved and whilst John remained at the premises at Cathedral Lane, Thomas returned to his occupation as under-agent for the lords of the manor of St Day. With a decline in the Cornish mining industry, the demand for scientific mining equipment decreased. Mass production techniques must have further eroded the business of hand-finished mine instrument manufacturing. By the mid-1880s, John Letcher was describing his business as watch and clock maker, along with the allied trades of jeweller and silversmith.[62]

Thomas Henry Letcher died at St Day in May 1908. He was described as possessing a 'scientific turn of mind', but had also established himself as a Methodist preacher 'wide and tolerant in his views'.[63] His son continued as land steward for the lords of St Day manor for several years after his father's death.

John Teague Letcher died in 1917 and the business premises continued in the name of his son who practised as an optician until his death in 1956. When the premises were sold and subsequently cleared in the same year, it was discovered that on the top floor, boxes containing clock workings, tools, clock parts, and similar items, littered shelves and the floor. On the middle floor, 24 boxes of minerals were found, which were deposited at Truro School and became known as the Letcher Collection. On the ground floor behind the shop were three rooms which each housed various lathes and their attachments. The whole atmosphere of the premises was of time frozen.[64]

There is little doubt that Wilton, Newton and the Letcher brothers were among a very few engineers and instrument makers, within an international market, who achieved advances in scientific

Scientific Instrument Making

Above: *Surveying instrument manufactured by William Wilton.*

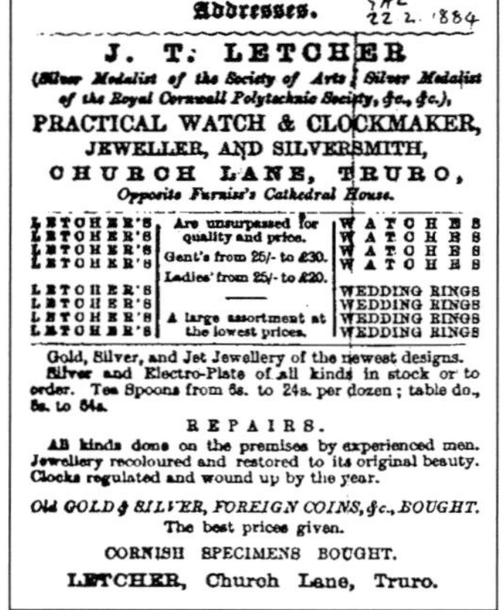

Addresses. 22 2. 1884

J. T. LETCHER

(Silver Medalist of the Society of Arts; Silver Medalist of the Royal Cornwall Polytechnic Society, &c., &c.),

PRACTICAL WATCH & CLOCKMAKER, JEWELLER, AND SILVERSMITH, CHURCH LANE, TRURO,

Opposite Furniss's Cathedral House.

LETCHER'S LETCHER'S LETCHER'S LETCHER'S	Are unsurpassed for quality and price. Gent's from 25/- to £30. Ladies' from 25/- to £20.	WATCHES WATCHES WATCHES WATCHES
LETCHER'S LETCHER'S LETCHER'S LETCHER'S	A large assortment at the lowest prices.	WEDDING RINGS WEDDING RINGS WEDDING RINGS WEDDING RINGS

Gold, Silver, and Jet Jewellery of the newest designs. Silver and Electro-Plate of all kinds in stock or to order. Tea Spoons from 6s. to 24s. per dozen; table do., 5s. to 64s.

REPAIRS.

All kinds done on the premises by experienced men. Jewellery recoloured and restored to its original beauty. Clocks regulated and wound up by the year.

Old GOLD & SILVER, FOREIGN COINS, &c., BOUGHT. The best prices given.

CORNISH SPECIMENS BOUGHT.

LETCHER, Church Lane, Truro.

Right: *Advertisement for the business of J.T. Letcher, 1884, after he moved premises to Church Lane, Truro.*

Right: *Brass protractor manufactured by William Wilton, St Day.*

Below: *Advertisement for the business of William Wilton junr who succeeded to his father's business, which he continued with his brother-in-law, E.T. Newton, under the name 'Wilton & Co.'*

Re WILLIAM WILTON, DECEASED.

ALL Persons having any claim on the Estate of the late WILLIAM WILTON, Mathematical and Philosophical Instrument and Watch and Clock Maker, St. Day, are requested to furnish particulars of the same; and all Persons indebted to the said estate, are desired, as early as possible, to pay the amount of their respective debts to Mrs. WILTON, St. Day, the executrix of the said estate.

WILLIAM HENRY WILTON begs to inform the friends of his late father and public generally, that the above business will in future be carried on by him and his brother-inlaw, E. T. Newton, under the firm of WILTON and Co., and also to thank them for the very liberal support which his late father experienced for more than 35 years, and in succeeding to the above business, solicits a continuance of their esteemed favours.

Having had the entire management of the working department during the protracted illness of his father, they are enabled to conduct it on the same principles, and to execute all orders entrusted to their care with the same promptitude and accuracy.

Dated St. Day, May 8, 1860.

instrument making. As with the invention of Humphry Davy's safety lamp and Bickford's safety fuse, they understood the commercial incentives. But in looking beyond the need to make a living, we see a competitive spirit, a striving for precision, and a humanitarian motive in the desire to produce items which would help save workers from the countless dangers of the Cornish and global mines. Today we can still view some specimens of their work, which proudly rest among displays at the County Museum, Truro, Camborne School of Mines and Geevor Tin Mine Museum, St Just. Like the judges and patrons of the nineteenth-century Royal Cornwall Polytechnic Society, we can marvel at the remarkable craftsmanship and ingenuity which these surviving pieces still illustrate.

Arsenic Production at Poldice

The production of arsenic was a subsidiary industry in many tin- and copper-mining districts. The processed mineral was used for a variety of purposes, including enamelling, and the manufacture of glass, colour pigments, dyes, insect pesticides and rodent poisons, adding to metals for finishing effects, sheep-dipping mixtures and tanning processes, amongst others.[65]

For many years miners had disregarded the usefulness of arsenic pyrites (often known as 'mispickel') but by the mid-nineteenth century a few mining sites began to process the mineral in answer to growing market demands. Nearby at Bissoe, the British Arsenic Company was reasonably well established by this time and at Trevince, a Chemical Works processing some arsenic was in operation by 1875.

The years 1897 and 1898 witnessed a sharp upturn in demand and output, and investment in an arsenic works (originally intended for Devon) was secured by Mr C. Pengilly and George S. Bray at Poldice.[66] Pengilly was to become the managing director of the Poldice works and the engineering advisor, whilst Bray was a large shareholder. Both men negotiated Poldice as the site on behalf of the Anglo-Peninsular Chemical Company, of Fenchurch Street, London, which was one of three new developments.

With £2,000 for investment, a cornerstone of the new calcining and refining house was ceremoniously laid in March 1897, with Mr Joseph Allen of Carharrack contracted for the construction. Although this was a new venture, some 'arsenic burning flues and houses at the place' had recently been acquired for the company and records of repairs to old flues suggest earlier arsenic processing and production before the Anglo-Peninsular Company takeover at Poldice.[67]

Production capabilities were estimated at 2,400 tons per annum and with 120 employed (on what hours or conditions is uncertain) by September 1897, output quickly reached 90 tons per month, although the works were in fact geared to produce around 200 tons per month. The average pay for all workers was £200, which was paid on a fortnightly basis. Precisely when the works were closed is (at present) not known, but operations probably ceased early in the twentieth-century as little mention of them appears after 1901.

Velveteen Manufacture

Around 1881, two Rochdale men, Mr J. Fitton and his partner Mr Gazy, established a velveteen manufacturing business in a small shop in the town of St Day, having been attracted by 'the cheapness of labour in [the] little Cornish town and neighbourhood.'[68] The business grew and soon moved to the dilapidated ironworks at Little Beside, which was rebuilt for the venture. Eventually, an average of 40 staff were employed and began work:

> *... in the long sheds of the factory,* [where] *from 40–50 girls were constantly moving up and down and thus covering miles in the course of a day's work. They were engaged in cutting the clothe with knives fitted with needle-like points. For this onerous task, they were paid at the rate of three to five shillings a week.*[69]

Expenses amounted to around £1,000 a year, of which '£138 went to the railway company who charged 58s.6d. a ton for bringing the fustian direct from Manchester' and the same for returning '1,000 yard lots of blocked velvet to the Manchester dyers, who then distribute it to the warehouses.'[70] By 1894, the business was struggling to make real profits. Changing fashions, in particular the move away from velvet, set the business into real decline, but it still continued until 1899 when T.R. Mills sold 'John Fitton's Velvet Factory and dwelling house' by public auction for £340.[71] Despite some hopes, the factory was never reopened.

Notes

Thanks to John Tonkin for his advice on china clay and brick production.

[1] *West Briton*, 12.2.1864.
[2] *Cornish Post & Mining News*, 28.1.1909.
[3] *Royal Cornwall Gazette*, 27.6.1879.
[4] Hunt, Robert, *Mineral Statistics of the United Kingdom in the 19th Century*. Also, Tonkin, John, communication/notes from St Austell, 1995, and Trevithick, Annie, *A Short History of St Day*, c.1897, p.17.
[5] Miners' Association of Devon & Cornwall, 1869, pp.36-37.
[6] Tonkin, John, Ibid.
[7] Mitchell, Frank, *Annals of an Ancient Cornish Town – Redruth*. Dyllansow Truran, Redruth, 1985, p.172.
[8] Barton, Rita, *A History of the Cornish China Clay Industry*, Truro, 1966, p.17.
[9] *Royal Cornwall Gazette*, 27.6.1879.
[10] Trevithick, Annie, Ibid, p.18.
[11] CRO. TL90. Account Book, The Cornwall Arsenic Co., Bissoe.
[12] Hill, J.B., and MacAlister, D.A., *Memoirs of the Geological Survey: The Geology of Falmouth and Truro and the Mining District of Camborne and Redruth*, London HMSO, 1906, p.111.
[13] *Royal Cornwall Gazette*, 27.6.1879.
[14] Ibid.
[15] James, Terrence (FSA), 'A Carmarthen Bay Shipwreck', in *The Carmarthenshire Antiquary, Vol. XXIX*, 1993, p.101.
[16] *Royal Cornwall Gazette*, 31.5.1879.
(See also Brickworks tradecard, 1880.)
[17] Bradford Barton, D., *The Redruth & Chasewater Railway 1824–1915*, 1978, p.26.
[18] Ibid., pp.71 and 79.
[19] Trevithick, Annie, Ibid., and *Royal Cornwall Gazette*, 27.6.1897 and 4.1.1912.
[20] Blewett, R.R., 'These Things Have Been', Inst. 64 (March, 1970). (See also *Royal Cornwall Gazette*, 1.6.1877.)
[21] *Royal Cornwall Gazette*, 24.5.1873.
[22] Francis, William, *Gwennap*, Privately Published, 1845, pp.162–63.
[23] Whittaker, *The Rise and Progress of the British Explosives Industry*, London, 1909, pp.412–13.
[24] Ibid. (See also Earl, Bryan, *Cornish Explosives*, 1968, p.79.)
[25] Earl, Bryan, *Cornish Mining, The Techniques of Metal Mining in The West of England, Past and Present*, St Austell, 1994, p.43.
[26] CRO. AD 642/12.
[27] Ibid.
[28] *West Briton*, 26.10.1871.
[29] Harris, T.R., A *Short History of the Cornish Explosives Industry* (ms), 1971, p.7.
[30] Trevithick, Annie, Ibid., p.18.
(See also *Royal Cornwall Gazette*, 27.2.1875.)
[31] *Royal Cornwall Gazette*, 27.2.1875, and *West Briton*, 25.2.1875.
[32] *West Briton*, 25.2.1875.
[33] *The Rise and Progress of the British Explosives Industry*, Ibid., pp.412–13.
[34] *West Briton*, 15.3.1875.
[35] *West Briton*, 25.2.1875, and *Royal Cornwall Gazette*, 13.3.1875.
[36] *West Briton*, Ibid., and *Royal Cornwall Gazette*, 27.2.1875.
[37] Trevithick, Annie, Ibid.
[38] *The Rise and Progress of the British Explosives Industry*, Ibid.
[39] *Mining Journal*, 1893, p.424.
[40] *Kelly's Directories*, early-twentieth century.
[41] James, C.C., *History of Gwennap*, Privately Published, (n.d.), p.139.
[42] *West Briton*, 26.10.1871.
[43] *West Briton*, Ibid., and 9.8.1875.
[44] *West Briton*, 9.8.1875.
[45] Francis, William, Ibid., pp. 62–63.
[46] *West Briton*, 7.5.1875.
[47] *Cornubian*, 13.8.1875.
[48] *West Briton*, 9.8.1875.
[49] *Journal of the Royal Cornwall Polytechnic Society*, 1890, p.86.
[50] Ibid.
[51] Ibid., and 1839, pp.101–2.
[52] *Royal Cornwall Gazette*, 26.6.1844.
[53] Trevithick, F., *Life of Richard Trevithick*, 1892, pp.108, 342–3.
[54] *Journal of the Royal Cornwall Polytechnic Society*, 1847, pp.23–24.
[55] *Journal of the Royal Cornwall Polytechnic Society*, 1890, p.89.
[56] *Royal Cornwall Gazette*, 11.5.1860.
[57] *Doidge's Directory of Gwennap*, 1866, p.8.
[58] *West Briton*, 26.3.1874.
[59] *Collectania Cornubiensis*, p.895.
[60] Ibid., pp.495–6.
[61] James, C.C., Ibid., p.83. (See also front cover of the J.T. Letcher Catalogue (Copy at RIC, Truro) and thanks to Mr R. Penhallurick, RIC, Truro, for his discussion of the Letcher brothers.)
[62] *Royal Cornwall Gazette*, 22.2.1884.
[63] *Cornubian*, 21.5.1908.
[64] *West Briton*, 9.2.1995. (Thanks to Philip Martin for kindly lending the author a copy of a J.T. Letcher catalogue. Information was also taken from the demonstration of blowpipe apparatus by Alan Cotton and the lecture by Philip Martin given at St Day Historical Society Meeting, February 1995.)
[65] *Journal of the Trevithick Society, No.15* (1988). (See also *The Rise and Progress of the British Explosives Industry*, London, 1909, pp.412–13, and Burt, Roger, *Arsenic – Its Significance for the Survival of South Western Metal Mining in the Late-Nineteenth Century and Early-Twentieth Century*, pp.5–19.)
[66] *Royal Cornwall Gazette*, 24.3.1898.
[67] *West Briton*, 1.4.1897.
[68] *Cornubian*, 5.10.1894.
[69] *Camborne-Redruth Packet*, 17.1.1961.
[70] *Cornubian*, 5.10.1894.
[71] *Cornubian*, 28.7.1899.

Shop front belonging to: 'T.R. MILLS. FURNITURE ESTABLISHMENT & SHOW ROOMS', c.1900.

Seventeen

St Day & The Emigration Experience

For some, the word 'emigration' conjures an image of St Day in the 1890s, the arrival of the South African mail, the distribution of bankers' cheques from Kimberley and Johannesburg, the rush to towns for wild spending sprees and crowded markets and shops burning lamp oil late into the evenings. The South African mines, like those at St Day a generation before, were opening one after another. Prospects for foreign employment and good wages had not been seen like this around Gwennap for over 20 years.

Emigration began from the early decades of the nineteenth century, when we find in 1827 a Captain Trebilcock advertising for two 'able bal carpenters' for the Bolivian Mining Company. By December 1831 Michael Williams of Scorrier House was advertising for a mine captain in Brazil. Carpenters 'capable of building water-wheels' in Brazil as well as other prospects for blacksmiths were offered with 'liberal wages' in the mid 1830s.[1] To some extent, this highlights a rather early but nonetheless shrewd investment by some mining adventurers. They were capable of looking beyond the long-term dangers of placing all their eggs in one basket at home in Gwennap, to involving themselves in global economic forces, which shaped the fortunes of mining throughout the next century.

Another early picture of emigration from St Day was very different from the simple demand on skilled labour abroad. With a large population, at least by Cornish standards, Gwennap became a concern for the Guardians of the Poor, who believed their responsibilities of providing for paupers were growing and becoming too expensive. A solution had been found by other regions that offered 'assisted emigration passages' where people could choose to emigrate to Australia or New Zealand. Their choice was based on the options of facing a difficult journey to a relatively unknown land, or facing more poverty and hardship and the possibility of the parish workhouse at Burnwithian. This early wave of community emigration appears to have attracted families rather than the skilled or semi-skilled labourers of earlier and later generations. R.R. Blewett gives a fascinating, though speculative account of the times. Below is a list of early emigrants who received assisted passage to Australia, and who appear in the Gwennap Parish Vestry minute-book:

William Lawn, his wife and seven children.
William Sprague, his wife and five children.
Charles Burn, his wife and four children.
Samuel Coombe, his wife and four children.
William Williams, his wife and seven children.
John Crap, his wife and three children.
John Moyle, his wife and four children.
Martha Williams, single.
Samuel Peters, his wife and six children.
Ann Harvey, widow and six children.
Nicholas Burrows, his wife and three children.
Elizabeth Benbow, widow and five children.
Hugh Long, his wife and three children.
Henry Rosewarne, his wife and three children.
Mary Gill, single.[2]

As the copper mines began to close in Gwennap during the 1860s–'70s, a few miners found employment in the tin mines of the Camborne district or at the St Day Brickworks. However, these industries could never absorb anything like the mass of miners who had previously been employed at Gwennap. For many, the only option was emigration, but to what extent this may have been considered a permanent or temporary solution by the local community is difficult to estimate. A steady flow of emigrants from West Cornwall was well under way by 1869; the bulk of travellers appear to have been 'miners and young women.'[3] By the early 1870s, St Day was experiencing the acute effects of the crisis, as a correspondent of the *West Briton* noted:

> *The working mines are ground to death's door, and... whilst the salaries of the agents are increased 20 per cent, the miners are not allowed to get enough to keep body and soul together. In fact, many of them have resolved, during the past fortnight to pick up their kit and start. If by any chance whatever they make in one month 50s. or £3, the next month they are not allowed to earn more than 30s.*[4]

One of the headstones of Gwennap and St Day emigrants who died abroad. This stone was erected for William Arundell Paynter 'Formerly of Gwennap, Cornwall'. He died at the Moonta Mines, Australia, 1873, aged 54.

The records of emigration details do not seem to feature heavily in the newspapers until the 1860s when a flow of St Day extracts from the *West Briton*, the *Royal Cornwall Gazette* and the *Cornish Post & Mining News* begin to appear more frequently and continue until the 1940s. A typical extract read: 'Thursday last Mr Michael Jeffery left St Day for Southampton where he will join *The Greek* which sails for Johannesburg on the following Saturday.'[5] Often these extracts would include other personal information. When used collectively as a sample of the times, a more distinctive picture of emigration emerges, and we can begin to chart the movements of a range of individuals. Male and female entrants are recorded along with their children; emigration was for some a family experience. Communications, shipping routes, boom and rush periods may be gleaned, as well as a host of other individual experiences such as biographical notes, successes and failures of individuals, deaths, adventure, travel experiences, transport, hazards, plus the persistence of culture and religion with emigrants abroad.

This study of the 602 emigration extracts available to date possesses inherent weaknesses. For example, the bulk of extracts appear from the 1880s by which time we know that a great deal of emigration had occurred from the St Day district (similar to earlier Cornish movements to both North and South America in the 1830s, Australia in the 1840s and South Africa in the 1890s). Reportage is not always consistent, and inaccuracies, with surnames for example, throw doubt on the identity of a few individuals. Also, access to other comparative data, specific to these particular extracts, is not easily available. However, an immediate general picture begins to emerge as emigrants naturally divide into departures and arrivals to and from St Day and district. The departures can be divided into three main destinations: South Africa, the USA and 'others' which include South America, West and North Africa, India, New Zealand, Canada, Turkey, Spain and Australia.

More acute analysis shows that 16 per cent of all extracts relate to women, whilst an overwhelming 84 per cent refer to movements of male emigrants. South Africa was by far the most popular emigration region for St Day miners from the 1890s, followed by the USA. Several extracts refer to miners having travelled to several different countries during their lives as emigrants. For example, Captain Thomas Chivell worked at mines in Mexico, Chile and California.[6] Others moved about whilst staying in the same country, such as William Pope who worked in mines at Ruby Hill, Eureka, Nevada, and California, all before 1881.[7]

Of the sample of females who emigrated, a different picture emerges as the dominant emigration region for this group was the USA, followed by South Africa. This suggests that South Africa was more of a 'lone-male' experience for St Day emigrants, with females less likely to consider this region than the USA. Perhaps South Africa, with its more hostile terrain and climate and less developed industrial infrastructure as well as occasional political hostilities, provided less attractive opportunities for females than the USA.

Arrivals home somewhat reinforce this picture; the vast majority of all returning emigrants came home from South Africa. It seems this region offered rather short-term solutions for most emigrants and was perhaps not a permanent option in overcoming difficulties back home in the St Day district. We cannot be sure how emigrants perceived the unpredictable nature of a mining-based economy which had undermined their own lives and communities up to these times. For many, it must have been a more gradual unfolding of opportunities, events, timing, planning and day-to-day expectations.

Those 'other countries' to which many people emigrated were similar to South Africa in that a huge percentage of emigrants seemed to return to the St Day district. For example, Mrs E. Williams and family returned to St Day to resettle after a stay of 20 years in Mexico.[23]

The *West Briton* recorded that from 1868–71, 2,750 people left the districts of Gwennap, Chacewater and Redruth seeking employment in the mills of the North of England, which at the time offered far better prospects, wages and conditions than anything available in Cornwall.[8] Undoubtedly, some St Day people would have been amongst them. Emigration gathered pace from 1896 to 1899, with new mines opening around that time offering real prospects. The increasing tension and eventual outbreak of the Boer War between the Dutch settlers in South Africa and the British prompted the return of many St Day men by 1899. St Day Institute was reported to be 'full with men returned from South Africa' around the time that hostilities broke out in October 1899, a fact borne out by the contemporary newspaper reports that mentioned a noticeable grouping of emigrants returning from that region.[9] Very little movement took place for the duration of the Boer War and the years immediately following it, as it took a while for life in South Africa to settle.

Several men found employment in the Gwennap United Mines around 1900 reworking the burrows for tin. The Poldice section of the St Day United became engaged both underground and at the surface, with 96 heads of Cornish stamps erected. Both burrow and underground 'stuff' was being worked.[10] The years 1905–08 showed a real 'rush' period of emigration; clearly emigrants from St Day and district felt safe to return to South Africa by this time. Despite this, several St Day men returned from South Africa during July 1907 because of a large strike in Johannesburg.[11]

Comparatively, this was the busiest period of all, but it was interrupted by another decline in 1909–10. Some local mines such as Parc-an-Chy and Wheal Gorland were being worked with reasonable success by this time, improving prospects at home, which perhaps had some impact upon emigration figures. St Day's Brickworks showed some peak years around this period and the Unity Safety Fuse Company was reopened under the management of Captain Bennetts in 1909. Emigration figures picked up from 1911–13, but the years 1914–18 show a sharp decline in newspapers reporting any real movement, with the exception of 1915, when 15 extracts are recorded, mostly relating to returning emigrants from the USA. With the German U-boat campaigns, travel became severely restricted. Also, new opportunities in military service, reopened mines and the fuseworks again offered better prospects.

Significantly, several St Day men appear in the ranks of foreign 'contingent' forces and responded with patriotic vigour to the Empire's 'call to arms'. The year 1919 saw an initial surge in the amount of emigration recorded (17 instances in total) in an attempt to recapture something of the pre-war optimism. However, this quickly gave way to a significant drop in such reports – newspapers included the rare reference (i.e. one, two or a maximum of three) up to 1948. New immigration laws, restricting entrants into the USA were fully effective by 1921. Canada appeared to be taking immigrants around October 1922; F. Morcom was among 100 Cornishmen who had just left for that region. By the following November, under the heading 'Good News For St Day', it seems that 106 unemployed men had either found full-time work, or emigrated. Perhaps Canada opened doors for immigrants which had been closed by the USA.[12]

Whilst newspaper extracts as a source present us with an important quantitative overview, other sources provide valuable insights into the very nature of the emigration experience itself. We quickly learn of a vast shipping network, administered at a local level by shipping agents such as T.R. Mills, 'Ironmonger, Auctioneer & Estate Valuer at Church Street' (and later Scorrier Street), and Theophilus Mitchell, a draper from Fore Street. The latter frequently travelled abroad for short spells, such as when he journeyed to Real-del-Monte in September 1900 to get married. In 1898, he reported back that prospects for overseas work and wages were very good.[13] No doubt such a first-hand experience could heighten his sales pitch amongst those still dubious about the potential of travel abroad. Money well may have been lent for emigration fares, but with miners going abroad, security of payment may at times have been stretched. Blewett reminds us of the 'unlicensed moneylender' who was always on hand to arrange a deal, 'with one Carharrack moneylender having done so much in business in South Africa, that he travelled out to collect the money personally.'[14]

T.R. Mills maintained a steady business in household and property auctions for customers in mid-Cornwall, many of whom had themselves emigrated. Both men were solid businessmen and equally quick to recognise and meet the demands of new global markets opening before them. By July 1894, T.R. Mills was advertising the sale of tickets to Cape Town, South Africa, for the considerable sums of £9.9s., £12.12s. or £15.15s. (the price being dependent on the class in which people travelled).[15]

The mass of emigration literature informs us that in earlier decades emigrants often departed from Cornish ports such as Padstow and Falmouth, although Plymouth may have been used at times. By the 1890s, Cornwall offered little compared to ports such as Southampton and occasionally Liverpool. By 1898, the Great Western Railway had added extra carriages for Cornish emigrants destined for Southampton, making this by far the busiest port used by St Day migrants as they travelled abroad.[16]

Another typical extract from this time reads:

> *Mr Theo Mitchell sent off T. Rowe, W.H. Johns and Charles Rodda of St Day to South Africa aboard the SS* Norman, *sailing from Southampton. On board from Penzance to Southampton were 100 men* [emigrants].[17]

We find that steamships such as *The Greek* and *Dunvegan Castle* departed Southampton for Johannesburg; while *The Scott*, *The Briton*, *The Sparton*, *The Guelph*, the SS *Norman*, *The Gaul* and the *Tantallon Castle* all departed for the Cape, South Africa. Departures for North America were often aboard *The Paris*, whilst the SS *Whakatane* sailed from London to New Zealand. Almost every week emigrants from St Day would join others on the platform of Redruth Railway Station to begin their long and unpredictable journey to 'the lands of alluring gold and glittering diamonds.'

Much of the Cornish emigration literature focuses on the colonisation by those travelling abroad at this time.[18] To a large extent, such infiltration could only have been made possible by effective communication between home and abroad and this was a key feature in the emigration process. The success of an immigrant worker would be corresponded or cabled home, which would often stimulate others to join him. Early successes would also mean financial assistance allowing others to follow. This was of course a much safer way of emigrating and not in the same spirit of the original pioneers who gambled their options. In this context we find Richard Carkeek leaving Scorrier Street for America in October 1908, where it was stated 'he [would] join his brothers'.[19] Mr W. Kestle who departed in March also joined his brothers. Once links were established, a 'commuter-type' emigrant seems to appear.[20] These emigrants returned quite frequently, as many as three times a year. For example, in 1906, we find: 'Joseph Annear of Telegraph Street, St Day, left on Friday for South Africa. After a stay of several months with his friends at home.'[21]

Moments of departure must have caused great anxiety for families, provoking intense pain and sorrow and a great deal of change to family life. It is not difficult to imagine the departing miner, often a dedicated father and husband, taking his place aboard the train, soon to vanish into the smoke, steam and piercing whistles. A family's life would change; so many women shifted to the role of head of household and the extra work and responsibilities of their departed husbands fell upon their shoulders. Some children would barely grow to know their fathers and consequently the community at St Day became much more matriarchal. Financial hardship continued, at least until remittances were sent home. Such scenes provoked St Day native Herbert Thomas to pen this emotional verse during these times:

Stand back, you wives and sweet hearts,
cease your kisses sighs and tears.
For the last 'good-bye' and a weeping eye
are the worst of the miner's fears.
He will face the blinding sun-glare,
and in deep weird caverns dwell,
But the anguish spent in parting,
seems a moment spent in hell.

Group emigration from a district community seemed fairly common and to travel alone was not the expected norm. For example, nine St Day men left Gwennap for South Africa aboard *The Moor* on 17 September 1896 and 12 departed for Johannesburg aboard the *Dunvegan Castle* on 3 December of the same year. Such a trend may indicate a 'rush' movement to those gold and diamond regions.[22]

However, it seems family groups of a husband, wife and children were much more the pattern of emigrants to the USA. Whilst several families travelled to South Africa, it was usually for a visit, unlike their American counterparts who often chose to stay abroad. Examples of family groups can be found in Mr and Mrs J. Murton who returned from South Africa after a stay of four years in 1907, and Mrs W. Wales who left St Day with her children in September 1913 to join her husband. Marriage also features in several of the extracts. News of various weddings abroad appear, as do newlyweds emigrating, perhaps romancing the notion and hope of a new adventure of life and love in a foreign land.

The stories of emigration covered in the newspapers are fascinating in that they chart the fortunes of departing men; their bravery, innocence, ignorance, and wit. Most survived, but several perished on such hazardous journeys. This report in the *Royal Cornwall Gazette* provides a flavour of the emigration experience in the Klondyke in N. Canada in November 1897:

Cornishmen all over the world are noted for courageous bearing in the face of difficulties, but surely the miners from St Day and district must face a superabundance of this quality to contemplate a visit to the Klondyke goldfields, in the face of particular hardships to be encountered in that district. Gold is there certainly, but in how many instances nothing but bones remain of those who went there to search for it. In many respects South Africa is not a desirable country in which to live for many years, but at present its goldfields offer a few more comforts than those of the Klondyke. Should the St Day men adhere to their present intention, it is hoped their energy will be rewarded.[24]

The possibility of death was always a real and feared factor for the immigrant miner and must have been evaluated against the harsh desperation of depression and hardship at home. Such risks were the same everywhere, if not so much on the surface, most definitely underground. To drown, be blasted or buried alive was the fate of several Gwennap immigrant miners. There are several extracts relating to St Day men who perished in the foreign mines. Thomas Launder was killed in the Carmelite Mines, Tocpilla, Bolivia. His popularity was such that over 150 Cornishmen attended his funeral abroad.[25] Thomas Henry Matthews was killed in South Africa aged just 20.[26] Fever constantly struck individuals who were often too weak to return home to loved ones before they died. The wife of Captain Simon Kinsman travelled urgently to Johannesburg with her daughter in November 1904, only just arriving in time to see him before he died of fever, mere hours after her arrival.[27] A Captain Gilbert died as a result of the climate whilst working in mines in West Africa.[28] Captain S.J. Hocking returned to his native St Day from South Africa in the same year 'for a rest from fever'.[29] Sickness could at times reach epidemic proportions or cut journeys short, as can be seen in this extract:

The foreigners are coming home from Africa, but not laden with gold. Some have not been gone long, but have decided to return quicker than they otherwise would have done owing to the sickness prevailing in that climate.[30]

Occasionally, news reached home of murder. In January 1907 William Blewett of St Day, who was employed at the Randfontain Mine, South Africa, was shot in the head whilst in his room. A sum of £22 was later discovered missing.[31] The reverberations of such an event would have stunned communities both at home and abroad and amply reinforce fears of families who anxiously awaited the safe return of relatives. In South America two St Day men were among a group of Cornish miners who were attacked by Bolivian mutineers.[32] When Willie and Albert Gay returned to their luggage at their arrival at Port Elizabeth, South Africa, they realised that they had been robbed of three fine gold rings, one pair of gold cuff-links, a £2 gold piece and many of their personal possessions, including a gold watch. Dutchmen were believed to have robbed them, but the men were left stranded to fend for themselves, probably only able to continue because of the support and generosity of other Cornish expatriates.[33]

Certainly another cause of frequent death was the dreaded mining disease, 'miner's phthisis'. Bad working conditions, especially poor ventilation and respiratory facilities meant that miners always stood the risk of infecting their lungs from the deadly rock-dust which polluted the atmosphere in which they worked. The result was often fatal. Such diseases did not discriminate against age. Many immigrant miners returned home, knowing in their minds that they had the disease, as breathing became more laboured; witness the Knuckey family in August 1908:

The death took place of Mr William Knuckey at Busveal. Deceased spent several years in South Africa, where he contracted miner's phthisis. He leaves his widow and three young children, and has over the past three years buried three sons, all young men.[34]

Reportage of death through such diseases was incredibly common (especially in connection with the miners in South Africa) from the 1890s through to the 1940s. The disease was uncompromising; miners such as James Matthews returned to St Day and died a few months later of 'the miners complaint' – in his case in July 1912, aged just 29. He left a widow and two children, but fate seemed cruel as a third child died within days of him and they were both buried together.[35] Michael Tangye interviewed the late Mr Percy Teague who commented on St Day during the period 1910–'30s:

They were bad days. When the mines closed it was either emigrate or starve. Thousands left for America and South Africa. Many returned to die, their lungs eaten out by mine dust. If you walked through the quiet streets of St Day on a summer's night the only sound to be heard was the coughing of the sick miners coming from the bedroom windows, which were always full open so that they could breathe. There were lots of widows in those days, young women left with large families to raise, with hardly any money.[36]

Phthisis was the 'widow-maker' and the rock-drill, heralded as the finest technology could offer, was simply the means of delivering death for so many. Little had been done to protect miners from the discharge of fine dust which they were forced to breathe. The subsequent effects would for many families be felt long after death, as they struggled with the social and economic setbacks which were the very nature of widowhood. Terrible fates awaited many families, including this one in November 1912: 'John Jeffery of Crofthandy died from phthisis after years in South Africa. He leaves a grief-stricken wife and ten children.'[37]

Even Theophilus Mitchell, the St Day emigration agent, died in 1916, aged 45, from phthisis contracted from spending years in Mexico and South Africa.[38] Other more natural disasters, such as the San Francisco earthquake, affected local families who had mining relatives living in that area. Such was the case for a Mr James who received a letter from his sister in May 1906, who explained the details. The letter was not only relayed around the local community of St Day, but also published for wider communication in the *Royal Cornwall Gazette* to help inform other Cornish communities. A similar earthquake disaster at Valparaiso, Chile, in August of the same year prompted the same reaction.[39]

Man-made disasters, such as war, also made a tremendous difference. There is little evidence to show that St Day men were defensive of the British cause during the Boer War. Most appear to have come home. For whatever reasons, be they political, financial or geographical, St Day man Thomas Ham found himself in action against the South African Dutch settlers at Spion Kop during the conflict, as did William C. Fairhurst who served in the South African Imperial Yeomanry.[40] St Day's Anglican Church began collections for the wives of the soldiers who had gone to fight in Transvaal and those at home worried as local boys waged war abroad.[41]

There were others who simply vanished and were never seen again. Whatever happened to the husband of Mary Inch who was never heard of after he last contacted her in 1900? By 1912 her distress had reached breaking point:

Mrs Mary Inch, widow of Scorrier, made an application in the Probate Court on Monday for leave to presume the death of her husband, a miner and sailor, in Chile. Mr W.T. Lawrence, for the applicant, said deceased in 1900 wrote from Cobiabo, Chile, that he was in hospital suffering from a bad heart. Nothing has since been heard of him. His estate amounted to £100 on an insurance policy. The application was granted.[42]

Despite such inherent dangers many emigrants achieved success. To balance the picture we have many accounts which show how emigrants fully supported their families back home with remittances from abroad. A few became extremely wealthy men. James Henry Paull, who died at Saltash in May 1940, left a creditable will including £26,456 net. He was celebrated a St Day hero for having led a group of miners out of a mine at Kimberley during a disastrous fire.[43] Others who decided upon remaining abroad achieved success in a variety of ways.[44] Captain Samuel Morcom established a Temperance coffee-house at Adelaide as early as the 1840s which he ran successfully until his death in 1881.[45] In 1906 we read of the death of William Beva Barnett at Iquique, Chile; he was a native of St Day. As one of the founder members, he was honourably buried in the vault of the British Mutual Benefit Society. F.W. Bawden of St Day, a successful miner at the North Randfontain Mines, was made a Fellow of the Geological Society for significant mining-related geological observations and discoveries in South Africa. He was a noted Anglican lay preacher abroad.[46] James Dunstan owned a successful hostelry in Butte, Montana, and was noted as a very successful businessman abroad.[47]

Edward C. Hall, a musician from St Day, also achieved great success at Butte, Montana. Captain W.J. Gidley junr travelled to Pachua, Mexico, with two rams from the Prince of Wales Farm, Sandringham, to continue his successful work in the selective breeding of livestock.[48] Nicholas Grenfell Kinsman died in July 1913 at Galt, Canada. He lived an adventurous life as a pioneering miner. He travelled early in his life to Mexico, as an engineer at the Mineral-del-Monte and other silver mines and then returned and married the eldest daughter of Captain Joel Whitburn in 1850. Other journeys followed, but by 1858 he had decided to settle with his wife and two children in Galt, where he lived for 38 years. Aged 96, just before his death, he was honoured as Galt's oldest resident. William Teague was appointed as JP for Yale (the British Columbia district) as we are informed from his obituary in the *Cornubian* newspapers for 6 May 1887. Many Cornishmen received promotions abroad, usually to management of the various different mines. These included individuals such as James Whitbourne of St Day, who managed the Nouse Mine at Johannesburg, and Mr B. Nicholls, who for many years was in charge of the Bolivia Silver Company. The list is too numerous to quote in full, but what it does suggest is that generally emigration was a successful experience for most miners.

Success or just a modest living allowed those abroad the opportunity to support a variety of community activities at home by sending back donations. Emigrants rarely forgot their roots. Mr W.J. Kitto sent 10 shillings each to the Wesleyan and Primitive Sunday schools in 1899. Donations for various Primitive and Wesleyan fund-raising events abound from several emigrant quarters such as that of a Primitive bazaar in February 1902 which netted gifts of £1 from Kimberly South Africa, the USA, Santiago and the West Coast of Africa.[49] Sunday schools seem to have done quite well out of such donations, as emigrants such as Jack Masters and Harry Morcom, two former St Day Wesleyan Sunday-school scholars, sent home 10 shilling donations in May 1915.[50] The building of the new pulpit was partly facilitated by a few donations from South Africa during the prosperous year of 1897, when emigrants were doing well abroad.[51] As early as 1890 that academic miner Fred Bawden of Poldice House sent home a parcel of literature for the St Day Free Library from Mexico.[52] The restoration of St Day's town clock in 1904 attracted several donations from emigrants in South Africa. Arthur Mills sent home £8.10s. from collections among St Day emigrants in South Africa for the Gwennap Show in 1912 and Arthur Teague also collected £8.10s. from 'the boys in South Africa' for the Gwennap Cottage Garden Society in September 1919.[53]

Naturally, trade flourished at St Day during the closing of the nineteenth and opening of the twentieth centuries. Directories and picture postcards reveal a good range of businesses. The market and the inns maintained a steady flow of custom. Returning miners boosted the economy with some wild spending. Apparently, miners threw 'gold sovereigns in the streets'. R.R. Blewett captures something of the spirit of the times in this abbreviated extract from his paper prepared for Selwyn College, Cambridge, in 1935:

> *Here is a picture of St Day – and of many other Cornish mining villages from 1890–1910. A large village half denuded of its men. Monday, the great day of the week, for the African mail comes in. Wives hitherto used to a domestic economy based on a pound a week or less, suddenly blazing in the glory for £20 or £30 a month – a bankers draft headed with the magic words 'Standard Bank of South Africa' – journeys to Redruth in a horse-drawn bus and a visit to the bank and the safe stowing of the bank book – miserly saving or mad spending – new furniture, a piano and all the children playing music... dress – Methodist chapels a tournament of fashion... ostrich plumes floating from head and neck – gold mounted lion claw brooches... gold rings set with valuable stones which sparkle in the lamplight of the evening chapel service... men are usually home on holiday with bronze faces and wearing 'Billy-cock' hats, and mustard-coloured shoes, and parading their knowledge of the Kaffir language...*

The remittances sent back home certainly boosted the trade and economy of St Day and other neighbouring towns. The St Day Post Office Savings Accounts reveal something of the value of foreign money in the town. By as early as January there were 114 accounts (£2,608 in accounts, which may have included Carharrack) compared to other Cornish areas such as Chacewater with only 15 accounts (totalling £58), St Just 70 accounts (£754), Scorrier with 55 accounts (£813) and Probus with 90 accounts (£1,286). This compared to towns such as Penzance with 1,081 accounts (£13,784), Truro with 1,015 accounts (£16,059) and Redruth with 553 accounts (£6,490.54).[54] This prompted a more serious consideration for investments returning better interest rates and in May 1885 T.R. Mills, working with the Redruth branch of the Star-Bowkett Building Society, and Messrs Tweedy (in the chair), C. Bawden, T. Rickard (directors) and G.S. Bray (solicitor) became their agent at St Day.[55] By May 1885 Post Office accounts had doubled at St Day to 203 showing a total balance of £2,798.56s.

It seems from a variety of evidence that the Cornish deliberately maintained their distinctive culture and identity when settling abroad. However, when we consider that Cornish pioneers were often the original settlers within many overseas communities, it is not surprising to discover strong characteristics of Cornish architecture, Nonconformity, sports and leisure, dialect, place names, customs and traditions, industry and work ethics amongst a host of other communal features. Many street scenes from picture postcards and photographs abroad bear a striking resemblance to Cornish towns. It is essentially this persistence to transfer their culture and preserve their identity that hallmarks the Cornish abroad.

In the transfer of such culture, newspaper reports reflect how there was a surprising amount of Anglican and Nonconformist clergy emigrating as a continued effort towards their evangelical mission. At Broken Hill, South Australia

> *... the first ever religious service was preached by Gwennap-born George Henry Paynter. A son of Captain William Paynter, George had arrived in Australia as a young lad and grew up at Moonta.*[56]

T.R. Mills organised the passage of his own nephew and assistant in his businesses at St Day, William M. Richards, to America in March 1899. Richards, who was a well-known local Wesleyan Methodist preacher, travelled to America to study for entry into the Methodist Episcopal Church. He returned to St Day occasionally, later of course as the Revd William Richards.[57] R.C. Colliver, who originated from Gwennap, was noted as a successful Methodist preacher in America as was the Revd J. Hall who settled in Butte, having originated from St Day and the Wesleyan chapel. The Revd Leslie Verne Jolly, vicar at St Day from 1943–46, had been ordained priest in Montreal, Canada, before taking a living at St James Old Town, Maine, USA.

Emigration became a way of life for people born in St Day for generations. Even today, elders within the community casually discuss the lives, journeys, adventures and successes of their relatives abroad. Relics from the times – such as jewellery made from South-African gold, or postcard photographs – still hold links to a distant and remarkable chapter in the history of St Day.

Notes

1 *West Briton*, 12.10.1827, and *Royal Cornwall Gazette*, 17.12.1831, 6.11.1935 and 21.9.1836.
2 Blewett, R.R., 'These Things Have Been', Inst. 54 (October, 1968).
3 *West Briton*, 16.5.1869.
4 *West Briton*, 16.5.1871.
5 *West Briton*, 3.10.1896.
6 *Royal Cornwall Gazette*, 23.3.1911.
7 CRO DRB WR 34, 1881.
8 *Royal Cornwall Gazette*, 13.6.1907, 18.9.1913 and 13.7.1913.
9 *West Briton*, 5.10.1871.
10 *Cornubian*, 27.10.1899.
11 *Cornubian*, 14.9.1900.
12 *West Briton*, 27.6.1907.
13 *Cornubian*, 15.10.1897.
14 *Cornubian*, 25.2.1898.
15 Blewett, R.R., 'These Things Have Been', Inst. 3 (May 1964).
16 *Cornubian*, 13.7.1894.
17 *West Briton*, 10.10.1898.
18 *Royal Cornwall Gazette*, 14.10.1897.
19 Dickason, G.B., *Cornish Immigrants to South Africa*, Pryor, Oswald, *Australia's Little Cornwall*, and Rowse, A.L., *The Cornish in America*.
20 *Royal Cornwall Gazette*, 1.10.1908.
21 Correspondence from Moira Tangye (1996), the former director to the Cornish emigration to the USA Programme at Murdoch House, Redruth.
22 *Royal Cornwall Gazette*, 27.9.1906.
23 *Royal Cornwall Gazette*, 17.9.1896 and 3.12.1896.
24 *Royal Cornwall Gazette*, 18.11.1897 and 25.11.1897.
25 *West Briton*, 27.5.1878.
26 *West Briton*, 6.12.1906.
27 *Royal Cornwall Gazette*, 10.11.1904.
28 *Royal Cornwall Gazette*, 11.9.1902.
29 *Royal Cornwall Gazette*, 26.6.1903.
30 *Royal Cornwall Gazette*, 19.5.1904.
31 *Royal Cornwall Gazette*, 3.1.1907.
32 *Royal Cornwall Gazette*, 23.4.1858.
33 *Cornubian*, 21.1.1898.
34 *Royal Cornwall Gazette*, 27.8.1908.
35 *Royal Cornwall Gazette*, 1.8.1912.
36 Tangye, Michael, *Redruth and its People*, Privately Published, Redruth, 1988, pp.72–3.
37 *Royal Cornwall Gazette*, 19.5.1904.
38 *Cornubian*, 16.11.1916.
39 *Royal Cornwall Gazette*, 24.5.1906, and *Royal Cornwall Gazette*, 23/30.8.1906.
40 Payton, Philip, *The Cornish Overseas*, p.359 and *Royal Cornwall Gazette*, 2.1.1946.
41 *Cornubian*, 17.11.1899.
42 *Royal Cornwall Gazette*, 29.2.1912.
43 *Cornish Post & Mining News*, 18.5.1940.
44 *Cornubian*, 15.10.1897.
45 *Cornubian*, 25.11.1881.
46 *Cornubian*, 15.10.1897.
47 *Cornubian*, 28.6.1917.
48 *Cornubian*, 12.11.1897.
49 *Cornubian*, 13.1.1899.
50 *Cornubian*, 6.5.1915.
51 *Cornubian*, 15.10.1897.
52 *Cornubian*, 21.11.1890.
53 *Cornubian*, 6.5.1915, *Royal Cornwall Gazette*, 5.9.1912, and *Cornubian*, 13.1.1899.
54 *West Briton*, 19.1.1882.
55 *West Briton*, 11.5.1885.
56 Payton, Philip, *The Cornish Miner in Australia*, Dyllansow Truran, Redruth, 1984, p.166.
57 *Royal Cornwall Gazette*, 23.3.1899, and *West Briton*, 12.8.1907.
58 *Royal Cornwall Gazette*, 4.7.1911, CE, 29.4.1904, and *Royal Cornwall Gazette*, 8.9.1898.

Street Scenes

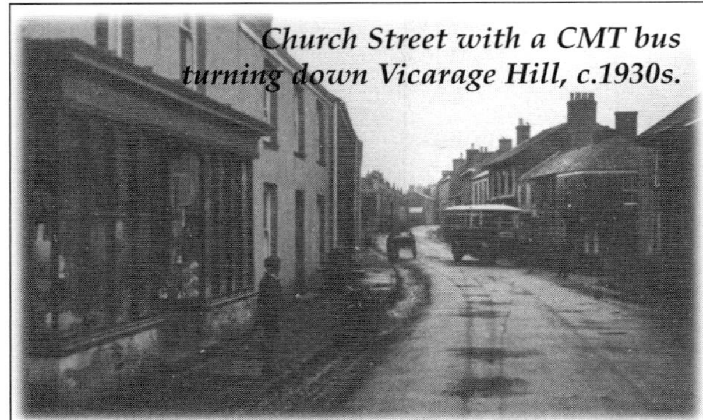
Church Street with a CMT bus turning down Vicarage Hill, c.1930s.

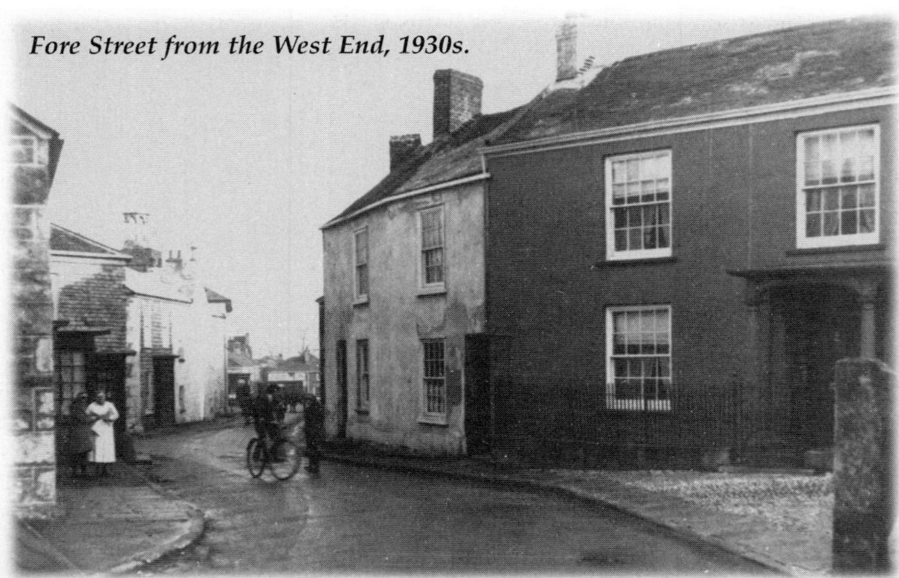
Fore Street from the West End, 1930s.

Above: *The shop at the corner of Mills Street and Scorrier Street, June 1930. The shop belonged to Mrs Williams.*

Below: *Church Street and a CMT bus, 15-seater Thorneycroft. Joe Mills rode to Redruth School in this bus. Note the boy's four-wheeled 'dandy' in the right foreground.*

Eighteen

The Depressed Years of Mining, 1870–1940

With the closure of almost every mine in the Gwennap district by the late 1860s, pumping operations ceased and many underground levels began to flood. This marked a point of no return for Gwennap miners. The subsequent unemployment intensified existing distress for those who felt mining was not simply their occupation, but effectively their only way of life. A few seemed prepared to diversify into other trades, but many sought to use their skills abroad. Others found it too difficult to manage either of these options and so chose to stay, perhaps hoping times would change or prospects improve. Others, the aged, infirm, single-parent or other vulnerable groups, probably had little choice but to stay and face whatever fate had to deliver. By mid-1877, the problems appeared more acute when it was reported that 'a few months ago, thousands of pounds were paid monthly in miner's wages, but the amount now does not exceed £90.'[1] Little had changed by November that year when it was recorded that 'many of the inhabitants and traders [at St Day] have been greatly reduced of late.'[2] Grim times, indeed.

The knock-on effect was the collapse of some other industries, such as the Tolgullow Ropewalk which completely failed by the mid-1870s. The fuse-works and brickworks (and, by 1881, velveteen industries) offered some relief, although, it must be noted, to a predominantly female workforce. In these places, the young female may well have begun to displace the older male as the family breadwinner, or at least bolstered the family income until the bankers' orders began to arrive from the foreign mines, sent by their young male counterparts.

The decline seems to have been gradual and fragmentary by nature over the decade 1860–70, in particular from March 1877, when the Revd Edward Olivey formed a committee at the Temperance Hall to help raise funds for those families experiencing financial hardship. People needing help could apply to the newly formed Miners' Distress Fund. This had received support from the Mansion House Inundation Fund in London in the form of a sum amounting to £240. It helped meet the needs of '73 special cases requiring immediate relief, as well as a large number of deserving cases.'[3] £110 soon arrived as well as other help from the 'principal residents in the neighbourhood', with families such as the Williamses, Beauchamps and Fords offering substantial amounts of money and support.

Relief seems to have been temporary and by May of 1877 128 families within Gwennap were considered to be on the 'verge of starvation'.[4] The Revd Olivey had by then received another £47.10s. and developed a plan (which he had recently seen in operation at Chacewater) whereby former miners were employed to repair and maintain important roads, being paid with distress relief money. The attitudes of many of those experiencing such apparent destitution seemed to be 'one of acceptance of such hard times'. In silent dignity few appear to have made any fuss about their hardship and Gwennap people at the time were generally considered 'rather timid about relief from the County Distress Fund', as well as being men 'who really don't [sic] acknowledge how desperate they are.'[5]

Many former Cornish miners were, however, forced to consider other options. The same mines in South America, Australia, South Africa and the USA which had challenged and defeated the Cornish stronghold on the global mining economy, now offered hope of jobs or entrepreneurial prospects. Be he labourer, artisan or highly-skilled expert, the Cornish miner could offer experience that was in considerable demand elsewhere. And so began the great exodus of the 'adventuring-type' of Cornish male, seeking to escape depression and possibly make some future or fortune.

The emigration trends gathered real pace throughout the 1880s and up to 1914 when war was declared. These were fairly successful years as miners abroad sent money to their families back home. St Day, as a community of traders, appears to have been economically buoyant during this period; for example, trade directories list a broad variety of traders, services and retail business, hardly typical of depressed times. Chapel buildings, extensions and renovations continued and picture postcards illustrate a reasonably content, indeed comfortable scene.

The impact of the First World War upon such a vulnerable economy was significant. As the British

Empire sent out a 'call to arms', many emigrants returned; such turbulent times offered new employment prospects in the military and mining. With the end of the war, emigration became a trickle compared to the former 'rush' periods. With so many casualties, especially of young males, St Day like all communities, had little left to offer the former destinations of emigration, and many of those left would have been reluctant to leave families experiencing further grief.

The demand for local copper, tin and safety fuse had eased unemployment during the war, but now these too ceased. With no revival of the foreign or wartime economy, the financial safety net which had staved off the first wave of depression for almost four decades, had now disappeared and the second depression would prove to be more savage than most could anticipate. By 1921, between 200 and 300 Gwennap men were to march to Redruth to 'urge the Council to help absorb unemployment.'[6] The 'dole' had been reduced to 15 shillings per week and by May of the following year between 800 and 1,000 unemployed miners from Redruth and district (including many St Day men) marched to the Redruth Town Workhouse, where a meeting to discuss 'out-relief' was being held. A similar march was held by 300 men at St Austell, and a concert given at St Day Wesleyan Chapel by the 'Unemployed Welsh Miners Choir', to help relieve their problems back in Wales, illustrate just how deep and extensive the depression was.[7]

By this time, around 205 people at Gwennap were applying for relief amounting to £103.13s.8d. Only a few men found employment in the meagre pickings of the occasional reopened mine. R.R. Blewett quotes up to 90 men in St Day being unemployed and several choosing to leave the district by 1921. Those who chose to stay were indeed facing critical hardship and degradation as they faced the scrutiny of the Gwennap Parish Council in their bids to be 'excused' from paying rates. Analysis by Blewett of the Gwennap Rates 'Excused List' from 1906–19 shows £44–55 each half year being considered. By 1922 this had risen to £140. Blewett recalls the meetings at the vestry of the old Burnwithian workhouse:

> *Our most memorable meetings were those at which we interviewed applicants for rate excusals. The lies that were told by some of the applicants for rate excusals. ('All men are liars'), the soul-searching questions that were asked by members of the Council; at the close we felt that very few, if any, had got away with it.*[9]

He also comments that by the late 1920s, over 40 men were unemployed in one St Day street, and the only man with a job was the postman. If times seemed bad, they soon paled against the cruel turn of depression over the next decade, which by 1934 included 470 Gwennap persons being excused the total sum of £469.13s.6d. Of these, Blewett extracts 189 persons as coming from St Day, who had been excused £185.1s.7d., with roughly 120 or one-third of the inhabitants unable to pay or contribute to local rates. Such times were to continue until the 1940s when the changing economy of the Second World War would take effect.

Destitution

A range of cases featured occasionally in newspapers from the 1860s which provide us with some insight into the growing social problems of the decline of mining. One common example was infanticide, where women (often young, or sometimes wives of absentee partners) tragically disposed of their newborn child by abandoning it in an isolated area or throwing it into a disused shaft. Sometimes children were beaten to death. Such tragedies often resulted in high-profile trials and severe punishments. Pauperism was all too apparent, as in the case of a mother and her four children found wandering around the edge of St Day for several days all 'seminaked, starved and in a wretched state of mind.' One man who 'resorted to keeping his house for lunatics' was sympathetically dealt with by local authorities after heavy complaints from neighbours, but he does appear to have opened his doors to the vulnerable and mentally ill. Begging was a common crime, and one case at St Day when a man was sentenced to seven days' hard labour for being caught seems typical of how the authorities dealt with such social difficulties. Such accounts make uncomfortable reading, whether they be of the extreme cruelties perpetrated by desperate people, the degradation they suffered or the equally cruel punishments meted out. Many of the details are too disturbing to quote and all references have been withheld to protect the sensitivity of such times.

Housing Problems

With over 60 houses (out of approximately 350) available to let, overcrowding would seem to have been an unlikely problem from the 1870s. In May of that year a correspondent noted that 'ten years ago it was a different matter to get a house [at St Day]', but during his visit noticed that there were 13 in Simmons Street, 7 in Scorrier Street, 1 in Church Street, 3 in Fore Street, 8 in Back Street, 7 in Chapel Street, 7 at Vogue, 5 in Moors [Pink], 4 in Jewell Row and 5 in Clock Street and Court.'[10] But while it appeared that several empty houses of emigrant families were available, there were still those who could not afford to rent. From the 1870s, families are occasionally reported to be living in overcrowded conditions, with notice to quit, which still left the authorities with the headache of offering suitable alternative accommodation. One local man at Govorow

(Gwennap) lived with his wife and two children in a shed measuring 11ft x 7ft. At nearby Porthtowan, around 100 people could be found living in tents, with only three conveniences between them, during the summer of 1913. By 1935, Blewett was again on hand to comment in his Social Survey that '16 households showed 143 persons living in houses containing [altogether] 47 rooms and sleeping in 25 bedrooms, an average of 6 per bedroom.'[11] He continued that in the last 50 years [previous to 1935] fewer than ten new houses had been built and about six had been demolished; 'the latter were clay built and straw thatched.' There are examples from newspapers, which discuss the most deplorable living conditions being tolerated by some families in St Day.

Overcrowding, poverty, unemployment and destitution led to pockets of squalor which in turn led to a rise in disease and infection. The research of Richard R. Blewett is hard to escape as he offered analysis of the Gwennap Parish Burial Registers for the years 1833–66. Significantly, Blewett highlighted infant and child mortality rates, as on average 'a child funeral a fortnight'. Frequent infections and resultant deaths from 'smallpox, scarlet fever, measles, whooping cough, typhus fever, cholera, inflammation of the throat (which sounds like diphtheria) and a disease described as 'swine pox' were discussed by him. A cholera epidemic killing 20 people seems to have occurred and the victims may have been buried in a mass grave 'on the right-hand side of the south path of St Day Church.'[12] Cholera rarely appeared after this time, but the other range of diseases continued, being given as the cause of death in many instances. As late as 1928, a measles and whooping-cough epidemic was to claim nine victims, all of whom were similarly buried in one grave in the churchyard.

The Response of Charity

The Gwennap Parish Vestry Account Book illustrates many cases where the parish overseers granted food, clothes or small amounts of money to help relieve poverty, undoubtedly much of it in St Day. This source continued until 1894, when the Gwennap Parish Committee was formed to manage the poor. A noticeable increase in charitable activity is evident from the 1870s, often led by the local gentry. For example, under the direction of the Revd Olivey, several leading local female figures such as Mrs Williams of Tolgullow, Mrs Harvey of Torquay, Mrs Ford of Pengreep and Mrs Andrews, as well as a few other prominent ladies, gave 20 tons of coal for the poor of the neighbourhood.[13] Coal charities were particularly important for the poor who were dependent upon a regular supply, not just for winter fuel, but also cooking. By 1878, a Coal Distribution Committee met regularly at St Day, where typically they organised 1 cwt. of coal for over 300 poor persons.[14] Little seems to have changed by 1896 when the committee distributed up to 5cwt of coal to over 200 poor people.[15]

By 1897, the Gwennap Coal Club subsidised coal for 187 poor widows, by collecting a half-crown from each and adding money sent in by local landowners and others. The same group were still supplying coal to over 200 people as late as 1903.[16]

The St Day Dorcas Society (probably affiliated to the Wesleyan Methodists) appears in 1876, distributing to the poor of the parish various 'blankets, sheets, calico, and flannel, as well as providing the occasional tea for aged women', at the St Day Town Hall.[17] They held an annual bazaar 'in aid of the poor residing in St Day and neighbourhood', sometimes at the velvet factory. With the money raised certain shops in the town were invited to tender for the supply of goods. Various charity entertainments and lectures frequently helped boost funds for the relief of the poor, with Church and Chapel all offering their resources in a spirited, ongoing community effort.

The Revd J.J. Murley was noted for his annual knife-and-fork tea, held for the children of Chapel Street during the 1890s. The Williams family of Scorrier held daily soup kitchens at St Day Church Mission Room from 1921–24 (when needed) for the children of St Day School whose fathers were unemployed. The kitchens were at times attended by up to 60 children, who were waited upon by Mrs Williams and other helpers she had rallied.

Charities played a vital part throughout the nineteenth and twentieth centuries. To some extent, they survive today in the subsidies left by W.J. Mills during the 1920s–'30s and the legacy bequeathed in 1882 by John Davey, a native of Gwennap. This has been made available for miners' widows residing in Gwennap and is paid annually, the profits of the fund being divided between the recipients.

Notes

1 *Royal Cornwall Gazette*, 9.5.1877.
2 *West Briton*, 29.11.1877.
3 *Royal Cornwall Gazette*, 16.3.1877, 23.3.1877, and 30.3.1877.
4 *Royal Cornwall Gazette*, 9.5.1877.
5 *West Briton*, 14.4.1879.
6 *Royal Cornwall Gazette*, 13.7.1921.
7 *Royal Cornwall Gazette*, 24.5.1922.
8 *Royal Cornwall Gazette*, 4.5.1921.
9 Blewett, R.R., 'These Things Have Been', Inst. 56 (March, 1969).
10 *Royal Cornwall Gazette*, 18.5.1877.
11 Blewett, R.R., Article produced for Selwyn College, Cambridge, 1935.
12 R.R. Blewett, 'These Things Have Been', Inst. 4 and 5. (August–October, 1964).
13 *Royal Cornwall Gazette*, 3.1.1879.
14 *Royal Cornwall Gazette*, 18.1.1878.
15 *Royal Cornwall Gazette*, 17.12.1896.
16 *Royal Cornwall Gazette*, 17.12.1903.
17 *Royal Cornwall Gazette*, 15.1.1876.

Archway at Scorrier Street, built for Queen Victoria's Diamond Jubilee in 1897.

Queen Victoria's Diamond Jubilee, 1897, with the burning of the tar barrels at Wheal Jewell.

Nineteen

Leisure, Entertainment & Self-Improvement

Scientific & Mining Associations

Most Cornish communities boast a range of clubs for the entertainment and leisure of their parishioners. At St Day, from the early part of the nineteenth century, several facilities made available for the education and enjoyment of the people are recorded. As the nineteenth century gave way to the twentieth century, pastimes became less formal in the course of providing educationally motivated activities. St Day has enjoyed a variety of other groups, clubs, team events, celebrations, festivities, carnivals and parades, which together are too numerous to record in this volume. However, a selection of traditional and modern leisure-, entertainment- and self-improvement-led organisations, provide us with a flavour of the aspirations of the community.

The establishment of the St Day Association for History and Science in February 1828, under the presidency of Mr John Rule, may well reflect the growing intellectual demands of a community at the forefront of mining technology and scientific progress. Rule, himself a surgeon, 'demonstrated the properties of the electric aura' amongst other lectures, highlighting the high levels of learning to which some people aspired.[1] Such organisations probably continued throughout the following decades, but tended to link with countywide organisations by the mid-nineteenth century. A typical example is the Devon & Cornwall Miners Association, which established a class at St Day in January 1862. Initially offering instruction in chemistry and mineralogy, the association focused on skills and knowledge central to mining and its related industries. Later, physiology, physical geography and drawing appeared as options. This group may have also been referred to as the St Day Science Class which offered similar courses and entered candidates for the Science and Art Department of the South Kensington Examination Board.[2]

Throughout the late-nineteenth century St Day seemed to offer a variety of evening classes including art with watercolours and drawing, geometry and freehand. Significantly from the late 1870s, the effects of the mining depression gave rise to some concern within the community with the Revd Edward Olivey establishing a reading room during the winter of 1878 for the benefit of 'young men' who could instruct each other in such a way that he hoped would 'be of some good' to them.[3] Olivey became very active in promoting educational instruction in the face of an uncertain future for a community potentially on course for economic collapse. With almost every mine around the St Day district closed, or on the verge of closure, Olivey and J.T. Letcher (a local scientific lecturer) undoubtedly attempted to equip as many young men as possible with formal skills and qualifications which might help ease them into better employment prospects abroad. As late as 1891, with little local mining activity or prospects, Letcher was still instructing a class of 18 students through Kensington chemistry and mineralogy examinations every Saturday afternoon, with Peter Jennings (St Day's board-school headmaster), instructing another 39 students in drawing and physiology on Thursday evenings.[4]

St Day Library & Institutions

In 1855 a meeting was held to form a library at St Day, which made little headway until the St Day Institute was established in October 1858. The opening lecture on astronomy was followed on a monthly basis with others such as 'Nineveh and her Palaces', comets, the history of Protestantism in France and the 'Advantages of Science to Working Miners'. Meetings were initially held in 'rooms at Scorrier', the committee being led by Mr Charles Hawke of Tolgullow (to some extent showing the patronage by local gentry). By 1863 the St Day Institute was meeting at the Temperance and Institute Hall and had attracted 80 members. A library had been well established by this time and was to be 'enlarged and popularised by the purchase of standard works.' A table was 'liberally supplied with newspapers' with *The Times* being lent the day after its publication by Mr Waters of Whitehall (Scorrier). William Wilton junr was the librarian at this time. The Institute hosted a very distinguished list of lecturers, among them regulars such as William Wilton, Revd Bannister and Professor Hunt. Throughout the following two decades, the Institute included a range of musical programmes for its members with various concerts by church and chapel choirs and musicians.[5]

Complaints from the St Day Mutual Improvement Society about the stocks of the Institute library and the acquisition of the Temperance Hall by the Primitive Methodists prompted a call for a new institute and library by November 1889.[6] Suggestions to convert the now-vacant Market Inn and the Old Market House amounted to little, despite frequent protests that there was 'no place where the inhabitants could go to see a daily newspaper.' Such criticisms were quickly acted upon by Mr Passmore Edwards who offered to donate a number of volumes if an institute to house them could be secured by the people of St Day. By September 1890 a committee was formed with a very distinguished panel including Mr George Williams of Scorrier, T.H Letcher, T.R. Mills, Charles Corfield, John Rooke, Theo Mitchell and C.A.V. Coneybeare, among 50 others. With the Revd Olivey as chair, a letter was sent to Mr Mallock asking for terms for a house adjoining Mr Charles Corfield's druggist's shop. The whole project was constructed on the basis of being 'unsectarian and non-political'. Another house became available in Church Street and both were acquired and remodelled. The house on the east side of Church Street became known as the St Day Institute (which survives today) and the property further along on the south side became known as the St Day Free Library. Both buildings were made available to members and became known as the St Day Free Library and Institute.[7]

The St Day Free Library was formally opened in January 1891 with a rather grand concert of musical events being given in the schoolroom. Over 400 volumes were donated by Passmore Edwards and Mr John Charles Williams donated a further 200 volumes. By the summer of 1891, a more formal arrangement of 'Ladies' and Gentlemen's' Institutes had been formed, with the men at the Institute and the women occupying the upstairs reading room of the library.[8] By 1892 membership had grown to around 90 with 50 books being loaned per week. It appears that the ladies worked hard to maintain the dignity and comfort of their exclusive domain by holding various bazaars and fund-raising events to furnish their room with 'easy chairs, curtains, and pictures'. Further, they enjoyed numerous magazines of the 'higher walks of literature' such as *Cornhill*, *Review of Reviews* and *Strand* among others, in their home-like and attractive surroundings. By contrast the men, who had the benefits of a room below, were referred to as 'miserable sinners' who revelled mainly in '*Comic Cuts*, *Tit Bits* and other frivolous periodicals' as well as playing draughts. At an annual subscription of 6 shillings and Sunday closing, it appears the men sought little in terms of value for their money.[9]

By mid-1894 the library contained 834 volumes including 'standard works of fiction, history, etc.' However, 'the semi-religious novel [was] the most popular.' This was not a 'free' library and the idea for a small free circulating library was mooted during the last decade of the nineteenth century. However, a library was to last at St Day right up to 1928. When R.R. Blewett arrived in St Day in 1921, he met the unpaid librarian Ellen Nicholls and her assistant Lottie Auld. Around this time the building had been blighted by a leaky roof, which had caused serious decay of many books upstairs.[10]

The Institute over at Church Street had by this time become known as the 'House of Lords' and with its chess and draughts tables, card games and daily newspaper, it settled into being a 'Public Institute' with much the same character that it enjoys today.

Political Meeting Places

Political reading rooms appeared in St Day from the 1880s. In February 1887 Mr Strauss, MP, opened a new Conservative reading room in Fore Street, near the town clock. In the same week, perhaps prompted by their political contemporaries' move, or simply having outgrown earlier premises at the West End, the Liberals moved to a new venue at Scorrier Street, 'near the Primitive Methodist Chapel', where they could enjoy the popular game of bagatelle.[11] The St Day Liberal Association maintained a reading room at St Day until just after 1919, whilst the Conservatives, by this time meeting under St Day Unionist Reading Rooms, had disappeared by around 1923.[12]

Music, Bands, Drama, Choirs & St Day Adult School

Many groups seemed to flourish at St Day during the nineteenth and twentieth centuries. The town's Philharmonic Society enjoyed many successful years up until the end of the nineteenth century, while the Amateur Dramatic Society continued a similar existence.

Choirs have contributed much to the richness and colour of life at St Day over the years. From early times, churches, chapels and schools have organised a variety of male, female and children's choral groups, which have entertained around the county and beyond. Much has been said of the choral successes of church and chapel groups, including St Day's 1920s Male Voice Choir. However, another such choir was started around 1964, by Mr May of The Cedars, Church Street. He became president of the choir and initially held practise sessions at his home. The group eventually grew to be around 40 strong, so practise was then held at the Primitive chapel at Scorrier Street. The accompanying pianist was Mr J.G. Gilbert and the conductor was Mr George Evans. The group travelled all over Cornwall and Devon and became a sought-after source of entertainment before they disbanded towards the

Main image: *Male Voice Choir, 1960s.*

Left: *Frances Mills and Tanya Dyer who sounded 'The Last Post' and 'Reveille' at the November Remembrance Day service at the War Memorial, 1980–'90s.*

end of the 1960s.

During the celebrations of the baronetcy of Sir William Williams of Tregullow, reference was made in the *West Briton* to the 'excellent Brass Band of St Day', which led the procession of miners from the United and Wheal Clifford Mines on 20 July 1866. Various bands appeared in the local press from the 1880s, usually revolving around the local musician and organist Thomas Cara. Queen Victoria's Golden Jubilee celebrations of 1897 also featured the 'St Day Band'.[13]

Several postcards of St Day tea treats and festive events show local bands. In the early decades of the twentieth century, Carharrack Temperance Band was often mentioned as supporting St Day Feast or Christmas-carol visits around the town. In these early years the Allen family were all involved in the formation and organisation of the band. Thomas John Allen was particularly involved and became bandmaster for many years. From 1932, after the gift of new uniforms and instruments from W.J. Mills, the band became known as Carharrack and St Day Silver Band. W.J. Mills also stipulated that a room of the new Carharrack Village Hall he funded must be set aside for the band to practise in and allowance was to be made for storage of their instruments and equipment. In 1937 Clifton Allen became bandmaster, a position he held until his resignation in 1960. Throughout the decades the band has competed in many festivals and competitions, achieving notable success. Strictly speaking, the band originates from Carharrack, where it still rehearses, but it has served St Day admirably and can still be seen around the streets at Christmas, as well as leading Feast-Day celebrations followed by a concert in the field.[14]

A branch of the Adult School was opened at St Day in August 1909, for young men. The group became affiliated to the Cornwall Adult School Union later in November. The group was supported by the Holy Trinity Church which appears to have given one of its rooms for meetings and a social club at Wheal Jewell, which attracted around 60 young men by the end of the year. The Adult School Social Club was equipped with a billiard table in November 1909, and from this time onwards a regular billiard team featured in various local leagues. Membership required attendance at lectures, usually given by influential locals. Among such lectures there were talks with such subjects as 'Reality and Religion', 'Love', 'Living Worthily', 'Personal Worship', 'National Worship', 'What Men Live By', 'Self-righteousness' and 'Humility'. A harmonium was installed and a choir formed in the same year. Often, the Adult School linked to the Primitive Methodists at Scorrier Street, where they held choir practise and listened to various addresses. Membership by 1910 stood at 103, but the First World War may have temporarily interrupted the progress of the Adult School. Despite a revival after the war and up to 1924, the group had disbanded by 1926, when the premises were taken over by the Ex-Servicemen's Club.[15]

St Day Feast, c.1940s. R.R. Blewett helps distribute saffron buns.

The St Day Shows

The St Day Show was a feature of leisure and life at St Day throughout the first half of the nineteenth-century. Its purpose was to generate local interest in agriculture, through the exhibition of livestock and working farm animals. The event, through patronage by the local gentry (the Williams and Beauchamp families) also looked to 'keep up that good feeling which should ever exist between landlord and tenant.'[16] A typical advertisement from the times read:

St Day Show Fair will be held on Tuesday the 29th July instant, when free ground and every other accommodation will be given to those who may bring cattle; and the following prizes awarded by just umpires: For the best fed oxen, £2.2s.0d.; for the best two working oxen, £1.1s.0d.; for the best bull, £1.1s.0d.; for the best fat cow, £1.1s.0d.; for the best cow and calf, £1.1s.0d.; for the best five-year-old saddle horse, £1.1s.0d.; for the best three-year-old colt, £1.1s.0d.; for the best half score sheep, £1.1s.0d.; for the best ram, £0.10s.6d. The above must be seen in the possession of the owners, for the space of two months. No inhabitant of St Day or Gwennap will be allowed any prize, which is done solely to encourage strangers, and it is sincerely hoped that no inhabitant will feel offended, the intention being pure.[17]

Most towns and villages also maintained a similar show, which collectively produced a busy seasonal calendar where prize exhibits could establish reputations for many farmers. Prizes were usually awarded during an after-show dinner at one of the local inns, and the Cornish Arms, Market Inn, the Commercial, and the King's Arms seemed to rotate the honours almost annually.

By the 1850s, the St Day Show had become known as the 'St Day Show Fair', and besides catering for labouring animals, this event included a category for 'the Labouring Man that [has] raised the largest families without parochial relief.'[18] The St Day Show Fair continued until the early 1880s when it took on the name of 'St Day Horticultural Show', extending to 'St Day Horticulture, Poultry, Cage Bird and Butter Show.' By this time, the show was less inclined towards livestock, but rather entries for plants, flowers, vegetables, wild flowers, poultry, game birds, cage birds and rabbits. There was also a local cottage gardens category.[19] T.R. Mills promoted the idea of a 'St Day Bird & Flower Show' by the mid-1890s, but this was elaborated on to become the 'St Day Poultry, Pigeon, Cage Bird, Rabbit, Cat & Egg Show', only accepting entries from within a 12-mile radius.[20] The Church Field at Vicarage Hill continued as the venue for the show which seems to have incorporated the Gwennap Show when the Gwennap Cottage Garden, Horticulture & Poultry Show began to meet at the Church Field from 1899. All the previous categories of crops, birds, dairy, livestock, flowers, animals, etc. continued, but by this time it was decided to maintain categories for 'timbering, butter-making and milking contests.'[21] Apart from a few brief periods such as the two world wars, the St Day Horticulture Society has continued to flourish until the present day. Still organised by a select committee, it is a very popular and well-supported show attracting entrants from far and wide. Enjoyed annually, with venues at the community centre, the Masonic Hall, the Church Mission Room and St Day School, the show continues a long run in the history of the community.

Top: *St Day Dairy School, 1914.*

Above: *Dairy Class, 1919/20.*

Dairy Classes

Although little reference is made to agriculture within the St Day district, demonstrations by travelling 'Dairy Classes' were organised by the 'Cornwall Technical Committee' around 1914. These were initially held at the Board School, before moving to the Wesleyan Sunday Schoolrooms. They were well supported at St Day. Instruction was given to young men, but mostly women, in the processes used in making dairy products. This continued into the 1920s, under the eye of Mrs Penrose.[22]

Recreation for the Youth

The Boy Scouts were very much in existence by 1909 and continued at St Day for many years up until the 1950s. In their early years they were heavily involved with recruitment parades during the First World War. Towards the end of their existence they used the Church Schoolrooms.

A club for St Day's majorettes was started in the late 1970s by the Dagley sisters who lived at Pink Moors. They were an immediate success and through tremendous hard work they quickly established a leading Cornish troupe at St Day, attracting girls from a wide area. At different times the group was led by Deborah Stapleton, Michelle Bray and sisters Paula and Melanie Harris. They trained at a variety of venues. The group became very well organised and enjoyed a range of successes at local, county and national levels, where many of the girls asserted their baton-twirling talents to win major competitions and coveted titles. With their own coach, outfits and equipment, the St Day Majorettes could often be seen at local carnivals, parades and shows and enjoyed great popularity until they disbanded in the late 1980s.

St Day Youth Club pantomime, Little Red Riding Hood, *performed at St Day Church Hall.* Left to right: *Regan Matthews (Dame), Ian Newcombe and Sally Pearce.*

A variety of youth clubs have existed at St Day over the years, usually supervised and attached to local church or chapel groups and venues. Both Primitive and Wesleyan chapels as well as the Holy Trinity Church ran youth and boys' clubs up to the 1960s. By then, a new initiative to form an independent youth club was led by Hayden and Mona George at St Day. It was formed after a public meeting in 1965 under a management committee including several leading community figures. The rooms were used until a more suitable, purpose-built club was opened in July 1971.

The Youth Club became very popular and a welcome meeting-place for many youngsters, not just from St Day, but also other neighbouring villages. It formed teams in football, cricket, table tennis and judo amongst a variety of other sports and pastimes. A great deal of young talent was nurtured there as boys and girls used the club as a springboard for greater things. Amateur dramatics was a very successful feature throughout the history of the club and various groups led local pantomimes for many seasons, with several young actors and actresses moving on to large-scale performances with major Cornish amateur dramatic groups. The group continued to be led by Hayden and Mona George, who motivated many others to contribute and support the youngsters at St Day. The club disbanded in 1982, due to a lack of funding for essential repairs.

St Day Historical & Conservation Society

At a public meeting held in 1987 to discuss the implications of the locality being designated a Conservation Area, planning officer Stephen Bott, of Kerrier District Council, requested that a local group should take an active interest in promoting conservation. His suggestion was taken up by Mark Johnson and Bernadette Fallon, amongst others, with the aim of also incorporating an historical interest in the community, balancing local history with concerns for the environment. Historical activities include an annual programme of events, involving speakers on local historical subjects and occasional guided walks or field-trips, as well as purely social events such as the annual Christmas meal and summer party.

The society is often consulted by local authors and visitors for help on local historical matters and it aims to maintain an archive of local historical material. Its most active role, however, has been in the setting up of the Old Church Project, in 1988, which aimed to save St Day's first listed building. The main stimulus for this idea came from a party of Breton friends, who came to take part in St Day's Feast that year. It took six years to obtain a faculty from the Church authorities to carry out phase I of the project, which was intended to stabilise the building. Funding was raised through various sources and grants, as well as specific fund-raising activities locally, such as a sponsored walk, a plant sale and car-boot sales. Paul Annear wrote and published a book, *Some Notes on the History of The Church and Chapel of The Holy Trinity St Day.* Sales are entirely for the benefit of the Old Church. Using these funds, along with a gift of £500 from St Day Parish Council, a lightning conductor was reinstalled on the church tower and a contractor was hired to help a team of volunteers clear invasive vegetative growth from the exterior of the building. Rose Lewis of the late lamented Kerrier Groundwork Trust then put together a funding package of £107,000 which financed the clearing out of the rubble of the roof from inside, and various structural repairs designed to help stabilise the building.

The church then had its official opening to the public in November 2000 and was reopened for daily public access from Easter Day until 31 October 2001, during which time a team of dedicated local volunteer stewards welcomed around 3,000 visitors, including people from all over the world.[23]

Freemasonry at St Day

Freemasonry was initiated at St Day in 1864, when a Masonic Lodge was formed at St Day, under the

Entertainment & Leisure

Left: *St Day Youth Club pantomime* Sleeping Beauty. Left to right, back row: *Garry Hill, Paul Annear, Ian Newcombe, Jackie Grenfell, Gary Parsons, Julia Dagley, Regan Matthews, Sally Pearce, David Newcombe, Peter Holland, Glen Parsons, Roy Peters, Andrea Croft, Peter Richards;* front (kneeling): *Donna Parsons, Alison Nicholls, Tracey Nicholls, Catherine Nicholls, Lisa Hillman, Tracey Cox, ?, Ian George, Andrea Parsons, Joanne Latham, Mandy Richards, Tracy Simmons.*

Right: *Paul Annear, Ian Newcombe, Gary Parsons, Regan Matthews and David Newcombe in the St Day Youth Club production* Jack and the Pasty.

Bottom right: *St Day Youth Club Table Tennis, 1970s.* Left to right: *Nigel Williams, Peter Harris, Peter Etherington, David Moyle, Colin Parsons, Christopher Peters.*

St Day Youth Club Management Committee, Christmas party, 1966. Left to right: *Ron Nicholls, Hayden George, Dick Clymo, Mona George, Nora Clymo, Bernice Williams, Penny Stead, Ken Stead, Annie Knowles, Renfred Knowles.*

name of Tregullow Lodge, No.1006. This was achieved through the early efforts of Frederick Martin Williams of Tregullow estate. The first meeting was held on 28 June, in the 'Hotel, St Day, when the Worshipful Master, W. Bro. Thomas Mills opened the Lodge.' The first return of members to the Grand Lodge totalled 21 names from Redruth, Perranarworthal, Scorrier, Truro and Penclawdd, as well as the St Day district. By 1866 membership had grown to 29. By 1865, the Lodge Rooms were in part of the present (2002) Masonic Hall, and despite some temporary movement, the Lodge was firmly established there until 1872.

In 1867 the Rose of Sharon Chapter No.1006 was formed at St Day from members of the Tregullow Lodge. Meetings were held at the Masonic Hall until 1888, when the group moved to the Druids Lodge, Green Lane, Redruth, to continue their separate freemasonry activity. The 12 minute-books of the Tregullow Lodge record much activity and growth of the freemasons at St Day, including various donations of furniture and artefacts, many of which still survive. In 1935, the Lodge extended to double its size. Freemasonry at St Day continues in 2002.[24]

The St Day Feast

The roots of the St Day Feast are lost in ancient tradition. However, in 1824, it was stated that the Feast of St Day should be held four weeks after that of Gwennap, suggesting that St Day had been a separate parish from Gwennap.[25] By the mid-nineteenth century, the St Day Feast had become an annual feature in the county press and was generally regarded as very significant. Newspaper accounts around this time present the event as more of a fair than a religious event, although religious observations and services were held. The Feast thrived throughout the end of the nineteenth century, and was held over several days. Often, a sporting event, such as the Cricket Club's Married Men's Team challenging the St Day Bachelors would be a highlight, along with the visiting fair, waxworks, hobbyhorses, side-stalls and other visiting amusements. Wrestling became a popular attraction during the Feast celebrations, continuing the more secular direction of the event through the late-nineteenth and early-twentieth centuries.

Traditionally, this was a time when houses were whitewashed, flags and bunting hung across streets and everyone dressed in their very best clothes. During the First World War, the Feast was temporarily stopped until 1917. It became a focus of the Community Council formed in 1926. From 1933, in appreciation of his many gifts to St Day, the Feast celebrations acknowledged W.J. Mills when the committee, community and children followed St Day Silver Band in procession to his monument at St Day Playing-Field.

Since that time the event has followed a similar pattern, with schoolchildren enjoying their 'shilling and saffron bun' (the token money has increased with inflation) and in later years a bottle of pop donated by Jolly's. Children's sports are held in the afternoon at the playing-fields, with various side-stalls offering children's rides, sweets, foods, toffee-apples and other festive products. Each year the fair returns and since the late 1970s the St Day Feast Dance has been held, choreographed by Mrs Linda Williams. Couples are welcome to join in the dance in formal dress, where they dance in groups of four to the special St Day Feast Dance tune, composed by Kenneth Pelmear. The St Day Feast is still a great focal point in the calendar of the community.

Other Festivities & Celebrations

St Day has shared in the celebrations of the historic events which have, over the centuries shaped the history of Britain. For example, the exile of Napolean to Elba heralded the final stages of the Napoleonic Wars by July 1814, so around the Gwennap mines the landowners, adventurers and agents provided dinners for all the miners. Triumphal laurel arches and flags were erected and massive dining areas assembled. At the United Mines, Michael Williams presided over 1,200 men, where 20 tons of beef, 1,200lbs of bread and 600 gallons of strong beer were provided to celebrate the event. Remarkably, the gentlemen, with their agents, assisted the labourers at their tables, nor did they sit down to their own repast until their dinner was concluded.[26] Such a show of gratitude and generosity by local gentry would have been generally considered unlikely, but clearly this occasion proved that they were capable of meeting all men on any terms. At Wheal Gorland Michael Williams provided a similar celebration, and other prominent local gentlemen did the same at the New Consolidated Mines, Wheal Damsel, Wheal Jewell, Treskerby, North Downs Mine, Wheal Unity, and Creegbrawse Mine.

The next major event, though not on that scale, was the passing of The Reform Bill, in 1832, when again triumphal arches were erected across the streets. We may wonder at the thoughts of the 250 poor and aged men and women who were treated to the tea and cakes, whilst the redistribution of the 'rotten boroughs' began and the vote became extended.[27]

When Sir William Williams of Tregullow celebrated his baronetcy in July 1866, over 1,300 miners alone entered St Day in procession from the Gwennap Mines, behind the brass band.[28] Undoubtedly, such a spectacle would have attracted large crowds.

Over 8,000 people assembled at the church for the laying of the foundation stone on 6 October 1826.

Jubilee celebrations in 1887 were well received at St Day, and the following account is typical of the events so patriotically observed by the majority of the town:

High Days & Holidays

Left: *St Day Trinity Church, Christmas 1948.*

Main: *Queen Victoria's Diamond Jubilee celebrations, 1897. A triumphal arch stands at the bottom of Fore Street – showing a remarkable effort, but such was the standard of the day.*

Right: *St Day School infants at the St Day Feast.*

Below: *St Day Dance. Pictured are Linda Williams (co-dance designer) followed by Evelyn and Stanley Martyn, and the Revd Timothy and Pamela van Carrapiett, 1980s.*

St Day Feast with the children enjoying their tea treat saffron buns.

Jubilee Day was kept up with much spirit, the Town being decorated with flags. The bells were rung and a service conducted in Church by Revd Olivey. The National Anthem was sung, accompanied by the Band. At three o'clock the children assembled in the Church Square and, led by the band, marched through the streets to Vogue, opposite Mr Davey's, where the National Anthem was sung, then they returned to Market Square, where they had tea in the streets. Afterwards all the aged, infirm, and the public partook of tea together. The Band then marched a crowd to a field kindly lent by Mr Apps, where various sports were held – conducted by Messrs Mitchell and Mills [prizes for events follow].

The Band then led the crowd to Wheal Jewell Row Burrow, where there was a huge bonfire, all the furze being presented by Mr John Davey of Vogue House. The bonfire was erected by Messrs Mitchell and Mills. Everything went off admirably. The only nuisance was a drunken fisherman and a half-idiot who tried to light the bonfire before the appointed time. The Devoran Band played splendidly throughout, and enlivened the proceedings until 10p.m. During the day a congratulatory telegram was forwarded to the Lord Lieutenant for presentation to her Majesty.[29]

Whilst Royal celebrations promoted such universal festivities, the death of a monarch meant widespread mourning and demonstrations of final respects, as was the case with the death of King Edward VII in May 1910:

On Saturday morning the mournful news of the death of the King was received with much regret by the inhabitants of St Day. At all the business houses, shutters were put up and the blinds drawn down on private houses. Acknowledged in Church and Non-conformist Chapel alike. The Dead March in 'Saul' was feelingly rendered by the respective organists.[30]

Clearly the celebrations at the end of both wars were mixed with great sadness and sorrow, as well as relief for peace. The end of the First World War may have been one of the very last times that bonfires or 'tar-barrels' were lit on the burrows opposite Wheal Jewell Row.

In 1977, Queen Elizabeth's Golden Jubilee attracted a considerable crowd and triumphal arches and flags returned St Day to times it had rarely seen since the turn of the century.

Christmas

The other great celebration in the calendar of the community at St Day are those of Christmas. Coconuts, oranges and bon-bons appeared in shops as Christmas gifts. Shop displays were described as 'very beautiful' and were commended by local newspapers throughout the late-nineteenth century. It was customary for mischievous boys to whitewash peoples windows, and swap window shutters around. On one occasion, the Primitive-Methodist minister woke to find a donkey chaise in front of his manse, as pranks abounded the night before.[31] Choir practice could be heard to echo carols around the streets, and in the 1920s and '30s unemployed men formed choirs to sing for donations towards their funds.

Christmas would not be the same for many without the 'St Day Carol'. It was noted by W.A.D. Watson, who heard the carol sung by Mr Thomas Beard, who took down the words and tune. It was then passed on to Dr Dunstan, who printed it in *A Second Book of Carols* (1925). Unfortunately, it was later published by *The Oxford Book of Carols* (1928) as the 'Sans Day Carol', which was a mistake. It has featured in the school carol services for decades and has a county-wide appeal.

Since the 1980s St Day has followed the new custom of erecting large illuminated Christmas trees, usually outside the St Day Inn, and adorning the streets with illuminated displays.

Notes

[1] *Royal Cornwall Gazette*, 1.3.1828.
[2] *Royal Cornwall Gazette*, 29.7.1876.
[3] *Royal Cornwall Gazette*, 15.11.1878.
[4] *West Briton*, 14.12.1899.
[5] *West Briton*, 29.10.1858, 19.11.1858, 3.12.1858, 23.9.1859, 16.12.1859 and 20.2.1863, and *Royal Cornwall Gazette*, 12.1.1879.
[6] *Royal Cornwall Gazette*, 24.7.1885 and 7.11.1889.
[7] *Royal Cornwall Gazette*, 31.7.1890 and 12.8.1890, and *Cornishman*, 25.9.1890 and 30.10.1890.
[8] *Royal Cornwall Gazette*, 30.7.1891.
[9] *Cornishman*, 31.5.1894.
[10] Blewett, R.R., 'These Things Have Been', Inst. 51. (July 1968).
[11] *West Briton*, 3.2.1887.
[12] *Kelly's Directory*, 1919 and 1924.
[13] *Royal Cornwall Gazette*, 1.7.1897.
[14] Mills, Joseph, *Carharrack & St Day Silver Band 65th Anniversary Booklet*, 1977. (A forthcoming publication on Carharrack will make further mention of this subject.)
[15] *Royal Cornwall Gazette*, 12.8.1909, 11.11.1909 18.11.1909, 2.12.1909, 9.6.1910, 11.8.1910, 8.12.1910, 26.1.1911 and 23.4.1924.
[16] *West Briton*, 1.8.1856.
[17] *West Briton*, 27.7.1823.
[18] *West Briton*, 29.7.1859.
[19] *Cornubian*, 24.8.1883.
[20] *Royal Cornwall Gazette*, 31.5.1894 and 21.6.1894.
[21] *Royal Cornwall Gazette*, 13.7.1899.
[22] *Cornish Post & Mining News*, 16.4.1914.
[23] M. Johnson and B. Fallon provided much of the material for this overview of the society. The complete account can be seen in the *St Day Community Newsletter*, Autumn 2002.
[24] Mills, Joseph, *Tregullow Lodge No.1006. 1864–1990*, Privately Published, 1992, St Day.
[25] Hitchens and Drew, 1824, *The History of Cornwall*, p.303.
[26] *Royal Cornwall Gazette*, 2.7.1814
[27] James, C.C., *History of Gwennap*, (n.d.), p.138.
[28] *West Briton*, 20.7.1866.
[29] *Royal Cornwall Gazette*, 24.6.1887.
[30] *Royal Cornwall Gazette*, 12.5.1910.
[31] *Royal Cornwall Gazette*, 3.1.1879, 1.1.1891 and 31.12.1891.

Church Street, c.1900, showing the Cornish Arms Inn. Note the folk outside, particularly the rather dandy gentleman, and the cobble-lined water-gulley.

Trap outside the Star Inn at Vogue, c.1895.

Below: *The right side of the Red Lion, otherwise known as Micky Duff's Beerhouse, c.1900.*

Twenty

Inns & Public Houses

By the eighteenth century a few references begin to emerge relating to various inns at St Day. Several are included in the *Sherborne Mercury* from 1768 when details of a 'survey at the house of Charles Hawke, Innkeeper, St Day' emerge. Another survey at 'the house of Mr Hitchens, Innkeeper, St Day' follows in 1783, and another almost certainly relating to his widow, Mary, appears in 1793.[1]

Gwennap: 17 Inns & 45 Beershops

Annie Trevithick refers to 'nine public houses being in the town and eight in the district – all doing a splendid trade' when the mines were in full swing. The Parish Constables Account Book covering 14–15 September 1837 refers to the serving of Magistrates Orders on 45 beershop keepers at 2d. each. On 30 August 1868, at the annual licensing meeting at Greenbank, 17 inns received licences in Gwennap. These were: the Queen's Head at Little Beside; the Fox and Hounds, Scorrier; the Six Bells at Gwennap; the Victory; the Miners Arms at Crofthandy; the Seven Stars and the Steam Engine, both at Carharrack; the Pick and Gad at Treskerby; the Hare and Hounds at Comford; the Cornish Arms at Frogpool; the Miners Arms at Lanner; the Commercial; the Cornish Arms; the New Inn; the King's Arms; the Britannia; and the Market Inn. The same licensing meeting also granted 45 beershops licenses at 7s.6d. each and these included seven at Carharrack, one each at Poldory, Pulla, Combe, Little Beside, Poldice, Tolgullow, Busveal, Lanner, Penance, Churchtown, Golden, Trevarth; two at Cusgarne, Crofthandy, Scorrier Gate and Vogue; three at Consols; and six at St Day.[2]

The number of inns and beerhouses reflects the prosperity of the mines. Such hostelries provided great temptations for miners, especially on pay day!

A rare view of West End, St Day, during the festive celebrations of Queen Victoria's Diamond Jubilee, 1897. The gabled building beyond the arch on the left is probably the Britannia Inn.

George IV (later the Star Inn), Vogue

At Vogue we find the George IV, named after the monarch who reigned from 1820–30.[3] *Pigot's Directory* of 1830 lists an inn at St Day as the George IV. It was later named the Star Inn as it appeared in *Slater's Directory* of 1852–53, when William Perriman was the landlord. It seems the inn was used as a venue for the occasional public auction or sale. Like many inns, the fields at the rear have been used for various sporting events, in particular annual wrestling from the 1870s to the 1940s. The inn has survived for so long probably because it served a wider, somewhat separate community at Vogue and strictly speaking was within the Redruth boundary. At nearby Pink Moors a 'Malt House' is known to have existed, but this fell into disrepair by the 1940s.

The Britannia Inn, West End

H.L. Douch, in his remarkable study *Old Cornish Inns*, suggests that the patriotic naming of inns Britannia is rather common in Cornwall.[4] The Britannia Inn appears in *Pigot's Directory* of 1830, situated at the West End of St Day. The inn was subject to a frequent change of landlords, typical of the majority of inns at St Day. It was stated to have 'good stabling, brew house, beer cellars, a large yard, piggeries and all the other conveniences.' Further, the Britannia maintained a 'good kitchen garden with fruit trees and a meadow of good pasture land.'[5]

A reference to a change of licence from James Hodge to Sampson Chynoweth, which appeared in the *Royal Cornwall Gazette* on 4 December 1869, seems to be the last record we have of the inn, which probably closed with the collapse of mining which many pubs and inns struggled to survive in the 1860s.

The King's Arms, Fore Street

Similarly, the King's Arms was well established by 1829, when the death of a Mrs Treweek was reported.[6] It is reasonable to assume that the inn was named after George III, who reigned from 1760–1820. It appears on the 1772 Survey of St Day and on the Gwennap Tithe Map of 1843. The latter shows the King's Arms situated in the gap between the current Spar shop and Post Office, almost opposite the St Day Inn. *Doidge's Directory* of 1866 lists the inn at Market Street at the south side.

William's Commercial Directory of 1847 lists a Queen's Arms at St Day with Henry Luke the landlord. However, he was the landlord of the King's Arms at this time so this serves to highlight how such directories are not always accurate. Interestingly, female landlords are listed almost as frequently as males – especially after the 1860s, with so many men abroad.

The inn had 17 rooms, pig houses, a cow house, coach-house, coal cellars, a stable, hayloft, dairy, large yard and a half-acre meadow at the rear. It was privately owned and sold to Richard Rooke during December 1869 for £386, compared to £462 in 1862,[7] a considerable decline in value probably because of falling trade and growing fears of depression. From July 1870, the licence may have been transferred from Richard Rooke to William Sowell. Reference is made to the Williams Arms during this period; this could be either an error or a change of name for the inn (possibly after the Williams family of Scorrier).[8] The Quarter Sessions refer to a 'robbery at the 'Williams Arms' St Day' in June 1870, and as late as 1877 local newspapers made reference to a 'row of houses known as flat tops and those at the back of Williams Arms' that were to be repaired. It is possible that the inn operated under this name into the 1870s.[9]

The St Day Inn, Fore Street

Apart from the Star Inn, the only other pub to survive today is the St Day Inn, first listed in *Pigot's Directory* of 1844, when Thomas Mitchell was landlord. Also known as the St Day Hotel and the Commercial, the inn has a long and reasonably well-documented history. There was also a Commerical Inn at Lanner. Auctions were held at the inn from 1851, which was let with a few acres of meadow. A more detailed account of the furniture and brewing utensils appears in an auction notice in June 1851:

> *An excellent malt mill and brewing utensils complete a large kitchen apparatus with smoke jack and conveniences for roasting attached; a large quantity of spirit and beer barrels, a very good patent mangle and various other articles.*[10]

Clearly the inn brewed some of its own alcohol, the utensils perhaps belonging to Mr Chester the landlord departing the premises at this time. Another auction in June 1868 refers to 'Brew Houses and Spirit Cellars' where a:

St Day Inn, c.1897, which was known at the time as Smith's Hotel. It has been called Bennetts Hotel and the Commercial, at different times. Note Paul Kruger's effigy above the door.

> ... *100-gallon copper furnace, cooler, mash tub, grain tubs, brewing utensils in general, beer horses, seven 72-gallon barrels, with smaller barrels, old timber, water barrels, wheelbarrow* [and other articles appear for sale].[11]

William Bennett, previous landlord of the Cornish Arms, moved in during 1851 and the Bennett family occupied the inn until around 1883, when the widow of William Bennett is reported to have died. On this basis it was known as Bennett's Hotel for a time. During this period the premises contained a 'parlour, dining room, sitting rooms, five bedrooms, a servants room, drinking rooms', and a 'bar parlour and mixing bar' as well as the brew houses.[12] The inn kept a skittle alley by about 1912. Skittles, otherwise known as 'nine-pin' or 'Kayles' in the nineteenth century, was common in many Cornish inns and was occasionally used for illegal gambling – as a few reports of St Day men being fined for this activity clearly illustrate.

An application to close the inn was presented in December 1911 by Penryn-based police Superintendent Nicholls, as the licence came up for transfer. However, he failed because expenses and evidence against the new landlord was not justifiable.[13] The inn was said to have closed for a time in 1921, and this seems likely as many pubs closed temporarily for a variety of reasons, such as the death of a landlord or the expiry of lease or contract.[14] Although the hotel was presented as a traveller's hostelry, offering comfortable accommodation and hospitality, the maintenance of a doorway providing access to the Masonic Hall adjoining caused concern to police who said on one visit that people could use this as an escape route.

The inn provided a venue for a variety of local functions. It was a regular venue for auctions, a meeting-place for the annuacourt of the lords of the manor and a place where inquests into local deaths were held. By the late-nineteenth century the inn had come under the ownership of the Redruth Brewery.

Hensley's shop, c.1900. Note the double lintel over the doorway of what was the Market Inn, which closed in 1888. The house on the far right may also be a shop, with the owner outside in their apron.

The Market Inn, Church Street

The Market Inn, situated on the south side of Church Street, does not take its name from Market Street (the former name of Fore Street where it lies opposite at the Church Street junction). A 'St Day Town Trail' plaque presently marks the site. It was advertised as a 'lucrative business for the past 20 years' in April 1849, so was well established by the 1820s.[15] It is not difficult to imagine the meeting between traders, farmers and other dealers who negotiated over a lunch at the inn, which served the weekly market interests. This inn also had its own brew house, cellar, yard and stables, as well as outhouses.[16] By 1875 the premises were being managed as an outlet for Treluswell Brewery who maintained the lease offered to tenant landlords. The fate of the inn seems tied to the mining depression and the brewery failed to secure the lease during 1888.[17] Certainly the inn had closed by 1889, when the premises were being considered as a venue for the new library.[18]

The Cornish Arms, Church Street

The Cornish Arms was listed in *Pigot's Directory* of 1830 and the name rather inspires a local recognition of allegiance to the county. (There was also a Cornish Arms at Frogpool.) This inn was situate at the top of Vicarage Hill on the corner next to the granite octagonal gatehouse of The Cedars. By the early 1830s it was a venue for the prestigious dinners of the St Day Show Fair. It was offered to let in 1858 with 16 rooms.[19] The inn survived the mining depressions but closed in 1915. However, it reopened in February 1921.[20] The opening was tentative and under the scrutiny of Superintendent Nicholls who, acting on behalf of the Brewster Sessions, recommended that it be closed. Unable to make any real headway, the Cornish Arms finally closed a few months later in July.[21]

The New Inn (site unknown)

The New Inn is recorded as early as 1813, when it was used as an auction venue for property sales within St Day.[22] By 1838 it is quoted as a 'well accustomed inn, with its own brewing utensils'. It was owned by Collan Harvey by this time and specifically referred to as The New Inn.[23] Harvey let the lease by tender for 14-year periods and some time after 1838 it was leased by Thomas Mitchell with whom it continued a rather uneventful existence. It is listed in *Pigot's Directory* of 1844. It evades further mention until it was granted a licence at the meeting at Greenbank held on 30 August 1868.[24]

The Red Lion, Scorrier Street

An inn that appears frequently from 1844 was the Red Lion. It was first licensed in 1839.[25] Early accounts show the assault of a constable and reported theft during the years 1848–9, perhaps hinting at a rather lively venue.[26] The Red Lion was also known as the Lion Inn and Mickey Duff's Beer House. Mickey Duff died in 1908 and was replaced by his son, Michael, who continued at the inn until 1912, when the Brewster Sessions refused to grant him a licence.[27] Evidence against Duff was presented by Superintendent Nicholls who testified to the rowdy nature of the inn and suggested St Day could well do without another inn to take money from those who could ill-afford the cost of beer, whilst their families were sometimes denied a basic existence.

A field attached to the inn hosted regular Cornish wrestling matches as mentioned in the *Royal Cornwall Gazette* on 5 May 1878:

> *On Tuesday as usual the annual wrestling took place in a field behind the Lion Inn, and after some tough tugs, the first prize was taken by Mr Stone of St Austell, 2nd W. Tresidder, Golden Lion* [Stithians?], *3rd S. Jackson of Redruth and James Matthews of St Day. Alfred Uren, the Featherweight Champion was at the ground but did not wrestle.*

Not all was so calm and collected during the annual Feast celebrations, when the inns and public houses of St Day presented a very different picture, as this newspaper report of 1889 reveals:

> *... not only were the streets thronged with hilarious townspeople and visitors but free fights were carried on with vigour in some of the public houses, from which the disputants were summarily ejected through the door or window, to continue their war of oaths and fists outside. There was no attempt at enforcing the Marquis of Queensberry's rules for excitement ran too high. If fists would not hit hard enough, sticks or boots got in their deadly work, and altogether, as was observed by many an observer, "Twas like owld times again yu. St Dye edn't dead yet."*[28]

The Queen's Head, Little Beside & The Miners Arms, Crofthandy

Others pubs served the St Day district during the heyday of mining. The Little Beside House boasted on the retirement of Mrs Elizabeth Richards in 1812 that for '20 years past [it] has had as great a business as any in the County'.[29] The business was privately owned over the years by a variety of individuals and in 1817 the proprietor was James Michael, a Redruth spirit dealer who kept the inn until he died in 1849.[30] The inn was then sold, advertised with an assay office.[31] By the early 1850s the name had changed to The Queen's Head[32] (perhaps highlighting patronage to Queen Victoria). In September 1861 the inn closed because its licence was not renewed.

Another early inn was the Miners' Arms at Crofthandy. A reference to 1819 refers to a 'well frequented public house between New Consolidated Mines and the United Mines on Cusgarne Common.' Two miners who had been drinking at the Miners' Arms in January 1832 fell down a shaft to their deaths whilst walking home. The Miners' Arms was one of the few inns to remain open throughout the depression years of the 1870s and appears to have kept a fairly low profile. However, like many other St Day pubs, the Miners' Arms fell under the scrutiny of Superintendent Nicholls, who worked hard to close several pubs in the area, presenting cases against them at the Brewster Sessions of East Kerrier Courts. By this time the Miners' Arms was little used and the landlord struggled to justify the continuation of the licence; it could offer a mere 18-gallon barrel of beer and a small measure of spirits. On a few occasions the Superintendent had called only to find the inn closed and the landlord tending his garden. Certainly he was raising a family of 11, but a busy occasion such as Boxing Day might only draw five or so customers. Superintendent Nicholls was concerned about the inconvenience of policing such remote outlying inns. It seems that the landlord hoped for better times, when a return to the former heady days of mining would mean great profits for any landlord of an inn. His licence was refused and in February 1912 the Miners' Inn closed.

Notes

1 *Sherborne Mercury*, 24.10.1768, 20.10.1783 and 14.10.1793.
2 The former curator of Truro Museum H.L. Douch's notes and references at the Courtney Library, RIC.
3 Douch, H.L., *Old Cornish Inns*, (1966), Bradford Barton, Truro, 1966, p.142.
4 Ibid., p.138.
5 *West Briton*, 12.3.1858.
6 *West Briton*, 27.3.1829.
7 *West Briton*, 23.12.1869.
8 Douch, H.L., Ibid., p.212.
9 *Royal Cornwall Gazette*, 8.1.1870, 23.6.1870 and 13.4.1877. (See also *West Briton*, 30.6.1870 and 7.7.1877.)
10 *West Briton*, 13.6.1851
11 *Cornubian*, 19.6.1868.
12 Ibid.
13 *Royal Cornwall Gazette*, 7.12.1911.
14 *Royal Cornwall Gazette*, 16.2.1921.
15 *West Briton*, 20.4.1849.
16 *West Briton*, 20.4.1849.
17 *West Briton*, 24.6.1875 and 13.9.1888.
18 *Royal Cornwall Gazette*, 7.11.1889.
19 *West Briton*, 18.6.1858.
20 *Royal Cornwall Gazette*, 16.2.1921.
21 Ibid.
22 *West Briton*, 16.4.1813.
23 *West Briton*, 5.1.1838.
24 Notes of Douch, H.L., Ibid.
25 *Royal Cornwall Gazette*, 29.12.1912.
26 *West Briton*, 4.8.1848 and 30.3.1849.
27 *Royal Cornwall Gazette*, 8.2.1912, 29.2.1912 and 1.8.1912.
28 *Cornishman*, 25.7.1889
29 *Royal Cornwall Gazette*, 25.1.1812.
30 *Royal Cornwall Gazette*, 24.1.1817.
31 *West Briton*, 24.8.1849, and *West Briton*, 24.8.1849.
32 *West Briton*, 25.2.1853.

Twenty-One

Prominent Personalities

The Williams Family

The growth of the Gwennap mines and St Day as a service town would not have been possible without two families, the Williamses of Scorrier and the Harveys of St Day. With the development of the mines came prospects and employment. From this a population grew which became dependent upon a whole range of provisions, supplies and services. Both of these families responded to the needs of such demands.

We do not know when the Williamses arrived in Cornwall but three brothers, James, Davy and Richard, were living at Stithians by the 1650s. Of these James makes the claim to the lineage which managed, toiled for, invested in, speculated upon and maintained much of the foundations on the basis of which Gwennap became one of the greatest mining districts in the world.

James' grandson, often referred to as John I, managed the property of the Hearle family, who were joint holders of the manor of St Day and Poldice Mine. This probably served as a springboard for his success as a mining adventurer, which secured enough finance for him to settle at Burncoose in 1715. It was his grandson, John II, who initiated the drainage of the Gwennap mines through the County Adit in 1748, allowing mining operations to continue and develop well below the inhibitions of the natural water levels. James I had a great-grandson, Michael I, who more or less resided at Burncoose until his death in 1775.[1]

The residence at Burncoose was then taken by Michael I's eldest son, John III. He was born at Lower Cusgarne. The year 1776 saw his marriage to Katherine, daughter of Martin Harvey of Killifreth, and the following year their first child John IV was born. The family moved from Burncoose to land at Scorrier, which became the family estate. John III managed his business from Scorrier until moving to Wheal Damsel Count House. Around 1829 he transferred business to offices added to Burncoose.[2] John III seems to have lived a fascinating life. Around 1800 he was said to have been visited by the Compte de Lille and the Compte d'Artois who later became no less than Kings Louis XVIII and Charles X of France. John III not only established the Williams family at Scorrier, but also purchased the manor of Calstock from the Duchy in 1809 and was one of the constructors of the Plymouth Breakwater in 1812. It was around this time that John III had a 'prophetic dream' about the assassination of Mr Spencer Percival, Chancellor of the Exchequer, in the lobby of the House of Commons, on 11 May 1812. Indeed, the Chancellor had been shot that same evening, but news of the event was not relayed to Cornwall until the next day, by which time John Williams had explained in detail the events in his dream to several family members, themselves prominent county figures. The dream became the talk of the county. John III's mining interests locally, nationally and internationally allowed him to build what was reputedly the finest collection of Cornish minerals ever assembled. After the death of his wife Catherine in 1826, John III remarried and moved to Sandhill House, where he retired. He died in April 1841.

John IV had already inherited Burncoose and became a Quaker by 1809. In 1810 he married Philippa, daughter of William Naudin, a French Protestant refugee, in the Friends' meeting-house in Perranwharf. The connections were probably made earlier during visitations by the French royalty in around 1800. He became a minister in 1831 and died a much respected man in 1849.

John III's second son, Michael II, was also born at Burncoose in 1785 and inherited Scorrier House from his father and enjoyed great success, contributing much to the development of the Gwennap mines. Michael II maintained business interests at Portreath, with harbour leases and tramroad interests, the Perran Foundry Co., copper-smelting interests in the firm Williams, Foster & Co., as well as numerous interests in mines both at home and abroad.[3] Michael also maintained family business interests in land at St John, Swansea and Llangefelach in Glamorgan around 1837, whilst residing at Trevince.[4] His brothers John IV (then residing at Burncoose) and William (resident at Tregullow House, which he built) also held these interests. Perhaps in recognition of the contribution the Williamses made to that locality, Michael was made Sheriff of Glamorganshire in 1839. He met his civic duties with such energy that he was presented with a Testimonial of Public Esteem at Redruth in June 1853, the year in which he was elected MP for West Cornwall, a position he held until 1858. In 1854 he purchased Caerhays, although most of his life was spent at Trevince where he died in 1858.

William was John III's youngest son, born in 1791 at Scorrier House. He built a house and estate at Tregullow and married in 1826. He was associated with a range of mines and mining-related industries, among them Williams, Foster & Co., Williams, Harvey & Co., Copper Smelters in Swansea, Williams Portreath Co., Timber & Guano Merchants and Williams Perran Foundry Co. He was also a partner in the Cornish Bank at Truro, Redruth, Falmouth and Penryn, and Williams & Sons, Tregullow Office, Scorrier, as well as the chief shareholder of Clifford Amalgamated, Dolcoath, Cook's Kitchen, Carn Brea, South Crofty and Wheal Basset Mines. He was deputy warden of the Stannaries and was created a Baronet in 1866.

Whilst William lived at Tregullow, Scorrier House was occupied by John Michael Williams, son of Michael II, who was born at Trevince in 1813 and appears to have dedicated himself to his father's business. Upon his father's death in 1858, he inherited Scorrier House and the vast range of business interests at Portreath and the various mines. He worked tirelessly to establish his own ventures and by 1862 he retired his interest as a partner in the Cornish Bank and was given the Redruth Branch. He was also head partner in the West Cornwall Bank at Redruth and Falmouth and became sole proprietor of the bank at Redruth from November 1877. His adventures in mines and their management, as well as his activities as a copper buyer, are clear from this testimony printed in the *West Briton* in October 1876:

I scarcely believe that mine agents of the present day know what work is compared with what used to be in former days. Forty years ago I used to be intimately mixed up with mining and know pretty much of the Williamses of Scorrier who were the architects of their own fortune. I can remember very well when Mr J.M. Williams was a young man, how he used to work in those days. I have seen him drive away from Scorrier House and set to the men at Unity Woods, finish there so far as the setting and other business was concerned and drive thence to Poldice, set there also a heavy setting, thence to Wheal Gorland, thence to Wheal Maid, thence to Wheal Jewell, from there to Wheal Damsel, thence to Wheal Spenser under Carnmarth and thence back to Clifford, setting at each place and working with a will at each mine. It seems but as yesterday so vivid is it in my memory when Mr John M. Williams accomplished all this work in one day bringing a clear and vigorous intellect to the business before him and dispatching everything in a straightforward manner. The setting was all clear and above board and there was a wholesome competition. After accomplishing all this work in one day, I have known Mr Williams take a fresh horse and ride to Truro and take a coach to London and after finishing his business in the great metropolis going on from London to Swansea and coming back again as soon as he could finish his business. I remember also hearing that in order to take advantage of the market, as it was then tending in certain directions, instead of going from Bristol to Swansea, he took the coach and then posted back to North Devon and was pulled from one of these ports across the Bristol Channel to Swansea in a few hours, thereby saving as many days. This was before the days of railways and telegraphs. It may be truly said of him that whatever he found to do, he did with all his might and a few of the Mine Agents of the present day who complain at being overworked, ought to take a leaf out of his book.

John Michael Williams was to see the end of the great copper-mining era, through which the Williams family had successfully steered Gwennap. By the 1870s practically all of the Gwennap copper mines had closed. John Michael Williams died in 1880, by which time he had become one of the richest men in Cornwall.

Michael II's younger son George inherited Scorrier House in 1862 from his brother John Michael. He too had been born at Trevince in 1827. He rebuilt Scorrier House and established himself Master of the Four Burrow Hounds in the same year. John, his son, later inherited Scorrier House. By the end of the nineteenth century several members of the Williams family were MPs, whilst others chose military service or pursuing business interests.

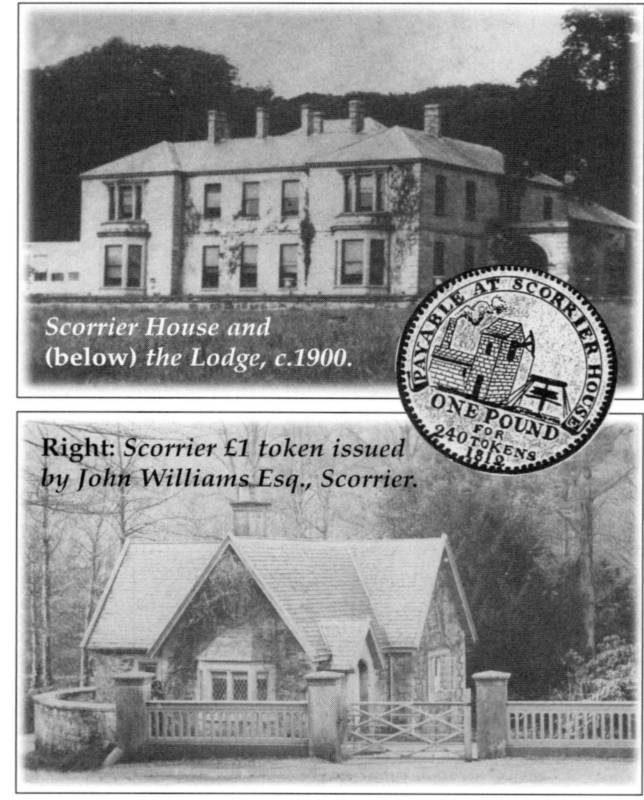

Scorrier House and (below) the Lodge, c.1900.

Right: *Scorrier £1 token issued by John Williams Esq., Scorrier.*

Carew House, St Day, the home of Collan Harvey in the early 1800s. The photograph was taken c.1910.

The Harveys at St Day

When, in 1776, John Williams III married Catherine Harvey, daughter of Martin Harvey of Killifreth, he probably never realised that her six-year-old brother Collan would become one his closest business partners. Collan began his working life as a cooper and by 1808 his brother James was an established mine adventurer. Some time after this the brothers set up as C. & J. Harvey, drapers, grocers, ironmongers, coopers and mathematical instrument dealers. They quickly built up the largest store in St Day.

By the Harveys' exertions and their links to the Williamses, St Day became the principal town and service centre for the Gwennap mines. Gwennap's population grew at an astounding rate from 4,594 in 1801 to 10,974 during 1841. Such an influx during this 'boom' period profited the Harveys to the extent that they were able to invest in the partnership with Collan's brother-in-law, through firms such as Williams, Harvey & Co., copper smelters, and Williams, Foster & Co., a tin-smelting firm. Consequently, they amassed a fortune.[5] Other business interests in Portreath Harbour, the Poldice–Portreath Tramway and the foundry at Perranwharf were established and continued under Collan's son Richard. By the early 1800s Collan had begun to shape St Day into what it is today. The present Masonic Lodge, erected 1809–27, was built by the Harveys as a flour store, from which two travelling clerks organised business.[6] The buildings opposite became the Harveys' store. Collan lived at Carew House and his brother James is said to have built The Cedars. Rock House was built around 1837 for the use of the Harveys' agent Richard Clift. The family also maintained business interests in the leases of the New Inn and St Day's market buildings. Both men were very successful adventurers in Wheal Gorland, Wheal Jewell, Tresavean, Trethellan, Wheal Brewer, Penstruthal, Consols, United, Wheal Damsel, West Seton, and South Francis, amongst other mines.[7]

The Harveys boosted their trade at St Day by managing much of their business through the 'truck system'. Miners who worked for the Williamses and the Harveys were compelled to purchase all their household and working supplies from the merchants store. Those who failed to oblige quickly found themselves struggling with an allocation of poor pitches on setting day. Ben Matthews was the first 'truck clerk' employed by the Harveys to go around each of the relevant mines on pay day and deduct what was owed from each miner's pay.[8] Matthews was vital to the operations of the Harvey family, and became a shrewd business agent himself. When Collan's son Richard died in 1870, Ben Matthews received a legacy of several thousand pounds.

Collan Harvey is reputed to have sold his share in the copper-smelting business for £300,000 before retiring to a wing of Pengreep House, Gwennap. He apparently made a gift to his son Richard of £300,000[9] in 1846 just before he died, by which time he was said to have accumulated 'half a million of money'.[10]

James Harvey died in November 1858 aged 78. His daughter Jane survived him and inherited his estate. She lived at The Cedars, her father's home, with her husband Zaccheus Andrew, RN, until she died aged 69 in 1880.

Richard Harvey, born in 1808, was the only child of Collan Harvey who survived him. Alongside his uncle James, he continued to work many of his father's business interests which he had inherited until James died in 1858. He was reputed to have left property worth £300,000. By this time Richard had purchased Greenway Mansion, near Dartmouth, from the late Colonel Carlyon of Tregrehan. (Greenway was the home of Agatha Christie in the 1930s.) He frequently resided there until in 1867 he bought the nearby manor and village of Galmpton near Brixham, Devon, for £37,000.[11] He took great interest in redeveloping the village; demolishing the so-called 'hovels', which were replaced with 'model' homes. Richard Harvey also maintained another prestigious seaside home at Rock End, Torquay, where he seems to have enjoyed an annual income of £70,000.[12]

Richard Harvey was said to be worth about £500,000 in property alone amongst a total estate worth £1.25 million when he died at Greenway in 1870.[13] With no children or particularly close relatives, he left almost his entire estate to his friend Mr P.P. Smith of the solicitors Smith & Roberts, Truro. He left his wife £20,000 and an annual annuity of £6,000. An interest in his will was later revived in November 1876, when a gentleman named Count von Howard informed a London merchant named John Harvey that Richard Harvey of Greenway, Dartmouth, had left him £40,000 in money and £10,000 in property. Count von Howard was an alias used by Charles Howard, an ex-naval clerk who managed to con £380 out of John Harvey before he was arrested, tried and found guilty and then sentenced to 12-months' hard labour.[14]

The Hawkes of Tolgullow

Edward Henry Hawke was born at Tolgullow in 1799, the son of John Hawke. By 1819, the family had established the Ropewalk at Tolgullow. Edward Hawke was one of the founder members of St Day's Freemasons' Tregullow Lodge. He was also a founder member of both the St Day Institute, which he and his son supported for many years, and the town's cricket club. Henry Edward Hawke junr was also born at Tolgullow in 1831 and was groomed for the business, which he managed successfully with his father, but he died in January 1870. He was the only child of Edward senr.

E.H. Hawke junr had a son who became Sir John Anthony Hawke. He was educated at Merchant Taylors' School and St John's College, Oxford, where he became an honorary fellow achieving a First Class MA in Law. He was called to the Bar in 1892 and became the Attorney General for the Prince of Wales before being appointed Judge of the King's Bench Division in 1928, when he was knighted. Among several prominent cases that Sir Anthony Hawke heard was the petition for divorce by Mrs Wallis Simpson at Ipswich Assizes in 1936 so that she might marry King Edward VIII. Hawke had enjoyed an interest in politics and became a Unionist (Conservative) candidate in various elections. He became MP for the St Ives Division in 1924. His call to the King's Bench led to his resignation from parliamentary representation in 1928, but upon his return to London he soon became President of the London-Cornish Association, a position he held for many years.[15]

Whilst Sir Anthony had moved away from Tolgullow early in his life, his sister Charlotte stayed, eventually marrying Henry Grylls, the Redruth solicitor.

Sir Anthony Hawke had two children: a daughter, Barbara, who married Major Sir Percy Simmons in 1931, and a son, Anthony Hawke junr, who followed his father's example and became a barrister. The two met at the Bodmin Assizes and enjoyed a little banter, when the son hinted that the two had met before, and Sir Anthony complimented the learned council on having profited from his valuable training![16]

The Mills Family

Three prominent members of the Mills family were particularly active at St Day throughout the late-nineteenth and early-twentieth centuries. They were Thomas Richards, William John and Joseph Mills, sons of William and Susan. Thomas, popularly known as T.R. Mills, was an auctioneer and valuer for many years at St Day. He also maintained an ironmonger's business and worked as an emigration agent at Church Street and Scorrier Street. He served on many different committees within the town, including the St Day Show, the Lamp and Clock Committee, the town-clock restoration appeal committees, the water-supply committee and various First World War committees. He led a group which attempted to connect St Day with the railways that ran through Cornwall. A memorial on the side of St Day's town clock is dedicated to him: 'Who was leader in all movements for the welfare of St Day'. Born in 1839, T.R. Mills died in 1915.

William John Mills started his working life as a blacksmith at Scorrier, but through illness was forced to consider less strenuous work. He then established a small dairy business, selling the produce locally. He moved to Devon in 1899 and established the Duchess of Devonshire Dairy Company. Within two years the company was processing the produce of between 4,000 to 5,000 cows and distributing milk, cream and butter all over England.[17] William John Mills paid towards the restoration and building of a monumental wall around the town clock, as well as providing a trust for its future upkeep during the early 1930s. By 1933 he had also purchased all 28 properties in Simmons Street, had them refurbished to a high standard and presented them to the Mills Trust for the elderly people of St Day. In his honour this stretch was renamed Mills Street. After Mills Street was officially opened on 3 July, a procession marched to the playing-fields where a new memorial to W.J. Mills was unveiled.[18] The event was tied to the town's Feast Day celebration, which still enjoys this procession today.

Joseph Mills built up the business known as the St Day Posting Establishment, at Church Street. From here a wide variety of brakes, wagonettes and landaus could be hired for weddings, excursions or for funerals.

Joe Mills, grandson of Joseph Mills modelled himself on the civic virtues of his great-uncle, T.R. Mills. He was born at St Day 1915, where he lived until he was on active service as an officer in the Fleet Air Arm from 1939–48. He was involved in enemy action during periods of the Second World War. From 1977 he was again in a leadership position; he was chairman of the Silver Jubilee Committee. He was then called upon to support St Day through the Telegraph Hill closure and he chaired the struggle for eight years. Joe Mills was immediately elected chairman when St Day Parish Council was formed in 1980, a position he held for 12 years. During this time he negotiated new wrought-iron gates for the War Memorial

Clock memorial gates

(designed by Hamish Miller of Hayle in 1987) and an extension of the burial-ground by 1988. He was pivotal in helping St Day secure Objective One Funding, which helped towards establishing a variety of heritage projects, including the regeneration of Market Square, improvements at Buckingham Terrace, the Old Church Conservation Project and the Town Trail. He still sits on several committees in the wider district.

Peter Jennings

Peter Jennings arrived at St Day in 1878 and was the first headmaster of the new Council Schools. He lived at Burnwithian House. He became a very influential member of the community; he was a noted Wesleyan Methodist preacher and an advocate of the Wesleyan Band of Hope temperance movement. Upon arriving at St Day, he immediately set himself about the task of recording the history of the town. He was a member of various committees and organisations within St Day and contributed several articles on the history of Truro to the Royal Institution of Cornwall journals. During the First World War he was a strong motivator in recruitment campaigns and supported the town's contribution to the war effort. Peter Jennings died in 1917.

R.R. Blewett

Another highly influential headmaster at St Day was Richard Rodda Blewett. Born at Leedstown, Blewett arrived at St Day, 1921. He immediately took an interest in the local library, conducting a report on its state. His first community position came as secretary and later chairman of the St Day Community Council, behind which he became a driving force throughout its formative years. He negotiated a great deal with W.J. Mills in helping secure funding for community projects. It seems he was something of a sociologist, and caused great controversy during the late 1930s with many of his ideas, writings and publicity about St Day. He retired from teaching in 1943, but was appointed as a civilian lecturer to the Armed Forces at Exeter University. It was during this period that Richard Blewett frequently broadcast and wrote articles about Cornish history, often with a reference to St Day. He completed an MA on 'Cornish Surnames' in his later years. Blewett was a Wesleyan preacher for almost 20 years. From March 1964 to May 1971, he wrote a series called 'These Things Have Been', as a supplement to St Day's church magazine. The series covered much of his valuable research and writings on the history of St Day, about which he was clearly passionate.

St-Day-born Arnold Hodge receives congratulations from his former headmaster Richard R. Blewett, as he becomes Mayor of Truro in 1969.

Herbert Thomas

Herbert Thomas was born at Pink Moors, St Day, in 1866. He began his career as a 'four shillings a week office boy' in a Redruth mining office, but eventually emigrated to America, where he became a reporter on the *San Francisco Examiner*. He travelled the mining camps of Butte and the Grass Valley, gaining much experience and knowledge of Cornish miners abroad. Upon his return to England he became a reporter for *The Cornishman*, but later became editor of the *Cornish Post* at Camborne, which he purchased shortly after, along with a financial interest in *The Cornishman* of which he also became the editor. He then bought *The Cornish Telegraph*. At one time he owned eight separate newspapers in The Cornishman Group.

As a journalist, Herbert Thomas enjoyed two remarkable achievements. Firstly, he was the first man to report upon the death of the Russian Tsar and his family at Ekaterinburg, six weeks ahead of any other national journalist; and secondly he was the only reporter to cover the funeral of King Edward VII along the entire route from Westminster Abbey to Windsor Castle. Herbert Thomas is also considered a worthy Cornish novelist, with publications such as *Romance of a Cornish Cove* and *Alan Pendragon*. He is considered among the finest of Anglo-Cornish poets, with such works as 'The Ballads of Evolution' and his celebrated 'Pasties and Cream'. Historically, his *Cornish Mining Interviews* is regarded as a classic amongst Cornish mining historians today.

Within his newspapers, he covered news, history and opinions relating to St Day and its district, often working under the pseudonym Springfield, named after his home at Carbis Bay, which was in turn named after his home at Pink Moors.[19] Herbert Thomas managed the publication of Annie Trevithick's *A Short History of St Day*, which was published in a serial form in *The Cornishman* around 1900 and again in the 1930s. Annie Trevithick enjoyed and researched local history at St Day, working from sources supplied by J.T Letcher.

Herbert Thomas was also a founder member of the Camborne Chamber of Commerce and the Camborne Student Association. In 1948 he presented

Arnold Hodge, born Buckingham Terrace, St Day. Mayor of Truro 1969–70, he was an Honorary Freeman of the City of Truro, 1987. Here he is conferred an Alderman, Freeman of the City of London, 1997, for dedicated service to Truro and Cornwall.

St Day with the gift of a new electric clock for the tower. Herbert Thomas joined the Gorsedd at its first assembly, after its revival in 1928 at Boscawen Un, and took for his name Barth Colonneck (the Friendly Bard) alongside the Cornish antiquarian Charles Henderson.[20]

Leonard J. Martin

Leonard J. Martin was born at Truro in 1882. The son of a local outfitter, his early life was spent in St Day. He was educated at Truro College, and at the age of 18 he began to make money. He graduated to a little shop in Lewisham which made motor-boat machinery. In 1908, with £2,000 capital, he bought the stock of an old bus company. He continued to buy 'dud' companies and began to ship the purchases abroad. This built his fortune. He then imported 68,000 agricultural machines and opened warehouses at Liverpool, Birkenhead and Bow, with over 800 machinery agents under him. During the war he 'put 3,000 farm tractors on English soil'.

In 1919 he made the famous 'linen deal', valued at £4 million, when he purchased 40 million yards of the finest linen from the Aircraft Dispersal Unit. The linen was of 16 different varieties and could be used for household goods.[21] Martin used his wealth to support St Day's Miners Distress Fund in 1921; he gave £1,000 to the cause in the form of coal and other necessities. He also purchased and donated a new Riley billiard table for St Day Institute at Scorrier Street.

Arnold Hodge

Arnold Hodge was born at Buckingham Terrace, St Day, in 1924. In his teenage years he moved to nearby Chacewater, where he became a member of Chacewater Parish Council for 18 years (never missing a meeting). He moved to Truro and became a member of the Truro Chamber of Commerce in the 1960s. During this time he was instrumental, with others, in securing a variety of corporate businesses in the city, making Truro the leading commercial centre of the county. He was also a member of Truro City Council for 35 years. In recognition of his efforts, he was made Mayor of Truro, 1969–70. Other honours followed when he was made an Honorary Freeman of the City of Truro in 1987 and an Alderman, Freeman of the City of London, in 1997. These prestigious titles have allowed Arnold special privileges, such as invitations to a variety of civic processions in both Truro and London, and in particular attendance at various royal visits and events. In 1988 Arnold was made a member of the Cornish Gorsedd and given the Bardic name 'Map Sen Day'.

Kenneth Pelmear

Kenneth was the son of W. George Pelmear, one of the founder members of Carharrack Brass Band. Born in St Day, he worked at Cligga Mine for many years, before entering into a musical career. He composed the tune for St Day's Feast Day Dance in the late 1970s. He has contributed to a range of musical groups, bands and other organisations, making himself well known amongst musicians within the county and beyond.

Like his father, he was a great rugby enthusiast; he published *Rugby in the Duchy* in 1960. A memorial plaque at his birthplace in Vicarage Hill commemorates his life and achievements.

Notes

1 James, C.C., *History of Gwennap*, (n.d.), pp.90–97.
2 Bradford, Barton, *Essays in Cornish Mining*, p.15.
3 Ibid., p.19.
4 Notes in author's possession relating to leases in these areas.
5 *West Briton*, 7.7.1870.
6 Annie Trevithick, *A Short History of St Day*, c.1897, and *Cornishman*, 25.5.1882.
7 Ibid.
8 Barton, Ibid., p.20, and James, C.C., Ibid., pp. 79, 225.
9 *West Briton*, 18.8.1870.
10 Barton, Ibid., p.20, and *Cornishman*, 25.5.1882.
11 *West Briton*, 24.3.1881.
12 *West Briton*, 24.3.1881.
13 *West Briton*, 18.8.1870 and 24.3.1881.
14 *Cornubian*, 3.11.1876.
15 *Cornish Post & Mining News*, 1.11.1941.
16 Ibid.
17 *Cornish Post & Mining News*, 28.1.1901.
18 *Cornish Post & Mining News*, 5.7.1833.
19 *Cornish Post & Mining News*, 1.11.1941.
20 *Cornishman*, 20.12.1951.
21 *Cornubian*, 26.6.1919 and 17.11.1921.

Twenty-Two

St Day Town Clock

Removal of market buildings, March 1911.

The town clock at St Day is so much more than a monumental timepiece. It remains central to the pride of the town and is representative of the image of St Day. It has inspired writers and poets, witnessed countless gatherings, ceremonies and celebrations, and has appeared on many souvenir plates, cups and other memorabilia. Importantly, our town clock harbours the roll-call of those sons of St Day who sacrificed their lives so that we may today live in freedom. Such is its place at the heart of St Day's history. If only it could tell us more than time itself!

The origins of the clock are well documented by many nineteenth-century historians. Lewis, writing in 1833, notes a 'neat stone tower, with a lock-house' that was erected in 1831 at an expense of £400.[1] No mention is made of a clock at this time, although William Francis writing in 1845 suggests a clock movement 'which the time seeker greets'.[2] The tower seems to have been incorporated into the market buildings that had been erected in 1797; here it took on a very different appearance from that of today, where it stands independent. Between the 1830s and the 1890s the town clock became the focus of a large market-place that served a thriving mining community, with the Gwennap mines in full swing.

The other use of the clock tower was as a 'lock-house' or 'clink', where those guilty of drunken or rowdy behaviour were imprisoned before being marched to the Magistrate's Court at Penryn.[3]

None of the nineteenth-century county historians tell us who actually built the town clock, or where the granite was quarried, or indeed who paid the £400. The clock (and probably the tower as well) seem to have been acknowledged as 'the property of the townspeople', but 'being enclosed by a market house and walls, which belong together with the grounds to the lords of the manor.' This caused problems for the repair and maintenance of the clock in its early history.[4] Some dispute resulted in the landowner exercising his right to deny access to the clock through his property of the market-place. The following anonymous verse appeared in the *West Briton* on 12 September 1851 and rather mocks the gentleman involved in the case:

Oh! Good Mr H----y I hope you'll attend
To the humble request which I venture to send,
And which I advise you to yield upon sight,
Lest by oft importuning I weary you quite.
Then sir to be brief, as I'm brought to stand,
I humbly entreat, that you'll give the command
To my friend Mr W----n to come with the key,
And at once set your humble petitioner free.
Let him give my hands liberty, if not my tongue,
Oh! Surely good sir this request can't be wrong,
For is it not hard for a clock in my case,
The first in the town, to be such disgrace?
To be left to run down, till I'm mute as a dummy,
With no more of life in my face than a mummy!
Whereas you know I'm still able and strong,
And willing to work all the day and night long,
That for years I thus laboured, and few minutes lost
But mostly was found in good time at my post.
Till lately the people looked at me with pleasure,
For the march of old time 'twas my business to measure,
So all knew when to go to mine, meeting and church;
But now I am idle they're left in the lurch!
For though most have got watches and clocks, yet you see
These smaller time-pieces can never agree;
Like mankind they want someone to give them the lead;
But where can they look when the Town Clock is dead?
So pray Mr H-----y revive me again
Occasion no longer, such trouble and pain;
The honours I'm sure of, ah! Prithee restore,
And then I promise to plague you no more.

The town clock and its bell became neglected and remained 'a long time idle' throughout the 1850s

St Day town clock and (right) *the Post Office window, c.1930s.*

Opening and dedication of the town clock garden, 1930s.

and 1860s until the problems were resolved in 1871.[5] The letters 'H' and 'y' at the beginning and end of the surname may refer to 'Harvey'. In 1851, Richard Harvey was an extensive property leaseholder within St Day and the Harvey family maintained early property rights over the market-place. Upon his death in 1870, much of Richard Harvey's property leases passed or reverted to the lords of the manors of St Day. It seems that the lease of the market access to the clock may have reverted to a Mr R. Chichester.[6] What the dispute was about remains unknown, but it was evidently so severe that Richard Harvey kept the grudge until his death.

Annie Trevithick suggests that the cupola of the clock had been struck by lightening and damaged around 1855 and was eventually replaced. It may be that the landowner did not allow access to replace the cupola until it was rebuilt by Mr Letcher in 1872. At this time the people of St Day and the lords of the manor entered into a new spirit of co-operation; the decision was taken to restore the town clock and at a public meeting in the Temperance Hall Mr R. Chichester sent a letter granting access to the clock and even offered to subscribe towards the restoration.[7] The clock was overhauled and restored by local clock and watchmakers John Veale and Edward Newton. Mr Letcher undertook necessary carpentry repairs.[8]

It is likely that the St Day Clock Committee was appointed around this time; it collected annual subscriptions for the upkeep of both the clock and tower. This became the St Day Clock and Lamp Committee in 1887 when public lamps were installed for the first time, in celebration of Queen Victoria's Golden Jubilee. Its job was to collect subscriptions from local businesses and townspeople, although the clock and tower occasionally needed a more thorough restoration, so various fund-raising bazaars and the like were held. One such restoration took place around 1905, when £100 was needed for the clock's renovation. It's rather touching to note how many St Day men working abroad in the mines of South Africa collected money to support the effort. Mr T.R. Tripp collected funds from St Day miners in South Africa, and a number of men, such as Edward Dunn and Arthur Strauss, sent a guinea. The Williams family of Scorrier were always generous, offering prizes for various competitions and donating sums of money.[9] It is probable that St Day was given the cupola and bell from Redruth during this restoration.

Attached to the town clock was of course the Market House, built in 1797. When the clock tower was erected it seems to have been attached to the market buildings. The market served the community at St Day for many decades, especially during the early-nineteenth century, when people came from neighbouring towns and villages to buy their provisions. Saturday night was particularly spectacular when:

> *... enormous quantities of beefsteak and onions were consumed by the miners on pay night at various public houses; the fry being washed down with beer. The mine girls also enjoyed themselves in the same way.*[10]

However, with the advent of the West Cornwall Railway, improvements in transport and an inconsistent economy, prosperity at St Day's market faded, as people travelled to other markets and towns. By 1897 the roof of the Market House had gone. In a meeting of the Gwennap Parish Council, Mr Theophilus Mitchell remarked that 'many years ago the old Market House had been given to the people of St Day.'[11] Despite attempts to revive the market, by 1909 the dilapidated site caused concerns but nobody wanted to accept any responsibility. Finally, in March 1911, the 'Old Market House' was removed. The materials were purchased by J.T. Letcher who also dismantled the building.[12] Postcards of the town clock around this time show a rather isolated building, similar to the building we know today.

Fund-raising for the town clock continued throughout the First World War, when the young people of the community held a carnival to raise money. They also revived the 'ancient St Day Feast' which had 'become a thing of the past'. In 1918, the clock tower had become a venue for Remembrance Sunday, when an open-air service was arranged for the United Sunday Schools, by the St Day Patriotic Working Party.[13] By November 1919 a proposal was made to make an addition to the town clock with an extension on the front, intended as a 'rest-house' inside which would be a tablet 'bearing names of the fallen soldiers and others of the parish who served their country.' The project cost around £350 and was largely led by Major John Williams of Scorrier House. His wife designed the structure and the Williams family paid for the granite and woodwork. Mr Leonard Martin, who had made his fortune in his famous 'linen deal', also sent a generous contribution. In April 1921 the new addition was unveiled by Sir Courtney Vivien as 'a painful record of the men who had fought bravely and served loyally.' He further stated that the monument was a fitting tribute by the people of St Day as a 'memorial raised by their hands from their hearts.' He continued:

> *This is only the beginning – its purpose was that their example, courage, endurance and love of these men should remain forever with you. You can so live and govern your lives and actions so that another war of this kind should become impossible.*[14]

In retrospect it is ironic to think that another generation of St Day men marched to another 'war of this kind' within the short space of 20 years. Their names were chiselled with the same pride into the same granite tablet.

Ten years later, a real boost was given to the future survival of St Day town clock by Mr W.J. Mills of Torquay, a native of St Day, who offered under certain conditions £125 to ensure the preservation of the clock. This was among many bequests W.J. Mills made to the community. By this time, the responsibility for the maintenance of the clock had fallen upon the St Day Community Council, who paid £5 per annum for having the clock 'wound-up and oiled periodically'. However, the council voted to pass the responsibility to Gwennap Parish Council, securing funding for the clock with Mr Mills' offer. In 1933 W.J. Mills paid for 'improvements' around the clock, including an ornamental wall and the planting of shrubs.[15]

By 1946 the responsibility of the clock's maintenance had passed to the Camborne-Redruth Urban Council, who recommended a new electric clock movement to replace the worn-out antiquated one, now beyond repair. In response to this Mr Herbert Thomas, also a native of St Day, sent a cheque for the full quotation of £265 to the council. The new electric movement was unveiled at St Day on 17 February 1948.[16]

Since these times, the clock and tower at St Day have continued to be ravaged by the weather and natural decay. The decades up to the present time have seen the responsibilities for maintenance and ownership shift from one governing body to another. St Day Parish Council, led by chairman Joe Mills, was faced with various dilemmas throughout the 1980s and '90s, when it was reported that the fabric of the tower was a serious cause for concern. Vivian Vanstone, who worked tirelessly at the preservation of the clock during this time took the author on a maintenance inspection conducted for the Parish Council in 1987. It was not difficult to see just how vulnerable this ancient building was to deterioration. Fortunately funding for the renovation has come, including for the replacement of the cupola in 1996, but the clock must be a priority for the future generations who inherit such responsibilities.

St Day town clock renovations, c.1905. Boys in South Africa sent home donations towards the fund.

St Day clock and War Memorial, c.1921. The War Memorial was designed by Mrs Williams of Scorrier, and her husband Major John Williams organised the project.

Inset: ***The War Memorial's handsome wrought-iron gates.***

Notes

[1] Lewis, *History of Cornwall*, 1833. (See also the St Day Silver Jubilee Souvenir Booklet by Joe Mills, 1977.)
[2] William, Francis, *Gwennap*, Privately Published, 1845, p112.
[3] Lewis, ibid., and Trevithick, Annie, *A Short History of St Day*, c.1897, pp13–14.
[4] *Royal Cornwall Gazette*, 14.1.1871.
[5] *West Briton*, 7.9.1871 and 29.8.1871.
[6] See *West Briton*, 4.8.1870 (p.5), which notes that at the 'Annual Court of the Lords of the Manor of St Day', which met at Bennetts Hotel, 'a considerable amount' of Richard Harvey's property had fallen to the lords of the manor. The town clock is not specifically mentioned. However, in the *West Briton*, 29.8.1871, Mr R. Chichester is mentioned as 'Lord of 1/6th of the Manor of St Day', which probably includes the Market House portion and rights of way to the town clock.
[7] *Royal Cornwall Gazette*, 14.1.1871.
[8] *Royal Cornwall Gazette*, 29.2.1872. (See also *Doidge's Directory of Gwennap*, 1866.)
[9] *Royal Cornwall Gazette*, 14.1.1871, 29.2.1872, 1.1.1886, 20.5.1897, 1.6.1905, 3.8.1905, 8.6.1905 and 21.10.1905, *West Briton*, 29.8.1871, and *Cornubian* 3.4.1905 and 22.7.1905.
[10] Trevithick, Annie, Ibid.
[11] *West Briton*, 17.5.1897, and *Royal Cornwall Gazette*, 17.6.1909.
[12] *Royal Cornwall Gazette*, 30.3.1911.
[13] *Royal Cornwall Gazette*, 15.8.1918.
[14] *Cornubian*, 20.11.1919 and 6.4.1921.
[15] Blewett, letters held at the CRO.
[16] *Royal Cornwall Gazette*, 15.8.1928, 7.8.1946 and 28.8.1946.

Twenty-Three

The 1881 Census

The census returns from 1801 provide us with a rather static picture of communities throughout the country. They allow us to glimpse a range of social features such as age structures, occupations, where people lived or were born, and gender differences amongst a host of other detail. From 1841 the census offers comparative opportunities for study – shifting or static patterns within society. The 1881 census provides a detailed, comprehensive snapshot of life at St Day by that time. The district of St Day is defined in the census as including Tregullow, Tolgullow, Poldice Lane and Crossroads, Crofthandy Road, Little Beside, Tripletts, Vogue, Tolcarne, Burnwithian, Church Street, Huel Jewell, Scorrier Street, Simmons Street (now Mills Street), Bunt's Lane, North Street (Telegraph Street), Market Street (Fore Street and Square) North Corner, The Gorland (Wheal Gorland), West End and Chapel Street.

In 1881, 64 per cent of St Day people were born in Gwennap parish. The remaining 36 per cent were born in a variety of areas. For example, the largest single concentration of people (both male and female) born outside St Day were born in Kenwyn and Truro; they made up around 8 per cent of the total. The Falmouth and Helston districts were where 6 per cent were born. St Austell and North Cornwall districts account for 5 per cent and Camborne, despite being a mining community, represented 1.5 per cent. The mining districts of Redruth, St Agnes and Illogan were the birthplaces of another 8 per cent of the population whilst the remainder of the British Isles added up to just 4 per cent. This means that 96 per cent of all St Day people born in 1881 were Cornish by birth. Some of those living in the town by 1881 were actually born overseas – the USA, Bolivia, Mexico, Brazil and Quebec account for 1.5 per cent.

Of a total of 1,335 people recorded as living in the district of St Day in 1881, 30.5 per cent of them were children aged 0–14 years. A further 33.8 per cent were adults aged between 15 and 35 years, while 23.7 per cent were aged 36–59. The final 14 per cent of the population were aged 60 or over.

The data illustrates a noticeable decrease in the adult male population of St Day. This is in part linked to the emigration that was taking place at this time. In addition, several young men died from diseases such as phthisis, and of course some young men moved to other areas temporarily to work.

In Church Street there were twice as many women as men aged 15–35, and four times as many aged 36–59. At Vogue there were twice as many females aged 36–59, three times as many in Crofthandy and Chapel Street, and four times as many in Scorrier Street. Not surprisingly perhaps, many of these women are listed as widows in the census; there were five widows aged 16–35 years, 42 aged 36–59 years and 25 aged over 60. Caroline Chenhall, aged 54, was one such single woman. She lived with her servant, Nanny Matthews aged 62, and Elizabeth Mitchell of North Street and her four children. Similarly, 38-year-old widower Grace Moyle lived with her five children.

In Chapel Street 36 per cent of all inhabited houses were headed by widows. Being predominantly mining-class housing, this suggests that husbands died through mining accidents or mine-related illnesses. Similarly at Huel Jewell, five of the nine inhabited houses were occupied by widows. At Pink Moors, another mining-class area, 31 per cent of houses were headed by widows, while in Poldice Lane three of the four houses listed were inhabited by widows. At Wheal Gorland (including some of Backway) 50 per cent of homes were inhabited by widows. Perhaps the most striking revelation is the fact that of a total 271 inhabited houses in the St Day district 105 were headed by widows totalling 39 per cent of the community.

There were several unmarried women, who inherited family responsibilities, including Emily Parry, 37, who brought up her three nephews (Philip, 16, William, 12, and John, 8) at Scorrier Street and dressmaker Nannie Mitchell of Chapel Street who looked after her 14-year-old sister Minnie.

Street Scenes

Everyone dressed up for the occasion, Chapel Street Treat, c.1900.

Above left: *Church Street, c.1900. The postcard is incorrectly marked. Note the cobbled pavements and water gullies.*

Left: *Vogue Hill with horse and water-barrel, c.1920.*

Below: *Vogue Hill with the children all dressed in their finery for the photograph, c.1915.*

Above: *Corfield's chemist shop, Church Street, c.1910.*

A horse and trap in Fore Street with J.T. Leverton, c.1910.

Making a Living

The census shows that 374 men were employed in the St Day district. Of these a surprising number are listed as tin miners and 33 are listed as copper miners. As such, miners accounted for 32 per cent of the male workforce in the district by 1881. Of these miners 27 per cent lived at Pink Moors, 18 per cent at Vogue, and 16 per cent at Chapel Street. Another 9 per cent lived at The Gorland. Among those listed were some particularly young lads (by today's standards) such as Edward Opie of Market Street. He was a tin miner aged just 13 years. Others included 14-year-old Charles Potter, Edward Kitto, a copper miner aged 14, John Williams, a 14-year-old tin dresser, John Galsworthy, a 15-year-old blacksmith, and Henry Lewis, a 13-year-old tin dresser.

Trade and retail represented the second largest employment sector, accounting for a total 18 per cent of the male workforce by 1881. This sector includes grocers, shopkeepers, butchers, hardware, sales, drapers, etc. These men total 67, and typical examples are T.J.T. Corfield, a chemist of Church Street, T.R. Mills Auctioneers & Ironmongers, also of Church Street, and John Edward, a grocer of Scorrier Street.

'General crafts' feature as the third largest group, representing 14 per cent of the male workforce in 1881. These include masons, stonemasons, carpenters, mechanics, engineers, wheelwrights and smiths, to name but a few. These men are not to be confused with 'mining craftsmen' which included all of the above-mentioned skills but those allied to the mining industry (i.e. mine masons, mine carpenters, mine engineers). It seems 30 per cent of these general craftsmen lived in Chapel Street and Scorrier Street. It is perhaps surprising that mining craftsmen, who represented around 6 per cent of employed men, did not live at Chapel Street or The Gorland – predominantly mine-housing areas – but a few appear at Vogue and one at Pink Moors.

Agricultural and farming occupations employed just 3 per cent of the male workforce in 1881. Manufacturing industries such as brick making, along with transport (including mines) barely make 3 per cent individually. Significantly, figures for agriculture, mining and manufacturing labourers account for less figures than their skilled counterparts in these sectors of employment at the time.

The professions offer just over 6 per cent of the employment figures for St Day. These include doctors, surgeons, accountants, stockbrokers, taxation officers, auctioneers and clergy amongst others. Such men primarily lived at Tregullow and Tolgullow, Vogue, Church Street, Scorrier Street and the West End.

A final group of note is that of the male 'domestic servant', which accounted for 3 per cent. These workers were found almost exclusively at Tregullow and Tolgullow; eight St Day men were among the staff of grooms, valets, horsemen, footmen and gardeners. Two men in domestic service lived in Church Street.

In total 509 women are listed in the census. By far the largest group amongst these are those entered as 'housewife' or 'at home'. These form 56 per cent of the total. This highlights the expectation placed upon women to stay at home and rear families. So where did these women live, in the trade and retail streets or in the mine-housing areas? Of the 282 women within this category, 57 per cent lived at Pink Moors, Vogue, Chapel Street and The Gorland – mine housing areas. Comparatively, 23 per cent of those listed as 'housewife' or 'at home' lived in retail and trade areas such as Scorrier Street, Church Street, Fore Street, Market Street and the West End.

The second largest employment sector for women was domestic service; 16 per cent of the total were employed in this way. With the exception of North Corner, these women could be found living all over St Day and district, but 15 were resident at Tregullow and Tolgullow. Again, mine-housing areas such as Pink Moors, Vogue, Chapel Street and The Gordon throw up a surprisingly small percentage of women employed in domestic service, with only 19 per cent of the 79 women. The retail and trade areas of Church Street, Scorrier Street, Fore Street and Market Street and the West End show a comparative 36 per cent. For example, women such as 15-year-old Emily Browning of Market Street was listed as a servant, as was Ann Blackler, aged 14, of Chapel Street.

The occupation of women 'making and selling clothes' accounts for around 13 per cent of the total female employment. Among these women were 47-year-old dressmaker Rosina Trebilcock, and 13-year-old tailoress Mary Jones of Tolcarne.

Around 5 per cent of women were listed under 'retail' and another 5 per cent were under 'laundry/charwoman'. Women in retail included the likes of 54-year-old widow Caroline Chenhall, innkeeper at Cornish Arms, 47-year-old Joanna Thomas, innkeeper, and 38-year-old Lavinia Duff of Scorrier Street, also an innkeeper.

Mining offered employment for 13 women and, although only accounting for 2.5 per cent of the total female workforce, it is an interesting statistic to quote, highlighting some persistence of traditional employment links. Among such women are listed Elizabeth Bartle, aged 62, a tin-mine labourer, and Harriet Barrett, a 37-year-old tin-mine girl who lived with her 80-year-old mother and 10-year-old son Richard; she was a single parent.

The presence of such ladies as Eliza Datson, an errand girl aged 14 from Huel Jewell, and Elizabeth Bray, a 79-year-old lodge keeper at Tolgullow Road, not only illustrate diversity in age but in occupation as well.

View from Lower Crofthandy towards St Day Church on the skyline and overlooking Crofthandy House and the tea-treat field behind it. In the foreground is a coalyard of the Devoran–Redruth railway, 1910.

Hensley's shop in Scorrier Street with a water carrier, early 1900s.

Twenty-Four

Making a Fortune, or Making Ends Meet

The Gwennap mines throughout the late-nineteenth and early-twentieth centuries became staggeringly wealthy, which gave rise to a new class of industrialists. Evidence of this new-found prosperity can be seen in the building of large estates, which began to appear locally at this time. A range of wills and bequests further highlight the heights of personal wealth achieved by some.

This boom period served as an economic driving force, necessary for the growth of St Day in several ways. The Harveys in particular invested a great deal of money in their rebuilding of several parts of St Day, and John Williams of Scorrier House was credited (by Cornish historians, Hitchens and Drew) in 1824 with finding 'the means to furnish thousands with employment, and their families with bread.'[1] Such men helped shape the physical growth of St Day from around 1800–40. A certain amount of exploitation occurred, but this was a ruthless age when fortunes could be easily won or lost.

St Day had little choice but to change at a rapid rate; all sorts of demands were made by the quickly growing populace, which increased almost weekly as people arrived to work at the mines. The following *Statistics of the Copper Mines of Cornwall* published in 1838 help to illustrate this:

Employment in the Mines

	MEN	WOMEN	CHILDREN	TOTAL
Consols & United:	1,730	869	597	3,196
Wheal Gorland:	53	12	21	86
Unity Wood:	206	80	138	424
Wheal Jewell:	212	53	94	359
West Wheal Jewell:	79	10	35	124
West Poldice:	80	Nil	Nil	80
TOTALS:	**2,360**	**1,024**	**885**	**4,269**

From the overall figures of the returns, we can see that the Gwennap mines offered employment to around 6,111 men, women and children. Those mines in the immediate vicinity of St Day accounted for 4,269, or almost 70 per cent, of the total. The mines listed above employed St Day people as well as miners from all over the locality. It is interesting to see that almost half the workforce in these mines was women and children who were, however, employed above ground.

Any reading of Cornish newspapers during the first half of the nineteenth century would show an almost weekly reportage of mining accidents. What is striking about these reports, however, is that individuals had to be killed or seriously maimed in order to be mentioned in the local press. We are left to wonder about the multitude of other serious accidents which were not considered significant enough to be highlighted.

Typical of these stories is one that appeared in July 1833, when James Olver fell over 200 fathoms, whilst ascending from the United Mines; his body was said to have been 'literally dashed to atoms'.[2] At Consols Mine a very unfortunate man fell into a cylinder. When the steam valves were opened, it blew him several yards out, and scalded two onlooking lads to death. A lad who was on the upper floor crawled along the engine 'bob' and held onto a capstan rope to save his life.[3] Children were especially vulnerable, as one account of an eight-year-old boy named Ede, who was working at Wheal Gorland mine in July 1832, shows:

... he went into the 'whim round' to speak to the boys, who were driving three horses, engaged in turning the whim to draw ore up the shaft. While thus engaged, the chain attached to one of the kibbles [metal buckets] *and occasioned a revulsion of the whim with such force*

that the horses were hurled backwards with such velocity. The boy Ede was struck by a part of the machinery and killed on the spot, as were the three horses, the other happily escaped with only a few bruises.[4]

Accounts similar to that of Hugh Long, killed during a 'premature explosion whilst blasting' at Wheal Gorland, often appeared in relation to the Gwennap mines, as did occasions when workers such as 14-year-old William Hitchens were buried alive at Consols. Both men were recorded as being killed in the same week.[5] William Maiden and Richard George were both also killed in a premature explosion, in January 1832, showing that accidents often caused multiple deaths.[6]

More spectacular accidents occurred from time to time. In April 1830, a 15-ton steam boiler was being removed from the Consolidated Mines. It was placed on a carriage being pulled by 20 horses, which had to negotiate a 25ft slide. Around 100 men were used to take the strain of the weight of the boiler during this difficult movement, when all of a sudden the ground gave way. A 'precipice' opened up and the boiler fell some way into the hole. Unfortunately, a man called James Northey became entangled in ropes and was dragged behind the boiler to his death.[7]

Gwennap suffered around 80 male deaths a year in the mines during the period 1830–40, similar to that of any other Cornish mining parish. However, Gwennap's female mine workers averaged 65 deaths per year compared to 77 in the Redruth and 51 in the Illogan districts.[8] This reveals the dangers of Cornish mining for those above ground as well as below. Similar figures for serious injuries are also recorded and a club was established at the United Mines, into which miners paid a regular contribution, so that if injured they could claim some money whilst off work.[9] If a miner died, money was usually paid to his widow.

The employment of children in the mines of Devon and Cornwall became a concern for the Government, who issued a report conducted by Dr Charles Barham in 1840. Several children from the Gwennap mines feature in the report. Barham provided a brief overview of each mine. He stated that at the United Mines levels in the 'ancient workings' did not exceed 5ft high by 2ft wide; with more recent workings averaging 7ft high by 4ft wide. The ores were mined from between 40 and 220 fathoms from the surface. Such tunnels followed veins which varied from an inch to 9ft in diameter. The Consolidated Mines had similar figures, but operated to nearly 300 fathoms from the surface. Ladders were usually about 8ft long.[10]

Barham commented on how the Cornish Mines were 'wet'. The 'principle tools' were the picks for working the rock and borers and mallets for making the holes for blasting. Usually these items weighed around 20lbs but they could be transported in the kibble, a large metal bucket that was used to clear rubbish. An interesting observation was made by Barham about the physical appearance of the West of England miner who:

... is a man of moderate stature, spare and muscular, with a chest and upper limbs rather more developed than the lower, and having the shoulders slightly inclined forwards. The complexion is sallow and rather sodden. The miner of a very large frame is seldom seen; a very fat miner could be hardly met with.[11]

A Gwennap miner's wages were usually around 55 shillings a month in 1840; however, with his wife and around four of five children employed, a family's monthly income might be around £7.10s. Outgoings, including provisions such as flour, barley, soap, starch, tea, and butter usually cost around £3.10s. Coals and candles amounted to 8 shillings, meat 1 shilling, shoes and clothes £1.5s., while other sundries amounted to £6.18s.[12] Presumably, the remainder went towards rent. A miner could expect to earn an adult wage by the age of 18. From this age, courtship was common, followed shortly by marriage and a family.[13]

Children were employed at the Gwennap mines from the ages of seven for boys and eight for girls. None were allowed underground until they were aged ten; when boys reached the age of ten they could go underground or remain at the surface, but females were never allowed underground. The hours of work for children in the Gwennap mines ranged from ten hours in the summer months, to nine in the winter. Work began at 7a.m. and finished at between 5p.m. and 6p.m. A short interval was permitted at 10a.m. followed by an half-hour-long break for lunch. If a mine operated 'piece work', then these hours could be affected, finishing earlier or later. On 'sampling days', which could last up to two weeks, when the ore had to be prepared and inspected before sale, children would usually have to work longer hours. A typical day for a boy or girl from nine to 12 years old would then be:

... to rise at about four o'clock in the morning, get a hasty breakfast, and after a walk of an hour or more – three or four miles – reach the mine at six. Work is continued till twelve, without intermission or refreshment, save what might be got by stealth. Half an hour is then employed in taking dinner. The child then works without interruption till eight; gets home, after repeating the walk of the morning, and may have supper, and go to bed about ten.[14]

Often children were given a day off after the sampling days were over.

The nature of the work described by Barham is exceptionally harsh. The first part of the process is the 'riddling' when pieces of ore were separated. The large pieces were 'ragged' or broken by men. Next the girls of '16 years or more' did the 'spalling'. Young boys then cleaned the stones in wooden troughs, with a stream of water flowing through. The ore was then 'picked', meaning the valuable pieces were separated from the rubbish. Young girls sat at a table sorting ore into boxes. The 'picking' was carried out in a shed or 'hutch' with open sides. The weather caused great discomfort to children in this part of the process; as did wet feet from the cleaning process. Girls of 15 years and above would 'cobb' the stone – place pieces on an anvil and break them again with a 'short-handled hammer', whilst rejecting inferior pieces. These girls could often be seen, sat at an anvil, with their feet and lower legs covered in broken rock. Next the ore was 'bucked' or broken down further with 'a broad square hammer, two or three pounds in weight'. This work was done at a counter and considered the hardest part of the process. It paid 10 pence or 1 shilling a day.

Finally the ore was taken away in barrows so as to be measured for sale.[15] 'Jigging' was a job for boys, and included sieving the finer parts of the stone, usually leaving the lighter, worthless stone at the top to be cleared. Throughout all processes a large amount of mud and slime was produced, and many young boys and girls were employed cleaning and clearing this.[16]

It usually took a man about 40 minutes to descend to the lower levels of the mine and about twice as long to climb up to the surface.[17] Underground, young boys were generally employed tramming and 'rolling', which meant barrowing broken earth and rock to a point where they loaded it into the kibble. Boys usually worked the 'windlass' or hauling tackle, winching the ore to surface. Other time was spent tending men and breaking ground. Boys were also used to 'tamp' clay into bore holes before they were fired. Progression from this led to them taking a turn at 'beating the borer'. This was often considered the time when long-term injuries could occur; pace, timing and nerve synchronised as the hammers took turns to beat the hand-turned bore drill. Teams were built around this process, with a boy 'coming of age' when he mastered the necessary precision.

The mines allowed no holidays, except for Good Friday and Christmas Day. On festival days a few were given. Work continued on Saturdays, but workers usually finished an hour early. On pay or 'setting' days held once a month, little work was done after dinner. Work at the mines was voluntary for children and young people, but family dependencies and competition for places caused few to miss the opportunity to keep employment.[18] Small girls might expect to earn around 7s.11d. a month, with older ones receiving 15s.6d. Young boys were paid 10s.5d. a month. A bonus of 1 shilling a month was paid for 'constant employment' and was often given to children as 'pocket money'. Wages were paid at the counting-house; often an older child was paid, who then distributed the money. Care was usually taken to pay children in sums small enough to save them from seeking change at the public house.

In terms of literacy rates among children and young people in the Gwennap mines, it appears 69 per cent could read an 'easy book'. Although there were ten 'Common Day Schools for the Elementary Education of the Working Classes' listed in the parish, to teach children from the ages of nine to 12, children would have been taken to work in the mines. As a result of the day schools charging fees, many children did not attend. Many did not even attend Sunday school, although the churches and chapels did strive to support their learning.[19] Nonetheless, Gwennap provided six Anglican Sunday schools, nine Nonconformist Sunday schools and five venues for evening classes.[20] Although much of the Methodist and Anglican Sunday-school curriculum would have been based on religious instruction and biblical text, it appears St Day and Gwennap were an exception within the county in providing 'reading, writing, arithmetic, grammar and geography' to many of the 'scholars'.[21]

Mary Verran informed Dr Barham of a typical diet of the times. Apart from a short break at mid-morning, 'crowst' (lunch) was the main break of the day, lasting around 30 minutes at Consols. Meals usually consisted of a pasty or potato, plums or 'hobban' (Cornish heavy cake). Barnham claimed, 'she (Mary) gets for supper, fish and potatoes: sometimes stew, roast potatoes and broth. Not many bring bread and butter.' A dry place had to be found and the children would sometimes huddle together in the cold, or enjoy the warmth of the mine-spoil banks in the summer.

Charles Barham's report is a remarkable document. Not only did he outline the various aspects of the lives of the working miners, their wives and children, but he presented 'evidence' for the Commission on the employment of children, by interviewing many people at their place of work. Some were older, but reflected back upon their early years of child labour in the Gwennap mining district. For example, he 'examined' William Trethewy, aged 13, at the Consolidated Mines. Trethewy had begun work at the age of nine, being employed 'jigging'. He later worked underground 'rolling' barrows of ore, which he considered the hardest work he had done. He was also able to 'turn the bore'. William Trethewy worked 'about six to eight' for a fortnight every month. Barham reported that he could read 'fairly' and that he never went to 'day school' except as a boy, but attended Sunday school, where he began to learn to read.[22]

Elisha Morcom was also 13 years old when interviewed at the Consolidated Mines. He had experienced 'bowel problems' and had recently been home for two days after a boy threw a stone at his stomach. He generally worked as a 'jigger' but was employed occasionally 'rolling'. Morcom enjoyed working underground and felt 'nothing from the powder-smoke or poor air' and 'did not spit black stuff'. He lived a couple of miles from the mine and usually got up 'at four o'clock or soon after'. He went to 'day school' and according to Barham he read 'tolerably'.[23]

Richard Jeffery was nine years old at the time of interview at the Consolidated Mines, where he had started work aged eight. He belonged to the 'boxes' behind the pickers; he sorted quality and sizes of ore and complained of 'sore hands'. Barham explained how he had to walk almost three miles to work, and often did not leave until eight o'clock. Richard's father died of cholera while in Mexico; a wife and four children were left behind in Cornwall. Richard was the youngest sibling; two sisters also worked at the mine and the other was a dressmaker. He never went to school and could not read.[24]

Elizabeth Curnow (24) was interviewed at the Consolidated Mines. She had been 'coming to the mines about eight years', although during a period of poor health, she 'went into service'. She was employed to cobb and was paid 8 pence for six barrows. Like the others, she complained about the cold and wet, especially when handling the stones in winter.

Christina Pascoe, aged 17, was also questioned at the Consolidated Mines by Barham. She had started five years before as a 'picker', then two years later 'went to the floors, spalling' and 'carrying'. She had been cobbing for several months; she was placed indoors after becoming short of breath. She got up at 6a.m. and worked extra time until 8p.m., then returned home to do housework and needlework to help her widowed mother. Pascoe's father had been injured in Wood Mine (Wheal Unity Wood) which led him to bring up blood. He later died of consumption.

Notes

1 *Royal Cornwall Gazette*, 9.5.1877.
2 *West Briton*, 29.11.1877.
3 *Royal Cornwall Gazette*, 16.3.1877, 23.3.1877 and 30.3.1877.
4 *Royal Cornwall Gazette*, 9.5.1877.
5 *West Briton*, 14.4.1879.
6 *Royal Cornwall Gazette*, 13.7.1921.
7 *Royal Cornwall Gazette*, 24.5.1922.
8 *Royal Cornwall Gazette*, 4.5.1921.
9 Blewett, R.R., 'These Things Have Been', Inst. 56 (March, 1969).
10 *Royal Cornwall Gazette*, 18.5.1877.
11 Blewett, R.R., Social Survey, 1935.
12 Blewett, R.R., 'These Things Have Been', Inst. 4 and 5 (August–October, 1964).
13 *Royal Cornwall Gazette*, 3.1.1879.
14 *Royal Cornwall Gazette*, 18.1.1878.
15 *Royal Cornwall Gazette*, 17.12.1896.
16 *Royal Cornwall Gazette*, 17.12.1903.

St Day and district, a view from Trefula, c.1900. Note the extent of the Brickworks by this time. The Wesleyan Methodist Chapel, town clock and Parish Church dominate the skyline.

Twenty-Five

Civic Amenities

Water

St Day was granted a remarkable opportunity for its own water supply, when the Harvey family established a scheme for the supply of water to the town in 1828. The people of St Day used two standpipes placed in the Potato Court and at Vogue Terrace.[1]

The water supply in question was a very elaborate system whereby water from Five-Shoots was forced up through iron pipes by a water-wheel at Burnwithian Pit. The water was then 'brought up to St Day into a reservoir built inside of one of the high walls surrounding Carew House' (the family home of the Harveys).[2] On 28 June 1839 Richard Harvey was allowed to have water:

> *... forced up to St Day for the two years from midsummer 1839, he paying the Lord 5s.0d. a year as an acknowledgement for the same and undertaking to keep the water home to St Day Fountain by Mr Harvey's House and allowing the inhabitants, Tenants of St Day Manor, for use of the same at fair rent.*[3]

The Harveys worked the scheme in conjunction with the lords of the manor who probably assisted in financing the £700 for the scheme. For example, the Harveys managed the scheme by overseeing payments for the use of the pumps by inhabitants, denying access to those who failed to pay and providing annual expenses and accounts to the lords. Significantly, the lords 'expressly understood that this arrangement [was] endorsed not with any view to profit Mr Harvey but for the general benefit of the inhabitants of the manor.' The reservoir at Carew House also served as a water source in the event of fires. Eventually the scheme collapsed and the standpipes fell into disuse, because so few inhabitants seem to have paid their annual subscriptions towards costs.[4]

From these times onwards, the community at St Day was left to rely on springs such as those at Five-Shoots, Vogue, Pink Moors and Carnmarth, from where a steady stream of men, women and children could be seen wending their way with buckets, pitchers and other vessels. Various 'hawkers' (as they were known) plied their trade in selling water door-to-door at a 'half-penny a pitcher'.

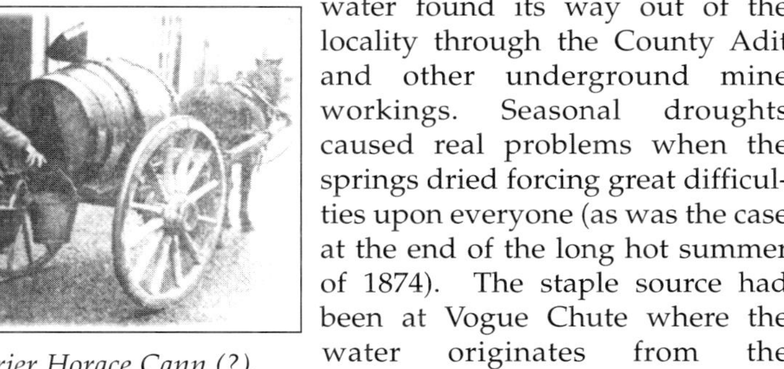

Water-carrier Horace Cann (?).

No wells were available at St Day because most water found its way out of the locality through the County Adit and other underground mine workings. Seasonal droughts caused real problems when the springs dried forcing great difficulties upon everyone (as was the case at the end of the long hot summer of 1874). The staple source had been at Vogue Chute where the water originates from the Cathedral Mine. During that year the shaft at the mine was sunk deeper resulting in the failure of water. Up until this time Vogue Chute had enjoyed the reputation of a 'never-ending stream of water' but the community was devastated at the consequences and inconvenience. Then began the first of many experimental ideas to introduce a consistent water supply to the town. It was immediately decided to investigate the possibility of sinking a well. However, the idea quickly faded as water at Vogue returned.[5]

The water issue caused little concern until a serious fire in 1891 made many people in the town feel vulnerable. Also around this time neighbouring areas such as Redruth and Truro were beginning to organise their own piped-water supplies. The ideal expressed at the time was for several standpipes to be placed around the town.[6] The problems were essentially that St Day was half a mile from the source at Vogue and, more problematic, it was uphill!

The question of water took on a more political outlook locally from these times, when the Revd J.J. Murley was recommended to lead the cause. Estimates for a new scheme varied from £500 to £2,300 around this time. Money could be borrowed from the Local Government Board for a term of 30 years with 3.5 per cent interest. Such quotations

Civic Amenities

Left: *Three 'ankers of water, Vogue Hill.*

Below: *'Blind David' Annear delivering water to residents at St Day, with his helper Russell Hosking.*

Above: *Former water reservoir of Carew House which also supplied pumps at 'Tatey-Court' giving St Day its own water supply in 1828. Today the site forms two properties. The photograph was taken in 1992.*

Above right: *Vogue Shute, St Day, c.1920. Horace Cann filling the 'anker' (barrel on wheels) from which he delivered water.*

Above: *A donkey and rider in Scorrier Street, c.1900. On the left is a window with the words 'OFFICE HOURS' inscribed. Was this the Manor Office?*

Left: *Fore Street Post Office and the postmistress and two postmen, c.1900.*

frightened most people, but with around 2,300 inhabitants the expense seemed to many to be worth considering. Quotes from the 1875 Public Health Act flavoured the debate and a special committee was formed from Redruth Rural Sanitary Authority to question the inhabitants of the town.[7] John Rooke of Carew House, a county councillor, estimated a considerable increase in local rates. C.A.V. Coneybeare and A. Strauss, local Members of Parliament, entered into the debate and were accused of using such a vital issue as a 'vote spinner'.[8] In November 1893, the Redruth Rural Sanitary Authority proposed a plan:

> *... to take the water from Vogue to St Day by means of the water-wheel now on the site, which could be rented from the Lord for £15 per annum. The water could be forced up to a high place at St Day, and thence allowed to gravitate towards such places in the town as might be most convenient for the erection of standpipes.*[9]

The main source was still considered to be Vogue Chute, owned by the Williams family of Scorrier.[10] However, with the unpredictability of the Cathedral Mines, other options were considered such as accessing Chygenter, the source which supplied the Cathedral adit. At the same meeting the possibility of levying the cost across the whole of Gwennap was considered. This, however, prompted a stern reaction from the other parishes, especially Lanner where Mr G. Bray explained that they were 'raising £60 by private subscription and would lay pipes for that village without asking the [Gwennap] parish for a single farthing.'[11]

In 1896, St Day was considered eligible for status as a 'Special Drainage District'. Under the 1878 Public Health Act, St Day was allowed to present the rates of the Gwennap parish as security for a loan, but only those who lived within 200 yards of the standpipe would have to pay. Understandably, the whole of the parish would not consent. At the meeting another elaborate plan was presented by Messrs Kitto, Nettle and Bawden, which showed bringing water from Vogue by various water-wheels, tanks, pipes, pumps, driving gear and launders, amounting to a total cost of £600.8s.6d.[12] Nothing came of this and the debate continued unresolved. By January 1898 another plan by Mr Trestrail, engineer to the Local Government Board, centred upon the idea of tapping into the supply at Cathedral Mine raising water by windmill power and gravitation to St Day. This was also rejected.[13] More ideas followed up to the First World War, such as a plan to sink a shaft at Chygenter, where water was discovered two fathoms above adit level and at a depth of 19 fathoms below surface level. However, 'pot-granite' meant possible drainage. A plan to build a 66,000-gallon reservoir at Treskerby that was filled by two streams (supplying water at 12–15 gallons a minute) and supply 530 houses materialised.[14] Pipes were laid, but the outbreak of the First World War placed a hold on progress. Work did not resume after the war and although other schemees were put forward in the 1920s, nothing changed; a pumping station at Tolcarne, heavily supported by Major John Williams of Scorrier House, failed to meet the approval of one senior Government Minister, Neville Chamberlain![15]

St Day continued to use the various chutes, but by this time the town had noticeably fallen behind in its number of civic amenities compared with other Cornish towns and villages. By the 1920s a host of characters began to attract the attention of local photographers and press. 'Blind David' Annear appeared in a special feature on the issues of water at St Day in 1928.[16] His own popularity stemmed from his ability to capture the spirit of struggle and denial of basic services long overdue in St Day. Blinded at Carn Brea Mine in 1891 at the age of 21, David, like so many other injured miners, resorted to making a livelihood by auxiliary occupations.[17] Every day he could be seen leading his pony and 'anker' (barrel on wheels) from Vogue Chute through the streets of St Day. Although a number of people collected rainwater in water-butts, for significant numbers people such as David Annear and John Downing, another blind water-carrier, represented the sole water supply. Horace Cann and his father were popular, as was the late Ronnie Williams with his father. Mr Heard and Russel Hosking are also remembered and the list is far from complete. The role of the water carrier can be clearly illustrated in a case during November 1924, when the RSPCA reported that David Annear's pony became unfit for work. When the pony was taken off the road, so too was the water supply as well as the livelihood of the carrier. Richard Blewett, realising the significance of this, immediately organised a whist drive and dance, with the RSPCA offering prizes, as well as a £5 grant, a new pony was purchased and the water supply resumed.[18]

The mains water supply was still slow to progress. During the Second World War a 5,000-gallon water tank was placed in the garden of the War Memorial in case of fire emergencies.[19] This was never considered adequate for a water supply and was dismantled in 1949. In March 1946, Mr C.O. Batty of St Day, representing the community, rejected any scheme proposed by the Ministry of Health to supply St Day with water from Vogue. In favour, it was suggested that St Day be allowed to tap into the 6-inch source at the top of Drump Road, Redruth, via Treskerby and Pink Moors.[20] This scheme was adopted and in 1950 water stands appeared in and around St Day for the first time. It took a few years to complete the supply, but by the mid-1950s St Day had piped water (although not without its problems). As late as 1950, the water carriers could be seen in the streets of St Day attracting the attention of the national press. However, they disappeared soon afterwards.[21]

Sanitation

St Day grew at an astounding rate during the first half of the nineteenth century. People built houses as they liked, with little thought for drainage and cesspits. Drainage presented few problems for the town as in most cases old mine workings carried away excess water and excrement. Such a system was still in effect in 1926, when the following extract from a sanitary report appeared in the *Royal Cornwall Gazette* on 30 June:

> *A large stone drain or culvert runs through the village; into this culvert enters the discharge of about 20 water closets, and it also carries the village drainage. There is no means of flushing the drain, consequently it lodges a large accumulation of filth and at times exhales noxious gases. The culvert finally empties itself into a cesspit at the bottom of the village. The overflow from the cesspit runs into a disused mineshaft.*

Such a primitive sewerage system had not changed from its original design well over a century before. This system was of course totally unacceptable for a community which had become an established township (by Cornish standards) by the middle of the nineteenth century. The following article appeared in most leading Cornish newspapers during the summer of 1866:

> *Unsanitary matters at St Day are said to require looking up. Some parts of the town have filth and stench that are abominable. There is one part worse than the rest, a block of five or six houses, flat roofed and covered with zinc, situated near Wheal Gorland, and termed the 'Rookery'* [defined as 'a cluster of mean tenements'].[22] *There are upward of 30 residents, who have no closet or privy; but adjoining the roads are 5 or 6 partitions (doubtless one for each house) into which are deposited the night soil and every conceivable article calculated to breed pestilence. Of course the smell arising from putrefying animal and vegetable matter can be imagined. In the West of England it would be impossible to find a hotbed for breeding and forcing fever and cholera equal to this.*[23]

Clearly, sanitary matters were worrying, but this particular area was extreme and not necessarily representative of all parts of the town. The casual disposal of night soil was also evident nearby at Wheal Unity, Todpool, where in a block of buildings forming six dwellings known as the 'Old Warehouse' none of the tenants were supplied with closets, so 'all the night-soil was emptied across the road, directly opposite the houses.'[24] Apart from the 'summer stench' this arrangement provided few real problems up to the 1870s, when it appears floods began to overflow adits in and around Scorrier Street and Simmons Street (Mills Street). Rainwater accumulated to a depth of 18 inches in this area and the local correspondent of the *Gazette* reported in August 1877:

> *My remarks in last week's paper, under the heading 'Nobody's duty' has discovered whose duty it was to attend to the drains, for on passing the street this morning, I found two scavengers busily at work repairing one at the end of the Lion Inn. A noted teetotaler says it would be a good job if the water was to surround the inn, so that the drunkards might fall into it and be brought to their proper senses; but I don't think there is much need of pon's in the streets of St Day for such a purpose, for to see a drunken man is a novelty, times are too bad.*[25]

The actual sewerage route overall was a mystery.

> *Pipes and open 6ft drains* [were] *discovered in the most unexpected places... permitting pedestrians to be effusively greeted by the effluvia from open stench holes, which are in some cases, close to peoples doorways.*[26]

Blewett, writing in 1935, discusses the sanitary arrangements for a row of 12 cottages where:

> *... there is one earth closet for two houses and these are places away from the houses and abutting on the public road. The drainage is primitive. A few drains empty themselves into open disused mine shafts and until 1935, one of the drains emptied itself into the open ditch of a main road.*[27]

The Second World War ended the plight of a community failed by local politicians. Sewerage, like water, continued as an issue for local politics until as late as the early 1960s, when funds were eventually made available and a mains system installed throughout St Day. Newspaper reports throughout the late 1940s and into the '50s were dominated by arguments and controversies over funding. Several Cornish villages experienced similar difficulties. Eventually, the main streets of St Day began to be dug for the laying of a mains sewerage scheme in 1965. St Day was consequently able to enjoy more modern conveniences.

Conditions of the roads

To facilitate the busy mining and commercial traffic through and around St Day, the maintenance of roads was critical. The condition of the roads attracted considerable attention in the local press from the early 1870s. The old system of a district surveyor responsible for inspecting roads seems to have lapsed by this time, much to the annoyance of the following correspondent:

> *The roads in St Day are a disgrace. Years ago they used*

to be laid about once a year. Now I think it is quite five years since Scorrier Street, Back Street and several other streets have had as much as half a coat put on them. From the Post Office to the Primitive Chapel the road is worn down to inches from the proper level. Can anyone inform me as to where the Inspector of Roads for the parish has been for the last two years?[28]

Dangerous shafts and abandoned clay workings could result in a severe fine for land owners. In and around St Day, dangerous shafts and 'a large clay pit several fathoms deep, half full of water, and very near the public road at Burnwithian' (almost certainly a water tank from the 1828 water supply) caused much uproar from the same correspondent. However, his criticisms were not in vain. He confirms:

... not only have the big boulders that were so prominent in our streets been crushed, but the poor old roads have a thin coat of mine stone provided them for the winter [and] *at Burnwithian... a hedge is in the course of building around this dangerous spot.*[29]

With plenty of mineral-waste dumps in the area, mine stone was a very cheap and convenient source for coating roads. As the mines closed locally, unemployment also caused problems for local communities of miners unable or less inclined to emigrate. During March 1879, at neighbouring Chacewater, over 40 unemployed men were paid by the local Distress Committee for the 'widening of [the] Chacewater–Twelveheads road.'[30] By May of the same year the Revd Edward Olivey, who led the St Day Miners Distress Fund, adopted the same idea for many roads and unemployed miners were glad of the work and a little extra relief money. Interestingly, the scheme was adopted again for unemployed miners at St Day in February 1921.

Throughout the late-nineteenth and into the early-twentieth century, the roads at St Day were given an annual 'coating', but by these times steam-rollers were used to crush and bed the mine stone. Of course, by the 1940s and '50s tarmac surfaces became more common.

Post Office & Communications

The Post Office was established in 1830 to meet the needs of expanding trade and industry. It was initially situated in Market Street, opposite the St Day Inn (more or less where it is sited today). Deliveries extended to Stithians, Ponsanooth and most of the villages within three miles.[31] The business thrived and by 1859 was handling upwards of 6,000 letters monthly, including newspapers. However, it had competition as a number of shopkeepers and carriers were keen to deliver post and parcel for a lower fee.[32] By 1892, the Post Office had outgrown this site and was 'removed to a more commodious and central position at the corner of Market Square.'[33]

The Post Office was given an even more prominent role when St Day was connected to the 'telegraph' from Scorrier Station in February 1871.[34] Communications were instantly improved as messages could be received immediately. As more St Day miners were emigrating, so too could money orders be dispatched from abroad. By the mid-1870s the telephone was beginning to be introduced into various parts of the county; what was probably the first demonstration of a telephone at St Day was exhibited by T.H. Letcher at a Dorcas Society bazaar held at the velvet factory, Little Beside, in January 1879.[35] By 1878, the Post Office at St Day also served as a 'Money Order and Telegraph Office'. In July 1915 the National Telephone Company erected 'overhead cables connecting the town with Redruth'[36] and in 1937 the new telephone exchange was opened at St Day.[37]

Notes

1 Blewett, R.R., 'These Things Have Been', Inst. 42 (October 1967). (See also Thomas, R., Map of Manor St Day, 1828.)
2 *Lakes Parochial History of Cornwall Vol II*, 1868, p.139, Trevithick, Annie, *A Short History of St Day*, c.1897, pp.15–16, and *Cornish Post & Mining News*, 16.4.1914.
3 CRO ref: DDWH4924.
4 Trevithick, Annie, Ibid.
5 *Royal Cornwall Gazette*, 5.9.1874.
6 *Royal Cornwall Gazette*, 4.6.1891.
7 *West Briton*, 8.9.1892 and 25.8.1892.
8 *Royal Cornwall Gazette*, 13.10.1892 and 16.9.1897, and *Cornubian*, 21.1.1898.
9 *Cornubian*, 9.11.1893.
10 *Royal Cornwall Gazette*, 8.9.1926.
11 *Royal Cornwall Gazette*, 8.10.1896.
12 *Cornubian*, 16.10.1896.
13 *Royal Cornwall Gazette*, 20.1.1898.
14 *Cornubian*, 20.5.1893 and *Cornish Echo*, 18.9.1914.
15 *Royal Cornwall Gazette*, 2.6.1926, and Blewett, R.R., 'These Things Have Been', Inst. 57 (May, 1969).
16 *Royal Cornwall Gazette*, 25.1.1928.
17 *Royal Cornwall Gazette*, 19.2.1891.
18 *Royal Cornwall Gazette*, 5.11.1924 and 12.11.1924.
19 *West Briton*, 4.8.1949.
20 *Royal Cornwall Gazette*, 3.3.1946.
21 Conversation with Mr Karl Bray.
22 *Chambers 20th Century Dictionary*, 3rd ed., 1901.
23 *Cornish Telegraph*, 1.8.1866.
24 *Cornubian*, 6.10.1899.
25 *Royal Cornwall Gazette*, 31.8.1877.
26 *West Briton*, 14.4.1892, and *Cornishman*, 20.10.1892.
27 Blewett, R.R., Selwyn College Notes, 1935.
28 *Royal Cornwall Gazette*, 26.10.1877.
29 For claypit and shafts see *Royal Cornwall Gazette*, 29.6.1877, 14.12.1877 and 1.1.1878.
30 *Royal Cornwall Gazette*, 28.3.1879, and *Royal Cornwall Gazette*, 4.4.1879.
31 *West Briton*, 24.9.1830.
32 *Royal Cornwall Gazette*, 2.12.1859.
33 *West Briton*, 4.2.1892.
34 *Royal Cornwall Gazette*, 11.2.1871, and *West Briton*, 14.2.1871.
35 *Royal Cornwall Gazette*, 3.1.1879.
36 *Cornubian*, 8.7.1915.
37 *Harrod's Directory of Cornwall*, 1878, 2nd ed, and *Kelly's Directory of Cornwall*, 1880s–1930s.

First World War

Left: *Trooper Tommy Mills of the Devon Yeomanry, 1917.*

Below: *Miss Elsie Stephens, First World War volunteer nurse, 1918.*

Left: *Trooper Tommy Mills of the Devon Yeomanry, 1917.*

Below: *Kitchener's recruits – the Miners' Battallion make their way to St Day from Redruth for parade, 1914.*

Twenty-Six

St Day During Wartime

Gwennap and St Day have sent men to battles and wars for centuries. However, by the turn of the twentieth century warfare was beginning to take on new dimensions previously unimagined. Military parades, jingoism and patriotism were all features from this period, as this extract from the *Cornubian* highlights concerning the Boer War, on 26 May 1899:

> *So the soldiers have passed down and our juveniles at St Day have been getting some guns. I see they have the end of Smith's Hotel for a target, but let me say, the soldiers as they passed through Scorrier in such weather, created a profound expression, just giving us a mild illustration* [of] *how arduous must be the task when marching on to actual warfare, and how thoughtful we need be as a country that we have such noble soldiers ever ready and willing to defend us.*[1]

The First World War, 1914–18

Following the invasion of Belgium by Germany, many Belgian refugees arrived in Britain, many of which ended up in Cornwall. Gwennap opened the door of hospitality and at Comford a house was immediately made available by Mr Beauchamp of Trevince. Several parishioners contributed £1 towards furniture, food and the general upkeep of the project.[2] St Day quickly followed the example, after John Williams offered a cottage at Tregullow and T.R. Mills offered furniture for some rooms. The community applied to host four Belgians and a further £20 was donated by Mrs Corfield's Patriotic Committee.[3] By February 1915 various sales of work by the St Day Girls Friendly Society and Mother's Union raised £20 for the cause and were typical of the fund-raising initiatives being organised locally.[4]

The war had gathered pace by December 1914 and hopes of a quick and decisive victory by Christmas were well and truly dashed. As early waves of volunteer troops were rapidly being wiped out, issues of conscription began to surface. At the annual meeting of St Day's Liberal Association in early 1915, attitudes against enforced conscription were stirring. However, it remained a likely option as volunteers became wise to escalating casualties.[5]

Despite this, the needs of voluntary conscription were reinforced by groups such as the Miner's Battalion who found favour in what was still a predominantly mining community. As they paraded to St Day Church, they were rapturously received by the vicar Revd W.W. Bickford and further marches around the town did much to raise morale and spirits. The sheer spectacle of the Miner's Battalion was to arouse patriotic fever which inflamed the desire of many young men to join their pals and swell ranks. Bickford continued to highlight the need for voluntary conscription with strong words from the pulpit, some of which occasionally found their way into the local press:

> *This month has seen three more men offer themselves for service, Cecil Braddon, Frank Wills and John Kinsman, and being intimately connected with them, as the two former are members of our choir, and the latter a regular attendant at church, I can testify to the excellent spirit in which they offer themselves. It is easy for us who sit at home to talk about the hardness of the soldier's life and which they must expect, but it is hard for them leaving comfortable houses and mother's care and to have associates many who have been bought up as they have, and whose manners and customs are very different from others.*[6]

He was also to comment 'I really don't see any more young men who could go and the response from St Day [to conscription] has been truly wonderful.' Clearly the Church promoted conscription as the Revd Bickford was further supported by the celebrated novelist Joseph Hocking as both men addressed crowds of young men at St Day to enlist with passionate pleas in defence of Belgian women suffering at the hands of marauding German troops.[7] Such events continued to be enthused by groups like the St Day Home Defence Corps, which held weekly drill on Friday evenings, before being led by Sergeant Buckingham and Lance Corporal Hawke on disciplined parades, instilling pride and confidence within the community. The Miners' Battalion was a popular regiment among Cornish mining towns such as Camborne, and the Redruth contingent often led the way at St Day from the Drill Hall at Redruth or met in the grounds of Scorrier House. Another popular battalion which attracted St Day men was the newly formed 'Pioneering Corps' who also trained at Redruth.[8] The return of casualties and fatalities from the Front Line, checked such enthusiasm as the stark realisation and recurrent echoes of family grief began to filter through community life. Recruitment figures for St Day appear healthy alongside most other Cornish towns and villages. By February 1915, we find 3 per cent of the population's men volunteering for armed service. Alongside Lanner with 1.5 per cent, Illogan with 2 per cent and Troon, with 1 per cent, these figures appear above average. However, compared to Hayle at 5 per cent and Camborne at 7 per cent the figures seem less encouraging.[9]

Trooper Tommy Mills of the Devon Yeomanry, 1917.

Another focus was the plight of the wounded soldier abroad, especially those blinded in gas attacks. Miss Mitchell frequently appeared on egg-collecting rounds as well as asking for people to spare pennies for wounded soldiers. Her efforts were warmly appreciated by letters sent home, which were advertised to the whole community. Such individual efforts merged into more formal group organisations which began to direct a collective effort to the support of men fighting in the trenches. Charitable acts also found an outlet with groups like Mrs Corfield's Patriotic Working Party which held various parties and fêtes, initially in the grounds of The Cedars. By September 1915 they had raised funds for making sandbags for the 'County Regiment' (The Duke of Cornwall's Light Infantry) which were promptly sent to bolster defence at the Western Front in France. Inspired and led by Mrs Corfield, this group was formed in November 1915, but later became known as the St Day Ladies Patriotic Working Party (St Day LPWP). The group met at a variety of venues, often the Methodist chapels, but they considered themselves to be strictly non-denominational. Visiting speakers like Miss Carkeek of Hayle who provided a talk entitled 'The necessity for the assistance of women's help in the present war' at the Primitive Methodist Chapel in January 1916 reinforced the new expectations placed on local women. The St Day LPWP could now be found organising food and clothes parcels. Within four months of being formed, the ladies' group had made 41 shirts, 57 pairs of socks, 30 mufflers, 19 pairs of mittens and 3 pairs of gloves.[10] This remarkable group of ladies remained loyal to their cause and worked tirelessly throughout the war and as late as August 1918 could be found organising an 'open air service' for a Remembrance Day event for the United Sunday School at St Day Clock Tower.

'Our Day' celebrations combined the community during these times in an effort to support the war. In 1915 a house-to-house collection and trade in flag sales raised over £30 for the Red Cross. Such days also benefited the St Day LPWP with similar amounts.

Central funding for the war effort was to some extent temporarily subsidised by schemes like the War Savings Campaign. In July 1917 Mrs Edward H. Williams of Fourburrow House presented each child in the Girls Council School with a savings book with 1 shilling as an encouragement to save.[11] These campaigns became more vigorous and a meeting at the Wesleyan Schoolrooms in December 1917 identified Hayle as a good example having raised £700. By this time there were two War Savings Associations in St Day, one in the school with 30 members and the general community fund with 103 members. In April 1918 the community could boast an account with £2,477 collected in the previous year and the School Association with £9 collected during the previous three months.[12]

A few local mines were reopened during the war. Though a slim shadow of their former times, collectively they were considered essential to the war effort. Equally, agriculture was to benefit (to some extent) from government intervention. Local mines and farms offered some employment with jobs considered vital to war economy and production. Volunteers for the Armed Forces began to wane after the initial battles of the war returned high casualty rates. To overcome the problem, conscription of all men between the ages of 18 and 41 was introduced through the Military Service Act in March 1916 and for married men two months later. Specific categories of workers in industry and agriculture became exempt from conscription because their skills and experience were considered necessary for the survival of the home front. Accordingly, men were classified in terms of their importance. Classes A, B, C and so on were further sub-divided into numerical groups 1, 2, 3 etc., with the A and 1 being considered least important (however, these changed as the war gave rise to different occupational demands). Miners appeared in Class C, whilst farmers appeared in Class B, mining being considered more skilled or with less experienced men available. Cases for exemption appeared before the Redruth War Tribunals who managed cases for the St Day district. As the war dragged on and the casualty rates increased men deliberately attempted to dodge conscription. Avoiding names, we have examples such as a St Day farmer, who was aged 30, married and managing 35 acres alone, and who was classified B1. When called up for military service, he was recommended for 'conditional exemption' for six months in this instance. Further draft papers would be issued once the conditional period was over and the tribunals would review the case. From 1917 tribunals became more difficult and the lower categories were being refused exemption more frequently. Despite this a Parc-an-Chy miner, aged 38, in class C2 was given a conditional exemption with 'the military bearing no objection'. A St Day carpenter was removed to class C3 and granted exemption on the grounds that a business depended on him, as did a community on his building, carpentry skills and the fact that he was the town's undertaker.

Peter Jennings, the school head teacher, played a key role in local affairs during the First World War by driving recruitment campaigns with rousing speeches, often in the streets, and being very instrumental in War Saving campaigns. His unfortunate death in April 1917 was deeply felt, but the community efforts continued undeterred. The school had not only developed a solid War Saving Association Scheme, but the boys also collected the substantial sum of £5 towards Sir Arthur Pearson's St Dunstan's Hospital for blinded soldiers.

Occasional reports of St Day men being wounded or killed in action appeared in the local newspapers. Those who survived and returned home maimed from the battlefields were a sharp reminder of the horrors of a new technological age where gases, heavy field guns, barbed wire and lethal machine-guns only served to increase the death toll. Sapper Richard Kinsman was captured by the Germans during their Spring Offensive of 1918. He was attempting to bring a wounded officer into the British lines on his back when he found himself captured. He was put to work behind enemy lines and paid 3 pence a day, but was poorly fed. After falling ill he spent time in a German hospital, but was discharged after the Armistice. Dressed in rags and shoeless, he became a refugee making his way across Europe, where he was picked up and helped. When his family received a 'wire' explaining his arrival at Paddington, the whole of St Day sighed with relief at the return of a lost son.[13] Not all were to tell such a tale and returning coffins served as reminders to the community making life more painful once again.

The community of St Day indulged in the jubilation and naïve enthusiasm of sending their sons to war, believing they would be home by Christmas 1914. They agonised through the cruel days and nights of Neuve Chapelle, Loos, Ypres and the brutal Somme, where on the first day, 1 July 1916, over 20,000 were killed and 57,000 wounded. The war had turned and twisted the emotions of the community, who braved the times through a probably insecure patriotism. Such losses saw a 'call to arms' across the Empire, where St Day expatriates rose to the cause from Australia, South Africa, Canada and New Zealand. The impact of these times would herald a new era, where traditional beliefs and trusts were shaken and a fear of new technologies applied to war embedded fear. Global affairs and personalities were now somehow closer to home. Eventually, the tide turned against the Germans and a peace was agreed for 11 November 1918.

The formal celebrations of 'The Triumphant Peace' was held at The Cedars, where a procession for all, led by a jazz band, followed by racing and sports, must have cut little though the grief which hurt so many mothers, sisters, wives, sweathearts and lovers, along with the host of children and other relatives who counted their losses. As the 'flare' blazed forth its message for peace at the summit of Wheal Jewell burrow, many slipped into the shadows of the occasion and loneliness to face a lifetime of remembrance. The St Day War Memorial was officially opened during April 1921. A sombre day passed and a community was wiser.

The Second World War, 1939–45

Within 20 years the world and indeed the community at St Day was to find itself preparing for war once again, but this time without the marked naïvety which characterised the loss of life before. It was with great reluctance and deep regret that Britain found itself at war in September 1939, as Nazi Germany invaded Poland.

At St Day, the standard issue of gas-masks for everyone quickly bought home the realisation of a war and the new threat of invasion. The Air Raid Patrol Wardens were formed by the St Day vicar Revd Thomas, who after some initial training in 'distinguishing incendiary devices', 'managing bombed sites', 'controlling gas leaks' and 'blackout procedures', began to train and prepare others for the host of potential difficulties which might lay ahead. Fortunately St Day was not bombed during the war, but the glowing skies of Plymouth and Falmouth could be seen from various points around the town. St Day fireman Joe Bray found himself amongst the flames fighting fires in both places. With no piped water supply, incendiary or other fires would have wreaked havoc, so a 5,000-gallons water tank was placed in the garden of the War Memorial in Fore Street to help extinguish any blazes.

Blackouts were of course very important in the defence against stray or rogue bombers who had missed their targets and resented the idea of a journey home without any opportunity to drop their load. Chapel services were held at the Primitive Methodist Sunday Schoolrooms, where blackout curtains had been specially fitted. There were only a few cars in St Day during the war, but all could be seen with their headlamps blanked bar a small strip, to allow just enough light to illuminate the road. Even torches were masked, with only a pinhole of light to guide the late-night traveller. The appearance of taped windows, criss-crossing glass also became a familiar sight.

A new wave of young brave soldiers found themselves departing, with a sense of fear carried over from the First World War; they were very much wiser to the possible horrors awaiting them, though no less determined to fight fascism. They soon swelled the ranks of Army, Navy and Airforce and began their long excursions away from St Day to a world most had only ever seen on maps or in pictures. The Far East, Europe, North Africa, the Atlantic and the Mediterranean all became the intense focus for their struggle to survive. Many saw action, some fell, all became heroes.

Very few evacuees arrived at St Day, perhaps a sign of the town's own difficulties in overcoming economic problems. Though the war would offer opportunities to escape from depression through conscription and other sources of employment, the benefits were a while coming.

St Day School took precautions by teaching at St Day playing-field, where pupils assembled every day, often under the trees, under the supervision of teachers to continue their regular curriculum, except that children were now also taught how to wear gas-masks, to observe their locality and report anything or anybody appearing to be suspicious.

R.R. Blewett designed plans which would facilitate escape from bombing or invasion. Parents were told that a tunnel under the Community Centre would lead them to safety in the advent of the German Army progressing into St Day. Most people followed the progress of the war by listening to one of the new range of cheap, mass-produced radios, which allowed them to hear the defiant speeches of their Prime Minister, as well as some light entertainment to ease the mood and tension of wartime. 'Lord Haw Haw' with his pro-Nazi propaganda taunted them, but the radio was more an ally than foe. Importantly the crowds around the radio awaited and listened in anticipated silence to the news; which was soon being discussed and relayed to the less informed.

The American General Infantry (GIs) arrived in preparation for the D-Day landings and camped in the grounds of Scorrier House. Segregated black GIs found themselves camped on land at Wheal Busy and in the grounds of Whitehall. Among them was Joe Louis, Heavyweight Boxing Champion of the World, a 'gentle giant' always happy to talk and hold up his palms for the boys to punch. Boys ran errands around the camps and were rewarded with cigarettes for their fathers and sweets for themselves. Occasionally a ham or other cold meats would be offered, a real luxury for many St Day families of the times. GIs frequented the pubs, where tensions between them and locals over the attentions of local girls occasionally erupted into a brawl. Over at the Seven Stars Inn, Carharrack, local boxer Bill Lewis was employed as a doorman.

Friendships evolved, but as 'D-Day' approached the troops began their long haul to the Normandy beaches and the liberation of mainland Europe. The black GIs left first. The tanks rolled through St Day as a farewell tribute to the locals they had become accustomed to and their tracks ripped the streets.

At the end of the war jubilation could be heard in the streets as victory flags were hung and people rushed to buy emblems. A United Service was held at the Primitive Methodist Chapel, offering thanksgiving and a reading of Psalm 46 for the end of the ordeal. In the evening a concert and dance was held at St Day Community Centre, organised by the St Day ARPs who collected a considerable amount of money for the 'Welcome Home Fund'. The families of those that did not return were given an amount from the fund, which did little to assuage the pain.

As the singing wound into the night, again there would be those unable to celebrate, sat silently behind closed doors and curtains to mourn the loss. Each year, the Remembrance Service allows the community at St Day to reflect and think of those who died; though memories fade, they still live on.[14]

Notes

[1] *Cornubian*, 26.5.1899.
[2] *Cornish Echo*, 23.10.1914.
[3] *Cornish Post & Mining News*, 12.11.1914.
[4] *Cornubian*, 18.12.1915.
[5] *Cornubian*, 28.1.1916.
[6] *Cornubian*, 11.2.1915.
[7] *Cornubian*, 29.4.1915.
[8] *Cornubian*, 3.6.1915, 1.7.1915 and July–Aug, 1915, and *Cornish Post & Mining News*, 29.4.1914.
[9] *Cornubian*, 11.2.1915.
[10] *Cornubian*, 21.10.1915, 27.1.1916 and 23.3.1916.
[11] *Cornubian*, 20.7.1916.
[12] *Cornubian*, 18.4.1918.
[13] *Cornubian*, 16.1.1919.
[14] I am indebted to the memories of the late Mrs Doris Hume, my father Roy Annear, Malcolm Hume and Karl Bray for their kind representation of an overview of life in St Day during the Second World War. (See also *West Briton*, 4.8.1949, and *Cornishman*, 17.5.1945 and 19.10.1945.)

Twenty-Seven

Sporting Traditions

For generations St Day has prided itself on the diversity and success of its sportsmen. Rugby, cricket, football, wrestling, snooker and billiards, pool, darts, euchre, tennis, table tennis, pigeon racing, athletics and cycling have all found themselves well represented at club level (junior and senior), county level and occasionally international level by St Day men, or equally importantly by those who have learned their skills and participated in clubs at St Day.

Wrestling

Wrestling was perhaps a link to the ancient Cornish organised sport (at least on record) within St Day. This was not like the wrestling we know today, but Cornish wrestling, where the tournament was conducted in a 'ring' and refereed by a 'stickler'. The sport was rowdy and from time to time the 'ring' was 'broken' (invaded) and play usually stopped. The sport was generally one of 'turns, spins and throws', and injuries could and did occur. A bout could last for over an hour. Tournaments were usually held as part of the St Day Feast week of celebrations. The earliest mention of wrestling where reference is made to Gwennap comes from 1817, when David Annear (of Gwennap, but almost certainly St Day) lost to James Hocking of Redruth in the final of a local competition.[1] Little mention is made of the sport until the 1860s, when a regular two-day competition attracted a first prize of £3. By this time St Day had several wrestlers, among them R. Tiddy, W. Pascoe, S. Cornish, A. Youren and another called Crowgey.[2] By 1875 the annual competition was well established, attracting a county-wide field of competitors including T. Stone and ? Bragg of St Austell. Such widespread attraction may have been due to the first prize of £4 on offer.[3] During this period St Day could still boast local and very competent wrestlers in James Matthews and Richard Gillard, and a County Featherweight Champion in Alfred Youren. The event took place at the rear of the Lion Inn and attracted large crowds. By 1881 the Star Inn at Vogue played host to what may have been a different annual wrestling match to that of the Feast celebrations, which were usually held in June or July. This tournament was held during August and again attracted a wide audience and wrestlers from across the county. This was also a two-day event as the following newspaper account reveals:

> *The annual wrestling took place on Monday and Tuesday 1st, in a field behind the Star Inn, Vogue, when some good play was shown, especially between Marks of St Austell and Richard Williams (alias 'Schiller') of Chacewater. After several splendid turns, Williams threw Marks with a heel. Good order was kept throughout both days. The following were the pize winners: 1st – Richard Williams, Chacewater; 2nd – Marks, St Austell; 3rd – Palmer, Linkinhorne; 4th – W. Thomas, Four Lanes.*[4]

Separate wrestling competitions were occasionally organised, such as the one in 1895 when Theo Mitchell staged an event in the 'Church Field' and offered a first prize of £2.[5] In 1897 the return of an 'old St Day boy', Alfred Bawden (commonly called 'Matt'), who was home from South Africa, attracted a great deal of attention. At this time tournaments were held on Mr Ball's lawn. Bawden reached the final of the tournament against another well-known Cornish wrestler, J. Tippett of St Austell. The match lasted 53 minutes and ended in a stalemate, with Tippet winning by the toss of a coin. The competition was particularly strong, being considered 'as good as ever witnessed at St Day.'[6] In 1906 a wrestling committee met at St Day and was chaired by Mr H. Ball. Their accounts showed a balance of 17s., which was handed over to the funds of Redruth Hospital that year.[7] Around this time the sport seems to have died out at competition level until it was revived in June 1924. The new competition at Vogue was now managed and organised by a formal committee consisting of a Gloucester-based president, Mr C. Glee, supported by local patrons who helped fund and stage events, including E. Long, G. Jeffery, H. Mugford, E. Matthews, F. Williams, Mr Whear, G. Knowles, C. Long and G. Trethowan. Sticklers were E. Matthews and C. Rowe. Competitors were confined to a five-mile radius and entered into weight categories of around 140lbs and 180lbs. R.J. Knowles senr won his category, much to the applause of his St Day supporters. C. Chynoweth of St Day lost in the second round of the 180lb class, whilst S. Morcombe lost in the first round of the 140lb class. Mr J. Triggs (an old Cornish wrestling champion himself) from Redruth refereed the events at St Day and also toured the county, not just officiating as 'stickler' but also doing much to advertise the sport.[8] Cornish wrestling seemed to be enjoying widespread popularity at local and county level. The last record we have of serious competitive Cornish wrestling at St Day is from 1926, when wrestlers from the western half of the county were invited to compete for the 'Insitu' cup, which had been 'presented by gentlemen from South Africa'. Significantly, the winner's honours went to Mr W. Morcom of St Day, who threw C.W. Hooper of the Camborne School of Mines in the final.[9] However, various smaller bouts and competitions were held up until the 1950s.

Cricket

A local cricket club was formed in the 1850s, initially as 'Tregullow Cricket Club', and played on ground provided by F.M. Williams. They later moved to Tolgullow.[11] A match is recorded against Perran, played at Tredea in May 1857, where St Day won comfortably by two wickets in a two-innings event. The club enjoyed some success and is reported to have consisted of 25 members by 1866, only two of whom were not residents of St Day.[12] The club had ceased by the 1870s.

In 1878 Revd Edward Olivey helped re-form the St Day Cricket Club by providing a field and general support in getting the community involved.[13] A friendly between the married and single men of St Day acted as practice and a warm-up for more serious competition against Devoran, and the thrashing of Redruth, as the *Royal Cornwall Gazette* highlighted on 26 July 1878:

> *St. Day cricketers defeated the Redruth team by 8 wickets! Can it be possible? Yes it is true enough; I was an eye witness, well done St. Day boys! When are the Devoran Men coming up to play the return match. I hope the above will not scare them.*

The team, known as Revd Olivey's XI, notched up some very creditable wins in these early years, defeating, amongst others, St Mawes at Falmouth and Chacewater. By the 1880s the 'St Day Wanderers' had formed a separate team. In 1909 proposals to amalgamate the two sides were flatly refused, perhaps illustrating some rivalry.[14] Both sides probably continued until the First World War, after which a single club was formed, which from around 1927 was considered strong enough to join the 'Junior League', being chaired by Malcom Hume senr and captained by G. Howard.[15] The club continued, with a lapse during the Second World War, and by the late 1950s had become part of the Falmouth and District Cricket League. A typical team of this time was chosen from Ken Harris, Donald Tangye, Malcom Hume junr, Donald Holmes, Ted Long, Peter Sowden, Ronnie Stokes, Brian Riddle, Tony Evans, Geoffrey Beskeen, Stephen Mills, Ronnie Veale, Alfred Peters, Raymond Reseigh, Tommy 'Taffy' Jones, Charlie Gay, Billy Williams, Thornley Richards and Michael Roberts, amongst others. Throughout the following decades Ronnie Stokes, Thornley Richards, Tommy 'Taffy' Jones and Alfred Peters merit special mention as dedicated clubmen. The 1960s saw the team settle at their new ground at Vogue, where they have played ever since.

The 1970s and '80s saw the team enjoying a range of successes in the Cornwall Junior Divisions, usually fielding two teams. Regular players by this time included Colin Clift, Lester Harland, Alan Curtis, Tony Mitchell, Neil Euctice, Peter Richards, Thornley Richards, Alfred Peters, Simon Medlyn, Ronnie Stokes, Roy Peters, Gareth Jones, Chris Bullen, Peter Smith, Peter Hillman, Brian Emmett, Alan Williams, Alan Smith, Paul Curnow, Kevin Jones, Neil Higginson, Lee Higginson, Robin Mitchell, John 'Kenny' Harris and Paul Harris, among many others. In 2002 St Day Cricket Club continues to enjoy the sporting traditions, challenges and hopes for the future.[16]

St Day Cricket Club, c.1980s and late 1950s.

St Day Cycling Club

In May 1894 a group of cycling enthusiasts proposed to start a cycling club at St Day, but the decision was deferred because of the possibility that some members might 'over-exert' themselves. However, the advantages of having the club were recorded as:

> *... a healthy out of doors exercise it arouses ambitions, and the members feel a degree of pleasure in possessing machines kept in good order, are imbued with a desire to proficiency, and are ever ready to run across country. A club or association possessing a strict code of rules ... where regulations are observed at all times, is a strict advantage in any town or village. Should the youths of St Day decide on forming a club, it is hoped that all cyclists should feel pleasure in joining it.*[10]

Arthur Beale Rowe arrived at St Day in the mid-1880s and could be found advertising as a watchmaker in the *Kelly's Directory* of 1889. Known locally as A.B. Rowe, he diversified into a range of goods associated with the trade such as clocks and jewellery, and kept a small sideline in bicycles. It was probably no coincidence that a cycling club was to be proposed and eventually organised at St Day, and Rowe himself was to become a leading stockist and supplier. The fact that few photographs appear after the turn of the century without someone propping up a bicycle is perhaps a testimony to his sales skills, as well as the fact that he kept over 100 'machines' in stock. By 1906 A.B. Rowe boasted a 'Cycle Saloon' near the bottom southern side of Fore Street, whilst still keeping his watchmaking and jewellery business in the building on the corner, a few doors down. He claimed to sell the most up-to-date stock of any cycle dealer in Cornwall, and at times the whole of the South West. Such claims seem rather excessive, but in all fairness Rowe did visit the cycle shows of London, Coventry and Birmingham.

A range of new cycles, among them 'Elswicks', Swifts, New Hudsons, Premiers and Singers, could be purchased, with Raglans at £5, through to Elswicks being the most expensive at £24. There was also second-hand stock which was priced from £2. Before selling them, Rowe tried and tested each cycle in workshops at the rear of his premises. He frequently advertised in the county press until the First World War, after which he continued working as a watchmaker until the late 1920s.

Rugby Football

Perhaps the earliest mention we have of the rugby football club relates to correspondence which appeared in the local *Cornubian* newspaper from a 'schoolboy' who felt 'it's a pity that young men and boys are standing around on street corners', and went on to comment on how 'the Revd Olivey has just started a cricket club, but why can't we have a football [rugby] club.'[17] The idea was not to fully marterialise for another three years when, in September 1883, a meeting was held to elect a committee for the formation of the St Day Rugby Football Club. Revd Olivey was nominated as treasurer, Mr W. Petherick was elected as captain, Mr W.F. Simmons was sub-captain and Mr W.B. Thomas was made secretary. A field was provided by Revd Olivey.[18] The team continued to play against a mix of village and town sides and the occasional church or chapel team, such as Camborne Wesleyan Chapel. The Lanner team also featured in these early years. The St Day club was still going strong in April 1890, when Revd Edward Olivey organised for the team to play in a rugby football tournament at Falmouth:

> *The first teams to meet were the Falmouth Wanderers and Mr Olivey's at St. Day. The latter, a smart little team, captained by a smart man, played a good game and won by a try and two minor points to nil. The Redruth Western Albions were now pitted against Mr. Olivey's team, and same pretty play was registered resulting in a draw.*[19]

It appears that St Day shared second place with Penzance – by no means a bad effort at what may have been the first attempt to play the sport by St Day men. The presidential successor was Revd J.J. Murley, who also took a keen interest in the club. He came to St Day in 1891 and appeared as vice-president of St Day Rugby Club by the 1909/10 season. By this time the president was Capt. S.H. Christy (M.F.H.). Other vice-presidents (early sponsors) of the club during this season were J. Williams, Revd W.T. Martyn, Dr L. Birchall, J. Smith, Frank Long, J. Letcher, W.J. Morcom, T.R. Mills, W.J. Mills, W. Gay, E.H. Williams, J. Hunt, J. Richards, S.L. Lanning, R.P. Wilde, T. Trethewy, J.C. Richards, W. Gilbert, R.H. Moore, J. Cannon and W. Smith. Captain for the season was T. Rule and vice-captain was F. Sleeman. Photographs of the team were usually taken at the vicarage and included members of the St Day clergy. In the formative years the team probably played at the Church Field (behind the Old Vicarage), but with the departure of Revd Murley in 1911 a new venue was required. Dr Birchall, a St Day rugby patron, offered his field behind Vogue House. Revd Walter Weekes Bickford, who arrived in St Day in 1912, appears in a St Day rugby club photograph, highlighting the continuous support some sporting clergy gave to the community during their stay.

Also in 1912, a meeting was held at the St Day Adult School Institute 'to consider whether it was advisable for the club to join the Cornwall Rugby Union', which was agreed. It is unlikely that St Day was affiliated before this time.

One player began to stand out. H. 'Topsy' Ham,

played as full back for St Day before moving to Redruth. He received 19 caps for Cornwall, playing between 1918 and 1925. In a three-mile race, organised by the landlord of the St Day Hotel, Ham won in 19 minutes, despite heavy going.[20] St Day managed to win the Cornwall Junior Cup in the 1920/21 season, captained by another of the club's most notable players, Renfrew 'Peano' Knowles. Playing at Vogue, they defeated Penryn Chiefs by eight points to nil. This remains the only time the club ever won the prestigious competition. Peano Knowles went on to play for the senior clubs at Redruth and Penryn, but is perhaps better remembered for being a county rugby football referee, and was for many years bound to St Day club as coach, clubman and committee member, continuing his interest throughout the decades up to the 1960s. He may qualify as one of the longest serving members of the club. Peano's son, R.J. Knowles junr, also moved from St Day to the senior club at Camborne and was capped six times for Cornwall. Another notable player from this generation was Tommy Harris, who went from St Day to play for Redruth and Cornwall, all in the space of a few weeks in 1919. He played six times for Cornwall from 1919–20, before he turned to the professional game and played for the Rochdale Hornets. While he was there Tommy became a rugby league international player.[21]

A photograph of the St Day team during the 1920s shows S. Rowe, S. Verran, F. Richards, P. Rowe, G. Knowles, D. Williams, M. Nettle, W.E. Williams, F. Wills (Hon. Sec.), G. Pelmear, A. Pengelly, E. Knowles, R.J. Knowles, J. Annear, J. Thomas, S. Rundle, H. Brown, Matt Nettle, J.C. Treweek and S. Penpraze. Harvey Brown and R. (Dick) Williams were also members. Other players also formed the nucleus of the team and included Bill Long, David Annear, Tom Hart, Harold and Bill Gerrans, Percy Rogers and exciting young talent Bill Harris. Bill Harris was spotted and encouraged to play at Redruth, where he spent most of his career, playing 24 times for Cornwall from 1935–52. By the mid-1920s the club began to play at a field donated by the Williams family of Scorrier, next to the present ground, which was later presented to the people of St Day as a recreational field by W.J. Mills in 1928.

The pre-war years at St Day witnessed a decade of changing faces, including regulars such as Joe Bray, Jack 'Jan' Hickey, R.J. Knowles senr, R.J. Knowles junr, Jack Annear, Bill Phillips, Percy Rule, Reggie Rule, Hugh Knuckey, Percy Knuckey, Johnny Chenoweth, Reggie Williams, Albert 'Ben' Williams, Henry Smith, Henry Vinnicombe, Nicky Pinch, Donald Pinch, Willie Wills, Frank Wills, Leonard Wills, Arthur Welham, Bill Penrose, Bill Mills, Carson Mills, Ken Waters, Frank Waters, Albert Harris, Jim Harris, Henry Smith and Percy 'Darkie' Ellis.

After the war the club re-formed, borrowing blue shirts for the forwards from the Falmouth 'One and All' players. This era produced a host of players, many of whom progressed to senior clubs. The nucleus of this side consisted of Dickie Wilton, Tommy 'Taffy' Jones, Kenny Lobb, Dick Williams, Dempsey Vinnicombe, Cecil Harris, Leonard Wedlocke, 'Whippy' Sweet, Ernie Mills, Henry 'Darky' Thomas, Arthur Matthews, Courtney Teague, Richard 'Dick' Clymo, Joe Bray, Jock Dabb, Jack Hickey, Tommy Burley, Charlie Pentecost, Albert Harris, Jack Thomas, Horace Wills, Ernie Hocking, Bill Pedley, Edgar 'Hunter' Roberts, Peter Tregonning, Peter Gill, Ely 'Taff' Griffiths, Peter Rogers, Bill Rickard, Fred Mitchell, Stanley 'Manna' Ford and Jeff Stubbs. Two local boys were to make an appearance for St Day around this time – the brothers David and Robin Andrew, who both played for the England Schoolboys XV whilst attending Truro School.

The 1950s saw several young players from the previous decade mature. A very talented St Day team, many of whose members chose to stay at St Day, was rewarded for their loyalty with several Cornwall Junior Group caps. The team around this time included Clifford Williams, Karl Bray, Roderick Martin, Baynard Martin, Ron Annear, Michael Phabey, Alan Phabey, Melville Annear, Roy Annear, Carson Mills, John Moyle senr, Wilfred Richards, Edgar Swan, Ernie James, J. Roberts, Desmond Downing, Kenny Lobb, Stanley Pope, Tom Hart, Ewart Matthews, Terry Downing, Courtney Butler, Tommy 'Taffy' Jones, Jack Willis, Desmond Hart, Sam Hill, Francis Matthews, Peter Bray, Norman Scoble, Jimmy Harris, Frank Jory, Dickie Wilton, Reggie Holland, Bill Wright, Thornley 'The Wisp' Richards, Henry Mitchell, David Hill, William 'Billy' Williams, Reggie Richards, Willie 'Jenks' Jenkins, Ben Francis, Denzil Hart, Jack Wills, Peter Rogers, and Ron and Kenny James. Notable at this time were the five sons of F. 'Roughie' Richards – Joe, Wilfred, Garfield, Tom and Frank. The sheer range of Cornwall Junior Group caps between these players is still listed amongst the finest achievements of the club. Young Henry Mitchell was one of the finest members of the St Day rugby club, where he played scrum half in the late 1950s, winning county cap honours for Dorset and Wiltshire whilst doing his National Service there.

The team of the 1950s was among those considered as the most feared in Cornish rugby. Alan Buckley, writing the biography of Howard Mankee, quotes his comments on St Day rugby during these times:

They Opies, Richards, Moyles, Matthews's, and Downin's didn't believe in givin' much away. They was bleddy 'ard men. Tough as old boots an' ard as bleddy nails. Half o' St Day was gypsies an lived out to United Downs an' down to Carharrack pound. I can remember Ewart Matthews and Frank an' Joe Richards now. Loved a scrap. As soon as fight [than] *eat meat, they lot.*[22]

Mrs Richards, wife of Joe, was a well-known character who would smash anyone with her brolly who dared score against St Day. Buckley continues:

> *'Twas like goin' in the lion's den. Every move you made you got shouted at, an' if you tackled a bit 'ard, my gar, the language was terrible. Even my own step-father, Reggie, when I bought down a player shouted: 'You dirty liddle bugger, Mank. Goos 'ome ter Camborne yer bleddy evil liddle bastard.' Rarely did highway finish a game against St Day unscathed. Howard and his mates would limp off the pitch, battered, bruised and bleeding.*

The 1960s saw an unbeaten run of 21 games, including a notable victory over touring side Coventry Welsh. Showers were installed at the ground in 1961 and no longer did players have to worry about getting changed at a local inn before walking to the field. Mr R.E. Dunster appeared a great deal in the local press, forging the progress of the club. 'Eric', as he was known, was the St Day Rugby Club secretary from 1958–71, and a Junior Mining Division representative of the Cornwall Rugby Union. One of Eric Dunster's greatest achievements was the establishment of the St Day Colts side, which was to nurture future talent and provide a springboard for many players who went on to become the regulars of the 1960s and who were given Cornwall Junior Group honours.

A few stalwarts of the 1950s continued their playing careers through the 1960s, such as John Moyle senr, Ewart Matthews, Sam Hill and Thornley Richards. Ewart was joined by his talented sons David and Michael. Other players who represented the club were Richard 'Dick' Mugford, Kenny 'Jock' Mugford, Michael Pheby, Joe Lawry, Alec Williams (Captain), Michael Tellam, Michael 'Mighty Mouse' Downing, Bernard Williams, Nat Long, John Blackwell, Colin 'Mousey' Mills, Donald Gunn, Allan Pheby, Paul Williams, Michael 'Scooby' Coad, Tony Matthews, C. Martin, R. Selwood, Chris Carter, Bernard Thomas, Roger Bray, T. Rowe, G. Gunn, A. Woodrow, Ronnie Annear, Tommy Ware, V. Martin, David Wedlock, John Bray, Barry Thomas, Kenny Jory and M. Dunstan.

From the 1960s, Michael 'Mighty Mouse' Downing was to emerge as the leading player in the club. By the 1967/68 season he had become a full back for the Cornwall Junior Group and soon established himself as one of the most talented young players in the county. A move to Redruth soon saw him appear as the regular full back for the senior club, throughout what may be considered to have been some of its most successful seasons. His reputation was formidable during this period and over the next 18 seasons he was to represent Redruth Rugby Football Club on 718 occasions, just surpassing the all-time club record set by Chris 'Bonzo' Johns. The record was confirmed after a recount found that Downing had played one more game. During his time at Redruth Michael was capped four times for Cornwall. In 1989 the club needed a revival and Downing was the tonic, as he quickly re-established himself as one of the leading players of the club. He was voted player of the year during his first return season and his efforts were greatly felt in fund-raising and promoting the club with local sponsors.

The 1970s again saw several of the late 1960s team members offer their experience to new players and a changing side. The nucleus of the team during this decade revolved around John Moyle junr, Tommy Ware, Kenny 'Jock' Mugford, Paul Williams, David Moyle, David Matthews, Michael Matthews, Paul Matthews, Peter 'Shreeds' Harris, Michael Bryant, J. Blackwell, Colin Parsons, Richard 'Dick' Mugford, Chris Johns, John Williams, Michael 'Scooby' Coad, Nigel Williams, Chris Carter, Rodney Flamank, Reagan Matthews, Colin Annear, Michael Williams, Bernard Williams, Donald Gunn, Tony Williams, Peter Etherington and Nat Long. Chris Johns was to receive England Schoolboy and Colts honours. Jack Williams continued amongst others to be a regular supporter of the club and was always proud to wear a St Day blazer and badge.

Another character appears in the club's history at this time. Michael Williams emerged as one of the best clubmen, as he still does today, for running the lines, organising half-time refreshments and always trying to motivate a struggling team. The 1970s saw club administration managed by several former club players, among them John Williams, William 'Billy' Williams, Tony Williams, Michael Williams, Sam Hill and Jimmy Downing, who was also the caretaker of the field and clubhouse facilities. By the late 1970s a host of new talent began to filter into the side and maintain the St Day tradition of quality rugby, with a side capable of beating any junior team. Chris Matthews, Tony 'Nini' Matthews, O. Vince, Phil Newman, Paul Richards, Dave Teague, Stephen Annear, Andy Thomas, Colin Annear, Garry Spargoe and Wayne James became big names within the club, many of whom began to assert reputations in the Cornwall Junior League, many capped with honours.

The talented rugby enjoyed during much of the 1970s was to give way to some difficult times during the 1980s, when club personalities and politics caused the occasional rift. Clubmen such as Clifford Williams, Ronnie 'Buck' Williams and Dick Clymo were always on hand to offer advice and encouragement to club, committee and players alike. After-match drinks moved from the Star Inn to the St Day Inn, and then over to Carharrack Club during this decade. Whilst all of these venues supported the club, loyalists felt that Carharrack should not be the social venue for St Day RFC. Carharrack quite rightly argued that they had invested money and several players over the years. New administrators, such as Les Chippett, Kenny Evans senr, Joe Lawry, Karl

Rugby Football

Left: *St Day Rugby Club, 1920s.*

Below: *St Day Rugby Club, 1920s.*

Below: *St Day Rugby Football Club, 1951/52.* Left to right, standing: *Leonard Wills, Carson Mills, Karl Bray, Billy Rickard, Ronnie 'Woodbine' Williams, Walter Harry (President), Fred Mitchell, Jeff Stubbs, Tom Richards, Edgar 'Hunter' Roberts, Reggie 'Dick' Williams;* seated: *Peter Rogers, Desmond Harry, Norman Scoble, Billy 'Jenks' Jenkins, Courtney Butler (Captain), Frank Richards, Henry Mitchell, Cyril ?;* seated on floor: *Stanley Pope, Dennis Williams.*

Above: *St Day Rugby Club, 1960s.*

Right: *St Day Rugby Club, 1970s.*

Team of the 1990s. Left to right, back row: *Stephen Mitchell, Les Chippett, Martin Opie, Ewart Matthews, Nigel James, Andrew Long, Mark Evans, Paul Matthews, Maurice Issacs, Sean Pegg, Derek Osborne, Ian Day, Chris Bullen, Paul Bawden, John Medlyn, Terry Chynoweth, Clifford Williams;* front row: *Kenny Evans, Michael Downing, Steve Annear, Phil Keverne, Karl Bray, David Moyle, Trevor Mankee, Chris Matthews, Mickey Evans, R. James, T. Trevena, Michael Williams.*

Top: *St Day Rugby Club, 1960s.*
Above: *St Day Rugby Club, c.1978.*

Bray, Frank Richards, Terry Chynoweth, Frank Opie, Paul Matthews, Kenny James, Paul Newcombe, John Bill and Paul Bawden worked hard to make the club the success it became. Michael Williams was always on hand to run the line or support the club in any way possible and Malcom Drew offered effective sponsorship.

Again many of these players were to lead St Day through the 1980s and pass on their experience to the new youngsters. David Moyle, Shaun Moyle, Andy Hales, Rodney Flamank, Reagan Matthews, Chris Matthews, Dave Teague, Phil Newman, John Webster, Chris Southworth, Wayne Gunn, Roger Walton, Andy Page, Clive Richards, Paul Newcombe, Rob Larter, Kenny Evans, Shaun Hook, Steve Annear, Tony 'Nini' Matthews, Andy Thomas, Garry Spargoe and Wayne James were now joined by a flood of new players, among them Steve Mitchell, Paul Annear, Ian Day, ? Rickard, Andy Page, Derek Osborne, Phil Keverne and Trevor Mankee. Colin and Doug Elliott made appearances during their stay in England. Typically of St Day, new faces began to appear which would remain for another decade, such as Martin McGovern, Salvatore Nucifaro, Mark Evans, Mark 'Tank' Stevens, David Bray, Chris Verran, Tony Mitchell, Martin Opie, Chris 'Skippy' Williams, Robert Risbridger, Michael Lawry, Stephen Mugford and Tony Dunstan.

The club saw the welcome return of Michael Downing in the 1989/90 season, along with the appearance of several new players to bolster the side. St Day were to show patchy form in the league, but enjoyed some fine rugby in defeating touring sides Bovey Tracey and Tongynlais during the 1992/3 season. Young Matthew Downing was now making his presence felt on the field, showing something of his father's flair. The team was joined by Damien and Tim Tromans, Sean Pegg and Mark Gillow around this time, and also welcomed Roy Peters who, with the Downings, was to become a leading point scorer during many matches.

Two further England Schoolboy honours were bestowed upon Steve Datson and ? Wright. The club enjoyed centenary celebrations during the 1994 season and looks set to continue well into the new century.

Billiards & Snooker

Snooker and billiards in St Day probably date back to the introduction of a new billiards table at the Adult School Social Club, three months after it was formed in August 1909.[23] The club was situated on land at Wheal Jewell, just behind the Church Schoolrooms (now the church). Local matches against various church and chapel teams, and village and town institutes including Gwennap, Lanner, St Agnes, Truro and Redruth amonst others, began to feature from these times. A typical team would include players such as F. Hensley, R.P. Annear, J. Annear, W. Webb, D. Annear, W. Webb and J. Richards.[24] Billiards continued at the Adult School Social Club throughout the war, with teams competing in the Gwennap League. After the war, the school seems to have picked up again, but had rather faded by 1926, when the premises were acquired by the St Day Ex-Servicemen's Club.[25] St Day Institute over at Church Street had acquired their new billiards table in April 1921. It was formally opened by Major Williams of Scorrier House, and had been a gift from the entrepreneur Leonard Martin. An exhibition billiards match between two county champions, W.G. Bailey and A. Thomas from Penzance, marked the occasion.

Both clubs were to provide a place of refuge for men during the dark winter evenings and became two very social focal points for men during the following decades. The St Day Institute had become known as the 'House of Lords' and the Ex-Servicemen's Club was known as 'The House of Commons'. To what extent this reflected the members' political loyalties or social status has at times been speculated upon, but only in jest. At some time during the 1930s the Ex-Servicemen's Club installed another table and snooker and billiards became very popular amongst the sportsmen of St Day.

The Second World War saw the closure of the Ex-Servicemen's Club as men were conscripted into the Armed Forces. As some were to return with injuries, it was decided to reopen the club in October 1943. The membership grew from 23 to 62 during the following year and, with £75 in the funds, it was decided to recondition the two tables and purchase a set of snooker balls for the youngsters who had been

Football

Left: *Football Club, 1952/53.* Left to right, back row: *Dougie Barber, Dennis Long, ? Nicholls, Arthur Teague, Rex Bray, Ewart Matthews;* front: *Ted Long, Hubert Heard, Don Hoyle (Capt.), Colan Dunstan, Charlie Gay.*

Below left: *St Day Football Club, 1949/50.* Left to right, back row: *Harold Cocking, Preston ?, Ewart Matthews, Roy Leah, James Williams, Desmond Harry, Rex Bray, Arthur Bray, Harold Teague;* front row: *?, John Heard, Teddy Bray (Capt.), Clive Blamey, Hubert Heard.*

Right: *St Day Youth Club, Cornwall Youth Club's Five-Aside Football Champions (Western Division), 1970s.* Left to right, back: *Francis Clarke, Gordon Henderson;* front: *Kevin Sheean, Mark Williams, Michael Jones.*

Above: *St Day Football Club, 1950s.*

Below: *St Day Football Club, 1972/73.*

Below left: *St Day Football Club, c.1975.*

encouraged to become members.[26] Snooker quickly became popular at club level within the county, partly because of the status and skills which the World Champion Joe Davis brought to the game. It was quicker than billiards, and whilst most young players were instructed in the rudiments of billiards, snooker was a much faster and more exciting spectacle. From this era, several leading St Day and eventual county billiards and snooker players were to emerge. Notable players were Doug Thornecroft (who also played a great deal in his home club at Carharrack Miner's Institute), Charlie Gay, Melville Annear, Francis Matthews, Alistair Bawden, Albert 'Ben' Williams, Tony and Peter Sowden, Percy Hosking, Tony 'Whippet' Williams, Ronnie 'Woodbine' Williams, Clifford Williams, Ted Long, Rex Williams and Malcom Hume. All of these players were capable of defeating anyone in the county over one frame on their night, but a few began to push ahead of the group.

By the mid-1950s the Ex-Servicemen's Club had closed due to a collapsed roof, and snooker and billiards became focused at St Day Institute. Soon, Francis Matthews was to win the County Youth Championship. Doug Thornecroft (though strictly a Carharrack man) then led the way with major success in the Heathcoat Cup (the Mining Division Individual Open – and we must remember that the Mining Division Leagues have historically been regarded as the strongest in the county) in 1954–55 and he began to dominate the County Billiards Championship from 1955 onwards. Thornecroft retained the Heathcoat Cup again in 1960, but not before Charlie Gay won the coveted title in 1958/59. The two players had asserted a stronghold on Mining Division snooker by this time. However, a very strong challenge emerged in the form of Melville Annear, who secured the Heathcoat Cup title during the 1961/2 season.

Thornecroft was to be the first to win the remarkable 'double' by being County Billiards and Snooker Champion in the season of 1962/63. This continues to rank among the greatest feats by any Cornish snooker player.

Both Gay and Thornecroft soon found themselves pitched against an even stronger force in the game. Jonathan Barron from Mevagissey appeared on the scene during the late 1950s as a County Youth Champion, and by the early 1960s had established himself as the leading Cornish snooker player. For the next decade, from 1963–73, Barron dominated Cornish snooker and appeared in two English amateur finals. Only Thornecroft could effectively challenge Barron's supremacy during this reign, when he won the county title in 1966/67. During the late 1960s Gay won the Heathcoat Cup on four occasions. By his own admission he played some of his best snooker against Barron, particularly in the 1971 County Final where he lost 5–0. Significantly, Gay was now playing the World and English Amateur Champion. Yet again Charlie Gay produced his finest snooker to lose the County Finals to the (then) World Champion 5–1 in 1972. A third consecutive final against Barron resulted in a 5–1 victory. Barron looked to step out of the game and this match may have been one of the deciding factors. It was now Gay's turn to dominate as he defeated his old rival and mentor, Thornecroft, 5–1 in 1974. He was selected for the England squad and travelled as player-reserve to an international lineup. Although he knocked on the door of the international game he was extremely unlucky not to play.

Gay went on to win the County Senior Snooker title for another four consecutive years from 1976–79. In 1976 he also completed the county 'double', winning both County Senior Snooker and Billiards titles, to equal the feat of Thornecroft. This he made even more remarkable by winning the Heathcoat Cup and the Carah Robert Mining Division Senior Billiards Cup in the same season. This achievement must remain the highest in Cornish county snooker. Other successes as county champion in 1979 and 1989 as county senior snooker champion probably hallmark Gay as the most consistent player of a century of Cornish snooker. From an administrative and player position he has led Cornish snooker from the front, remaining captain throughout the 1960s, '70s and '80s.

From the late 1970s another remarkable young player hit the scenes. At the age of just 16, Lanner-born Barry Scarlett was to re-write the record books by winning the County Senior Snooker title in 1980. He was encouraged to play first-division snooker at St Day, where he contributed much towards the club's success of the 1980s. He went on to win two County Youth titles from 1981–83 and continued his good form to win the County Senior title in 1984, by which time he had established himself as a regular in the County Senior team. In an attempt to turn professional Scarlett moved to London in around 1984, where he soon found himself in the London team (which consisted of only four players). Not quite fufilling his ambitions, he decided to stop playing after the late 1980s. Fortunately, he returned from a premature retirement in the late 1990s to enjoy his old boyhood game of billiards, which he still enjoys at club level in St Day with Charlie Gay and his old friend Joe Graham.

Whilst Melville Annear has been considered by many to be the most unlucky snooker player not to win County Senior selection, his cousin David Annear has enjoyed considerable county success. Though never to achieve individual honours, he did emulate his cousin by also winning the Heathcoat Cup in 1981. He formed a strong pairing with Charlie Gay when they became County Snooker Pairs Champions in 1975 and for three consecutive seasons during 1980–83. Another player to achieve County Youth representation was Paul Annear, who captained the County Youth Team in 1983/84. He was joined to represent Cornwall youth by Steven Beard, who moved to St Day from Mount Hawke in the early 1980s to compete in Mining Division One, after winning a string of titles in other leagues. A very stylish cueist and superb all-rounder, Beard has remained loyal to St Day for two decades.

Whilst some have achieved county honours, there remained at St Day many players who dedicated themselves to successful team performances. Ronnie Williams was content to enjoy team snooker for 50 years at St Day. An outstanding first-division player, he was reputed to never miss a blue off the spot. Alan Repper appeared and also won the R. Grigg Trophy in 1981; he later established himself as a leading first-class referee, working among leading amateurs and professionals in the game. Neil Keen was another player from the early 1980s who proved to be a superb pairs player, winning several championship titles with Paul Annear. Brian Payne joined the club in the late 1970s to compliment a strong first team. Other experienced and successful first-team players were Clifford Williams, Paul Annear, David Annear, Nigel Williams, Neil Keen, Ivor Curnow, Alec Littlejohns, Tony Williams and Keith Manley, who completed a squad that was to win the Mining Division One Championship from 1980–82. St Day had won the same league in 1971 and seldom moved out of the top three for almost another two decades.

Success was spread across many competitions with St Day winning every County and Mining Division Team Championship, including the Joe Davis County Seven-A-Side Team Snooker Championships on four occasions, Cornwall County

Above: *Devon and Cornwall Mayflower Cup winners, 1975.* Left to right, back: *Keith Manley, Charlie Gay, Tony Williams, Melville Annear, Ronnie Williams;* front: *Bill Manley, Norman Jory, David Annear, Gordon Gilbert.*

Right: *Mining Division 2 winners.*

Above: *St Day Snooker Team, 1980.* Left to right, back row: *Alec Littlejohn, Ronnie Williams, David Annear, Brian Payne, Keith Manley, Paul Annear;* front row: *Barry Scarlett, Courtney Trevithick (Chairman), Bill Pullen (President), Neil Wills (Secretary), Charlie Gay.*

Above: *St Day Snooker Club.* Left to right, back row: *Colin Mills, Keith Manley, Ronnie Williams, Ivor Curnow;* middle row: *Johnny Chenoweth, Charlie Gay, Doug Thornecroft, Melville Annear, Desmond Harry, Tony Williams, David Annear;* seated: *Gordon Gilbert, Reggie Stephens.*

Five-A-Side Team Snooker Championships, County Team Billiards Championship, Mining Division Two Team Championship and the Mining Division Five-A-Side Team Championship. The fact that St Day won the Mining Division Two League on no less than five occasions shows something of the range of talent that constantly looked to challenge first-team places. Here, players such as Desmond Harry, Peter Sowden, Mervyn Wills, Richard Angove, Roger George, Percy Hoskin, Colin Mills, Steve Annear, Colin Annear, Robin Mitchell, Stephen Mitchell, Roy Peters, Nigel Jones, Reagan Matthews, Craig Lopez and Robert Braddon could find themselves called upon to stand in for any team.

Considering these achievements, billiards and snooker must rank among the greatest successes of any sport ever played in St Day. The clubs, and latterly the Institute, have opened their doors to youngsters. They have always nurtured examples of clubmanship, as well as sportsmanship, through outstanding servants such as Dick, Herbert and Norman Jory, Bill Manley, Bill Pullen, Charlie Pearce, Neil and Archie Wills, Freddy Keen, Barney Smith, Len Dagley, Ray Pheby, Keith Manley, Gordon Gilbert, Alec Littlejohn, Ivor Curnow, Richard Angove, Robert and Baynard Braddon, Clifford and Tony Williams, and David Beard. To these and the others we owe a debt of gratitude as the club strives on.

St Day Amateur Football Club

A soccer club was set up at St Day by c.1910 and was certainly well established by 1912. A Football Supper was held in the Church Schoolrooms in May of that year, with Mr E.H. Williams as President, and F. Sleeman, T.R. Mills, J.T. Letcher and T. Rule as the organising committee.[27] Captain G.P. Williams gave free use of a field at Tolgullow Farm, along with a ball and a hut. As with all of the sporting clubs at St Day, both wars had a considerable impact upon the game and little is recorded until the late 1940s, when the club was re-formed. In July 1948, Don Hoyle and J. Waugh placed an advertisement in a local hairdresser's shop and received a good response, despite comments that 'St Day has always been a rugby village' and predictions that a football club 'would not last six weeks'. St Day adopted the colours of black and white (some say yellow) stripes and came runners-up in the 'Dunn Cup' competition in this first season. Further successes followed in 1953/54, when St Day won their Junior Cup Section.[28]

From the late 1940s and throughout the '50s regulars in the St Day Football Club team included Peter Davey, Brian Davey, Charlie Gay, Hubert Heard, John Heard, Ted Long, Eric Littlejohns, Alec Littlejohn, Clifford Williams, Francis Matthews, Trevor Waugh, Sam Waugh, Dennis Long, Searle Hill, Ben Ford, James Williams, Roy Leah, Clive Blamey, Dennis Hillman, Teddy Bray, ? Preston, Desmond Harry, Rex Bray, ? Nicholls, Dougie Barber, Don Hoyle, Colan Dunstan, 'Neighbour' Davey, Owen Teague, Arthur Teague, Charlie Harry, Leonard Cocks, Ewart Matthews and Ely 'Taffy' Griffiths.

The 1960s and '70s saw the club playing at Vogue, where they continue in 2002. Throughout this decade the teams have included members such as Colin Parsons, Mark Williams, Clive Brown, Michael Roberts, Peter Prisk, Leslie Vanstone, Brian Davey, Peter Mallet, Peter Grenfell, Roger George, ? Bawden, Rob Nicholls, Monty Hillman, Steve Edwards, Derek Leigh, Ron Veal, Terry Harry, Roger Hayley, Regan Matthews, Steve Annear, Kerwyn Prisk, David Searle, Clive Jones, Michael Jones, Peter Etherington, Brian Etherington, Nigel Williams, John Bawden, Simon Martin, Nigel Mitchell, Michael Moyle and Tony Mitchell. The late 1970s and early 1980s saw players including Robert Braddon, Roy Peters, Peter Hillman, Clive Roberts, Gareth Jones, Neil Ryan, Dave Thomas, Garry Parsons, Robin Mitchell, Paul Curnow, Michael Peters, Lionel Pooley, Chris Bullen, Wayne Carlyon, Chris George, S. Martin, J. Salmon, Shaun Wills, P. Nichols, J. Lee and B. Williams.

Outstanding clubmen have been Kerwyn Prisk, who has served the club for more than 40 years continuously, and David Searle, who has a similar record. Others have included Sheldon and Tony Mitchell. Throughout the decades, St Day Amateur Football Club has competed in a variety of leagues, divisions and competitions, during the course of which it has enjoyed a range of successes.

Notes

1 *West Briton,* 1.8.1817.
2 *West Briton,* 25.6.1868.
3 *Royal Cornwall Gazette,* 19.6.1875, 24.6.1876 and 8.7.1876.
4 *Royal Cornwall Gazette,* 12.8.1881.
5 *Cornishman,* 4.7.1895
6 *Royal Cornwall Gazette,* 1.7.1897.
7 *Royal Cornwall Gazette,* 23.8.1906.
8 *Royal Cornwall Gazette,* 23.6.1924.
9 *Royal Cornwall Gazette,* 16.6.1926.
10 *Royal Cornwall Gazette,* 24.5.1894.
11 *Penzance Gazette,* 21.4.1858.
12 *Royal Cornwall Gazette,* 26.7.1866.
13 *Royal Cornwall Gazette,* 31.5.1878.
14 *Cornubian,* 29.4.1909.
15 *Royal Cornwall Gazette,* 12.1.1927.
16 Thanks to Mr Tony Mitchell and Malcom Hume for kindly supplying me with names and the club's history from the 1950s.
17 *Cornishman,* 15.1.1880.
18 *Cornubian,* 17.9.1883.
19 *Royal Cornwall Gazette,* 10.4.1890.
20 *Cornubian,* 20.6.1919.
21 Newcombe, Paul, *St Day Rugby Football Club – The First Hundred Years,* 1894–1994.
22 Buckley, J.A., *A Miner's Tale: The Story of Howard Mankee,* 1988, p.68.
23 *Cornishman,* 18.11.1909.
24 *Royal Cornwall Gazette,* 30.11.1911.
25 *Kelly's Directory,* 1926.
26 *Cornishman,* 2.11.1944.
27 *Royal Cornwall Gazette,* 23.5.1912.
28 Notes supplied by Tony Mitchell and Keith Manley, extracts from *A Brief History of the Mining Division Football League Clubs, c.1950.*

Subscribers

Bob and Stephanie Acton, Penpol, Devoran, Cornwall
Tracy and Grant Anderson, The Corner Shop, St Day
W.L.L. Andrew, Trelawney, Vogue
D.N. Andrew, Trelawney, Vogue, St Day
F. Mona Andrew, Crofthandy, Cornwall
J. Andrew, West Trevarth, Lanner
Sylvia M. Andrews, St Day, Cornwall
Henry C. Angove, Trevethan House, Near St Day
Richard and Angela Angove, Redruth
Juliette Angove, Redruth
James C. Angove, Lanner, Cornwall
Cher Annear, Park Bottom
Steven and Heather Annear, St Day, Cornwall
Hetty Annear, St Day
Roy Annear, Brighton
Irene Annear, St Day
Barbara Baker, former Headteacher St Day C.P. School
V.W. and D. Baldry
Myrtle Bartle, St Day, 1918–2003
Helen E. Bartlett, Scorrier, Cornwall
David, Hazel and Mark Beard, St Day, Cornwall
D. Beard
Professor Stephen C. Bell, Leicester, Leicestershire/born St Day 1950
William Peter Benbow, Redruth, Cornwall
Nichola and Alan Bentley, St Day
Eric Berry, Busveal, St Day
Nicola M. Bicknell, Rosudgeon, Cornwall
Madge Blamey, Frogpool
Barbara Blamey, St Day
Baynard Cecil Braddon, St Day
Nona and Karl Bray, St Day
Peter Brew, St Day
Mrs Daphne J. Brinkley, St Day, Cornwall
Annie Brown, Troon, Cornwall
Philip Burley, St Day
Stephen Burley, St Day
Mrs Gloria E. Burley, United, St Day, Cornwall
Christopher Burley, St Day
Sally Burley, St Day, Cornwall
K.J. Burrow, Bucks Cross, Devon
Mr and Mrs Kenneth Bushell, St Day, Cornwall
Mr and Mrs M.R. Butcher, Leicester
Margaret and Stephen Caldwell, Litchfield House, St Day, Cornwall
Valarie Chown, Carharrack
Cheryl Christopher (née Field), Herefordshire
Lucie Clarke, St Day School 1977–1982
Roger and Maura Clarke, Crofthandy
Mr Clifton, Willoughby, Redruth, Cornwall
Sue Cockle, Falmouth
Judith D. Cocks, Camborne, Cornwall
Delia J. Collins, Taunton, Somerset
Mr and Mrs B. Cook, St Day, Cornwall
Marie and Ross Cookman, St Day, Cornwall
Philip G. Copley, Milborne Port, Somerset
Pete Corbett, Perran-Ar-Worthal, Cornwall
Mary R. Cornford, St Day, Cornwall
P.G. and K. Cornford, St Day, Cornwall
Robert and Marilyn Cragg, 2002
Julia Crichton (née Bennett), Kent/Gt-Granddaughter of William Bevan
Maurice W. Cross, Redruth, Cornwall
Ms S. Cross, Arkansas, USA
Mr Tony Cumberland, Vogue, St Day, Cornwall
Philip Curnoe, St Day, Cornwall
Leonard S. Dagley, St Day, Cornwall
Eileen and Roy Davey, Redruth, Cornwall
Mrs E.A. Davies (née Slocombe), Cheddar, Somerset
Derek J. Dowling, St Day, Cornwall
Margarett Drage, St Day
Susan and Stephen Edwards, St Day
Mr K.M.J. Evans, Bissoe, Truro
Mrs L. Fiander, Cove, Hampshire
Sarah Field, Gloucestershire/ Lanner
A.O.J. and V.M.St.J. Fitzmaurice, Vogue, St Day
Mr and Mrs G.C. Frewer, St Day
Aine Furey, Dublin, Ireland
Sonia M. Garry, St Day, Cornwall
Haydn George, St Day, Cornwall
Fr Andrew Gough, Vicar of St Day, 1994–
Alan Green, Mount Hawke, Cornwall
Rosemarie Grenfell
Denis Arthur Gribbin, Carharrack, Cornwall
Gumma Family, Crofthandy
Miss Margery D. Hall ARCA, Tolgullow, St Day, Cornwall
Robert G. Harris, St Day, Cornwall
Sue Harvey, St Day
Mr D. Carol S. Harvey, Lanner
Edmund D. Hill, Shangri-La, Green Lane, Redruth, Cornwall
Denny Hill, St Day, Cornwall
Lisa Hillman, St Day
Mike and Annette Hillman, St Day
Arnold Hodge, Truro, Cornwall
Steven Holland, Pink Moors, St Day, Cornwall
Dr Hugh C. Hollingworth, Redruth
Alison C. Homer
Mr Ron C.A. Hooper M.V.O., Redruth
Audrey James, Carmarthen
R.E.A. James
D.A. James and Sons Ltd,
Tom and Arana Jeffereys, General Stores, St Day
Stanley M. Jewell, Carharrack, Cornwall
C. and J. Johns
Beryl M.A. Johns, Redruth, Cornwall
Mr Nigel Jones, Camborne, Cornwall
Richard Jones
Clive and June Jones, St Day, Cornwall
Michael V. Jones, St Day, Cornwall

Betty Jones, St Day, Cornwall
Ronald C. Kellow, Redruth
Kay Kemp, Swansea, Wales
Dawn R. Kilroe, St Day, Cornwall
Anne Kinsman, Trenow, St Day
Anne and Rodney Knight,
Robin Knight, Halwill Barton
Lesley Critten and Brian Knowles, Townsend, Cornwall
David Laity and Janet F. Rowe, The Cedars, Church Street, St Day
Richard C. Latham, St Day, Cornwall
David Lay FRICS
Tony Lewis, St Day, Cornwall
Dr R. Little, Oxford
Fran and Reuben Long, Scorrier, Cornwall
Jill Luff, St Day
Mr and Mrs J. Luker, Tresaddern Farm, St Day
Ken and Pat Magor, Carharrack, Cornwall
Joan C. Malyan, St Day, Cornwall
T.R. Mankee, Redruth
Miss H.L. Manley, Oxford
K. and S. Manley, St Day, Cornwall
Leslie H. Martin, St Day, Cornwall
Dennis J. Martin, St Day
Evelyn Martyn, St Day
Chris Massie, Goongumpas, Redruth, Cornwall
William G. Matthews, Camborne, Cornwall
Barry F. Matthews, Carharrack, Cornwall
Mr and Mrs Barrie S. May,
Pat and David Maynard, Manor Road, Carharrack
Malcolm McCarthy, Padstow
The McEvoy Family, St Day, Cornwall
R. Ann Medlyn
Bryher Kerris Mehen, St Day, Cornwall
P. and S. Micklewright, St Day, Cornwall
Simon Mills, Kingsbridge, Devon
Hazel M. Mills
Agneta Mills, Exeter, Devon
Rebecca Mills, Exeter, Devon
Mrs R.M. Mills, Illogan
Jonathan Mills, St Day
Jenna Mills, Kingsbridge, Devon
Jasper Mills, Exeter, Devon
David B. Mitchell, St Day, Cornwall
Peter Mitchell and Joan (née Beard) deceased, Chacewater, Truro, Cornwall
Mr and Mrs Moores, (S. James), St Day
E.J. and P. Moyle, Redruth, Cornwall
Kenny F. Mugford, Nr Crofthandy
Christine A. Mullan, Crofthandy
Lester, Jill and James Nankivell,
Upper Westwood, Bradford on Avon, Wiltshire
Geoff, Diane, Ben and Peter Nankivell, St Day Post Office
Matthew Nettle, St Day, Cornwall
Mr and Mrs J.C. Newcombe, St Day
Norman D. Nicol, Shavertown, USA
Mike and Sarah Noakes, St Day, Cornwall
Gary S. Parsons, St Day, Cornwall
Elizabeth Peebles, Norway
Alison Peebles, Glasgow
Marion Peebles (née Mills), St Day, Cornwall/now Edinburgh, Scotland
Valerie Pellowe, St Day, Cornwall
Joan Pender, St Day, Cornwall
Mr E.J. Penglase, St Day, Cornwall
John and Elizabeth Pepler, St Day, Cornwall
Mr J.T. Peters, Bissoe, Truro
Ivor J. Peters, St Day, Cornwall
Ed Pettett
Charles J. and Sallie M. Phillips, Illogan, Cornwall
Mary and Dave Phillips, Crofthandy, Cornwall
The Phillips Family, Poldice, St Day
Jackie Pitt, St Day, Cornwall
John C.C. Probert, Redruth
Robert P. Radley, St Day, Cornwall
Raymonde A. Reeve, Higher Trevethan, Redruth
Marlene Richards, St Day, Cornwall
Mrs W.S. Rickard, Todpool, St Day
Julie and Robbie Risbridger, St Day
Mr A.J. Roberts, Redruth
Philippa Roberts, St Day, Cornwall
Miss Patricia and Mrs Eleanor J. Roberts, Pennance, Lanner, Cornwall
Robert W.T. Robins, St Day, Cornwall
Roy Robins, St Day, Cornwall
Vivienne A. Robinson, Vogue, St Day, Cornwall
R.S.W. and E.S. Robinson
Geoff and Tessa Salmon, St Day, Cornwall
Mr John G. Sandow, St Day, Cornwall
Ann S. Saunders, Wembley. Laura Williams' granddaughter
Darrin and Christine Sawyer, St Day, Cornwall
Donald L. Schiele, unofficial Puckey Historian – Pittsburgh, PA, USA
Sharron Schwartz, Redruth
Peter and Alex Seabrook, Pinkmoors, St Day
Mary Sedgemore, St Day, Cornwall
Joan H. Shaw, Perranporth, Cornwall
Ray Smith, Peterborough
Richard Snell, Crofthandy
Gary B. Spargo, Redruth, Cornwall
St Day and Carharrack Community School,
The St Day Historical Society, St Day
The St Day Inn, Fore Street, St Day
George Stephens, St Day, Cornwall
Warren and Sue Stevenson, St Day
Pauline Stimson, Pulloxhill, Bedfordshire
Beryl Stockwell, St Day
Mrs E. Joyce Stokes (née Parsons), St Day, Cornwall
P. and K.D. Temple
Joe Thomas, Illogan, Cornwall
Gilbert H. Thomas, Idless, Truro, Cornwall
Patricia Thomas, St Day
Peter Thomas, Redruth
Graham Thorne, Maldon, Essex
Margaret E. Thorpe, Formby, Lancashire
William G. Thorpe, Formby, Lancashire
Peter Tregoning
Roy and Linda Trelease, St Day, Cornwall
Dr Leonard Trengove, Ting Tang
E. Alan Trevethick, St Day, Cornwall
Murray J. Verran, Waipukurau, New Zealand
Paul Leslie Vincent, St Day, Cornwall
W.E. Walley, Ponsanooth
John F.W. Walling, Newton Abbot, Devon
Tom Watts and Angela Watts (née Stone), Perranporth, Cornwall
Alan Whitburn, formerly Wallasey/now Durham
C.N. Wiblin, Shrewton, Wiltshire
Wilfred William Williams, St Day, Cornwall
Denis G. Williams, St Day, Cornwall
Mr G. Williams, Newcastle-under-Lyme, Staffordshire
Ian Williams, formerly of St Day, Cornwall
D.C. Willis, St Day, Cornwall
R. Willoughby, St Day, Cornwall
Anne Wills, St Day, Cornwall
David and Christine Wilson, Trefula, Cornwall
Elizabeth Ann Wilson, Tiverton, Devon
Nancy Woodley (née Richards), St Day
Monica K. Wren, St Day, Cornwall

Community Histories

The Book of Addiscombe • Canning & Clyde Road Residents Association & Friends
The Book of Addiscombe, Vol. II • Canning & Clyde Road Residents Association & Friends
The Book of Axminster with Kilmington • Les Berry and Gerald Gosling
The Book of Bampton • Caroline Seward
The Book of Barnstaple • Avril Stone
The Book of Barnstaple, Vol. II • Avril Stone
The Book of The Bedwyns • The Bedwyn History Society
The Book of Bickington • Stuart Hands
Blandford Forum: A Millennium Portrait • Blandford Town Council
The Book of Bramford • Bramford Local History Group
The Book of Breage & Germoe • Stephen Polglase
The Book of Bridestowe • R. Cann
The Book of Bridport • Rodney Legg
The Book of Brixham • Frank Pearce
The Book of Buckfastleigh • Sandra Coleman
The Book of Buckland Monachorum & Yelverton • Hemery
The Book of Carharrack • Carharrack Old Cornwall Society
The Book of Carshalton • Stella Wilks and Gordon Rookledge
The Parish Book of Cerne Abbas • Vale and Vale
The Book of Chagford • Ian Rice
The Book of Chapel-en-le-Frith • Mike Smith
The Book of Chittlehamholt with Warkleigh & Satterleigh • Richard Lethbridge
The Book of Chittlehampton • Various
The Book of Colney Heath • Bryan Lilley
The Book of Constantine • Moore and Trethowan
The Book of Cornwood & Lutton • Compiled by the People of the Parish
The Book of Creech St Michael • June Small
The Book of Cullompton • Compiled by the People of the Parish
The Book of Dawlish • Frank Pearce
The Book of Dulverton, Brushford, Bury & Exebridge • Dulverton & District Civic Society
The Book of Dunster • Hilary Binding
The Book of Edale • Gordon Miller
The Ellacombe Book • Sydney R. Langmead
The Book of Exmouth • W.H. Pascoe
The Book of Grampound with Creed • Bane and Oliver
The Book of Hayling Island & Langstone • Rogers
The Book of Helston • Jenkin with Carter
The Book of Hemyock • Clist and Dracott
The Book of Herne Hill • Patricia Jenkyns
The Book of Hethersett • Hethersett Society Research Group
The Book of High Bickington • Avril Stone
The Book of Ilsington • Dick Wills
The Book of Kingskerswell • Carsewella Local History Group
The Book of Lamerton • Ann Cole & Friends
Lanner, A Cornish Mining Parish • Sharron Schwartz and Roger Parker
The Book of Leigh & Bransford • Malcolm Scott
The Book of Litcham with Lexham & Mileham • Litcham Historical & Amenity Society
The Book of Loddiswell • Reg and Betty Sampson
The New Book of Lostwithiel • Barbara Fraser
The Book of Lulworth • Rodney Legg
The Book of Lustleigh • Joe Crowdy
The Book of Lyme Regis • Rodney Legg
The Book of Manaton • Compiled by the People of the Parish
The Book of Markyate • Markyate Local History Society
The Book of Mawnan • Mawnan Local History Group
The Book of Meavy • Pauline Hemery
The Book of Minehead with Alcombe • Binding and Stevens
The Book of Morchard Bishop • Jeff Kingaby
The Book of Newdigate • John Callcut
The Book of Nidderdale • Nidderdale Musuem Society
The Book of Northlew with Ashbury • Northlew History Group
The Book of North Newton • Robins and Robins
The Book of North Tawton • Baker, Hoare and Shields
The Book of Nynehead • Nynehead & District History Society
The Book of Okehampton • Radford and Radford
The Book of Paignton • Frank Pearce
The Book of Penge, Anerley & Crystal Palace • Peter Abbott
The Book of Peter Tavy with Cudlipptown • Peter Tavy Heritage Group
The Book of Pimperne • Jean Coull
The Book of Plymtree • Tony Eames
The Book of Porlock • Denis Corner
Postbridge – The Heart of Dartmoor • Reg Bellamy
The Book of Priddy • Albert Thompson
The Book of Princetown • Dr Gardner-Thorpe
The Book of Rattery • By the People of the Parish
The Book of St Day • Joseph Mills and Paul Annear
The Book of Sampford Courtenay with Honeychurch • Stephanie Pouya
The Book of Sculthorpe • Gary Windeler
The Book of Seaton • Ted Gosling
The Book of Sidmouth • Ted Gosling and Sheila Luxton
The Book of Silverton • Silverton Local History Society
The Book of South Molton • Jonathan Edmunds
The Book of South Stoke with Midford • Edited by Robert Parfitt
South Tawton & South Zeal with Sticklepath • Radfords
The Book of Sparkwell with Hemerdon & Lee Mill • Pam James
The Book of Staverton • Pete Lavis
The Book of Stithians • Stithians Parish History Group
The Book of Stogumber, Monksilver, Nettlecombe & Elworthy • Maurice and Joyce Chidgey
The Book of Studland • Rodney Legg
The Book of Swanage • Rodney Legg
The Book of Tavistock • Gerry Woodcock
The Book of Thorley • Sylvia McDonald and Bill Hardy
The Book of Torbay • Frank Pearce
Uncle Tom Cobley & All: Widecombe-in-the-Moor • Stephen Woods
The Book of Watchet • Compiled by David Banks
The Book of West Huntspill • By the People of the Parish
Widecombe-in-the-Moor • Stephen Woods
The Book of Williton • Michael Williams
The Book of Witheridge • Peter and Freda Tout and John Usmar
The Book of Withycombe • Chris Boyles
Woodbury: The Twentieth Century Revisited • Roger Stokes
The Book of Woolmer Green • Compiled by the People of the Parish

For details of any of the above titles or if you are interested in writing your own history, please contact: Commissioning Editor Community Histories, Halsgrove House, Lower Moor Way, Tiverton Business Park, Tiverton, Devon EX16 6SS, England; tel: 01884 259636; email: katyc@halsgrove.com